Advice from a Dead Man

Richard Tabler

Cadmus Publishing
www.cadmuspublishing.com

Copyright © 2023 Richard Tabler

Cover art by Francisco Moraga – fjmoragaproductions@gmail.com

Published by Cadmus Publishing
www.cadmuspublishing.com
Port Angeles, WA

ISBN: 978-1-63751-128-2

All rights reserved. Copyright under Berne Copyright Convention, Universal Copyright Convention, and Pan-American Copyright Convention. No part of this book may be reproduced, stored in a retrieval system, or transmitted in any form, or by any means, electronic, mechanical, photocopying, recording or otherwise, without prior permission of the author.

Table of Contents

CHAPTER ONE 1
CHAPTER TWO: Positive Change. 41
CHAPTER THREE: Looking Through New Eyes 51
CHAPTER FOUR: What Do You Know About Respect? 67
CHAPTER FIVE: Lockdown 78
CHAPTER SIX: Who's Really Your Friend and Who's Not? 91
CHAPTER SEVEN: Let Us Laugh 103
CHAPTER EIGHT: Before We Went, We Had One Last Word of Advice for You 116
CHAPTER NINE: Being a Cutter Doesn't Mean You're Suicidal. 124
CHAPTER TEN: Being Tested by Fools Still 136
CHAPTER ELEVEN: The Nasty Cage and Its Attacking Tenants 158
CHAPTER TWELVE: "Respect for Authority". 167
CHAPTER THIRTEEN: Why Couldn't It Be Done? 179
CHAPTER FOURTEEN: Just Another Day, Or Is It? 183
CHAPTER FIFTEEN: "Voices from the men and women who work inside these walls…" 200
CHAPTER SIXTEEN: The Prankster and Those Who Do Violence . 205
CHAPTER SEVENTEEN: Family 217
CHAPTER EIGHTEEN: Special Section 237
"Storytime for a Trip". 244
"Canvas of Time". 245
Testimony of Alan Wade 247
MORE TO LIFE: Testimony of Jimmy D. Smith 251

Bonus Book: Within the Shadows of Life

Chapter One. 257
Chapter Two: Things Become Worse. 265
Chapter Three: Going to Jail and Learning How to Fight. 270
Chapter Four: Gladiator School. 277
Chapter Five: Road Trip. 290
Chapter Six: Teazer's Gentleman's Club 300
Chapter Seven: Not Finished Yet 307
Chapter Eight: Bell County Jail 311
Chapter Nine 321
Chapter Ten 335
Chapter Eleven 346
Chapter Twelve 352
Chapter Thirteen 355
Part 2: TEXAS DEATH WATCH 359
Chapter Fourteen 360
Chapter Fifteen 376
Chapter Sixteen 382
Chapter Seventeen 387
Chapter Eighteen 392

CHAPTER ONE

On Tuesday, January 11th, 2022, I decided that my life sucked and that I was ready to end things by taking my own life. I had been locked up in Texas now for 18 years and the whole time it's been spent in total isolation from other prisoners. That was partly due to the safety of others in the county jail and me because of the kind of case I had. Capital murder. So, for the time I was in the county jail, which was about two-and-a-half to three years, and then here on Texas Death Row since April 5th, 2007. Everyone who is on Texas Death Row is housed by himself in the Polunsky Unit's 12-Building. We spend 24 hours a day, seven days a week inside a cage no bigger than a dog pen, though with a working toilet, sink, light, desk, and a couple of shelves, as well as a single bed that is no wider than 30 inches and six feet long and two inches thick.

Before COVID-19 hit the world, I would spend 22 hours a day inside this cage. I have been denied visitation with loved ones for the whole time I have been on Texas Death Row because of a situation that I got into after I landed on Death Row. To know more about that you should read my first book titled "Within the Shadows of Life." Back to what I was explaining to you about the 11th. I was ready to get everything over with because I was just tired of doing time. I was escorted earlier that afternoon down to make a telephone call home to my mom because her health isn't too good these days, so I had been approved a telephone call to her every Sunday but had been told that I wasn't allowed such a call that previous Sunday that passed. Missing that call and being told that I was lying set something off inside of me. So, I sat back and typed out a letter to my mom explaining that I had reached that time.

Because of a situation that took place in "Within the Shadows of Life," my first book, all my outgoing mail went through the Warden's office, who in turn sent it via email scan to a Director in Huntsville, Texas before being allowed to be mailed off the unit (prison). This meant that everything I wrote aside from my legal mail, which is sealed, is read by the Warden and Director. So, knowing this and knowing that it would cause heat to land in the laps of those who messed me over on my telephone call home, I wrote that I was finished. That following morning, I was sitting in my cage when Field Minister Troup was visiting me cell-side at my cage. (A field minister is another prisoner that has gone to seminary at the Darrington Unit and can now walk around sharing God's word or talking to other prisoners or doing whatever the Wardens ask of them.) Thus, Field Minister Troup was sent to talk with me to find out what all is going on with me. I had known Troup for about one year at that time.

I went smooth off on him explaining that I was tired of everything. I went off on him about my restrictions and the isolation, everything. I felt like God was mad at me and wasn't answering my prayers because I was a condemned prisoner. When he left, I was in tears, and I could tell he understood that I seriously was finished with doing this time. He could relate to what I was going through because even though he's doing time and is a Field Minister, he is also serving time for a capital murder. He's not on Death Row, but he could have ended up here with me and many others, but God had other plans for Brother Troup.

After he left from speaking with me, I placed my headphones on and started listening to my radio and pacing the five steps I was able to take in my cage from my bed to my door and back again while listening to some music on my radio, all the while thinking how I was going to end my life.

A few hours passed, and I started thinking about continuing to fight and not giving up. As I was thinking these thoughts now, Officers Amos and Matthews showed up at my cage door. When I removed my headphones to ask them what was up, I was told that all the ranking Officers were just given notice from the Warden's office that I was to be given a telephone call every Sunday to my mom. This was emailed to everyone so nobody could say otherwise. I told him okay and went back to my radio only to notice that they were still standing at my door. Once again removing my headphones, I asked them what was up. Officer Amos informed me that they were told to escort me down to the legal booth to make a telephone call home to my mom for the call I was denied on Sunday. I knew this was from the letter that I had mailed out that morning.

I stripped out butt-naked so that my clothing could be searched and returned to me to get dressed again before placing my hands behind my back out the slot in my cage door so the officers could place handcuffs on me. My cage door was then rolled open by the Officer working the control picket. I stepped out backward and was escorted by both officers down the stairs from 2 Row and off of A-Section Death Watch and off the Pod. Walking down the hallway to the legal booth down by the LT's office, they were told to call my mom and that I was to get only five minutes.

Once I was in the legal booth and the restraints were removed, Officer Amos made the call to the switchboard or central control who made the telephone call to the outside and my mom before handing me the phone to talk to her. While I was talking to her, those first 30 seconds or so, she told me about how her ex-boyfriend drove from Orlando, Florida, which was about one-and-a-half hours away, and in the middle of the night decided to act like a child and toilet paper both my mom's car and my sister's. Then she went on to explain to me that she has some further bad news for me. She went on to tell me that her sister, who is my auntie, Great Aunt Lena was rushed to the hospital out in California for a heart attack, and while she was in the hospital, she contracted COVID-19. She had flat-lined twice before they were able to get her stable. Though she was now in a coma, they still sent her home to die.

As soon as my mom told me this all we heard on the telephone was laughter before my phone call with my mom was rudely disconnected! (Note to the readers: whenever we're given a telephone call here on Death Row the calls are always listened to by rank.) Getting this news and being disconnected like that and with everything else already going on within my head and heart, I lost my temper and went off yelling at the ranking Officers I knew who were sitting in the LT's office right next to the legal booth before throwing the phone out the slot in the legal booth's door and punching the safety glass, which broke.

When all the ranks came running out of the office filled with laughter, they were no longer laughing when they saw the glass on the door or my face and the verbal assault, I was throwing at each of them! One of the Sergeants after they all left returned and with a mute nod towards me and asked me what my mom's number was so that he could get the switchboard/central control to redial my call home. Soon as I was connected to my mom, I saw him get on his walkie-talkie (radio) and order the escort team to come back and get me and return me to my cage as I was losing it.

Talking to my mom, she asked me what that was on the phone before we were disconnected. I explained that they thought it was funny when you told me that our loved one was now dying at home while in a coma from contracting COVID-19 at the hospital. I told her that I loved her, but that I was finished with this time. I asked her if she would please give my love to my older and only sister and little niece and contact my lawyers and let them know I was checking out that night. This is the last thing any parent would want to hear from their kid regardless if they say they understand and will support whatever their kid decides to do when in such a tight situation.

Then the escorting officers were back and I had to get off the telephone. Telling her goodbye and that I loved her was one of the hardest times for me since being locked up. The escorting officers could tell I was seriously upset by the simple fact that without stripping out I just placed my hands behind my back to be cuffed and they took notice of the safety glass that is 1-1/4 inches thick and now has a crack going down the middle of it.

Usually, I will speak with whoever is escorting me and vice versa, but on this day they and everyone else we passed on my return to my cage could see that it would end badly to try and say anything to me. I was placed back into my cage and the handcuffs were removed and the officers left. I jumped right back under my radio and headphones and pulled out this typewriter of mine to write/type some letters to my mom and lawyers and friends. I was beyond pissed off and tired of everything. I couldn't fathom the loss of another loved one of mine while I was locked up doing this time.

When I was placed on Death Watch from the regular Death Row sections, it was done as further punishment by numerous directors and wardens. It also happened on the very day I was given the news from a friend out at visitation that my mom's other sister died from breast cancer on January 2nd, 2011. Auntie Donna Bird, may you rest in peace up there in Heaven with God, His Son, and the angels!

It was now around 3:00 in the afternoon of January 11th, 2022, and as I was sitting on my bunk typing letters out on the desk, here comes Field Minister Troup again to check on me. I got up from typing and removed the headphones and before he could say anything to me, I explained what happened on the telephone as tears are now pouring down my face. I went on to further explain to him that I loved him and the other field ministers and greatly appreciated him and them always coming around to talk with me, but man, I was so finished with doing this time and was going to check out tonight in the early morning hours when nobody would be here in medical. He left because he knew there was no talking to me anymore, as he said I just had the look that tells everyone I'm done.

Not 20 minutes after Brother Troup left my cage door, here comes someone from medical asking me some questions about my sanity and if I was okay, and if I was planning anything. I asked them who told them that I was not okay. They explained that security said something about getting bad news on the telephone this afternoon and then about a letter that both the Warden and Director read, thus they were sent to speak with me. For the very first time since I have been on Texas Death Row, I told a lie to medical/mental health. I told them that I was okay and that I had nothing planned. They left, but not before telling me that someone from mental health would be around to speak with me tomorrow sometime as it was too late today.

After they left, I got back, yep, you know it, back under the headphones and on my typewriter to finish my letters! Right around shift change among the officers, which is 5:30 p.m., though in this case I was bothered at 5:24 p.m. by two officers knocking on my cage door to get my attention. When I looked up and removed my headphones, I asked them what was up, meaning what did they want? I was told that they were to escort me down to speak with the Assistant Death Row Warden. Not hearing them, I said who? They said the Warden. I said which one? They said the black one. I said Assistant Warden Rigsby? They said yeah, that one. I knew that this was a bogus stunt to get me out of my cage but went along with the whole song and dance and got butt-naked, then redressed and allowed them to cuff me up before escorting me down to the major's office where they usually talk to prisoners. Once we got off the Pod, I walked past 12-Control where numerous officers were getting ready to change shifts. Many tried to say something to me only to see the look in my eyes and on my face to know that now was not the time to try and talk with me about anything.

 I kicked open the door to both the major's office and the captain's office, which is in the little room off to the side from 12-control. Getting inside I take noticed that neither office has a warden inside of them, but one of the general population's captains was sitting behind the desk in the major's office. She told the escorting officers to bring me in there and for me to have a seat. Doing so, she looked at me and said what was up? Looking directly at her, I said nothing. She said, well I heard you were showing out. That was the wrong thing to say to me. So, when she again asked me how I was doing, I think she knew that she messed up because I'm now no longer looking directly at her but showing her the same disrespect, she spoke to me with by no longer acknowledging that she is even there. Instead of looking at her when she is trying to ask me questions, I'm now looking directly at the base of the floor and the back wall. Out of the corner of my eye, I can see her looking at me and escorting officers. She goes on to tell me that the warden sent her to talk with me and find out what is going on. So, what is going on with you? I said nothing, tell the wardens I'm doing great and that everything is copacetic. Still, I refuse to look at her and give her an honest answer to anything she says. I can see her look up at my escort team and then she tells them to take me back to my cage. As I get up, I still refuse to even look at her before leaving the office.

 Out of the office and returning to my cage passing by 12-Control once again people are trying to say, hey what's up Tabler?! I pay no attention nor say anything which is so unlike me. Everyone around 12-control gets quiet until I'm out of sight.

 Back in my cage and as the officers are leaving, I say that she'll be out of a job by morning. Unbeknownst to me at the same time I was down in the major's office speaking with the captain per the orders of one of the wardens, Field Ministers Troup and Solley are way down the hallway on the other end talking with LT. Highfill. I would find out later that Brother Troup and Brother Solley were waiting to be stripped out at 12-Control for about two hours. While Brother Solley is sitting down, Troup is pacing back and forth. That's when Solley asked Troup what was up. Troup went on to explain to him about my talk and how I said that I was finished and was on my way out. Solley told Troup, "Come on! We have to go let the lieutenant know something because you and I know that he's going to do something." Thus, they went off to talk to the lieutenant before the shift change was over.

While down there, Brother Troup went on to explain to LT. Highfill that she needed to place someone on me tonight because I was going to do something. Her response to him was that she's taken care of it, and she would have someone watch the video camera inside his cell. Troup told the lieutenant that that wasn't good enough and that she needed to put someone on me now. "You know that he has a history, and he will do something. I'm telling you LT. Highfill, he got bad news on the telephone and was disrespected by staff this afternoon during that call, it will be on you if and when he does something."

That was when she finally got some sense and picked up the telephone and placed the call.

Ten minutes after I had been placed back into my cage, here came one of the escorting officers with a chair, radio (walkie-talkie), flashlight, gas mask, MK-9 chemical agents, and logbook. I had been placed on "SO" (Security Observation). This is where an officer is now assigned to sit in front of my cage 24 hours a day, seven days a week until I was taken off by medical or mental health. As soon as I saw this officer and found out that I was placed on SO I told myself that it wouldn't stop anything that I was planning that night in the early hours of the morning.

It didn't matter that I had an officer watching me 24/7 now nor that I had a video camera that watched me 24/7 for the last 14-1/2 years! As the officer sat in front of my cage, I made sure to allow him to see me walking or moving around inside with my headphones on. He was sitting about 10 feet from my door, thus far enough away that he couldn't see what I was doing. Timing was everything as there were also two other officers working this pod, one in the control picket and another one making her rounds walking around doing the security checks. Without either of them being the wiser, I was slowly packing up all my personal property, then placing a drop-sheet over everything in the event they ended up using chemical agents on my corpse. They had been known when rank shows up at the scene of a nonresponsive prisoner to utilize chemical agents upon their dead bodies. No idea why other than to make sure their loved ones and the funeral homes smell the chemicals and are also burnt when they handle or touch the body.

At 11:45 p.m. I pulled out the razor blade that I had hidden and turned towards my cage door while sitting halfway on my desk with my right boot resting on my toilet. Looking at my watch I knew that the officer walking around was due for her security checks as she was long overdue. Ha-ha, right then she walked by. I lifted the razor towards my throat on my right side to cut and it was as if somebody took hold of my hand! I could no longer move the hand that held the razor blade to my throat. Just as I started to question why, my conscious decided to open full blast and thoughts about the officers and how what I was fixing to do would destroy their lives. When bad things happen inside prisons it runs downhill, meaning that it's not the ranking officers that get into trouble, but the lowly officers. I tried to tell myself I didn't care, but I knew that I was only fooling myself because even though the officer assigned to sit in front of my cage was doing so from 10 feet out, he was still a new officer, only being here maybe six months, while the female officer had been here for years and we were somewhat friendly as prisoners and officers are known to get at times. Her job would be finished too. And what about their psych? I knew that within the Texas Department of Criminal Justice, I'm what is titled a high-security prisoner or high profile because of my actions from back in 2008. I have to be housed under a video camera 24/7 inside my cage until the day I die of natural causes or my execution is carried out by the State of Texas at that time. I still tried to shake off these thoughts and cut my throat, only for the thoughts to continue and the tears to start pouring down my face freely.

Getting up from my half-standing, half-sitting position and lowering the blade in my right hand down to by my side, I walked the very few steps to my cage door and told the officer sitting there to tell the female officer to contact the field ministers and let them know that I needed to speak with one of them right away.

He flashed his light at the control picket and when she lowered her head down by the window and said what he was able to yell at her that I wanted to talk with a field minister. She said okay she would get it done, meaning she would contact her lieutenant in the lieutenant's office which is #836478. Once that was done, I went back to sitting/standing at my desk until the other female officer walked by so that I could get her attention now that my plans were defeated by my consciousness and thoughts for others instead of myself. They still had a very serious situation on their hands, though they didn't know it.

When she walked by, I asked her to please get my letters out of the outgoing mailbag, at which time she looked down at my right hand and saw what I was still holding—the blade. Trying to get me to hand her the blade, I told her I would flush it after she brought me my letters because if I give it to her then she can write me up a disciplinary case for either contraband or having a weapon.

She went to get my letters from the mailbag in the control picket then returned to speak with me about giving up the blade. By this time, it's now after midnight on January 12th, 2022. When she returns to my cage with my letters in her hand, she tells me to give her the blade. I tell her that I'll flush it once she gives me the letters because even though we are now at this point, her writing me a case would still cause me to go off even though it would be my fault. She told me that she wouldn't be writing me a disciplinary case for it, but she wanted me to give it to her, please. I asked her if was her word that she wouldn't write me up for it. She told me yes, that she was giving me her word. (Giving your word in prison is the only thing a person really has. Either the prisoners or the officers, each has to stand on his/her word inside prison walls or face getting hurt. It's just the way things are run inside prison, kind of like a law within these walls.)

Just as she says this to me, here comes the Field Minister, which happens to be Troup coming up the stairs, and right behind him is the new Sgt. Justice (that's really his name!). Brother Troup stands back by the railing and the dayroom bars taking off his thermal shirt and allowing the sergeant and the female officer to continue talking to me about things. Knowing that Sgt. Justice heard what we were talking about, I turned my eyes upon him at my cage door and asked him if was he going to have her write me up for this. That's when he too took notice of the blade in my hand. At that time, he could have ordered me to either drop the blade or give it to them and threaten to use chemical agents on me. Instead of doing either of those things, I think because they knew it would move things forward in a very negative way and they knew that chemical agents don't bother me, he allowed the female officer to remain in control of the conversation that was taking place between her and I and now he. He did say that he wouldn't have her write me up and that he was also giving me his word that he wouldn't write me up himself.

I took a step forward and gave up the blade to the female officer and she gave me my letters. (I wanted the letters because I knew that if they got mailed I was going to find a way to go through with things regardless.) Before Sgt. Justice could walk away and before Brother Troup could come to my door to talk, the little female officer stopped them all in their tracks and told them this bit of news. She told them that she has known me for years upon years as she has been working here for that long, and right now she is beyond happy to still have her job and that she was able to talk me into giving the blade up because this is the very first time she has ever heard or seen me do something like this, as usually when I set my mind on doing something, either cutting or running the Seven Man Team in riot gear after being gassed with numerous cans of chemical agents, I always go forward with it because that is how I'm wired.

With that said, she and Sgt. Justice left and Brother Troup came forward to speak with me. I could see right away that he had been woken up out there in the general population where he lives and sleeps on W-Pod which is dorm-like living with numerous others. Rubbing the gunk from his eyes, the first thing out of his mouth is, "Put some hot water on for a cup of coffee, would ya?"

"No problem," I say and dig out my Hot-Pot to get the water started then start talking with my Brother.

As he and I are talking, I'm slowly unpacking all my property that I had packed up, getting my cage back into some order and the way I like everything. We talk about the Bible and God's word as I explain to Troup how I was ready to go and even had the blade in my hand raising it towards my throat to make that final cut when my conscience and this loud voice started screaming in my head, making me stop and think about everyone else.

You should understand that I don't hold the officers that work here responsible for me being here. How can I? My own actions placed me where I'm currently at today in life, Texas Death Row. This is just a job for most of the officers that work here, a way to provide for their loved ones, put food on the table, and pay the bills. I cannot be mad at them for that as it's more than I'm currently doing for those I love and care about. At least they're doing something honest and not out there on the streets slinging dope or walking the streets as a hooker/prostitute. They're holding down something that is legal by law and allows them to have a roof over their heads.

Troup and I talk long into the early morning hours before I send him back to his dorm/pod letting him know that I'm okay. We part ways telling one another we love the other and to keep our heads up. He goes on to tell me if I need to talk again don't hesitate to let them know you need to speak with a field minister.

After Troup leaves, I return to placing my things back into their spots and into order before taking a short nap as I have been awake for going on 36 hours now. Not being able to sleep, I just lay there thinking about everything, as I know that even though I was able to talk with Brother Troup, I wasn't out of the woods yet.

Shift change comes and goes and the day-shift officer that is now assigned to sit in front of my cage is another one that I know and talk with. This time though with this officer, he's coughing up a storm and telling me that he's under the weather and doing overtime today. The first thing I say to him is, are you vaccinated? Nope. Great, I think to myself, even though I have been fully vaccinated and had a booster shot, that doesn't make me safe from everything. As he and I are talking, we hear this female officer way over on another section screaming her head off and slamming the crossover doors that lead from one section to the other around the pod. When she gets to the section I'm on, which is A-Section, also known as Death Watch, she's going full out as if she's done lost her mind.

Her name is Officer Tiffany Pech. She is an officer with a very smart mouth, and I don't mean that she speaks intelligently but rather with foul language and a negative attitude toward some prisoners and other officers. She is the kind of person that talks major trash and does so because she knows that there is no real way for someone to get at her and let her know how it really is and that she should talk to people the way she would want to be spoken to.

As she comes before my cage and starts talking with the officer assigned to me, and as usual she's complaining about having to work A, B, and C pods alone because they are so short-staffed thanks to COVID-19. Normally there are to be three officers working each pod on 12-Building which houses both Death and Ad-Seg prisoners. These are all single-man cages. After she leaves, it's about two hours later when she returns with another officer, and they are doing showers now on the pod. Only when she comes around full circle do I ask what's up with my shower. She starts screaming at me with her foul mouth telling me that I don't get a shower because I'm on CDO (Constant Direct Observation)! I tell her that I'm not on CDO, but SO (Security Observation). She goes on to act like she knows everything and continues to scream at me and curse me telling me that she's not giving me a shower and that is that!

Shaking my head knowing that to do anything to her is wrong even though she was the one to start disrespecting me by calling me a little b---- and another foul word because I simply asked about something that I was and am entitled to, I decided to make sure that she had to work the same three pods tomorrow because by then having to assign an officer to sit in front of my cage daily until Mental Health took me off it, it would keep the staff on shortage and thus having to work more pods than normal.

After she and the officer with her walk off, I tell the officer sitting in front of my cage to open that log book by his feet. He does so, and I tell him to go to the left side of the log sheet and tell me what it says. As he's doing this he gets to the spot I was waiting for him to get to. It says: is the inmate in the shower? If so, check using bath! Who is the moron now? Both the officer and I start laughing at this, then I explain to him that her actions just caused me to see to it that tomorrow (meaning the following day) I would make sure that I still had an officer assigned to sit in front of my cage 24/7.

As we are standing there talking, the Necessity's officer, Officer Marlee Watson, comes walking up the stairs to relieve the officer with me because 12-Control wanted to speak with him. He's gone about 30 minutes before coming back and telling us both, myself and Officer Watson, about how Officer Jamie Brewer in 12-control told him that she was contacted by the warden and that he needed to shut up and stop talking with me because if he stopped talking with me and to me, then I would come off this Security Observation. She didn't know that Tiffany Pech and I had already gotten into it and that I had already told the officer that I was going to screw this shift over again tomorrow.

Sure enough, just as he finishes telling us what was said, here comes Mental Health Clinician Jeannette Harden. This woman is a very beautiful African American that makes every man that knows her salivate at the mouth! She is also a very good friend and she and I have known one another for years and years. After we talk a little bit, I explain what all took place in the night and how I and my mom were screwed over on the telephone when she was sharing the news with me about her sister, my auntie, being in a coma after contracting COVID-19 and sent home with her son, my cousin Damon, to die out there in California. I told her how these people disconnected the call right after she told me this bad/sad news and how I blew up at rank and everyone and punched the safety glass, breaking it.

She asked me how I was doing and what I wanted to do. I said since I still had all of my property and that this was something new being done (I could have come off Security Observation right then but thought of how Tiffany Pech spoke disrespectfully to me), I told Mrs. Harden to just leave me on this Security Observation for another 24 hours and come talk to me then and we'll see how I feel. She said okay and left.

After she had gone the officer and I laughed harder than heck because now Tiffany Pech and others like her would have to work numerous pods the next day. Less than 30 minutes later a Regional 1 Officer had been sent to my cage to change out with the officer that had been assigned to sit in front of my cage that day. When this took place I had been trying to lie down and get some sleep. When I was just starting to fall into a deep sleep, a flashlight beam hit my face and back wall, waking me up right away. The light didn't last but a few seconds, but it was enough to make me peek out from under my sheets and blanket towards my cage door to see who was sitting there now as I didn't watch the change but heard them speaking and talking about why he was being replaced with this Region 1 Officer (for talking to me).

When I looked out, I saw this short, stocky little guy with a baseball hat on his head and the look of a soldier. Diving back under the covers to try and sleep some more but being unable to, I decided to get up and move around as sleep was evading me for some reason. Plugging in my Hot-Pot to make some water for a cup of hot coffee, as that was heating, I washed my face and brushed my teeth, read my Daily Bread for the day, then as I'm filling my cup with hot water and instant coffee, I get the feeling on the back of my neck that this dude is still seriously looking at me. Peeking over my shoulder I see him still looking directly at me with a really intense stare that only a soldier knows how to pull off.

After a while, I decide to engage him and see what's up. I find out his name and out of respect for him, I'll just call him S. Sgt W. as I don't wish for him to get into any kind of trouble because once we got to talking, we easily fell into a respectful conversation and laughter with one another. I did find out that he was in the United States Marine Corps and did serve overseas a few times and that he loves M&M's with peanuts, lol!

He watched me clean my cage from floor to wall and asked me if this was something that I did daily and I told him yes. I asked him if he wanted to listen to some music and he said sure, and I tuned into a station of rock and roll which he greatly enjoyed. Then after a while, I shared some jokes with him so that he could share them with his coworkers as they traveled from prison to prison, as they were called or ordered to go to, to assist with operations there because of short staff or to shakedown certain cells of prisoners for contraband.

Just before the shift change at 5:30 p.m., I pulled him up by my cage door by asking him to step closer so I could say something to him. He said what's up? I told him that I'm sure most people in prison don't say this if ever to him, but I wanted him to know I was thankful for his service as a soldier. This lit his face up with a smile as one of his coworkers came upstairs to get him because about seven of them drove there together.

His coworker had a bag full of goodies from the prison Commissary and the first thing he pulls out is a pack of M&M's with peanuts and then a Mt. Dew soda. Standing out there by his coworker I overhear him telling him that I was the best Security Observation/Constant Direct Observation that he has ever had to sit on. I was respectful and the two of us were laughing at jokes and talking like people instead of prisoner and officer. When he finally left, I knew that I had made an impact on him and that he would remember me in a positive way instead of a prisoner that was disrespectful. After all, we're all human beings with a beating heart underneath our skin.

I thought about not sharing this but have decided that it needs to be told because the truth can be used as both a weapon and a learning tool for others. That night that Sgt. Justice was at my cage door giving me his word that he wouldn't write me a disciplinary case nor would he have his officers write me one for that razor blade, he did something that both stunned me and blew my mind. So, let me take you back to Sunday, January 9th, 2022 in the evening around 7 p.m.

That night the officers that were assigned to work A-Pod were Picket Control Officer Roark who was sick and would stay in the picket for the night, Officer Hays, and Officer Cassey (female). Earlier that afternoon we were supposed to get a telephone call but were told that they would happen on night shift. So, when these officers came onto shift and this pod to work, the other inmates hit them up about our telephone calls. When Officer Hays came up to 2-Row the first thing he says to me is, "Tabler, I asked rank about your telephone call to your mom and was told by both LT. Todd Tolar and Sgt. Justice that you do NOT get a telephone call."

I just looked at him and shook my head and said, "That's cool. I'll take care of everything." That night I got on this typewriter and sent out letters that I knew as always would pass both the warden's desk and his boss's, the director's, desk. I explained in my letters to loved ones about how I'm constantly getting screwed over by the same shift and how it's always LT. Highfill's shift on days and then night shift on both cards, Lieutenants Todd Tolar and Kent Glassel. After these letters were typed up, I stuck them in my door to be picked up with the outgoing mail and went to sleep, nothing I could do about it.

That is the reason that those officers showed up at my cage door on Tuesday, January 11th, 2022 telling me that everyone has been notified that I am to get a telephone call every Sunday to my mom due to her health. From there occurred the disrespect on my telephone call when I got bad news about my loved one slowly dying at home while in a coma from COVID-19. Fast forward to the next day when S.Sgt. W is now sitting on me for SO/CDO.

Around 3:45 p.m. a female captain whose name I don't remember and LT. Highfill came to my cage door and told the officer sitting with me, S.Sgt. W to go and take a break, that they were there to escort me to speak with Warden Dickerson in the major's office. Once we were down in the major's office and the two female ranking officers were sitting on the bench to my right and Warden Dickerson sitting behind the desk with me sitting in a chair directly across from him, Warden Dickerson and I started having a long and deep conversation.

I explained about everything going on: how I'm constantly getting screwed over on Sundays when Captain Gibson had given a direct order to Sgt. John Hardin and LT. Watson that they let others know I'm to be given a phone call every Sunday to my mother. Captain Gibson was in line with what the warden had already issued but other rank aside from LT. Watson's shift refused to, stating that I was never told by rank or the warden that I'm to be given a telephone call every Sunday to my mom.

I explained about the disrespectful telephone call on Tuesday with my mom and how I was given bad news about my loved one in a coma at home and given days to live, about how the sergeants that were listening into the call were laughing at our situation, and about how I went off and punched the safety glass. Then I told him about how the captain had me escorted down to this very office the day before under the guise of talking with a warden about how she said what she did and how I reacted to her after that. This whole time that same captain is sitting to my right nodding her head and saying that is exactly what was said and how I responded.

Taking a breath, it was then that the captain spoke up and apologized to me because she had no idea what was going on and said she shouldn't have come at me like that. I told her in front of Warden Dickerson that it was all good and that I also wanted to apologize. She accepted my apology as well. That was when I looked directly at LT. Highfill, who was now standing by the door instead of sitting down on the bench with the captain. I explained to the three of them, while looking directly at LT. Highfill, about last night and the razor blade situation and how I wanted to cut out and end my life because I was sick and tired of doing time and of the treatment by those who hold an attitude/grudge against prisoners and myself in general. I said the thing that affected me the most about last night though is that when Sgt. Justice came to my cage, he said he was doing so because he wanted to apologize to me! Sgt. Justice went on to explain to me that his lieutenant, LT. Todd Tolar, lied to him and his officers on Sunday night, January 9th, 2022 when Officer Hays asked about my telephone call. LT. Todd Tolar was told face-to-face by LT. Highfill to give Tabler a telephone call to his mother that night and he was also sent an email from LT. Watson as were all lieutenants and sergeants by LT. Watson. It was LT. Todd Tolar's actions and choice to do what he did by screwing me over and in doing so lying to his own sergeants and officers in turn. Such actions could cause all kinds of problems had he done this out in the general population or any other prison. "That said," I told LT. Highfill, "I want to apologize to you because I felt like it was you screwing me over for some reason that I couldn't understand, and I ask you all to not just take my word for this but question this young Sgt. Justice when he comes on shift tonight."

After I said all of this there was a moment of silence before Warden Dickerson asked both women to leave the office and close the door so he could talk to me alone, please. They did so and once the door was closed, Warden Dickerson and I started talking about just daily things and life. We laughed a little when I explained that I could have come off the SO/CDO today but wanted to remain on it after Officer Tiffany Pech was disrespectful towards me and screwed me out of a shower. He even said I was supposed to get a shower, lol!

We spoke about his diet that he's on and how his wife makes sure he eats a salad daily instead of all the food he loves to eat. I asked if it were possible if he could please call my mom to let her know that I was doing okay because, after the phone call I had with her, she is under the impression that I'm fixing to check out. I would like her to not worry any longer, please. He said sure and grabbed the telephone on the desk, but it wouldn't work right, so he called in LT. Highfill and explained that the telephone wasn't working right, could she please get another jack for the phone so he could place a call? This was done right away, and after she left with closing the door behind her.

I took notice of two large pizzas sitting on the bench now that I hadn't seen earlier. Looking at Warden Dickerson I asked what's up with the pizzas. He said that they weren't his and I said, "Well, what the wife doesn't know doesn't hurt. What do you say we split them real fast?" He laughed and said nope because those women out there that were in here would surely beat us up. He then placed a call to my mom and we got to speak for about 20 minutes. I explained that the telephone situation has been cleared up and that according to Warden Dickerson, I would be given a telephone call to her every Sunday afternoon or evening. We hung up after giving one another our love and she thanked Warden Dickerson for everything.

After the telephone call, Warden Dickerson and I spoke a little bit about the new tablets that were coming into the Polunsky Unit prison and to Death Row prisoners from Securus Technologies, the JP6S tablet, and how they should be here within the next couple of months and that he was trying to get Death Row prisoners access also to the telephone hookup on them as this would greatly help him out with everything.

Once we were finished and I raised from my seat to walk out (with cuffs still on behind my back) I looked lovingly at the two pizzas and tried one more time with Warden Dickerson saying, "You know, you can always look the other way as I'm walking out and I can do the five-finger discount, seeing that I'm in prison already, what can they do?!" He just laughed and I thanked him and walked out to my escorting ladies, the lieutenant and captain.

After returning to my cage, I was still on SO/CDO and the Regional 1 Officer, S.Sgt. W was there waiting for me. The next day I would ask to be taken off of SO/CDO, which would happen. It was now January 13th, 2022. Thirty minutes after being taken off of it, LT. Watson came by my cage to talk with me as she was making her rounds on the pod. Starting on 1-Row and walking around so that she came from F-Section 2-Row, I was the last person she would pass by.

When she passed by my cage, I took notice that she was walking with another officer. She stopped for a few minutes just to make sure that I was okay because when she came on shift that morning and heard that I was on SO/CDO she couldn't believe it as nobody else could either. I told her I was okay but still in a dark mindset, so now I was going to just take it one day at a time and that the only reason I told the Mental Health woman (who wasn't J. Garden) was because she always rubbed me wrong and thus, I could not speak with her openly. I knew that she would end up shipping me out to another prison where I would be butt-naked for anywhere from one week to three weeks before being allowed some boxers and any other clothing. She had the bad habit of doing this to anyone that spoke with her.

The other prison is called Jester-4 and it's a Mental Health prison for prisoners losing their minds or showing signs of doing so. I never could understand why they would want to ship a Death Row prisoner to such a place. I would try my best to point out to them (Mental Health staff) that it made no sense to do so because what are you going to do there? Place us on medication so the State can say that for those of us that are mentally ill, we are now being medicated and have an understanding of why we're being executed? What could they possibly do for someone that has been handed down a sentence of death?!

My second reason for coming off of it was because it was a new shift card and it was LT. Watson's shift. She is the only lieutenant that not only did her job but did so with a heart of gold and compassion for those of us on Texas Death Row. That's not to say that she was showing us favoritism, because she wasn't. Allow me to explain why and how I know this to be true and correct.

One afternoon I was out in the legal booth waiting for a legal telephone call with my lawsuit lawyer, David A. Lane of Killmer, Lane &

Newman, LLP out of Denver, Colorado when I noticed LT. Watson standing outside the legal booth door talking with someone. After she was finished speaking with an officer, I asked her a question. I said, "LT. Watson, how is it you can treat every one of us prisoners the same? What I mean is how can you continue to always show us such compassion when I'm sure numerous other prisoners, both Death Row and Ad-Seg, have caught Code-20s from you? I'm asking you this because I would like to write another book to help troubled teens/young adults and others about this kind of life."

    She took a step or two backward and stood up against the wall that was directly across from the legal booth I was in. This way I could stand up and look at her directly. Looking back at me and making sure to make eye contact the whole time, as this is a sign of respect between the both of us, she told me that, "Tabler, I'm able to treat you all the same like you've pointed out because I strongly believe in God. It's not my place to judge anyone here within these prison walls. I believe that everyone is capable of changing his/her life if they so choose to do so. Knowing this and knowing that I have a relationship with God, I'm able to treat you all the same day in and day out."

    I told her thank you and as she was getting ready to walk away and get back to whatever she was doing that day, I saw that she was now smiling. It wasn't long before I found out that she was going to be doing escorts with numerous other officers because they were running Classification for the Ad—Seg prisoners that were housed in 12-Building. My wait would be a few hours after my legal call with David A. Lane, Esq.

    After my legal call with David, I had been standing there for some time now, I stopped Assistant Warden Rigsby who was also walking by. I asked Assistant Warden Rigsby how he was doing and if I could ask him something for my next book. Sure, he said, what's up? I said what is one thing that you would like everyone out in society to know about yourself that they don't know? He told me, "Tabler, you tell everyone in your next book that I'm allergic to B.S." I said are you serious, that's what you want me to say about yourself? Yes, he said.

    About an hour or so later after watching numerous prisoners being escorted back and forth from in front of the legal booth I was waiting in, I witnessed the following take place in the hallway. They had just escorted this huge African American prisoner from down on F-Pod to the place where they were holding Classification, which consisted of at the time

Captain Gibson, Mrs. Runnels, some other person I didn't know, and Assistant Warden Rigsby. As I listened to what all is going on, I hear someone ask this prisoner what his name and number was and what he had to say. Not hearing that response but only the response of A.W. Risgby telling the prisoner to walk back to his cell, I can see the escorting lieutenant that is with Regional 1 and another officer walking back towards my direction. Before I can see the prisoner stop and start talking trash to everyone, telling them all that he ain't no punk or a B---- and that they need to show him some respect, he is now being ordered to walk back to his cell by A.W. Risgby.

After about five minutes he starts walking back with his escorts. Passing me by I just look at him and shake my head. Not even 10 minutes later I see another Regional 1 team escort going past where I'm standing in the legal booth and not three minutes later here comes the prisoner that was just talking trash to the Classification and A.W. Rigsby.

As he gets closer to where he was during the Classification and A.W. Risgby, I hear A.W. Rigsby say put him in the legal booth then go and shakedown his cell and take everything. As they go to walk back in my direction and place him into the legal booth, they see that they cannot do so because I'm standing right there, as I have been for almost four hours now.

They explain to A.W. Rigsby that someone is in the legal booth. Just as they say this, the big prisoner that not long before was talking trash, starts screaming that he's suicidal and that he's going to hang himself when he gets back into his cell on F-Pod. Not being able to help myself, I yell out the legal booth door, "I thought you said you weren't no punk and that you weren't going to be treated like such!"

Everyone is now silent from hearing what I said, then they just escort the dude back to his cell. Next thing I know I'm being escorted back to my own cage on A-Pod, A-Section. Passing the Classification and A.W. Rigsby, I say to him, "I thought you told me to tell everyone out in society in my next book that you're allergic to B.S. What do you call how you just acted, lol!"

After speaking with LT. Watson at my cage door on Thursday, January 13th, 2022, she walks off to do her job and I go under my headphones and listen to my radio. The next few days pass by and I sink deeper and deeper into the darkness.

Another Sunday comes around and goes by without being able to make a telephone call home to my mom because Major Taliesin Stern has locked up the cordless telephones in his office and because it's the weekend and he's working out in general population instead of 12-Building, the telephone call cannot be made until Monday the 17th of January, which happens to fall on Martin Luther King Jr. Day.

When I'm finally able to speak to my mom this day, I found out that my Great Aunt Lena had just celebrated her 92nd birthday on that Sunday while she was in her coma dying. It hit me a bit harder because it just reminded me that we inside prison are not the only ones suffering from COVID-19, but our loved ones and everyone around the world are having a really difficult time surviving out there in society.

Monday turned into Tuesday and Tuesday turned into Wednesday and Wednesday turned into a darker place as shift change came on and for no reason I could understand, another officer who had become a friend too stopped by my cage before heading over to work in 11-Building. When Officer Losoya got to my cage door, he had tears in his eyes and told me, "Tabler, just know my friend that a lot of people in here and out there care about you, and don't give up because God is right here with you. It's gonna be okay, my friend."

Not having any idea why he had come by and was saying this to me, I told him I understood and that I was thankful for his kind words as usual. Ten minutes after he left, another officer walked up the stairs to 2-Row with a chair, walkie-talkie (radio), gas mask, a huge can of MK-9 chemical agents, and a logbook. I had been placed on SO (Security Observation) once again. This would be the second time in less than one week. I tried to ask the officer why I had been placed on this once again in less than one week and was told that as the lieutenant was giving out who would work where during that shift (night) he was called out of the turnout room being told that he had a telephone call from someone.

Leaving for about 10 minutes to take the call in the lieutenant's office, he came back explaining that he had just spoken directly with the general population Assistant Warden B. Jackson and that it has been ordered that Alpha 10 was being placed on Security Observation. No reason was given. I would remain this time on SO/CDO from that night of January 19th, 2022 till Friday, January 21st, 2022.

Another Sunday would pass without a telephone call home to my mother until Monday night, January 24th, 2022. During this call, I found out that she (my mom) had contacted the warden's office on Wednesday morning the 19th only to have to speak with a secretary because the wardens were not in their offices. When the message was left and received later that night, A.W. Jackson had me placed on SO/CDDO for safety/security reasons.

On Tuesday morning my Great Aunt Lena died. May she rest in peace with all the angels in Heaven and our other loved ones that went before her. That was on Tuesday, January 18th, 2022 that she passed and the news reached the warden's office on Wednesday the 19th, thus me being placed on SO/CDO.

From that telephone call on the 24th with my mom, I would continue to sink further and further into a dark place within my mind and soul. I was tired of being locked up in prison, tired of fighting with lawyers from the Capital Habeas Unit's Federal Court Division in Philadelphia, tired of suffering from survivor's guilt. I knew it was only a matter of time before I slipped so far backward that I started cutting on myself to relieve myself of the pain and heartache of everything.

Later on that same afternoon of the 24th, LT. Watson would stop by my cage one last time before having to go through shift change with the night shift LT. Kent Glassel. When she stopped by to ask me if I was going to be okay, I told her one way or the other. I could tell that she didn't like my answer because this is a woman/officer that I have known since she was only an officer with no rank. But I knew she also cared about some more than others.

On Thursday the 27th, 2022 I was set to have a legal visit with Cassandra Belter of the CHU (Capital Habeas Unit) who I thought was a friend, but actions came to show that she was just another lawyer/investigator. When I was finally escorted out to the visitation building for a legal visit with her and placed into legal booth A-5, she was finishing up with a legal visit with John Balentine. As Balentine was being escorted out of visitation, he told me that Cassandra had something she was going to tell me from him. Not knowing what to expect, I said okay and then he was gone out the door.

Waiting for Cassandra to take a seat across from me, the first thing she tells me is that everyone at CHU had told her this morning that she wasn't to visit with me, but she was there anyways to let me know something I mailed to her was out of line. Before she could go any further, I told her I knew that as soon as I mailed it and explained that when I wrote it, I was messed up but that's no excuse and I want to apologize. She accepted the apology and then told me that John Balentine said to tell me hello and God bless and that everything would be okay. I wasn't expecting this from Balentine because he's always laughing or cutting up jokes, but I guess he had been hearing from everyone and officers what was going on with me lately and how I was sinking into a dark place.

After she said that, though I could tell that whatever friendship I thought we had was no longer there, she tried to tell me that she was worried about me, but from the time she said what she did about her bosses telling her not to visit, I had locked down my thoughts and kindness. I started planning more of what I was wanting to do. She left after 30 minutes as this is about the longest she's been visiting with me for some time now, short visits or getting further and further away from the friendship we had at one time, that of like a li'l sister to a big brother, but it was now dead. I always knew that I was for the most part just another paycheck to my lawyers, but a small part of me just wanted to be loved and accepted as a person and not for the actions I was doing time for on Texas Death Row.

After she left and I was once again back inside my cage, I started packing up all of my personal property into my mesh bags. I had made up my mind that I was finished with everything and I'd either end my life come Friday the 28th of January or I would go back to cutting on myself to release my anger and pain from everything that I held from long ago and currently in my life.

Friday morning came around and because of COVID-19 the prison was once again short staffed and the officers that did show up, which were very few, were working between two and three pods instead of only working on one pod with two other officers. Around 11:30 a.m. I started to pace back and forth in my cage trying to either talk myself out of cutting or going through with it to kind of hit a reset button within myself. Before I knew it, I had cut myself on my left arm 120 times and when I had gotten up to 100, I started cutting deeper and deeper.

I don't know why or what caused me to stop at that number, but I did so, allowing the blood to clog up and harden enough so that I could clean my cage up of the blood all over the floor and wall. Once I had cleaned everything up, I tried to figure out why I did it and what I really wanted to do. I hadn't cut on myself for years.

Just as I was thinking these thoughts, here comes Warden Dickerson and two wardens from another prison. Once they came on the section, I'm thinking to myself, please stay your butts on 1-Row because I didn't want to cause an issue for Warden Dickerson. I was now feeling bad that I did this to myself because he out of everyone has done what he could to help me and many other Death Row prisoners in ways that nobody could ever imagine.

Sure enough, they walk up to 2-Row and when they get by my cage I had my cage blacked out so you couldn't see inside while standing in front of my door, though I was also standing right by my door so I could speak with Warden Dickerson if he decided to stop at my door and ask me how everything was going. He did in fact stop after the other two wardens with him walked further down the run.

When they were out of sight, I turned so that he could see my neck and where I had started to cut my throat before showing him the razor blade and that I was now flushing it down my toilet. That was when he saw the major part and my left arm. When he saw this, he literally sagged against my cage door. It was then that I knew from deep inside myself that he really cared about me and others here and that my cuts and self-harm affected him in such a profound way. The last person I wanted to hurt, or thought that my actions against myself would hurt, was Warden Dickerson. I never thought my self-harm would have the effect it did on him.

I told him that I was good now, I just needed to hit the reset button on my life and within myself as I had always been in some way or another what society calls a cutter. I just needed some medical attention if possible but if not, I could clean it up myself.

He couldn't talk because he was so hurt, and I felt so bad. I had known Warden Dickerson for a long time since I got to Texas Death Row and he wasn't a warden but a jerk. Now I was seeing for real that he was a Christian. Nodding his head and walking away from my cage and myself as well, he spoke to LT. Highfill and then sent a text message to A.W. Rigsby about what I had done and what he wanted to be done for me.

About 30 minutes later Sgt. Amanda Maddox and Sgt. Scott Grimm are knocking on my cage door telling me to come on, that A.W. Rigsby wants to talk to you in the major's office. Cuffing up and exiting my cage, we walk down the stairs and off the section, and then the pod. As we enter the major's office, I see A.W. Rigsby sitting behind the desk and the captain and lieutenant sitting on the bench to the right inside the office. Now along with these ranking officers, you have myself plus two sergeants who brought me into that office.

A.W. Rigsby asks me what's going on. As I explain that I just needed to hit a reset button, he surprised me with this. He explained to me that he understood because he had a family member that used to rub an eraser on his arm to burn himself. It was a way to reset himself and not actually hurt himself to kill but just to release his pain and anger. When he explained to this family member that he needed to find another way, he started choking himself instead. He went on to explain that he understood that I and others did this as a way to cope and deal with everything when we feel burdened with life and all we go through. That said, he asked, "Are you okay, Tabler?"

I told him that I was okay now and that I just needed to reset. He told me okay and that I needed to make sure and not make him look bad because he was going to take me at my word. He could have had me downgraded and my personal property removed from my cage. Instead, he told me that I was being given a second chance because he was told to do so by Warden Dickerson and because he also understood that punishment wasn't the right thing to do because he was pretty sure it would only push me all the way over the cliff.

The sergeants were ordered by the A.W. to take me to the Emergency Room there in the prison to get cleaned up. Once over at 10-Building which is the prison Medical/Hospital, I was escorted into the ER Room and told to take a seat on the bed/gurney which I did as told. When one of the staff came into the ER Room and saw what I had done she asked me a million questions and I told her I just needed to hit reset and that I'm dealing with a lot both inside these walls and outside of them thanks to COVID-19. She started to try and wipe the blood from my arm so she could see what had been done when I said to her why don't I step over to the sink and use the water to slowly wipe it away? Good idea she told me, so that is what we did with some bottle of what is like blood remover/soap and warm water directly spraying onto my arm. While the sergeants are sitting off to the side, they knew that I wouldn't do anything, but they couldn't help but ask, "Tabler, doesn't that hurt when she is washing it off and really scrubbing it with warm water?" Truthfully, I said that my mind was shut off right now and that I can block or turn off the pain from feeling anything. Thus, I'm not feeling it right now, so I'm good.

It took her about two hours to get my arm cleaned up enough so we could all see the damage done to my arm and it was bad. The provider entered the room and said that I would need staples. Do you want to take something for the pain? No. Just get it done because right now I don't feel the pain as I turned that part of my mind off.

They all looked at me like I was crazy but went to work getting the staple gun out and I laid my arm down so he could work on it. I ended up with 27 staples in my left arm. When the report on how much damage was done was relayed to the captain, all she said was god----!

When I was escorted back onto 12-Building everyone was told to put me back inside my cage. Questions were asked, who is going to watch him on SO/CDO? They were told that I wasn't being placed on it and that I wouldn't be disciplined because they (wardens) understood what was going on within me. To say that everyone was stunned is nothing short of a miracle.

That following Saturday morning when the new card (shift) came on it was none other than LT. Watson's card, and when she was making her rounds on the pod and got to my cage, I could see that when she found out when she arrived at the prison and saw/viewed pictures, they messed her up too. She couldn't believe that I wasn't on SO/CDO, but everything was kept hush-hush. But when she stopped to talk to me it was with tear-filled eyes because she was so hurt by my actions and yet she shared with me that she honestly understood too because she has been dealing with depression herself.

Throughout the next few days, I would learn from numerous officers that they too would deal with depression at one point in their lives by self-harm. Those talks from these officers would help me in letting me know that there was nothing wrong with me and that we all go through life and deal with things in our own ways. It's what we do after we learn these things in our lives that matter.

Knowing this though and doing it are two different things. As much as I wanted to get back on the right track within myself and these prison walls, I just couldn't seem to get there. It was like every time that I started to get traction under my feet, I would get hit with something else that would bring me to my knees.

Because the mail out in society is backed up and it is always bad within prison walls, a letter that was written and mailed to me on Tuesday, January 25th, 2022 from a very dear friend who started out as a spiritual advisor to me named Mary from Austin, Texas. On the very Monday that I was making a telephone call to my mom and finding out that my Great Aunt Lena died, my friend Mary's mom also died that day, may she too rest in peace with all the angels in Heaven.

Throughout my years spent on Texas Death Row (16 years as of this writing), I have been up to my neck in trouble within these very walls. From constantly being gassed with chemical agents to having a seven-man use-of-force team run into my cage after being hit with said chemical agents, I have caused nothing but trouble when certain officers went out of their way to cause me trouble as well.

Any time I was escorted out of my cage to either the shower or down to the disciplinary captain's office where they hold the hearings and always find us guilty regardless, I would either sit down on the run refusing to walk back to my cage, thus ensuring that they would have to carry me, or I would jack the disciplinary captain's office refusing to walk the long walk back to my cage. This would not only make everyone mad but would see to it that they now had to do further paperwork because once they touch me with their hands it becomes a major use of force and a video camera must become involved in everything.

The following pictures are a taste of what I went through within these prison walls. You'll see what I did to myself when I would cut or in one incident actually tried to end my life after being given an execution date that I had volunteered for only for it to be taken away without my asking for it.

If you think that prison or jail is fun, it's not and you're a fool to think that it is. Think your friends that are running the streets with you are going to be there for you when you fall and get yourself locked up? You're not only lying to yourself, but they are also lying to you. They're only your friends when you're down for doing stupid things out there in society or doing illegal garbage.

Do you think it's cool or that you're someone to respect and fear because you can pick up a weapon such as a pistol? If this is something you believe, you should take your young butt down to the local hospital and see up close and personal what happens to those on the receiving end of gun violence from being shot by another gang member or some idiot involved in road rage or some racist act in their lives.

And if that doesn't do it for you, you or your loved ones that are trying to save your young life from such violence should take you down to the city morgue so that you can see and smell what a dead body looks like. They should make you sit in on an autopsy. This way you can see firsthand what your actions can and will cause another person if you continue down the path you might currently be on.

If these thoughts aren't enough to make you pause what and how you're acting in life, think about that body being someone you love such as your own mom, sister, brother, father, boyfriend or girlfriend, or spouse, one of your kids. What is it going to take to make you see that what and how you're behaving is the wrong way and the wrong path in life? Yeah, yeah, I'm sure that you're saying this would never happen to me or mine because nobody would ever find where I live or where my loved ones live. Do you honestly believe that stupidity?

I found somebody I had been searching for from the time I was 17 years old until I was 25 years old and found him from within prison in California and was on my way to end his life in Chicago before my actions here in Texas got the best of me and cost others their lives instead of the man I was seeking in another state. My actions here in Texas caused family members of my victims to lose their husbands, brothers, and fathers as well as others. It cost me my freedom and the freedom of my codefendant who is innocent of any serious crime and only acted because he feared for his life from me.

To this very day, I'm trying to make amends to those I've hurt or caused pain to as well as trying to help get my codefendant out of prison or a new trial because he shouldn't be in prison for what he is in for. He shouldn't be serving a capital life sentence. More about that in the later part of this story I'll be sharing with you. For now, think about what I have shared with you here on these pages and look and read over the following pages and pictures and imagine what your loved ones would be going through if these pictures were of you or someone you know. How do you think that would make them feel? Take your time and I'll see you all in the next chapter.

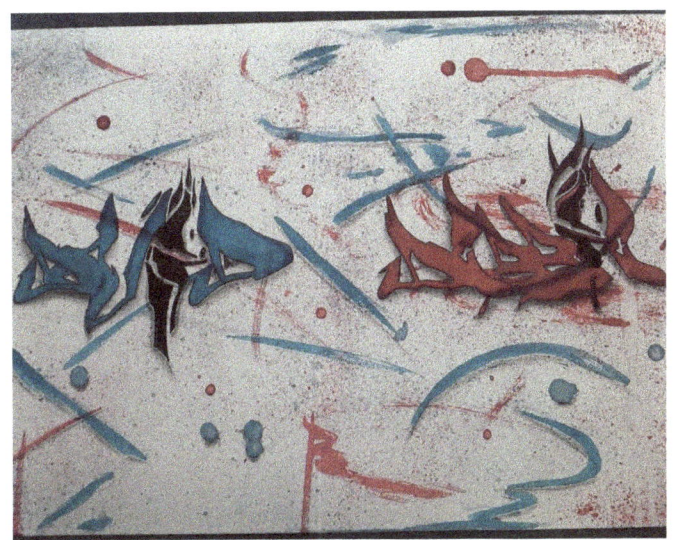

Abstract 1

Colored pencil drawing Karen and Tim

Colored pencil drawing of a Parrot

Colored pencil drawing of hummingbird

Colored pencil drawing of a butterfly

Colored pencil drawing

Cross with wings

Farmhouse

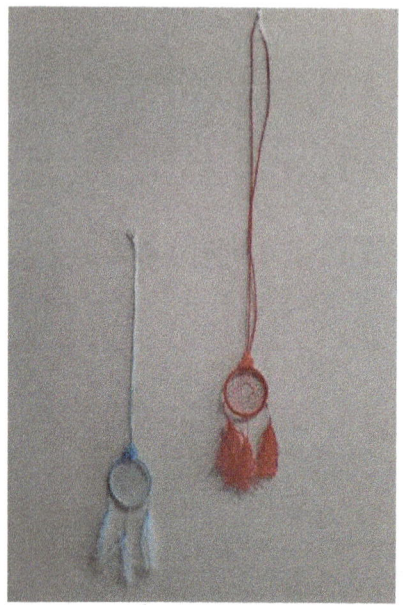
Dreamcatchers

House on island

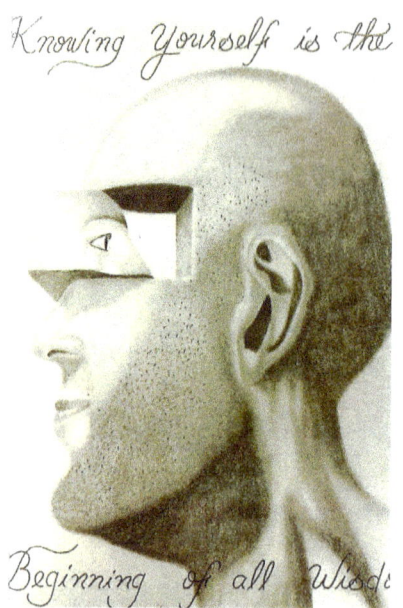
Knowing yourself is the beginning of all wisdom drawing

Pencil drawing and thoughts on Donald trump 2020

Field Minister- Brother Troup Foster handing me my certificates

My friend, Josina and her cat in Germany rading my first book

My Life Coach-Brother-Friend, Jimmy Smith

Jimmy Smith and his beautiful wife, Stacey

NEW PHOTO SENT 6-6

My little friend Sasha of Atlanta Georgia

My mom, sister and Niece 2022

Overcomers Certificate and Large Pizza and Puppies

Teacup pup

Pencil drawing of Sasha

Pencil drawing of the sorry
Eagles QB

Watercolor painting of Jesus
Christ 2020

pencil drawing of Cassandra Belter

Pencil drawing of Master Hopkins, Cassandra Belter's owner

pencil drawing of someomone's cat

You want to smoke weed, go purchase it legally.

Pickup

River

Watercolor painting of woman rising out of water

watercolor painting

CHAPTER TWO

POSITIVE CHANGE

"Some sat in darkness and the shadow of death,
Prisoner in affliction and in irons,
For they had rebelled against the words of God,
And spurned the counsel of the Most High.
So he bowed their hearts down with hard labor;
They fell down, with none to help.
Then they cried to the Lord in their trouble,
And he delivered them from their distress.
He brought them out of darkness and the shadow of death,
And burst their bonds apart.
Let them thank the Lord for his steadfast love,
For His wondrous works to the children of man!
For He shatters the doors of bronze
And cuts in two the bars of iron."
Psalm 107:10-16

On Saturday, February 5th, 2022, as I was reading a book while laying on my bunk, I could hear my name being called. "Tabler! Tabler! Tabler!" Getting up and walking the few steps to my cage door I yelled out, "What's up?!" That's when I hear all 14 men on C-Section start singing aloud to me, "Happy birthday to Tabler, happy birthday to you, happy birthday to Taaaabbblller, happy birthday tooo yooouuu!!!"

Thanking each of the fellas on that section, I went back to my bunk shaking my head while also being hit very deeply and emotionally by that simple song to me for my 43rd birthday. It was the very first time in 18 years since anyone has sung me or wished me a happy birthday, and to have 14 grown men sing it to me with God in their hearts was a whole 'nother thing. Little did I know that that simple act of kindness would start to break through the darkness that had been pulling me down every time I started to get my feet under me and feel like I was standing on solid ground.

The following Sunday, after speaking to my mom on the telephone and making a friendly mother/son bet on the Super Bowl, I would also make a $10 bet with "Spider" as I would bet that the Bengals would win. After losing by three points, I tuned into this FM radio station on my radio called "The Word." This station is always airing church services and other shows, one being "Oasis" on FM 100.7 on Sunday nights from 10 p.m. to midnight Texas time. It's run by a family of believers in Jesus Christ and Pastor Lonnie. The loved ones of prisoners can call into this station and give a shout-out to their loved ones over the air while also listening in on a live church service and mini service. It's a real blessing for all involved. The number to call "Oasis" is 800-808-5548. For those of you reading this that would like to call into the radio station and share how God has worked in your lives or how this book has touched you in a positive light, I would recommend that you call in or just tune in online and listen to them speak because I promise you, you'll walk away feeling 10 times better than you were!

As I was laying on my bunk late that Sunday night and listening to the brothers and sisters speaking to everyone, I started to be moved deep in my heart and soul and took the step to rededicate my life to Jesus Christ by saying the Sinner's Prayer. From that day until the present, I have become stronger in my walk with God and His Son Jesus Christ. I have stopped using foul language and writing such curse words in any of my letters to friends or lawyers or family. Instead, I find that I'm sharing God's message with everyone I write, even a radio station out in Houston, Texas called KRBE and the Roula & Ryan show along with their coworkers Special K, Eric & Samantha (Sam).

I have fully forgiven myself and for the first time in my 43 years of life, I love myself and am showing and sharing love with everyone else and doing my faith-based programs such as Bridges to Life and Overcoming Life-controlling Problems. I and 31 other Life Row (Texas Death Row) prisoners will be graduating on March 11th, 2022 from both these programs. On this day there will be a special service taking place as we each are given our certificate of completion and a meal for doing so. Special guests will be coming such as Dennis Martinez who is the world and U.S. skateboard champion, Darlene Bahr who is a singer and songwriter, Bill Corum who is an author, and lastly, we will be having Christian rap artist Dontae and about 15 other people from the Texas Department of Criminal Justice such as directors and wardens of other prisons to see and hear everything that will be taking place that day.

None of this would have ever happened had it not been for God and His Son Jesus Christ working in and through Warden Dickerson, Assistant Warden Rigsby, Assistant Warden Jackson, and Director Hazelwood who is the Regional Chaplaincy Director. The prison chaplains here at the prison, Chaplain Gay (pronounce Guy) and Chaplain Martin as well as the many volunteer chaplains and speakers that come from out in society to share their stories with us from Bridges to Life, none of it could have happened without the love and push from our field ministers Troup, Solley, Mann, Gomez, Gallardo, Lee, and the other brothers that are not field ministers but are a part of the prison church and come back here every Wednesday evening to hold a mini church service and many songs that are sung by Carlos.

The Polunsky Unit (prison) also has its very own radio station that is called "The Tank" which is run by prisoners for prisoners and our very own Megamind. This station has everything from different church services as well as Muslim services. It gives everyone a chance to listen to a certain kind of music during different times and announcements from the unit warden, Warden Dickerson, and other speakers. Without all of this many prisoners would still be sitting in darkness, and I could very well be one of them. A lot of work goes into running such a radio station, and even more work is constantly put in by all our field minister brothers. It matters not the time of day or night, but if there is an issue or major situation that calls for a field minister to be called out, then they are called out to speak to prisoners that are having a difficult time or got news of the death of a loved one. We all have days that feel like they will be the last, but we all also have heart and strength and the will to continue fighting and making a difference in our lives and those around us.

Throughout the coming days and weeks, I would be pushed to limits that I never expected from committing myself to walking with Jesus Christ and doing my best to abide by His Words in the Holy Bible. I knew when I first decided to fully walk in His light that I would be tested by the devil. Every chance he got to tear me down he would because he doesn't want me to be good or to follow what Jesus Christ tells us each to do in His Word. Evil is like a disease. It rubs off, scrapes off, gets airborne, and breathed in. It gets picked up from living hard or from being hurt. It comes from need, everybody's need!

I have found that a great place to ask yourself what kind of follower you are is by reading Matthew 13;1-23. This is where Jesus Christ is speaking to the crowd. In this chapter, He tells us the story of the parable of the four soils. Nope, just because I am a follower of Him doesn't mean that I'm going to do your work for you. If you want to know what it says then go and pick up a Bible and read it for yourself. You cannot be lazy your whole life.

I will tell you this from my own experience though. It's easy to agree with Jesus's words, but it's also easy to let life's pressures and attractions to that kind of life that you are currently living crowd Him out of walking in a positive light or way than what you're used to. Distractions can easily rob a new believer of his/her time to dive deeper into God's word and grow from it. That kind of life can stifle the guidance and support you'll need to mature. Business, worries, and the desire to show off for that special someone in your life or make more money will only downgrade God's priorities so your life continues to produce nothing of value.

If you think I'm lying, just stop for a second and think about where I'm writing this book for you from… See what I'm talking about? This is no life for anyone, and I wouldn't wish this kind of life on my worst enemy! Even now I have thoughts that I shouldn't be having, but I know that I'm not perfect and will always sin in my life no matter how hard I try and how hard I tell myself that I can do better. I will always fail just as each and every one of you will. But that doesn't mean we get to give up and throw in the towel. It just means that we have to keep fighting for something that is beyond all our understanding!

Day in and day out I listen on my radio the news on NPR and I hear about all the killings going on out there and the violence, people screaming out about how cops are getting away with murder and racism, etc. I'm not saying that I agree with what the cops are getting away with, but have you ever stopped to think about why they are all of a sudden acting this way or people in society are acting?

I've been places and seen things long before I came to prison my first time out in California and Florida, and long before I landed my butt on Texas Death Row 18 years ago. One thing I have noticed is that the police become callous, which is a fact as old as time. They're constantly overexposed to death and cruelty in the world, and in turn, they just stop believing in the general goodness of the human heart and all that greeting card crap, and they look upon depravity and murder as being common to the human condition. They stand by talking or laughing while one of their own kneels down on the throat of George Floyd, not paying any real mind. They act this way and have become this way because we as a people have shown them that it's okay to kill and murder by our own actions.

I'm not saying that I'm a saint because I'm far from anything close to that, but I know and have seen firsthand how gang members are out there killing one another over turf or some other idiotic thing and in the process accidentally murder a child in a drive-by. But not all cops are bad just like not all human beings are bad. There will always be good and bad just as there is Ying and Yang, salt and pepper, light and dark. It's part of life and until we are willing to come together as a whole we will continue to fail and kill one another until nobody is left.

Stop screaming bloody murder and start looking into the mirror for a change! All it takes is for one voice to start a movement or seek out peace. If you are at peace, then there is at least some peace in the world. Then share your peace with everyone and everyone will be at peace. God intends for you to openly share with others your peace of mind and freedom from life-controlling problems that have resulted from your relationship with Jesus Christ. You should tell those you meet who are also struggling like you once did, or like I did and am now sharing with you here on these pages, how you found peace of mind and release. If you are already experiencing God's love and hope, then share it with someone that isn't so that they too can know what you're feeling and going through!

Recently here on Texas Death Row, we held a mini church service that the field ministers do for us every Wednesday evening. On this Wednesday though it was extra special because a friend to many of us here named Spider was set to be executed on March 8th, 2022 at 6 p.m. by lethal injection. This Wednesday evening though on March 2nd, 2022, while the service was taking place Field Minister Terry Solley went around with the open mic asking/allowing anyone who wanted to do so to say a few words to Spider. Every one of the 14 men housed on C-Section said something to Spider which was mainly that each of them was praying for him and sending him their love.

Then Terry Solley entered into the other faith-based section, B-Section, and again every one of the 14 men in that section also said something to Spider, letting him know that each of them was praying for him and sending their love along with a little joke here or there.

Then Terry Solley came over into A-Section where only three of us are enrolled in the faith-based courses and two who are not. First, he went to CB in #1 cell and he said a few words to Spider before Terry moved on to RG in #7 cell and he too said some things to Spider, letting him know that he too was praying for him to get a stay of execution. Then Terry came upstairs to my cage in #10. I told Spider that I had been praying that he would soften his heart towards God and allow Him to come into his life because if He can work in my life and save my life, then what does Spider have to lose? I told him that I loved him and prayed he would do this and that God would grant him a stay of execution.

Then Terry walked down to run two cells to ask another prisoner named Kosoul if he wanted to say something Spider, and he said no.

Field Minister Terry Solley then walked down the stairs to Spider's cell in #6 where Field Minister Troup was standing also. There he asked Spider what he had to say to all the love and prayers he just heard from his friends that have known him for over 10 years. All we could hear was Spider, this big guy that is from Odessa, Texas, letting his emotions run freely now for the first time since any one of us has known him. This side of the pod was dead silent, you could hear a needle drop if you had one to drop.

Then Spider shocked us all by sharing his life story and how things have been happening in his life. He shared some serious gut-wrenching issues, but then he shared how he was ready and that was when he shared with us that Field Minister Troup had told Spider that whenever he was ready to take that next step to let him know and he'd be there to walk him through it.

That time had come, Spider told us. He then called Troup and told him that he was ready to accept Jesus Christ into his life! After Brother Troup walked him through what to say from the Holy Bible, this place went wild with joy and shouting and telling Spider how proud we all were of him for taking this step in the right direction. He was now a part of our family in Christ Jesus and no matter what happened on his day of execution, whether he got a stay or was executed, he would win because God is in control!

For over the next hour-and-a-half, this pod and my brothers sang songs and even did some freestyle singing when Terry Solley came around with the mic for them to do so. The only bad thing? The field ministers forgot to record it all, lol! You need to understand this though. Spider did not have anything pending in the courts and his lawyer wasn't trying to file anything, so more or less there was a good chance that Spider was going to be executed on March 8th, 2022. However, unbeknownst to all of us humans, God had plans and He showed each of us just who is in control!

The next morning while I was in the dayroom here on A-Section and talking to both RG and Spider, I was telling Spider as I had been for the last few months, that he was going to get a stay of execution and when he moved to another part of this pod I would send him a couple slices of my graduation pizza on Friday, March 11th, 2022.

We were each laughing about the pictures that my Ndugu Oba sent me of himself. Oba, who is my li'l brother (Ndugu) likes to smoke once in a while and he did so legally. So, in this picture I'm sharing with RG and Spider he's high as a kite wearing a skull cap and holding up a small bag of weed with a blunt in his mouth! He's so high he can barely keep his eyes open. Before I know it, my time is up in the dayroom and it's time to be escorted to the shower directly from there. So, off I go saying later to both RG and Spider.

About one hour later as I'm just finishing up a letter to one of my lawyers, I hear Rick in the dayroom screaming out at everyone that Spider got a stay of execution! Spider got a stay of execution! Sure enough, here come the field ministers and it's true, he got a stay of execution, but he doesn't know this because he's out at visitation with his loved ones for his all-day visits that had started that day, March 3rd, 2022.

When I saw Brother Troup, I asked him to tell Spider when he saw him because I thought they would be moving him off the section to another part of the pod, so please tell him I told him that he was going to get a stay of execution and that NOTHING IS IMPOSSIBLE WITH GOD! God was just waiting for Spider to ask Him into his heart and once he did that, He would show Spider who He was and what He could do with nothing pending. God is in control of everything, and we mere humans are just spectators in His ultimate plans!

It is now Saturday and Brother Troup brought around the 60-inch big-screen TV along with a little one and the DVD player and showed one of the DVDs I had sent into the prison from Amazon.com. I had ordered Boss Baby #1 and #2 for some humor and laughter as we are always locked down around here because of a shortage of staff due to COVID-19, and also Black Hawk Down for some action and suspense to liven things up for us, and the last one was Dirt, which is about a young teen who gets a second chance at life after being caught boosting cars to provide for his little sister. Today though we watched Black Hawk Down which for those of you who don't know, it was based on the true story of soldiers in October of 1993 and a Black Hawk helicopter going down. Very good movie to watch and to remind us what our soldiers go through out there in real life while you're all sitting at home enjoying the creature comforts of life. You should check it out if you have the time to do so. If you enjoy these kinds of things, then you should also check out the book called "A Dog Called Hope" which is also a true story about a Special Forces soldier and his service dog Nepal. Beware though, it's a tearjerker.

Not every day inside these walls is filled with movies or church services taking place back here because we are very much still inside of a prison and things do happen that are out of our control within these walls. So, don't think from reading about the good things I share that this is a life you want to see one day because you or your homies and friends think it's cool because it's not and you can end up just as dead within some prisons as you can out there on the streets you think you run freely!

Take a real good look at what is going on right now out there in Ukraine. These people just want to live their lives in peace and Russia and their President Putin, who has ruled that country for 22 years, 22 years too long I might add, wants to be the next bully. Ukrainian President Volodymyr Zelenskyy, who is also Jewish and was once a comedian, is now fighting for his and his country's lives. And for what? He shouldn't have to be fighting for this right now because he and his people were enjoying life and living, then out of nowhere a bully who wants to be heard and when he doesn't get his way, he tries to take things by force. I'm speaking about that trash President Vladimir Putin. But he bit off more than he could chew, and this fight reminds me of the fight in the Holy Bible that took place between David and Goliath.

David was just a little kid with a slingshot, but he knew that God was with him, while Goliath was this nine-foot-tall jerk and had a huge javelin army behind him, but he underestimated David and his God and was defeated by David with a single stone slung from his slingshot. Read about it in 1 Samuel 17:1-51.

So, it is my prayer that the Ukrainian people will hold off the Russian military and President Vladimir Putin who is nothing more than a bully. When someone is bombing women and children it shouldn't matter if Ukraine is a part of NATO or not. They are asking for help and we as a people should help them. President Joe Biden is weak and a coward and never should have been appointed as the President of the American people. He screams about sanctions against the Russian government, but this only happens after Ukraine is bombed and people are now getting slaughtered because that is what is happening to the people in Ukraine!

Why do I care so much about another country so much you might be asking? Because I have two friends that live and work in the capital of Ukraine, Kyiv. Plus, nobody should have to fight for their freedom and lives when they are in their own country or because they were and are thinking about joining NATO. The American President had no problem with invading Iraq. But now when another country is asking for help, only because they're not a part of NATO you are refusing to send American soldiers over there to help fight against Russia. When another country is bombing schools and hospitals because he is unable to get through to the state capital of Kyiv to kill their president, he begins to bomb everyone and everything because he's so little-minded.

This is how not to act. While I'm on the topic of American presidents, the ex-President Donald Trump, I don't understand how he is still out there running his mouth off about everything instead of being thrown into prison for the January 6th riots in the nation's capital. Everyone wants to talk about how the cops and court systems are ruling in favor of such bad people, well you only need to blame yourselves because you people had this man placed into the White House. When you did that, you allowed an undercover racist into the house and those who run with him.

If it were up to me everyone who is in prison and has a death sentence should be allowed to choose to enter into the military for a second chance to fight overseas in such places as Ukraine or any other place that either a soldier or a fighter is needed to defend the helpless or the ones that don't know how to fight or fire all kinds of weapons. If the American president doesn't want to send over military Troupes, then allow those of us in prison and on Death Row to sign up if we want to. Sounds crazy, but at least it would give those who need help a fighting chance instead of being thrown to the wolves and America refusing to help.

Hearing the Ukrainian president asking for help and about how children and women are being killed makes me sick at heart to be called an American. If it was my choice, I would be shipped over there with the clothes on my back to fight for Ukraine!

CHAPTER THREE

LOOKING THROUGH NEW EYES

This morning after I woke up and had washed my face and said my prayers for the day, I did as I usually do every day and that is clean my cage, but first and I cannot stress this enough for each of you reading this book if you're religious or not, you should become so. After saying your prayers, be sure to go that extra mile regardless of how you're feeling. What I mean is do a little bit of reading from either your Bible or a Daily Bread. You can purchase a copy of the Daily Bread by either writing directly to them at: Our Daily Bread Ministries, PO Box 2222, Grand Rapids, MI 49501-2222, or online at: ourdailybread.org. I have found this to be of great help to me each day as I start my mornings, and if it can help me walk in the right direction each day from within these prison walls; then imagine what it can do for you out there in society each day.

After doing these things I then cleaned my cage from the floor to the walls and the toilet/sink combo as just because I'm in prison doesn't mean I need to become a nasty person that lives like an animal. Keeping yourself and your place of living clean will also allow you to continue feeling this way and allow others to see that you are properly dressed and/or smell good.

I then stood up on my desk and toilet and yelled down to Billy Tracy in my air vent that he and I share to see if he was ready. Billy was getting baptized this morning as were three other "Life Row" (Texas Death Row) brothers. What takes place is the field ministers bring this giant kiddie pool that is about 10 feet long and four feet deep and place it out on the outside rec yard around 6 a.m., though he and another brother brought the pool over to the pod yesterday so that they didn't have to deal with it this morning.

So, when Brother Troup got here this morning at the above time, he also brought with him a hose to hook up and start filling the water into the pool. This process took about a half-hour or so. While the pool was filling up, I hollered down to Brother Troup and asked him if he wanted some coffee. He said yes! Less than one minute later I hollered back down to him and said come on up as it's ready now.

Once he was up here, I placed a funnel made from some plastic wrap out the side of my cage door so that I could use this to pour a hot cup of black coffee with no sugar to my Brother Troup from a cup inside my cage. Billy Tracy doesn't drink coffee, that's why our brother has stopped growing at around 5'9". Just more for people like Brother Troup and me and half the prison population!

After that, Brother Troup went back to getting everything ready for the day as Warden Dickerson would be coming to witness as well as Chaplain Martin and his wife and another chaplain I have yet to meet. Numerous field ministers came and so did our brother Megamind who runs the prison radio station called "The Tank."

Climbing back up into the air vent to speak with Billy, I also asked him if he was ready for that cold water. He said he could take it, no problem. Laughing as I got down from speaking with him, I couldn't help but think, yeah right!

Just a little after 10 a.m. everyone entered the pod from Warden Dickerson, Chaplain Martin and his wife, other chaplains, the numerous field ministers, and Megamind who held the video camera to make a recording of all the guys being baptized that morning. LT. Sliger and Sgt. Hardin were the escorting officers for this event. They came and got Billy first and escorted him outside to the pool with everyone present. He was standing outside in the cool air of the morning in only his shorts and t-shirt with a belly chain wrapped around his waist which was in turn connected to a pair of handcuffs in front of him.

Once he stepped into the pool, he said it was kind of cold, but when he sat down in the water, he was singing a whole other tune! He said that the water was freezing cold, and then before he knew it Brother Troup was laying him backward under the water baptizing our newest brother in Christ Jesus, Billy Tracy!

After he exited the giant bathtub as I call it and was returned to his cell, it was Bigfoot's turn to be escorted outside to be baptized as well. Bigfoot is this giant guy who is Native American that stands about 6'7" and 300 pounds with his Steven Segal ponytail.

After he was baptized then it was Crazy J's turn to get baptized. Now, Crazy J is only about 5'6" give or take, and wears glasses with a full-face beard. He too is escorted outside in front of everyone who is witnessing this huge event in only his boxers and a t-shirt. Maybe two minutes later as he takes his step into the pool you don't hear anything, but when he's told to have a seat down so he can be baptized, we can clearly hear him, "Ahhhhh!" Yes, that water is cold, isn't it?

After he's been baptized and is being escorted back inside, I tell him congratulations just as I did with the two before him, but I also say to him that I heard him yell after sitting in that water. He said yeah, it was cold! That I think is an understatement because the water that was used to fill that pool came from the water tank on the prison grounds and that water is ice cold because the temperature lately has been down in the 20s and 30s as of late.

As everything was finished and the witnesses reentered the inside from the outside rec yard, I saw Chaplain Martin and asked him from up here on 2-Row when he was going to grace us all with some of his singing again. He said what about right now? Off he went singing a song of praise to our loving Lord and Savior Jesus Christ! Chaplain Martin has a voice like an angel and can sing really well. Afterward, he came and spoke with me for a few minutes and explained everything that will be happening on this coming Friday the 11th of March 2022 as 31 of us brothers in Christ Jesus celebrate graduating from the two faith-based programs we've been working on for the past 90 days.

After he left then Warden Dickerson came up to speak with me as well, along with LT. Sliger with him. I spoke to the warden who just so happens to also be our brother in Christ Jesus. This time though I was talking to him in regards to a signed letter he sent back to me on Friday in the mail regarding some typewriter ribbons that were shipped to me from the company Swintec. He asked me if I had gotten them all. I had typed out a response letting him know that I did not and that the property officer told me she was going to get with him to make sure I could have all of them, but I found out from him she never did. I told him it was just a simple misunderstanding on her part, but if he could make sure I get them this week it would be great. He said he would make sure this took place while also explaining to LT. Sliger that when I was making my telephone call home this afternoon that I was to get 15 minutes along with everyone else making calls on this section.

One thing I'll never understand is how some officers when they don't know something automatically assume that they know it all. Instead of contacting the lieutenant about the telephone calls, an officer working in the picket named Rodgers explains that I'm only to get five minutes, not knowing that this is wrong. Thus, when Officer Holmes comes around to do the telephone calls a little before noon time, she tells me I only get five minutes. I explained that I was told just this morning by Warden Dickerson who told LT. Sliger that I'm to get longer than that. She left to check and now there is no telling when she'll return with the telephone for me to make my call home.

This should also give you something to think long and hard about. If you screw your young life up and enter into prison for any amount of time, you will have no control over anything that you do from the time you enter into prison until either your release or your death. So, make sure you stop and think before you act at any time! You might remember a time in life when at your school there was also a police officer who showed up to teach about drugs and what they do to your life. The program when I was in school a long time ago in Turlock, California was called D.A.R.E. Years later I would recall this program and though I don't remember what exactly D.A.R.E. stands for I made one of my own and you would do good to take heed from it: Drugs Are Really Expensive.

Ever since the Capital Habeas Unit's Federal Court Division lawyers became co-counsel to my lead lawyer Marcy who is currently working for the Georgia Resource Center in Atlanta, Georgia, I have always felt like they were just telling me what I wanted to hear. Even though they would try to tell me otherwise, I just knew in my heart that I was in many ways just another paycheck to them. Look how many other prisoners they have had to work with; you can imagine that they have been burned over and over and over again. Thus, they treat each of us the same up to a certain point, always thinking that they know everything about prison and what goes on inside such places. You and I know this isn't true though because that would be like saying you know everything about life, and the only One I know that knows that is God alone and His Son Jesus Christ!

Don't get me wrong, in a courtroom every lawyer thinks he/she knows everything as if they are God themselves, just ask the judge or the media. But we know the truth and they say the truth shall set you free!

Prison life is difficult on so many levels, from doing your time in total isolation to having to deal with being treated like an animal or worse and learning how to let go of your pride. Pride is a very major part of one's life both inside prison and out. As long as you let pride control your life, you'll always fail and find yourself on the wrong side of the law or worse…dead. But I don't want to get off track as I was talking about my lawyers or lawyers in general.

One of my lawyers/investigators had broken my trust and in doing so after we had spoken face to face the friendship that had formed between the two of us over a little over seven years or so was now finished. Long before this took place though I had stopped reaching out to this set of lawyers because I was feeling like they just never listened to what I was trying to tell them about my time in prison and the situation. Then one of them reached out to me wanting to come visit with me on March 8th, 2022 at 9 a.m.

I told myself that I was finished with these lawyers and that if they wanted to reach me, they could do so through my lead counsel Marcy or my lawsuit lawyers at Killmer, Lane & Newman, LLP, namely my friend David Lane. So, I wrote to this lawyer and explained that I was not going to see her when she came and that she could contact my other lawyers as could the rest of her office.

I felt disrespected that I could take the time to reach out to my lawyers/investigators/paralegals and not one of them would take the time to let me know that they got my letters or if they could send me the legal work or set up a legal call or anything like that. I was constantly having trouble with the outgoing mail at the time as well as incoming legal mail, so I would ask them to please let me know either through a snail mail letter or by dropping me a short JPay letting me know that they got the letter, etc. Not one time would they do this, so in a way it showed me that they didn't care nor respect me as a person, so I decided I was finished with them.

Then I rededicated my life to Jesus Christ and many things changed within me as a person in the most powerful and amazing ways. Once I decided that there had to be a better way to do this time and that I should just trust Jesus Christ to lead my life as He knows what's best, I also decided that all my lawyers and loved ones and friends would take a backseat in my car or ride in the bed of my truck because God and His Son would now and forever be my #1!

Let's take a look at scripture so that you may see also and not just take my word for it. In Romans 3:21-29, "But now God has shown us a way to be made right with him without keeping the requirements of the law, as was promised in the writings of Moses and the prophets long ago. We are made right with God by placing our faith in Jesus Christ. And this is true for everyone who believes, no matter who we are."

For everyone has sinned; we all fall short of God's glorious standard. Yet God, in His grace, freely makes us right in his sight. He did this through Christ Jesus when he freed us from the penalty for our sins. For God presented Jesus as the sacrifice for sin. People are made right with God when they believe that Jesus sacrificed his life, shedding his blood. This sacrifice shows that God was being fair when He held back and did not punish those who sinned in times past, for He was looking ahead and including them in what He would do in this present time. God did this to demonstrate His righteousness, for He is fair and just, and He makes sinners right in his sight when they believe in Jesus.

Can we boast, then, that we have done anything to be accepted by God? No, because our acquittal is not based on obeying the law. It is based on faith. So, we are made right with God through faith and not by obeying the law.

After all, is God the God of the Jews only? Isn't he also the God of the Gentiles? Of course he is. There is only one God, and he makes people right with himself only by faith, whether they are Jews or Gentiles.

If we all would only believe in Him things in and throughout our lives can change for the better faster than you can imagine. But I noticed that when I failed to place my trust in Him my life was garbage, and I couldn't find that place within myself that made me feel complete and happy with any sense of peace within myself. Once again, let me take you to scripture that has helped me see and understand that there is nothing wrong with me. It's as if the inner soul of self longs and knows that we belong to God and He's just waiting for us to come to Him when we're ready.

I want to walk you along with me and learn about how when we fail as a people (individual) we'll never find that happiness or peace of mind, we'll always be miserable in our lives, and we'll always fail at everything we want to do in our lives or for those we love. This kind of life stinks.

Let's check out what it says in Hebrews 3:15-19: "Today when you hear his voice, don't harden your hearts as Israel did when they rebelled. And who was it who rebelled against God, even though they heard his voice? Wasn't it the people Moses led out of Egypt? And who made God angry for 40 years? Wasn't it the people who sinned, whose corpses lay in the wilderness? And to whom was God speaking when he took an oath that they would never enter his rest? Wasn't it the people who disobeyed him? So we see that because of their unbelief, they were not able to enter his rest."

I can honestly tell you that before I accepted Him fully into my life I was always restless and depressed and just short-tempered with everyone as well as myself. I didn't love myself and would self-harm to release my frustration and I didn't know how to let go and forgive myself for all the harm I have caused throughout my life and the hurt I caused others before coming to Him. This isn't the kind of life you want to continue living if you're sitting there reading this book and telling yourself that this is you or that my words are also speaking to you. It's the worst way to live and it's unhealthy in every sense of the word.

Now let me take you back to what I was trying to share with you until you caused me to go offroad! On the morning of March 8th, 2022 just before my alarm clock went off at 5:30 a.m., I rolled over and slapped it to the off position, then told myself aloud that I wasn't going to go to the legal visit with Claudia. There was no point because I had already written her a letter and told her not to come and my lawyer Marcy had also sent an email letting her and the rest of her coworkers know that I wasn't going to come out for the visit. I was finished with everyone at the CHU office in Philadelphia.

So, as I rolled back over to snuggle deeper under my covers and get back to sleep, wouldn't you know that the man above just wasn't trying to hear what I was saying!

"Ahhh, okay, okay, you win! I'll get up, God!" Rolling over and planting my feet on the ice-cold concrete, I was soon awake from the cold in my cage. Getting up and plugging in my Hot-Pot to make some hot water for coffee, I went to making up my bedding area and folding my blanket and sheets and putting them away (I like having my cage clean and in order). Then turning to my sink, I locked on my hot water button to wash my face and brush my teeth. Drying and hanging my towel up, I grabbed my coffee mug that has a huge sticker on it that says: "STOP TRUSTING COPS" and put a single spoonful of instant coffee into it and then turned around and added a little water from my Hot Pot to dissolve the grounds. I then set my cup down and reached for my Daily Bread. Reading for that day, I then grabbed my Jesus Calling by Sarah Young and read from it while marking down the scriptures from her book (devotional) to look up in my Bible afterward.

Once this was done, I did just that, I read the scripture from my Bible which is a Life Application Study Bible NLT. Only once I was finished with my morning time with God did I pour hot water into my coffee mug to enjoy my first cup of coffee. Like always, that first sip…no, it's nothing like heaven, but it does take me outside these prison walls and lets me remember what all I'm missing and how much I crave to do right by Him from this day forward and to always strive for better in my life and to help others see His light. Plus, the coffee helped to wake me fully up.

While I was sitting there enjoying this cup of coffee, I made a deal with God. I said, "God, let your will be done on earth as it is in heaven this day. If the escort team comes and gets me out for this so-called legal visit you want me to go to before 9 a.m. or a little after that time, I will go out there and share my testimony, and what all You are doing back here in Texas Life Row (Death Row). About the lives you are changing and saving, the men you are bringing to their knees seeking your love and forgiveness of their sins, and how we had four baptisms on Sunday, March 7th, 2022. I will also share Your word with this lawyer and bring her back into Your loving grace. This is my word to you God, but if it's after 9:30 a.m. I'm not going out! I will only go to my legal telephone call with David."

Wouldn't you know that God loves it when we dare Him to do something? You can say whatever you like and plan your day however you want, but if you have God in your life, then you're planning your days and nights to His schedule! Proverbs 19:21, "You can make many plans, but the Lord's purpose will prevail."

At 8:45 a.m. two escorting officers were knocking on my cage door, Officer Amos and OJT (Officer Junior Training) Patty. Officer Amos let me know that they were there to get me for my legal visit and that I also had a legal telephone call at 11:30 a.m. Mumbling to myself I said you sure right God, lol!

On our way out to the visitation building, we have to walk under a metal walkway next to 11-Building outside. But just as you pass under it there is this little gap where rainwater is constantly pouring down on whoever walks beneath it, having no choice but to pass under it and through the rain that is now pouring down from a major thunderstorm that has been pounding this area lately. The OJT Patty rolls open the gate to the walkway and Officer Amos is trying to hold me back before pushing me right when the rain starts really pouring down through there, thus my back and neck are now soaked with ice-cold water. But that works two ways because just as I go through, I stop right on the other side, forcing Officer Amos to have to stop right underneath the gap thus getting soaked as well! You know how it is, he started it, I finished it!

So, as we're walking down this walkway that is around 250 feet, I'm slowly leaning towards my right side where the OJT Patty is walking while holding onto my right elbow. Doing this I keep slowly pushing him closer to the fence where the rain is now blowing through. Having Officer Amos on my left side, he's just walking along as if he's going for a ride. Wherever I go he goes and whichever way I lean he has to lean. Officer Amos catches my eye and sees me smiling. When I look at him I look toward the OJT Patty and that is when Officer Amos sees that he's soaking wet and says, "Ahhh, Tabler that's messed up." So, I pull the OJT back towards my left towards Amos so he's out from under the rain blowing through the fence. That's when he catches on to what I was doing and starts laughing. Next thing you know we're all laughing, and I said welcome to Death Row.

Knocking on the visitation's back door until Officer Moore opens it up for us, she tells them to put me in legal booth #A7 which they do. Once I'm inside, I have to wait about 10 minutes before my lawyer Claudia is there. Once the visit between the two of us starts, I allow her to start it off because she is the one that asked for this visit, or I should say stated that she was coming on this day and would like to see me.

Sitting there I listened to her talk to me and explain to me that she wants to apologize for what she did, meaning that she was the one who sent Cassandra an email telling her not to visit with me and that she needed to remind herself that everyone at the CHU office are adults and should be treated as such.

I was a bit shocked that she would own up to her mistake and what she has caused to happen between Cassandra and me. I told her right then that I accepted her apology and that I also forgave her for what she had done, but she's not the only one that is responsible for what happened between Cassandra and me as Cassandra is also responsible for not responding to my letters since. However, she shouldn't thank me for coming out to the visit, but she should give thanks to God because He is the reason I'm currently visiting with her right then.

That's when I went on to explain to her how I had rededicated my life to Jesus Christ on February 6th, 2022, and that I have completely turned my life around for the better and how God is working back here on what was at one time called Texas Death Row but has now gotten a new name by those of us living within its walls. It's now called Texas Life Row because God is working in each of us and we're no longer waiting to die one day but are living for Him!

At that point, I asked her to go and grab one of the Bibles that they always have out there in the visitation. Once she had one and had returned to her seat, I walked her through many scriptures in the Bible after finding out that she had become a Christian back in 1975, asking her when she last spoke to God and gave Him thanks for everything He has done in her life from her children to her current grandbabies. It was time for her to thank the Man above.

I was sitting out there walking this little tiny thing of a lawyer through God's word because I made a deal with God before coming out to the visit, and when you make a deal with God you make sure to always fulfill them!

Let me see what scripture I can find for you to give you an example of what I'm speaking about because after all, the Bible is the blueprint for life and how we should live it. Everything that is spoken about in the Holy Bible can be found to relate to what is going on in each of our lives right this very moment. Here we go, my friends. Proverbs 20:25 says, "Don't trap yourself by making a rash promise to God and only later counting the cost." What this Proverb is pointing out to you is that it's dangerous to make a promise impulsively and then reconsider it. God takes promises very seriously and He wants them to always be carried out. Just as if you were in prison here or anywhere around the United States, if you failed to keep your word (promise) to someone, you could end up dead or seriously beaten up or even raped. Just as you would keep your word in here so you should always keep your word to God because He holds your whole life in His hands.

Just before my visit was over with Claudia, she told me that she would go home and rededicate her life to Jesus Christ. After that, we parted ways and she left letting me know that she would also share with the other lawyers and investigators that if they wanted to rebuild their relationships with me, if it mattered to them, then they could do so by reaching out to me and trying to mend things between us as they would have to start all over and earn my trust back because I no longer trusted either of them. Sure, I forgave them for their ignorance, but I can tell you that nowhere in the Holy Bible does it say that we are to forget what someone does to us. It says that we are to forgive those who wrong us or trespass against us just as God has forgiven us our trespasses against Him. It tells us to love one another just as He so loved us, even our enemies, but it does not tell us anywhere in all 66 books that we are to forget. I believe the reasoning for this is simple, by not forgetting we can use how we were treated or wronged as a lesson in our lives so that it may help us become a better person and shows us how not to treat someone else. All I can honestly say is to follow your heart but always trust God and pray and ask Him for His guidance before setting out to do something that you are unsure about doing or don't know how to do. If you always come to God and are sincere in your asking of Him, He will never lead you astray.

As I sit here typing this all out to you, I'm listening in on the prison radio station. Yes, you read that right, we here at the Polunsky Unit/Texas Life Row have our own radio station called The Tank which is run by the prisoners for the prisoners. It has numerous different radio shows on it throughout the day and night from music to church services for every religion and it has an update for what is going on around the campus as we call this prison. It's run by our Brother Megamind and a few other brothers. On Wednesdays, they have this show called Dirt Road which is filled with country music and some talk from the brothers out there in the general population.

As I'm listening to them talk about what is going on, one of them says, "Hey, I just heard that President Joe Biden is in the hospital." One of the other guys there says, "What for?" The brother says, "They say he can't stop Putin (poopin')!" The joke was funny, but only if Joe Biden would seriously help the Ukrainians push back Russia. I cannot seriously call Joe Biden the president because he acts nothing like an American president should, nor did the one that was before him. The only president I had any respect for was Obama. We all know that Russian President Putin is nothing but an animal mixed in with cowardice. His soldiers are acting like the very animals we see in zoos and while they destroy the cities around the capital of Kyiv, Ukraine committing unspeakable atrocities against the Ukrainian people and the bombing of a children's hospital, Joe Biden still refuses to help. This is sad and upsetting.

After my legal visit with Claudia, I was escorted back onto 12-Building and down to a legal booth at the end of a long hallway where I would have a legal telephone call for one hour with David Lane, my lawsuit lawyer. Once I was on the telephone with David, the first thing he says to me is, "This is Tabler's personal secretary, how may I help you?" How many lawyers do you know out there that would say this to one of their clients, let alone a prisoner? Yeah, that's what I thought, not too many if any. But David isn't like other lawyers, he's more down to earth and has over the years become like an older brother or really good friend whom I can speak with freely without having to watch what I say and without worrying that he's going to run off and tell the whole wide world. He also gives just as good as he gets!

After laughing off his greeting to me, he hits me with a bomber I never saw coming nor ever expected to ever be asked. He says, so, my wife wants to know if you'd be willing to write her because she wants to write to you. I told David to stop playing, man. He goes, I'm serious, Richard. She wants to write to you. David, just what the heck have you been telling your wife about me?

The thing that David didn't know, as I'm asking him these questions, I have tears pouring down my face because he has always spoken to me like a human being and not a killer or criminal, and when he told me that his wife wanted to write to me, it truly touched me in a way I never knew I could be touched. As if I were really alive and breathing, that someone could want to have something to do with me for me and not what I have done to land me where I am now. So, we agreed that I would write a letter to his wife and let her decide after reading it if she still wanted to correspond with me. No doubt one day she'll be reading this letter and who knows what she'll think then. If by chance you're reading this Debbie, thank you for showing me compassion through your husband and for showing me love through our Heavenly Father, God, and His Son Jesus Christ.

Returning to my cage after our telephone call, I sit back and type out a three-page letter to his wife even though I'm scared to death by the idea of writing to her. The rest of the week goes by fast and then on Thursday the 10th I'm being escorted out to the visitation for my monthly visit with my friend Mary from Austin, Texas. During our visit for a change the tables have been turned and I'm having to be centered and grounded for Mary because she's having a tough time lately.

Back on January 24th, 2022, just one week after I and my loved ones lost a loved one to COVID-19, she's losing her mother as well. I cannot even begin to imagine what this must be like and to be honest I never want to have to go through losing my own mother while in prison. It's hard enough losing my aunties from COVID-19 or breast cancer, as well as my grandma.

That right there should give you pause to think about things and how you're running around doing stupid stuff. Take a minute to think about everything that I'm sharing with you within these pages. Could you handle everything, such as the loss of loved ones, while in jail or prison? Yeah, right. Most if not every one of you reading this book couldn't handle losing your cell phone or iPad. No more driving your car or truck to wherever you want to go, no more going out with friends or family. Everything as you once knew it is no longer going to happen because you refused to listen to what I'm pouring out to you on these pages.

Do you like being able to take a shower or a bath in your house? Could you handle it knowing that someone was watching you while you were butt-naked or using the restroom? What about not being able to control the temp of the shower and some days having to take ice-cold showers because the water line is broken or having to sit through the days and nights with your toilet backed up because the water has been shut off because the main broke?

No more fast-food joints, no more anything as you once knew it. No more enjoying a simple meal with family or friends or lover, no more contact from those you love and care about because you were too stupid and kept telling everyone you knew it all. Now your life is filled with lawyers and judges and many others who think they know what is best for you or where you should spend the rest of your life, that is if they deem you should be kept alive to do your time in prison and not sentenced to death because the District Attorney and the people on the jury are told lies. The jury is being told by the District Attorney and your lawyer is not speaking up and you do not know any better as to what all is now taking place…nothing serious, just your own life! But the jury is being told to predict the future and that you are so evil that there is no chance for you to be rehabilitated in prison.

Can you tell the future? Yeah, me neither, but the jury sure could or they thought they could just as the District Attorney and District Judge allowed them to get away with. Witnesses will take the stand against you and will be allowed to lie under oath, warrants that don't exist will be allowed. LEOs (law enforcement officers) will get away with lying under oath on the stand and will say anything to help the State. Yet, when you or your lawyers ask for proof or recordings of these claims, they cannot provide them because they don't have anything but hearsay.

Hearsay will convict you faster than a cop busting you for a speeding ticket! Then you are handed a sentence of death and you go through the appeals and numerous other lawyers who think they too know what is best for you. It all starts to get old, and it starts to wear you down mentally and spiritually. Just when you think you can do it no more for any reason, you notice something in your trial transcripts and the crime scene pictures. The thing is when you notice these things and ask your legal team to send you the crime scene pictures in color instead of black and white, they refuse to do it. This stops you in your tracks again because you got the impression that these lawyers cared about you. After all, they said they did. They told you that you were more than a paycheck to them because they cared about what they did and that's to keep guys like you and I from being executed which is just a legal term for State-sanctioned murder. They couldn't care less if you spend the rest of your life in prison slowly losing your mind and going insane as long as they were able to keep you from being executed because they don't believe in lethal injection.

It no longer matters that you can prove to your lawyers that certain law enforcement officers got on the stand and lied during your jury trial. It doesn't matter that you could prove this! Do you know why? Because in their eyes you're a convicted killer, period.

People who I thought were friends were not really friends but were just good at fooling prisoners like myself. Appeal lawyers can be a ruthless crowd. I sit here now because they think they know everything and when you explain that you can prove certain people got on the stand and lied under oath just to get the jury to sentence you to death, nobody wants to listen. Not one time have I said that I was innocent of my crime, but I do believe that I should have been tried for a lesser charge than capital murder. But that is beside the point.

Try as I might to get colored pictures of my crime scene pictures instead of black and white, I'm told no by lawyers. What is their reason for denying them to me? Who knows? You'd have to ask them, so feel free to contact their office in Philadelphia, PA. Just look them up under the Capital Habeas Unit, Federal Court Division or call them directly and ask them at the telephone number you find.

Why do I want the pictures in color you might be asking? That's simple really. The crime scene is wrong, and the number of evidence tags that they have on the ground marking shell casings fired from the weapon they said I used is wrong. Looking at the black and white pictures you can see numerous tags on the ground marking so-called shell casings from the so-called gun. I'm telling you now right here in these pages that if you could take me to trial and convict me cleanly then that's great, but to do so under dirty tactics and lying so that a 12-person jury is being played so that the scene makes it look like I'm a monster is wrong.

Let's take in the fact that for whatever reason way back in 2004 I fired a total of three shots from a pistol. Two of those shots were taken inside of my truck and one outside of it. Those first two shots, the shell casings landed on my dashboard inside my truck! The single shell casing that was outside should have been the only one found at the crime scene, but the District Attorney and other law enforcement officers provided numerous shell casings at the crime scene. The question is, how did these shell casings get there and why are they there?

During my time being locked up in the Bell County Jail, another person was facing serious time too for assault and threats on officers. This person would be housed in the back isolation cells with me during my time there. This same person could be heard talking on the recording devices there threatening the female officer's family and naming them each as well as her because they knew one another personally. This person was heard making threats to this officer's family and children, but instead of taking the stand and telling the truth, they say that it was I talking and threatening this officer and her children.

When asked about the recordings, all of a sudden they don't exist, but that's okay 'cause it must be true in the eyes of the jury because I'm such a monster. Then just before being found guilty, this person who had said these things and made the threats ended up assaulting this officer in the jail and catching a 10-year sentence for assaulting an officer!

Think about all of this because I want you to understand that if you decide to throw your own life away for whatever reasons, you're going to get screwed in every way possible by the legal system, so why do it? What is worse is you end up hurting all those who love and care about you that you thought didn't because you were too busy living your own life how you wanted to without listening to others.

CHAPTER FOUR

WHAT DO YOU KNOW ABOUT RESPECT?

Before I get into this next chapter deeply, I would like to bring your attention to the following because I feel that it's really important in all of our lives.

I had this friend who was also a serious person on my legal team named Cassandra. For some reason or another, things between us fell apart really fast and it was over something so small that it's no longer important. She had started out as just another member of my team on my appeals, but somewhere along the way I started to look at her differently; like I could trust her enough that she could be a real friend.

Do you have someone in your life that has become close to you like this only for something to take place between the two of you that has now caused the friendship you held dear to fall apart? What about your marriage to your lover or the relationship between your girlfriend or boyfriend? Or that something between your friend and you that you just cannot seem to get past because the rift just seems too big?

Though it's not looking like I can save the friendship between my little friend who I love and care about dearly, kind of like my little sister that I never had, just maybe I can help you see how to fix your issues because God would want you to just as much as you want to.

In the book Song of Songs in the Holy Bible, you'll find the story of two lovers talking about one another and how God can help you make amends. The little things can sometimes feel like the biggest thing even though it's not. Song of Songs 2:15: "Catch all the foxes, those little foxes, before they ruin the vineyard of love, for the grapevines are blossoming!" These little animals can cause so much trouble because they're always digging out the dirt trying to get at grapes, and just when you think you have one of them cornered, they dart right back into the woods. But if you could catch them ahead of time or prevent them from doing damage to your vineyards, life would be so much easier.

Just like in your life as in mine, it's the littlest thing that can cause the most grief or destroy friendships. What's more, God can help us fix things in our lives if we would just come to Him. Look at how He has forgiven us, don't you think it's about time that you ask that someone in your own life for forgiveness and grant it even if they are not willing to take that first step? Forgiveness is needed to nourish the vineyards of our heart and soul. It's just like the topic nobody wants to discuss aloud because they're insecure about themselves.

Love. What does it mean to love and be loved? Sometimes I think we overcomplicate it. Analyzing how we feel from moment to moment, we forget that love isn't primarily a feeling; it's a way of living and being in the world. We don't learn how to love through willpower or good intentions; we learn it through experiencing it and we learn it through living it.

I remember over one decade ago a story I had been reading about a husband and wife. For some reason or another, the husband turns to his wife and asks her if she loves him. The wife screams at him, "Do I what?" Thus begins a prolonged exchange that eventually leads to the wife conceding that if 30 years of working and struggling together and raising their children together isn't love, she doesn't know what is! After that part in the story, you read about the two of them soaking in a tub knowing that they've been loved all along.

I have never been married but know many people who have been or have had a serious relationship with someone they loved and cared about deeply. In knowing these people and seeing how they communicate with one another just like the story, I've realized the joy that one is loved and an understanding that love is forged through everyday ways we and they share life together. When we live for the good of others as we share our lives with them, then love follows and surrounds us, even if we don't fully realize it at the time. That is a perspective on love that echoes the kind of self-giving that Paul calls "live a life filled with love" (Ephesians 5:2). Once we realize that we have been loved all along, "Let love be your highest goal!" (1-corinthians 14:1).

The sacrifice of Jesus Christ established that once and for all and that right there changes everything. I never would have been able to share this with any of you had it not been for the close attention I paid to friends that started out as part of my legal team. People such as Luis and Joycet, Tiana and Tyler, Mary and Stuart, David and Debbie, and even the friend I have lost her parents, Jim and Karen. Thank you to each of you as your spouse shared their love during numerous legal visits and telephone calls.

Now, let me share something with you that in many ways you can say is a part of history. On Friday, March 11th, 2022 I and 31 other Texas Death Row that we now call Texas Life Row prisoners graduated from a 90-day course after enrolling in the faith-based programs back in December of 2021. This course was called "Overcoming Life-controlling Problems." Those of us that graduated received a certificate of completion and were thrown a party that was approved by the administration and directors. Along with our certificates, we were also blessed with a large Little Caesar's Ultimate Supreme Pizza!

No doubt you're like so what, a pizza isn't a big deal to get happy about. Well, it is when you've not been able to enjoy such for 18 years and counting! To enjoy eight slices of deliciousness instead of cold or spoiled food that you have no earthly idea of what is in it (prison food), was almost as good as knowing that you are fully and wonderfully loved by God!

We heard from the Regional Chaplaincy Director Hazelwood and another director along with Warden Dickerson and the chaplains. Each let us know how proud they were of us and that we made a part of history because of what we've managed to do back here on what society knows as Texas Death Row, even though we now call it Texas Life Row. To know that each of these men, though they have a job to do, can take the time out of their lives to share God's word with each of us and allow us to enroll in faith-based programs that have never before been offered to men sentenced to death, is great.

The feeling of knowing that I and my 31 other brothers put in the work and completed something of this magnitude, to hear Director Hazelwood share his story of Moon Pies with us as if we were his own family, in which in a way we are because we are each a part of his family and the family of Warden Dickerson and the chaplains and each of you who are believers in Jesus Christ!

Through the grace of our loving Father God and His Son Jesus Christ, we also got to listen to some speakers that traveled from all over the United States to party with us. People such as the U.S. and World Skateboard Champion Dennis Martinez; Meet the Author Bill Corum; Singer and Songwriter Darlene Bahr; and Christian Rap Artist Dontae! Everything was filmed by numerous people either on video cameras or on their phones (wardens and directors). I have known Darlene Bahr and her husband Joe Bahr for over 11 years because they used to be a part of Bill Glass Ministries and as you know Bill Glass used to be with the NFL way back when!

It didn't end with that though because after the celebration of us graduating and everyone left, the field ministers Troup and Solley returned with two 60-inch TVs and the DVD I had ordered and sent into the prison. They showed the movie Dirt over in B-Section and those of us on A-Section listened in on our radios because they now had an AM receiver that allowed us to listen on the radio on the AM station 1400!

Once that was finished and the weekend had started and went by fast, Sunday afternoon ol' Troup and field ministers Gomez and Gallardo returned with the TVs again and this time played the movie on A-Section also known as Death Watch. This was another movie I had ordered for the whole prison but was being played because Billy Tracy heard that it was funny as heck from listening to me saying so. Nope, I never saw it until this day and the movie was boss, baby! That movie was beyond hilariously funny.

Once the movie was finished and the field ministers left, it was back to writing letters and catching up on other things. Then before we knew it, Tuesday was here and this day would also be another graduation for us and the faith-based program called Bridges to Life where we each received another certificate of completion, and this time we were given a minute to say something on a mic that was brought up to our cell doors by one of the field ministers. In my case, it was Brother Troup and I hadn't but a few seconds for him to explain to me what was going on because I had been down in the legal booth in the hallway talking to David Lane on a legal telephone call before I was able to strong-arm Captain Neyland (not really) into escorting me back to the pod so I wouldn't miss my graduation for Bridges to Life.

She had escorted me back and had just removed my handcuffs from behind my back and closed the slot on my door, then Brother Troup was there with the mic explaining to me what was going on and that I was next! Just as I start talking on the mic, I look up to see Chaplain Martin holding a video camera filming me, and down below him using his phone was Director Hazelwood! Talk about feeling the pressure! After our graduation though we each were blessed with a giant slice of cake and soda poured into our cups. I sent my graduation cake to my amigo and brother Fabian Hernandez, also known to us as Spook.

Now, I have been thinking to myself as I sit here typing all of this out to you trying to decide just what the younger readers are wanting to see within these pages that would grab their attention as I feel that what I have said so far isn't enough. The problem nowadays is that most of our youth only understand one way and thing in life, though it saddens me to say it's no less true because I used to be just like them and craved it too. What is it? Violence. Respect. Being feared. Being accepted. Being the center of attention.

In my first book and now knowing how to seriously write and express myself through my words, I shared little about myself other than what I went through when I was young. Running away from home, being homeless at one point in life, and breaking and entering into homes and buildings before becoming a driver for a friend named Danny who was someone back then with MS-13, better known to its soldiers as Mara Salvatrucha, before finding him in his own home doing his best to hold his insides in after being hit with a shotgun blast.

What's not shared in the first is how I spent most of my life on the run from the law and from myself. From one coast to another coast, I ran and was involved with illegal activities. To meeting real OGs near 102 and Town Avenue in Los Angeles, California to GDs (Gangster Disciples) in Chicago, and back down into parts of Florida where some friends were with the Latin Kings. To knowing and even being in the car driving down the road on a major street in Tampa Bay, Florida with our lights out waiting for that unlucky someone to flash their lights on us letting us know our lights were off and to turn them on only to have their car opened up on with a Tec-9 pistol. Doing time in prison in California and being introduced to the real players now fighting for one's life and learning how to survive in the jungle that is man-made. Fighting and landing on a short stint in the SHU at Pelican Bay State Prison.

Is this the kind of life you want to live and face? Is this the kind of life you want to put your family through because you think it's cool and that being in such a place will get you respected? Having your loved ones wondering if you're alive or dead because they're not getting your mail. Is this what you want? What will it take for you to understand that the track you're running on right now will more or less lead to your very death if not serving a life sentence in prison?

What are you running from in the first place? What, you think you're the only one that's had it rough growing up? Feeling like you're unloved by family and friends so you feel the need to go out and prove yourself in some way or another? Let me share something with you, as many of you no doubt feel that it all comes down to respect. Maybe you believe that someone not paying for the food as promised or reneging on a gambling debt or taking your car or truck without asking is a sign of disrespect. If you believe this way and you can't put up with the disrespect, you may do to another person what you think they deserve and expect that next time they'll show you respect.

Or maybe you can respect the dude who is on top of his game and seems to have a glamorous life—he's got the gold necklace, the big house, the newest and fastest car or truck, the smokin' hot girl, and all the dope he needs for himself and his friends. You then do what it takes to have what he has for yourself because you want to be like this. The bottom line is this, you want to be respected and may fight, steal, sell drugs, become gang affiliates, or whatever else you feel is needed to gain that respect. But is this really the way things work? What really is respect?

Let me tell you from an OG's point of view. True respect is admiring or holding esteem for an individual because of their worth or excellence as a person. Respect has great importance in everyday life. Most of us have been taught to respect our parents, elders, the law, and other people's feelings and rights, as well as other things that are important to maintain a good and peaceful life.

Importantly, respect cannot be demanded or forced, though sometimes people mistakenly believe that it can. Pay close attention all you lawyers and investigators and people in general. Respect is something that is earned! One earns another's respect by voluntarily doing things that show respect. It's like a boomerang. What you send out will come back to you.

You can show respect to others, and most will show respect back to you. You can show disrespect to someone and they will in turn show you disrespect in return. In most situations in life nowadays you will learn the cost of disrespect in a very bad way: diss me fool, and you'll suffer.

Back in 2004, I felt like someone that I was dealing with had shown me disrespect by simply turning his head away from me when we were speaking. Something that most take for granted cost me my freedom and another person his life. Nothing in life is worth taking the life of another. I don't care what you think or what someone else is trying to tell you. Don't ever think that it's okay to take someone else's life because he or she disrespected you or someone you know!

Now, let's look more closely at two important aspects of true respect. First, respect involves admiring or holding esteem for another as an act of free will. You cannot force someone to respect you and another person cannot force you to respect them. It is a belief, not an action. However, respect can be shown through behavior, as we can act in ways considered respectful. On a practical level, this includes giving worth and value to someone's feelings, needs, thoughts, ideas, wishes, and preferences by acknowledging them, listening to them, being truthful with them, and accepting them as an individual, unique person of value.

Second, true respect involves admiring worth or excellence as a unique human being. It recognizes the good and the honorable in a person, and it does not mean giving in to another's physical threats or being influenced by another's money or social status.

The fact that one person gives in to another does not mean they respect them. Think about what often passes as respect in many of our lives. Perhaps one person respects the bigger, meaner person, or a person with a reputation as a fighter, or a person with a pistol, or that dude with a gang backing him/her. When someone is asked why they carry a pistol, they reply, "Before I had this pistol, I didn't have no respect. Now I do." Someone wants the same things a big-time drug dealer has, not because they respect the dealer as a person, but because they want what the drug dealer has or is jealous of his/her status among others.

This, my young readers, is fear and envy, not respect. Fear and envy are poisonous and tear us down, while respect builds us up. Fear is life-threatening, but respect can make life better. Fear is forced, respect is earned. Envy is self-centered, while respect is a positive focus on another. We learn to fear and envy, but we earn respect.

Respect and self-respect are deeply connected. Self-respect is often defined as a sense of worth or as due respect for one's self. It includes self-esteem, self-confidence, dignity, self-love, a sense of honor, self-reliance, and pride. It is the opposite of shame, putting one's self down, arrogance, and self-importance. It is very difficult to respect others if we don't respect ourselves, and to respect ourselves if others don't respect us.

A person who wants true respect lives as an honorable human being with the hope that others will voluntarily come to admire them. How this goes depends on whether you respect yourself. What are you doing closing your eyes?! Are you falling asleep from what I'm sharing with you, or do I still have your undying attention?

Do you know anyone out there in the town of Modesto, California, or Turlock? This is in Stanislaus County or area code 209. Back in December of 2002, I led numerous LEOs (law enforcement officers) on a foot chase out in the country right on the outskirts of Modesto, California that was being led by then police officer Phillip Roman with the assistance of DEA (Drug Enforcement Agency) agent Douglas Ridenhour. What you couldn't know was that I was wanted for questioning in regards to being a drug dealer of cocaine. The night this took place was December 24th, 2002 and I was getting ready to make a deal for two kilos of pure cocaine. Pure cocaine is off-white, more of a pinkish color. This stuff, had I been able to complete the deal, was so pure that just simply touching the wrapping that it was in would light you up. But as I was walking to the meet down this dirt road because my lowered truck wouldn't clear the ground, I was hit with numerous lights from flashlights and police cars and told to hit the ground.

How many of you hit the ground when you know it's either a one-way ticket to jail or your grave? Yeah, that's what I thought, half of you reading this have never been in this kind of place and I sincerely pray that you never end up in it either! Long story short, I was tackled by DEA Agent Douglas Ridenhour and taken to jail in downtown Modesto which is off H Street. Paperwork got messed up, and I was let out before my parole officer Peter Leu knew that I had violated.

Not even three weeks later I would be captured by Parole Agent Peter Leu of the Stanislaus County Parole Office in Modesto. Caught my butt slippin' and blocked my lowered blue S-10 truck in the driveway of my girlfriend's. Unknown to me until months later, she had called my parole agent and told him that I was violating my parole. See, take this as a lesson to you too. If you disrespect your woman or fail to make her happy, they can and will get even with you in the end and you'll be paying the cost for your screw-ups.

Just look at the beginning of time in the Holy Bible if you don't want to take my word for it. Adam's wife Eve threw him to the wolves after she listened to a serpent about eating the forbidden fruit. Instead of listening to God or her husband, she listened to a snake and then when they were found out by God, she blamed it all on Adam! Read Genesis 3:1-19! Thought you had it bad now, poor old Adam had it worse. Then again, the women in our day and age no doubt can come up with worse ways to deal with us men.

What?! Ladies, ladies, I had to give our readers something to laugh about as life is too short to always be serious. If you want seriousness, I can give you the number of numerous lawyers to call!

Back to being trapped in the driveway of my girlfriend in January of 2003. I remember it was a Friday night around the 10th. Slipping up and having to be placed in handcuffs by Agent Peter Leu, he failed to search me well and missed tons of stuff but thank God my pistol was inside my truck. I was soon placed into the back of Agent Leu's car before he started driving to the county jail in downtown Modesto.

About five minutes later while he was busy typing into his laptop computer, we had just turned onto McHenry Avenue which is a six-lane heavy traffic thoroughfare, coming to a stop at a red light but behind numerous other cars and trucks, I was able to slip my handcuffed hands from behind my back to in front of me. Though I was unable to get into my pocket and handcuff key to take the handcuffs off, I was able to open the car door and escape without stopping to think about where I was or who was around me, nor about my safety or anyone else's.

The light had turned green and everyone was now driving forward and here I was blasting my way handcuffed straight through heavy traffic, trying my best to get the few blocks to my truck where I knew I could get away all the way; but it wasn't meant to be. An off-duty CHP (California Highway Patrol) officer named Gowan and his wife were driving along in his lifted truck and just happened to see me running through traffic with no less than a pair of handcuffs on! Without thinking, he and his wife drove me down and were able to pin me between their truck's bumper and a concrete wall to an apartment complex just off McHenry Avenue behind the bowling alley.

That was the end of my Friday night, though it would cost the city police a new car window on one of their police cars after they tried to transport me to the jail for my parole officers. Who else comes to their rescue than none other than DEA Agent Douglas Ridenhour who was riding with the local police that night. I was placed in this device they call a wrap, which is supposed to prevent me from escaping or moving around much, only I was determined to get away. Around the same stop light on McHenry Avenue that I had escaped from Parole Officer Peter Leu, I was able to escape the wrap they had placed me in and kick out the back window, but before I was able to flee again, they hit the top lights and went through the red light. I still tried to make a run for it but didn't get very far as cops were now everywhere. I made it maybe 30 feet before being tackled by an untold number of police.

With a busted nose that won't stop bleeding, some busted-up ribs, and a bruised shoulder, I go with them peacefully. They have a paddy wagon pick me up to transport me the rest of the way to the jail thinking to myself that I would have one more chance at escape, but I would need to be on point, and it would be fast and a long shot but possible.

The Modesto Jail is or was off of H Street in downtown Modesto, but when the police are taking people in, they enter through an underground entry. They drive down the back way and the big rolling door rolls up and the cars or vans pull inside, and the door rolls back down. Most of the time though the police think it's a done deal and are secure in the fact that most of their suspects are not going to run anywhere. So, they walk around to the back of the van and open the doors. I guess they forgot that my handcuffs were still in front of me instead of behind my back. I figured I was already messed up, so I might as well give as good as I was getting, right?

As the officers and DEA Agent Douglas Ridenhour pull down into the underground entrance and the door is rolling up still, they have exited the van and are walking back to open the doors for me to get out. By this time the door is now rolling down to close. These fools open the back door of the van and I come bursting out the back and diving under the rolling down door, making it and running up the hill that is the driveway to the underground entry. I take a second to look back at them two fools and in doing so miss seeing the police car coming down with a suspect in the back. Yes! I was laid out flat on the hood and down for the count that Friday night!

I decided to just stay right there on the cop's hood, handcuffs and all, because I was too tired and had blood all over the place. Sometimes it's just not meant to be, you know what I mean?

Now, let's get back to the topic of respect. The value of self-respect may be taken for granted. We may discover how very important it is though when our self-respect is threatened or we lose it and have to regain it or when we struggle to develop or maintain it in a difficult environment. Some people find that being able to respect themselves is what matters most about avoiding bad behavior and getting their life together.

Confusing respect with fear or envy causes many problems while having self-respect and truly respecting others fosters peace. A person who truly respects another person does is because they see them as an honorable human being, not someone they are afraid of or envies because of what they have or how others see them in society. They want to be like the person they respect, and this means that they want to be honorable as well. You don't have to cause problems to get or show respect and foster peace in your life and those around you.

On the other hand, demanding something from another through fear fosters conflict, fights, and criminal behavior. And a person who wants what another has or wants to be seen as another is seen in society will often do what is necessary to get what they want. This approach to life also fosters conflict, fights, and criminal behavior.

Have you ever confused respect with fear or envy? Be honest with yourself. Perhaps you flew off the handle or hurt someone when you claimed they didn't show you respect, whereas the truth is they didn't fear you enough to submit to your control and behave as you wanted them to. Or have you done things that are wrong and illegal because you wanted to be like someone who in reality did not deserve your respect? The real truth though is that when we claim someone does not respect us, we need to look closely at ourselves and decide whether the real truth is that we don't respect ourselves…

CHAPTER FIVE

LOCKDOWN

No matter where you go in life, nor what it is you're doing, there will always come a time when things seem to be going and running too smoothly. This happens to all of us in prison as well, so don't feel like you are the only one having a bad day or night or that everything that you're going through is the worst it could be. Because I can assure you that you have no idea what bad is or just how bad it can really get for someone not living your life, nor that of my own.

Today as I sit here typing these words out to you, I cannot help but think about what is going on with my friends over in their country of Ukraine, where one such person works and lives in the bombed maternity hospital in Mariupol, Ukraine. I have no idea if she and her family are still alive. Or my other friend who is a cop in the capital of Ukraine, Kyiv. These are people that I have been corresponding with and knowing for over a decade, and to have no clue about their health, only to be able to listen for updates on my radio as I listen to the news 24/7 and pray that God allows all of the Ukrainians and their President Volodomyr Zelenskyy to push back the Russian soldiers and their cowardly leader Vladimir Putin. This man doesn't deserve to be called nor hold the title of president, and though I no longer condone acts of violence; I would be a liar if I sat here and said that thoughts of what should be done to Putin have not run through my head.

The best I can do for my friends over there and all of the Ukrainian people and their president is pray for them believing that God the Almighty will bring the Ukrainian people through in the end, but at what cost to the people and in turn the world? My heart goes out to each and every one of the people of Ukraine and those who are going to their rescue to help fight for them, and I don't mean from sitting behind a desk or running your mouth off to the media but taking your butt and fighting in the flesh with these people! I know it's dreaming, but if I was given the choice or the chance to go and assist these great people and their country, I would be on the first thing smoking to fly over there and place my life for not only my friends, but for all the Ukrainian people and the children because it's the proper thing to do.

Talk is what everyone can do and is doing, but actions are what count the most. I cried for this little girl and her family that are in a bomb shelter in Kyiv, Ukraine as she started singing in this bomb shelter the song from the movie "Frozen." The song is one of Disney's "Let It Go." As I know my little niece would know this song well, I cannot stop but think of her or my sister or mother in a situation like this while I'm sitting here in prison, feeling so helpless with no way to help nor provide for those I love and care about because this is how we as humans think.

To read how this USA Today columnist was able to capture the story of this young girl and the video that was shared on Facebook is so moving that you can do nothing but shed your tears for the pain these people are going through and what these little children are having to endure when they should be growing up and going to school and playing with their friends and learning about God. Sitting at their kitchen table and enjoying a meal with their family for Passover and other holidays. Instead, they are hiding in bomb shelters or fleeing without their own family for 600+ miles to the border like the 11-year-old boy.

Yet, each one of you reading this is crying about gas prices going up or not getting through on your cellphone or a boyfriend/girlfriend giving you problems. We complain about the parent that abused us or drank too much and beat someone we love. We say that President Joe Biden isn't doing enough or is screwing things up when the truth of the matter is we have become so passive that we are now taking things for granted.

These things are not only happening out there in society but within prison walls. Prisoners complain about everything as well. The food is too cold or we're locked down too much and too long. We should be getting this or that, or my loved ones don't really love me because if they did, they would be visiting me more often. The list goes on and on and on without end!

All it takes is for one voice, one person to set into motion change. That's all it takes to change how everything is going, almost like the ripple effect when you toss a pebble into a pool of water. It hits the water and then the ripples start to go out from its center, making wider and wider circles in the water slowly moving outwards from its center. That is what I'm praying my book that you now hold in your hands will do, have its own ripple effect on those of you in society, to assist in changing the way things are going for all the people of the world.

I'm in the situation I'm in because I broke the law and took action against others because I felt disrespected and owed, and for what? NOTHING! What I mean is that nothing in life is ever worth throwing away your freedom for, and nothing can be justified in taking another person's life, ever. And now I sit in my own kind of hell, though it was once so that I did see my situation as a hell, I no longer do. I'm more alive now than I have ever been in my whole 43 years of life.

Yeah, I know. You're reading this going dude, you're crazy! How can you say being locked up for what could be the rest of your life or even your death by lethal injection makes you feel so alive now than if you were out in society?! Hope. Hope and my trust and faith in God and His word which can be found throughout the Holy Bible.

Would you like to know how this is possible and how you can feel the same way or help someone you love and care about feel the same? Then please allow me to continue, but remember, you asked for it!

First, whenever we struggle with something in our lives, most of us will pray, and prayer gives us hope. When we pray to God, we open our minds to Him and help several elements in the healing process work together to give us hope. We all typically ask for help when we pray. In doing so, we acknowledge our weaknesses and accept that we are not all-powerful and that we need help from God. We acknowledge our belief that His power is boundless and limitless. Believing this means that we also believe anything is possible, even forgiveness from someone we have hurt or reconciliation with someone who has no rational reason to reconnect with us.

Furthermore, prayer helps us construct a mental image of what can be. We picture success and construct a vision of what our hope really is. When we do this, we believe more strongly and work harder and more intelligently, often many times in very small ways, to do our part in making our hopes and dreams a reality.

Secondly, hope is that faith in God will bring success in our healing process. Most of us have not only hurt another person in some way, but we have also sinned against God. The bad treatments towards our parents, siblings, friends, or people we don't know; our alcohol and drug use; our fighting and thefts, burglaries, assaults, or murders, and all other offenses violate God's commandments. But all we have to do to heal our relationship with God is to ask. When we do so and work our problems out, we have success. We have mended an important relationship and seen the evidence of doing so is possible. While hearing, loving, and forgiving God is easier than dealing with the hurt of an abused human being, mending the relationship with God suggests mending that other broken relationship is also possible. Doing this gives hope.

Lastly, the influence of hope is that God is constant and always in our lives, and if we believe in Him we know that He will be with us through the ups and downs in our lives. Often we're scared and lonely, but our belief in God means that He is there inside of each of us and is not afraid to deal with our losses. Healing relationships with another person is rarely easy, and there are always both good times and bad. But God is always present, and He never changes. We can always depend on Him or rely on Him for strength when we're facing difficult times, and this I promise you will give us all hope as it does for me within these walls knowing that I could one day be strapped down to a gurney and injected with a lethal dose of drugs until I'm dead.

One thing about being locked up in prison is that we're always going on a lockdown for some reason or another. During these days of lockdown, there is little to no movement by the prisoner population except to be escorted out to take a shower every other day, meaning Mondays, Wednesdays, and Fridays only. The weekends don't count according to the Texas Department of Criminal Justice. Each of us has to make do with his or her time in prison, and when these lockdowns do happen, they can get out of hand fast. From not being fed properly because we're always fed only a paper sack, also known as a Johnny-Bag, which consists of a peanut butter and jelly sandwich, one meat sandwich of some kind, and either raisins or prunes. This is what we are given most of the time during lunch and dinner. Breakfast is only a little different as we get two cold pancakes or maybe a biscuit. That's why if you find yourself coming to prison, you should always make sure you have some kind of outside support or you have a trade to make you some money inside prison walls. Without either of these, you will more or less starve.

Men think that we have it the worst in prison but let me share something very serious with you that you probably have failed to take into consideration because you're too focused on yourself and your needs instead of others. Women prisoners have it bad and in many ways worse than the men in prisons around the world. Not only do the women have to fight against their fellow female prisoners for one reason or another, they must also protect themselves against the male prison guards. Not all male officers are bad, but it's only a matter of time before one of them is trying to forcefully take something from the woman, and because their loved ones don't fully understand how prison is run; they end up turning a blind eye from ignorance rather than intelligence.

Thus, some woman somewhere in prison is being raped by a male prison guard or the woman is turning herself out to the male officers for better food or longer visits. But you also have female officers that prey on prisoners as well. Then during the lockdowns, the female prisoners have to deal with PMS (premenstrual syndrome). Being on a lockdown for them during these times can be beyond difficult because they're not allowed to bathe/shower properly and I have no doubt the smell can get very bad for them and those around them.

For those of us in a men's prison, lockdown can and will cause temptations to rise up and thoughts of anger or lust towards the female staff as well as verbal fights among one another. The isolation can become so bad that you feel like you can't take it anymore, reading the books that were ordered for you by family or friends or lawyers or by yourself no longer seem to hold your attention and you're getting restless because you want to move around and do something.

If you're having trouble sitting still out there in your own home or at work and you are feeling like going off or walking away, consider this—if you break the law and land yourself inside the justice system or an American courtroom, you won't have to ever worry about any of those things and feelings again because you'll have just become another statistic in the penal system and lost to those in society as just another person who broke the law or made a mistake.

That mistake is what everyone will now know you by and look at you for. It doesn't matter how good you've been or what you have done to correct that mistake because you will NEVER amount to anything more in the eyes of society, but you never have to worry about this if you walk with and have God in your life. You never have to worry about other people loving you because God loves you no matter what. Come, take a walk with me as I share with you the kinds of love there are.

The first love is what we call a need-love. This is a reflection of our physical, emotional, intellectual, and other needs. It is the love that sends a lonely or frightened kid into his/her mother's arms. Need-love is more than a selfish desire to be loved, but instead is the basis of a person's spiritual life and love for God. Need-love recognizes that we are incomplete and are often hurting inside, that our whole being is one of great need. This longing leads us to ask God for His forgiveness and support in our troubled lives. Need-love leads people who are spiritually isolated and lonely, waiting for another's affection either from family, a lover, or others in general.

Regardless of how unlovable your behavior has been, you can seek all the love you need and want with certainty that God will love you and with that hope that others will too. Our need for love from others motivates us to improve our lives because we want to please someone who loves us. Our parents, siblings, lovers, and friends, or God. If we accept that God loves us, we want to continue to please Him by living the way He wants us to. We think about our lives and our faults, focus on what we want to change, and make an effort to change to please the ones we love and those we think love us.

The other kind of love is God's love. God-love is of Himself working through a person. It is goodness and a Christian life exhibited in a relationship with another. Examples are the love that our parents or parent has for us even when we have violated their trust and caused them serious problems, or the love a kid has for their mother even though the mother is absent most of the time. God-love has a few important characteristics.

Someone showing God-love often shows love to the unlovable. Many of us have done some seriously bad things in our lives: lying, drugs, speeding, bullying, fighting, and thinking bad thoughts against another who has wronged us in some way or another. But we are also God's creatures, each with our own special story of humanity, and in most cases our own side of good. Those of you showing God-love look beyond our faults and show us love.

Those showing God-love often engage in risky love too. We give our hearts to people who have little experience with love of any kind and a poor track record, which is ultimately a recipe for betrayal and distress. Loving someone without a track record is like lending all your savings and car to a total stranger. It's not a safe investment. Unlike lending such funds or a car, however, the more love we give, the more we have. Loving another who may betray us is like God's love for us. He knows without a doubt that we will all let him down sooner or later, but He continues to love us anyway!

God-love only desires what is best for the other person. It has no agenda and expects nothing in return. It's just that loving another person is loving God, as Jesus Christ said in the book of Matthew 25:40, "I tell you the truth, when you did it to one of the least of these, my brothers and sisters, you were doing it to me!"

It's currently a little after 7 a.m. and I have now been awake for two hours and some change but didn't actually roll my old butt outta bed until 20 minutes ago. If I had gotten up as I do now every day out there when I was younger, I probably would have graduated high school with everyone else instead of doing so at a continuation high school for troubled teens. See, you're not alone in thinking that I have no idea what you have gone through. Everyone has issues in their lives, some just don't let their secrets out of the bag or they have money and can go get help right away. But we have ourselves and maybe someone that loves us just a little bit that can help us in some way or another, and if not then we got the system and this life. But in all honesty, I wouldn't wish this life on anyone, not even my worst enemy!

It's Sunday the 20th of March 2022 and we've now been on lockdown for one week and have been told that some big wig from Huntsville, Texas is supposed to be coming through the prison/Texas Life Row (Death Row), though nobody has any solid clue as to just who this person is. I was thinking about washing some of my laundry this morning but will wait until after this so-called big wig.

Do you still wait hand and foot on your parents to do your laundry for you, or are you old enough to be doing it on your own now? Or are you so lazy that you have your girlfriend or boyfriend picking up after you? If this is the case, it's only a matter of time before they say that enough is enough. Stop being lazy and do it for yourself. Life is too short not to do for oneself or even for someone you don't know.

Go for a drive in your car or ride on your bike and do some kind of random act of kindness for another person. It'll make you feel great inside after you've done so. Now, if you cannot see yourself doing this, then how about closing your eyes for a minute and picturing yourself washing your laundry in a stainless-steel sink with a hot water button you have no control over. Can you picture this? Doing your best to wash your clothing so that it's clean and then rinsing it out in this very same sink and having to deal with the water not going down the drain fast enough for you so you have to stop and allow the water to drain before continuing. Once you have each piece of clothing washed and rung out, you then place it up on your homemade clothesline running across the length of your cage (about the size of a dog kennel) so that it can dry before folding up and placing it into a mesh bag that you have hung up on the back wall so everything is in its place and out of the way.

The whole time that you're doing laundry you're jamming out to some music that is on your old school radio, not some iPad or phone or CD player that has cordless headphones, but the big bulky ones that make you deaf to everything else going on around you. The stations you pick up are so crazy that most of the time you have no choice but to listen to some ol' honky on your radio screaming about his tractor and his woman who threw him out of the house with his dog. Either he or she is drunk again, and she cannot get the dishwasher running and the kids are tracking mud into the house! This music, I tell you, is nothing but straight torture! Can I not listen to some old-school jazz or blues like BB King or even some music by Adele, Charlie Puth, or Imagine Dragons? And if I must listen to some country then maybe something that can be understood when listened to like Sam Hunt, Eric Church, Luke Combs, Kelsea Ballerini.

But some seriously great Christian music can be found too! Artists like Toby Mac, Danny Gokey, Ryan Ellis, Crowder, For King & Country, etc. But no! I'm stuck with some redneck I cannot understand with his woman screaming bloody murder because the kids are tracking mud into the house and the husband is more concerned about his coon hunting dog! Tell me these folks aren't butt-backwards, and what is worst of all is that someone gave these people airtime on the radio!

If that doesn't beat it all, picture yourself going to sleep one night only to wake up the next morning with some of the things you left on the floor floating around! Floating around I said. That is what I said, and it's not in clean water, but sewage water from a toilet that has backed up in another prisoner's cell and while he continues to flush his toilet, pushing dirty, crappy water and urine out of everyone else's toilet, there is no way to stop the flood of this sewage water because this other prisoner refuses to stop flushing his toilet! Can you imagine waking up to this, and I'm not talking about a little water but four inches of this stuff all over your cell now and flooding out under your cell door just as it is from everyone else's cell and now flooding the whole run (tier)?

And if that's not bad enough, remember that you're in the big house now and you no longer have someone to pick up after you or take care of you because you wanted to throw your life away. You wanted to break the law, so now instead you get to either soak the rest of the morning/day in this stink or you can clean it up with your own hands and a rag. That's what I said, put your hands to work and clean up another adult human being's poop and urine, then reclean your cell with soap and water and a clean rag. Then use hot water to wash, wash and wash your hands until they're red from the water temp and being scrubbed almost raw to get them clean but you still feel like you got poop on them from another dude!

You can either live and be respectful in a clean cell of your own or you can live and be disrespected the rest of your life while living like an animal, the choice always comes down to you in the end. My advice to each of you that this book has been handed to is if you're on the path to destruction and jail then prison, I would take the time to figure out how to make a change within yourself for the better because while you're out there living in society, whether it be in a halfway house, at home, or on the streets, you still have a chance to make something of your life in a positive way. Because once you end up in a jail cell, the chances of you getting out or making something of yourself becomes almost less than zero percent, and it's only a matter of time before the court sends you to prison, and once you get here, especially in Texas, you may as well have whomever you still have out there in society purchase you your own funeral clothes because you will die inside this place and that is no joke.

If I could hit a rewind button like when you watch a movie, I wouldn't hesitate to do so, but this isn't a movie and you don't get a second chance to make amends once the court decides that you are a continuing threat to society and those that live in it. What little of a life you had is now nothing, you no longer exist to those out in society. You're not only a nobody, but a never was.

Texas lawyers and judges and LEOs (law enforcement officers) will do everything they can to get away with tweaking the law to fit themselves, and if you don't believe me, do your own research on the following lawyers who are District Attorneys and one of my own lawyers here in Texas: Paul R. McWilliams SBOT No. 13877300; Leslie McWilliams SBOT No. 19857270, Rebecca A. Depew SBOT No. 00784021, and Robert O. Harris III SBOT No. 09098800, and District Judge Martha J. Trudo of the 26th Judicial District Court of Bell County in Belton, Texas. Had these people handled my capital case legally and properly, as well as my codefendant's, neither he nor I would have been charged with capital murder. I wouldn't be on Texas Death Row fighting for my life and a new trial or sentencing and he wouldn't be sitting in prison at the Darrington Unit serving a capital life sentence. But that is just what both of us are now doing, and because when you look and get right down to it, it's our fault for breaking the law, but it's their fault for not upholding the law of court. They each cut corners and lied to the jury. That is how Texas courts, their lawyers, and District Attorneys legally get away with murder in a sense.

Unless you have millions of dollars, you're going to remain in prison until you're either old or dead. So, I would in all honesty think long and hard about listening to your parents or good friends that are only trying to help you go down the right path in life because you only get one life and how you live it and what you do throughout that one life will be all that matters in the end.

Now, for the first time in over seven months, I was able to speak with all three of my loved ones on the telephone during my 15-minute call on Sundays to my mom. It was a little after 10 a.m. my time here in Texas but for them, it was after 11 a.m. once I was able to get my mom on the telephone where she tells me, you're calling early. I said that was because of the big wigs that were coming through this afternoon. They wanted to get the telephone calls out of the way, so we were being allowed to call now.

After speaking for a few minutes and talking about the new flooring they had put in earlier in the week and laughing about my niece's dog Eve not being able to throw on her brakes like she was able to with carpet flooring, I asked where Sis and Pey were. She told me that they were still sleeping. I said, would you please go and wake them up in their rooms? Jokingly she said, they'll kill me for waking them up, to which I told my mom; well, they can only do it once! Thus, she walked into my sister's room and woke her up, and handed her the phone.

Let me tell you, at first she was cranky but slowly she started coming around after her little brother was able to lay it on thick with the reverse psychology about not hearing from her and my niece for over seven months nor getting any pictures of all of them. Before we said our goodbyes, I asked her to read Matthew 13:1-23 in her Bible. Then before I forgot I asked if it was okay to get her and my little niece's phone numbers from mom. I was told yes and that she would try to get around to sending pictures. Giving each other our love, she was now sounding awake and maybe she had a smile on her face. I mean, how often is it she gets woken up by her little brother she hasn't been allowed to see in over 15 years?

Once my mom had her phone back, I talked her into going into my little niece's room and waking her up too. I figured she was already in the pool with me on waking up her daughter, my sister. Why not jump into the deep end and wake up her granddaughter, my li'l niece, too?

Let me tell you something. I'm a few thousand miles away from where they live but being on the telephone allows one to feel like we're right there with one another and hear everything, listening to my mom try and wake up this sleeping beauty who is my little niece. That took some serious work! Once she got her on the phone though and she said hello, I had her feeling like her mom as I said, hey, what are you doing in bed still at 11:10 a.m. on Sunday? Don't you know I have been awake since 5 a.m. and if I can do it so can you? Just hearing her talk I knew she was smiling, and as I learned from her that she likes to read books and watch TV/movies, I couldn't help but feel a great sadness inside my heart for all the years of her life that I have missed as her uncle, let alone the years of my sister raising her and my mom being with the two of them.

But being able to share this love with them about God, as they're each very religious and have their own relationship with God, allows me to also be gratefully thankful as well because I know that one day when our lives end in this life, I will see each one of them again in the Kingdom of Heaven! While being honest though, just hearing my little niece speak to me, I came to a cold-hearted truth. Though she may be little to me and will always be so in my eyes and to her mother and grandma, you wouldn't be able to tell from talking with her that she's a young teen because she sounds as if she's pushing 30 with a maturity and intelligence beyond her young years!

Passing the telephone back to her grandma so she and I could continue to talk for the few minutes we had left, it felt so great being able to talk with each of them, and without God, this wouldn't have happened because with Him all things are possible!

Can you imagine not being able to talk to, let alone touch, your loved ones ever again because you are now spending your life and time in a state prison? Stop and take into serious consideration the things and people you'll be forced to walk away from because you didn't stop to think about the effect it would cause not just you but everyone who knows you. I promise you, it's the littlest things in life that you'll come to miss the most and you won't even realize how badly you're missing something until you've had it taken away from you for the rest of your life!

How is it that every time someone says that certain people will be walking around (i.e., big wigs) they never come around until the very end of the day? And it's right after you've placed everything that you shouldn't have sitting out back into where you would have it to begin with. Plus, the towel on your light and the jacket rolled up tight and placed into the back window so that the light from the sun and the giant prison lights at night cannot enter your cage through the window, thus preventing you from being able to get to sleep.

So, this was what happened in the situation today. We wait, and wait, and wait until we think they're not going to walk through, and…bam! Here they are walking around with our very own brother Warden Dickerson. It's one thing seeing this brother walking around for those of us that can call him our brother from talking with him throughout our days working each of the faith-based programs and then graduating from Overcomers and Bridges To Life. We all know Brother Dickerson is one of us…a true believer in Jesus Christ and a new creation in Him. But what was a shocker was seeing Major Tolly walking around wearing a suit!

Now, I know for a fact that earlier that morning as he was walking around with the lovely LT. Watson, that Major Tolly was wearing his TDCJ-ID uniform, but when he came around with the big wigs walking around, it was like he took off into a telephone booth like...Superman Major Tolly! No more uniform but a transformation into a suit-wearing lookin'-business man. Craziest thing I ever saw.

If that doesn't beat all, the man himself, along with some sidekicks I guess you would call them, was the very man himself over all of the TDCJ-ID, Director Bobby Lumpkin, who just so happens to be the very one that I have a federal lawsuit against. Walking with this man are his sidekicks, though not really, a couple of state senators like Ted Cruz and some other along with some of their staff no doubt as they came onto this section of A-Pod, also known as Death Watch, to show them what the inside of the cells look like over here.

I heard them enter into the #2 cage and it wasn't long before somebody caught them a sucker. This time around it was one of the female staff. I can clearly see it in my head as she is standing in front of the toilet/sink combo and one of the males tells her to push the button on the sink so the water comes out, not knowing that the water pressure is way up and that if you don't have something to use as a nozzle the water will shoot straight up at you hard. Well, this is what happened and the next thing you hear is this woman squealing like a stuck pig while everyone else is now laughing at her expense. This all took place at 5:45 p.m. on March 20th, 2022.

Then right after they left, we all tuned into The Tank on our radios which is the prison's very own radio station on FM 106.5 where Megamind our DJ was playing the second part of the movie I had sent into the prison for everyone...Boss Baby Part 2! Hey, just because we're all men in a grown man's prison doesn't mean we don't like to have some laughter in our lives too and there is nothing wrong with wishing you could still be a kid 'cause God knows if we could all get a do-over in and with our lives we would all take it without a second thought!

Listening to this movie though had each of us laughing aloud and feeling even better about the weekend about to be over and the start of another week of...lockdown. But hey, showers in the morning 'cause it's Monday!

CHAPTER SIX

WHO'S REALLY YOUR FRIEND AND WHO'S NOT?

During my many, many years in and out of jails and then prisons, I would meet a lot of people who would say they were my friend only to find out later on down the road that they were nothing of the sort; and that I was nothing more to them than a stepping-stone in their life or a way for them to get something from me that they otherwise couldn't have gotten.

When I was just a kid and into my teens, I had a single friend that was like a brother to me and I to him. His name was Adam Enos. Adam's parents understood that I had issues as a kid, but they didn't let that stop them from allowing their youngest son, who was my age, from being friends with me and allowing Adam and I to do just about anything. We played on the same soccer teams numerous times and even went for tryouts on what was called back then for the under-19 years age group Modesto Ajax soccer team. Though neither one of us made it, Adam did make it for the Turlock Tornado's soccer team.

But I'm getting ahead of myself. Adam and I met when we were both around six years old and were going to the same school. From day one it was friends, and we would remain so for the longest time until I started going in the wrong direction with my life. If we weren't out riding our dirt bikes up in the hills at this off-road place called La Grange up in the mountains, we were riding our mountain bikes up into the same hills after riding from his house out in the country.

Riding the back roads and going up and down this road called Roller-Coaster Hills on our way out towards Turlock Lake we passed the lake before one of us got a flat tire and had to fix it out in the middle of nowhere and decided we should ride back. On the trip back to his house some 20 miles or so away, we took a different route from the one we did on our ride out. I should mention that both of us during this ride and time were both in high school and had been attending Turlock High School, and if I remember correctly, we were juniors, so 11th grade, though it was also around this time that I had to enroll at Roselawn High School.

So, as we were on our way back to Adam's house and on a different road than what we came out on, we notice that the trees all around us are those of apples, green apples. As we decide to take a break and walk out into the apple orchard, we both notice how big they are. These aren't normal-size apples but are the size of 1-1/2 softballs! They were huge and juicy. Adam had a backpack with him and before we left, we made sure to fill his bag with these apples. These are just one of the many memories I have of my friend before things started falling apart, and not because of Adam, but because of my choices in life.

It was during the summertime and Adam was working out at Napa Auto Parts in Delhi, California. Senior year of school for both of us, though I was no longer really attending school at this time. I was with a girlfriend, and we were driving in a friend's lifted Blazer. Thinking to make a detour and stop to see my friend Adam at work to see if maybe he wanted to get some lunch, I drive us there which is also out in the country off of Vincent Road but running parallel with Highway 99. Having traveled from just up north of Turlock near Modesto but now having to drive south, I take the exit for Delhi and take the road that turns off onto Vincent Road and the Napa Auto Parts store.

Parking and telling my girl I'd be right back I hop out and run inside and ask Adam if he wanted to get some lunch. He said he couldn't because they had too much to do at the shop. Understanding, I said okay and walked out, getting back into the Blazer. I looked over in the passenger seat and noticed that my girlfriend still had her seatbelt on. Backing out before turning onto Vincent Road to take it back into the town of Turlock from the country, I don't bother to put my seatbelt on and turn the CD player up that's playing 2Pac's "All Eyes on Me."

    If you've never lived out in the country, let me lace you up on something. It doesn't matter what time of the day you're driving out there because there will always be fog as it takes a little longer to go away than it does in the city. Some spots cannot be seen because of orchards or cattle crossings, all kinds of hazards that we when in the city don't stop and take into consideration. It didn't matter one tiny bit that I knew this road like I knew the back of my hand because nobody can control one's own fate. It didn't help that I was also speeding, as most who drive out in the country do.

    I was a little more than two miles from Adam and Napa Auto Parts and just as I was passing a slower car, it dawned on me too late that I was doing so right at a crossroads used by dairy trucks (semis). Right when it dawned on me, I saw the front end of just such a truck, only this one is a cattle truck and he was turning onto the road in my direction.

    Due to my size/lift and hitting him almost head-on, the impact allowed me to climb the right front corner of the semi before my push bar caught his engine. I came to with the sound of whoop, whoop, whoop, and spitting up blood into an oxygen mask. I was flat on my back with a neck brace on and strapped to a gurney. The sound I was hearing was the blades from the Medi-flight that was landing in the field to the side of the wreck which was heard by Adam and his coworkers two miles away.

    My girlfriend would walk away, but the lifted Blazer was totaled, and I would later be told that had I been wearing my seatbelt it would have ripped me in half. As it was, my head broke the steering wheel. Do you know who it was that came and visited me and checked me out of the emergency room/hospital many hours later? Nobody from my own family because the man that called himself my dad didn't care one way or the other if I died as he never wanted me in the first place, even after he was told by Adam's family and Adam himself and some police officers he knew. This man didn't even notify my mom who was living in Las Vegas at the time.

    The ones who came to check me out of the hospital were my friend Adam and his parents. They took me back to their home way out in the country over an hour away and another town over. To think I had one of the best friends a person could have, and in the end, I lost it because of my stupidity and poor choices in my life. Adam gave me every chance to change my path in life, but I just couldn't do it and it cost me my friendship with someone closer to me than my own blood brothers.

I not only miss my friend to this very day but have so many regrets for letting him down as well as myself. I pray that if you're reading this and have such a friend in your life that you don't lose your friendship behind bad choices in your own life because we only get one life and though we cannot change our lives we can change what we're doing. A true and sincere friend will only come around once in a lifetime. Please don't throw yours away and make amends with the friends you have that are like either a brother or sister to you before it's too late.

Not even one month later I would take off on my older brother Sean's Ninja 600RR motorcycle and ride to my mom's in Las Vegas, Nevada. (Note: Read my first book "Within the Shadows of Life" by Richard Tabler, ISBN 978-1-63751-128-2.)

After my trip to Las Vegas and return to California and my trip to CYA (California Youth Authority) and my run to Florida, where I would land on the streets in many ways, and here during a break-in of someone's home in Key West, Florida, I would make another friend over time. His name was Danny, though this isn't the kind of friendship one should have nor want.

Danny was someone that taught me the ins and outs of the drug trade, illegal arms, and how to evade either the police or someone giving chase in both cars and trucks and from a boat. I would also learn a trade that I wish he never had taught me—how to fire any weapon with accuracy while either standing still or moving. It was Danny that would bring me inside his circle and teach me how to survive the streets and on the run. This isn't something you should want to know to do in your own life because it can and will only lead to one or two places just as it did for both Danny and later on myself. Either you'll end up dead or spending the rest of your life in some prison or another as I'm currently doing.

After Florida, I would return to California where I would land in jail for a short time before once again fleeing to Fort Myers, Florida. There I would land in jail and I would meet another friend named Q. Q, as I called him, who would teach me how to fight. Those lessons would be with me through my walk into the jungle, also known as the California Department of Corrections, or as it is better known, the penitentiary, and I promise you it's nothing like your Hollywood movies or TV series.

My first major fight, if you want to call my beating somebody and dragging his body down three tiers of stairs a fight, took place at DVI in Tracy, California. (Note: Read my first book.)

From there I would go to many other prisons in California, and I would land in many fights, some where I feared for my life and had no choice but to become what is called a human torpedo. This is what one is called inside a California prison when he accepts a shank that is slid under his cell door. Sometimes it's for someone trying to make a name for himself and sometimes it's simply because someone has let it be known that the new guy was going to be tested and would certain sets (ethnics) step in for him.

Not all fights are reported in prison by correctional officers because, for the most part, California prisons are run by prisoners and officers who want to go home and don't step into something that doesn't concern them. Back then doing time in prison was very dangerous and in some places it still is. I would learn how to protect myself by wrapping magazines around my upper body area and hips, mainly my back area and stomach. This would prevent another prisoner if he caught you slipping or he was able to get inside and stick you with a shank, it would prevent most shanks from penetrating your flesh.

You can have somebody on the inside that you're tight with or such as your cellie who must also have your back because you and he are to stick together. It's the code between prisoners in California, but if you're in the wrong on something or you brought undue heat to the cell, your cellie and you could end up fighting or he stepping out letting you fight whoever came for you and vice versa.

You think you have everything covered but in all honesty, you don't! There have been times when I was placed into a situation because of my ethnicity and beliefs. I was tested numerous times by other prisoners to see if I would stand up and fight or if I would back down.

At CTF Soledad (Correctional Training Facility Soledad State Prison) you have to walk down this long hallway after exiting the block you live on to get to the yard or the chow hall during each meal. Knowing that I was fixing to be hit (tested), I did the unexpected and hit the person first from behind. I'm not proud of this, but in prison, it's either you or them. After I hit this man repeatedly with a metal shank when I caught him slippin' along with those walking along with him, I handed off my shank and watched as he hit the ground with a friend, and the weapon used was taken away by others that had provided it for me. No weapon, no charges, only an investigation if someone snitched. But I made sure to be fast and not get his blood on my body nor hands because that is one of the things checked for by officers.

This is not the kind of life you want for yourself or a loved one. If you think it's bad for only the prisoners, think again. NOBODY in prison is safe from violence at one time or another, period.

In another prison in California, I took a step when the offer was placed and became gang affiliated with a serious prison set known as Kumi Afrikan Nations or 4-1-5, our area code for Oakland, California. We spoke only in Swahili so that outsiders couldn't understand us when we spoke to one another. After joining up with them, I took out some revenge on two white prisoners with a shovel that was at hand.

It was a very bad place to do such a thing, but I was driven by anger and not thinking. This action cost me more months in prison and a one-way ticket to the SHU (pronounced shoe) in Crescent City, California where Pelican Bay State Prison is. I would be placed upon my arrival into a cage outside in the snow and sleet in only my boxers for hours upon hours until I thought I would freeze to death.

Throughout my life and time in prison and out of it, I would be stuck with shanks, I've been shot with a .22, and I've been hit with tasers numerous times. I have been held underwater and I've been suffocated. I have had plenty try to kill me both in prison and out, and you know why? Because I placed myself into these kinds of situations as a result of the kind of life I chose to live, such as breaking the law, dealing drugs, or being a driver for someone who I knew was doing bad things but couldn't let go of the rush from it all. I blame nobody but myself, and I tell you here and now, this is not the kind of life you want to live or allow someone you know to live, let alone one of your very own loved ones.

Before long I found myself once again on the move/run. I knew that by running I would be wanted again, but in my mind, I no longer cared. I was either going to make a life and name for myself or I would die. Who would have known that in a way I would die, but not like you're thinking, and I would make a name for myself, and again, not in the way that you're thinking but in a very negative way.

My mind was set, I had information on a man that hurt me, though not directly. His name was Terry Brotherton and when I first met him, he was living in Las Vegas and enjoyed beating helpless women while they were trying to sleep (read my first book). I had been tracking this grown man since I was 17 years old, and through bad connections I finally found him, and that was the sole reason I had for coming to Texas, which I planned to just pass through to where he was in the northeast.

I stopped here in Texas to visit with my mom and sister in Killeen, Texas. I hadn't planned on staying. Things never work out the way that we would like for them to though, do they? I cannot tell you why things took place here in Texas like they did because other than my mom and sister I didn't know anyone in this state and had only been through it once before in passing and saying hi to my sister then.

It's almost as if something else knew what was going to happen. I don't want to say God because believe me, what happened here had nothing to do with what my Father would want done. When someone is killed, writing a book and putting one's thoughts into words for others to read is NOT easy, so please bear with me as I try to form words that you'll understand…

I believe that all our lives intersect. Death doesn't just decide to take someone while missing out on another. But in the chance of either losing your life or continuing to live it, lives are changed. If the men whose lives were lost at my hand didn't die, then Terry Brotherton's life would have been taken by my hand and possibly any and every one I found with him. Think of it like this, when another car or truck crashes in front of you, that could have been your car or truck had you not slowed down. Or being a soldier over in Ukraine right now and the man right next to you is hit and killed, but you are still alive and breathing. Or when your loved one contracts COVID-19 but you don't, and you are in the same house together. Everyone thinks these are random acts, but there is a balance to everything. Just like life and death are a part of living on earth, everything happens for a reason…even though we may never understand them, they do.

My last trip was coming to Texas and I'm sure many people wish that I never did, but had I not, I never would have gotten to know God the way I do now. I never would have known what it was like to live and feel alive, nor would I have been allowed to meet some very good men who have now become my brothers and not only my friends. I'm hoping that some of them will take me up on my offer to say something within these pages as I have told them to write something for all of you to read within these pages about their lives and how they came to be here and why

YOU don't want to find yourself or your loved one here. If because of their appeals they don't write anything, then I will share some with you about them.

For now, let me tell you about some other people that I have met outside these walls. I thought about telling you about this woman that came into my life after reading about me on a pen-pal website called Wire of Hope. This woman's name is Amy. When she first wrote I was able to read in between the lines of what she was really trying to say. When I responded in kind, she was blown away by everything and explained as much. Here was another woman that had been abused by her spouse for years and years but could never walk away from him because she thought this was how she should be treated by men.

As our writing grew deeper and deeper for one another, so did our feelings for one another. Taking a chance, I sent her some flowers (just because I'm in prison doesn't mean I cannot get things done). When she got them, she again was blown away because she couldn't understand how someone on Texas Death Row could treat her better than someone she's known for half her life.

She was in the process of getting separated from her abusive spouse and he wasn't living with her and her kids as we started writing. Before you knew it, we were talking about hooking up, but I deep down couldn't understand why I was allowing myself to want to get involved with a woman while doing the kind of time I had been sentenced to…death. This wasn't fair to her nor her kids even though they are grown and have families of their own except for one of them who is only 13. So, I took a step out of my comfort zone, and the next thing you know, COVID-19 is full-blown in the world and her ex is now back in the house even though she doesn't want him there. Because he was on the lease she couldn't legally kick him out, but she said it wouldn't be a problem.

In the end, she got another job though she didn't need to work. She was doing so to get away from her ex and out of the house. This sounded good, but then he started getting my letters to her and reading them. She started pulling further and further away from what we had going. She would no longer let me know she was getting the artwork I was sending her. There was no communication between the two of us anymore.

In running from her ex, she ran away from me too and it cost us both a friendship, though she has tried to reach out to me, just as friends have tried to reach out to her to make sure she's okay, even one such friend that I used to run with but is currently wanted in the U.S. so he doesn't live in this country anymore. When I reach out she does the same thing and fails to respond. So, I let her go and decide that if she was meant to be in my life then God, when He was ready, would bring her back into my life, but maybe He was just using me in His way so that I could lift others up and show them that no matter what someone else might say about them or how they look or talk down to them and abuse them, that that is NOT the way they should be treated and in the eyes of God they are all beautiful and loved and cared about. So, Amy has run away from not only me but from herself and everyone who wants to help her and someone that even loved her for who she was as a person.

Around the same time that I met Amy, another young man named Oba would become a part of my life. In many ways, Oba, whom I would come to call my ndugu which is Swahili for brother, is like the little brother I never had. Knowing him and reading about everything he has done in life (always moving or traveling) makes me stop and think, is this how my older siblings saw me but in a bad way?

He would ask my advice but then would go against it anyway, only to say later on that he should have listened to me! How many times have your loved ones or a friend told you this? One thing though in life in general is like an old Swahili proverb: "Kupoteya njia ndiyo kujua njia," which means, "To get lost is to learn the way." If we never traveled and lost our ways in life we would never learn. Sure, we can learn things about life and history in a classroom, but hands-on experience is far more exciting, don't you think?

As time would pass, I would meet other people outside these walls, and I would remember things I did and people I knew in society as well. It's crazy how for the life of me I might not be able to remember someone's name for a long time because certain situations that took place were better left unthought about or remembered because they were during things that were being done illegally or against the law. So many times in my life I wish that my older siblings had accepted me as their loved one and brother. This way I could share things with them and they could with me, but the cold, hard truth is I know nothing about my two older brothers and their families. I have nephews and a sister-in-law but know nothing about them because my brother Sean refuses to acknowledge that I'm alive, just as my older brother Greg and his son, my other nephew, refuse to have anything to do with me except for one time back in late 2009 or early 2010.

Both of them wanted to come and watch my execution when I was given that very first execution date, as I had volunteered for execution. My execution date was set for May 20th, 2010. What kind of brothers would want to watch their little brother be killed? They reasoned that they wanted to be there for me so that I wasn't alone. If you didn't want me to be alone, then how come after all these years that I am still alive and talking and trying to reach out to each of them numerous times they return to me with nothing but silence?

Not one time have either Sean or Greg responded to my letters. To this day as I sit here sharing this with you and the world, I wonder what I did to either of them that was so bad that they would wish me dead because that is how I look at them wanting to only watch my execution but not offer letters or assistance with anything all the years I have been locked up in Texas, which is now 18 years and by the ending and publishing of this book will be 19.

The one thing I might have wanted to speak to Sean about years ago before I came to Texas and had even passed through his place in 2004 but didn't think to say anything to him about it then, was about a situation I was in for a few days. Sean at one point in his life I know took Scuba diving lessons. I don't know what he did afterward, but I thought I might have been able to talk to him about something that happened to me, as I have never been able to share it with anyone because nobody in my family has ever lived a life like mine.

But there was a time when I was working for Danny that wasn't on land but off the coast of Miami, Florida. I ended up spending about 15 hours inside a hyperbaric chamber for decompression after being underwater for more than two days at a little more than 100-feet. How can I best describe what a hyperbaric chamber is to someone that has never dived before? Here is the gist of it.

Decompression sickness is what is known as the bends. Under normal air pressure, the body respires most of its excess nitrogen. However, under increasing pressure as a Scuba diver as he descends, nitrogen increases in the bloodstream. As a diver ascends and the surrounding water pressure decreases, pure nitrogen bubbles form in the blood and eventually become too large to pass through the tissue. For the bubbles to diffuse and pass through lung tissue, the diver must sit inside a chamber that very slowly decreases pressure while breathing 100 percent oxygen, all the while being watched/monitored by a hyperbaric physician. I think if I remember it all correctly that is how it goes.

So, at one point in my corrupt life, I had to go through this myself and it was one of if not the scariest times of my life, and I thought maybe one day I could have spoken to Sean, my big brother, about it. In the end, both my older siblings and my dad would become nothing more than a stranger in passing before dying off within my thoughts and life. I'm sure that in their eyes I'm already dead but know this if you find yourself or someone you love in the same situation: you are not alone and you never have been, nor will you ever remain so because God is always with us.

Let me share this with you, and if nothing else, learn this from me, please. Holding anger in is a poison. It will eat you from the inside. We all think that hating someone is a weapon that attacks the person that hurt us. But hatred is a curved blade and the harm we do, we do to ourselves.

The best thing you can do for yourself is forgive them. "If you forgive those who sin against you, your heavenly Father will forgive you. But if you refuse to forgive others, your Father will not forgive your sin." (Matthew 67:14-15).

Pain can and often does turn into anger, but have you ever stopped and wondered about when you or someone around you was born? Nobody in this life or any life is born with anger, and when we die, our souls are freed of all the anger we ever had. But right now, and in this moment, in order to move on and forward with your life, just as I did, you need to forgive those that have hurt you.

Though I state that my older siblings are dead to me and I to them (brothers) that doesn't mean that I have not forgiven them because I have. I have even written letters to them apologizing for whatever they feel I did to offend them while also letting them know I forgive them but have moved on with my life now. Just because we do this doesn't mean that those we reach out to will respond, but don't let that get to you as I'm sure it will. As long as you know inside yourself that you tried to mend that gap and have forgiven them, that is all that matters because believe me, God knows that you have done so and He's proud of you for doing so, just as you are now proud of yourself and feel good inside about taking action in this regard.

"To say to you, 'Please forgive your brothers for the great wrong they did to you—for their sin treating you so cruelly.' So we, the servants of the God of your father, beg you to forgive our sins." (Genesis 50:17)

CHAPTER SEVEN

LET US LAUGH

Regardless of who we are or where we find ourselves in life, at some point in that journey we need to laugh because you have heard the old saying that laughter is good for the soul, but I tell you that laughter is not only good for the soul, but it is also a means of release from everything life throws at us. Just as we all have played one kind of prank or another on someone we know or love in society, I tell you that my brothers within these walls with me do the same.

When most in society think about those of us in prison, they have the bad habit of believing that it's just like what they watch on TV or in the movies, but the only movie I know about right now in this day and age that comes close to what prison is like is the movie that's out called "Attica" about the Attica prison riots in 1971. People should not believe what they see on TV or in the movies because where I have been for the last 18 years here in Texas, I've not been able to sleep in a normal bed like you. I don't go to the bathroom to take a shower whenever I would like to or a bath to soak. Neither I nor my brothers here with me can walk out to the kitchen and make something to eat or spoon ourselves some ice cream or pop some popcorn for a movie with family sitting on the couch.

My toilet doesn't have a seat that we need to worry about putting down after we use the restroom so our girlfriends or wives who get up in the middle of the night need not worry about falling into it. We don't have carpet on the floors nor many of the other creature comforts one has in society.

What we do have is concrete floors and walls along with a stainless-steel door that has a slot in the middle of it that can be opened for cold food trays slid into it for us three times a day. We have a stainless-steel sink/toilet combo without a lid and a caged-in light built into it as well. We have a steel bunk that has shelves built into it underneath so we can place our clothing or some property and we also have two shelves, one that can be used as a desk and the other right above it. Our mattress is less than 30 inches wide and made of plastic and no longer than 5-1/2 feet long and two inches thick.

Every time we exit our cells or as some of us call them, cages, we do so only after being completely stripped butt-naked in front of officers so that they can shake out our clothing before handing it back to us so that we can dress. Once this is done, we turn around so our backs are now facing the door and officers and squat down and place our hands out behind us out the slot in the door at which time the officers will place handcuffs on our wrists and double lock them. Only then are we told to stand up and the door is rolled open and we step out backward before turning around and walking under escort to wherever by two officers and sometimes more.

This is the ONLY human contact we have with another living person. To only have an officer or two grab onto our upper arms as they escort us to and from places, whether it be the shower, to visit, or to rec, or to talk to the captain, major, or wardens, or to be taken out of our cages so that they may enter into our cages to do what is called a cell search, day in and day out this is the life of a prisoner on Texas Death Row though now I and my brothers in Christ Jesus call this place Texas Life Row because though society sentenced us each to death for our crimes, God has given us LIFE!

Unlike out there in society, all kinds of creatures can and do walk inside this place, and if they can walk into this place they can surely walk into our cages at will. Though most of my brothers and I keep clean cages, it matters not to the creepy little things that crawl on the floor in an attempt to sneak up on you when you least expect it. Who is to say that creatures of all walks of life don't have a sense of humor too?

About two months ago Field Minister Troup and I were talking, and he explained to me how to make a roach trap because all over the place at night these things come out in force…cockroaches! What we do to stop them, or in our case catch them, is we take an empty plastic jar that was used with either a sandwich spread or a peanut butter jar. Once we clean it out, we take a finger's worth of Vaseline and wipe it around the inside of the rim of the jar. Then we take a piece of writing tablet or typing pad backing, tear a chunk off and fold it up and soak it with water. Then we drop it inside the jar and set it close to the door of our cell. We leave it alone and go about our days and nights. I did this one day after speaking to my Brother Troup, and the next day when I got up to do my routine, I picked up this jar, and lo and behold it had some roaches inside.

Brother Troup came around later on that day as well and I showed him the catch. What happens is these roaches like cardboard backing that is wet for some reason and climb into the jar, but when they hit the Vaseline, they slide down and are unable to get out, thus becoming stuck. Usually, when you have some you turn around and flush them down the toilet, but for those of you who don't know any better, that doesn't kill them! If anything, it just makes them want revenge when they figure out how to get back into your cage and not someone else's. Most days though when we didn't have the whole COVID-19 pandemic, the administration would have pest control walk around and offer to spray the inside of our cages. But since COVID-19, that has come to a standstill of sorts or they walk around but don't enter into the cells to spray.

I had been allowing these things to fill up numerous jars in the same week I put them out for them to climb into. One day as Warden Dickerson, who as I will share with everyone is our brother in Christ Jesus, was making his rounds on the pod. When he came to my cage and stopped cell-side, we got to talking about life and the faith-based courses some of us were currently enrolled in when I reached down and showed him my roach jar showing him all them little ugly things crawling around in the jar and over each other trying to get out but not having any success.

He got on his cell phone and sent a text to someone else about getting pest control to come through and spray. When he left, I thanked him and went back to doing my own thing in my cage thinking nothing more about it all. A couple of weeks went by and still no pest control and I was now getting tired of emptying this roach jar when I decided to have some fun because I just couldn't help myself.

Grabbing the jar of roaches, I walked over to my desk and set the jar down upon it. Turning to the side and digging through some of my other property, I pulled out a clear plastic bag, a roll of white medical tape, an envelope, and a sheet of paper. Placing the bag over the top of the roach jar, I then turned the jar upside down so that all these little homies fell into the bag. Once they were inside, there were about 40 of them in all, I folded over the opening before taping it closed. Setting them to the side, I wrote on a sheet of paper, "To Warden Dickerson, I know it's not your fault because I saw you text somebody about the roach issue in my cage and on this pod. But maybe if the ones you texted had to deal with them too they would take care of the issue sooner than later. Toss these around on others' desks and see how they like them running around!"

I mailed that through the mail here at the prison in what we call "truck mail" the next day/morning. What do you know, while I was out on a legal telephone call with one of my lawyers, which I think was David Lane of Killmer, Lane & Newman, LLP, pest control came flying through directly to my cage! The roaches have gone away to roach heaven. That is just one incident where I took it upon myself to have fun at others' expense.

Though we laugh and even nowadays are singing praise to God who is our Father in heaven, and the Holy Bible is the word of God and His Son Jesus Christ, it's also a book of love and compassion for its readers/followers. To show you in the Bible that it's okay to laugh, I give you the following verses and scriptures: "We are filled with laughter, and we sang for joy." (Psalms 126:2 NLT) "But the Lord just laughs, for He sees their day of judgment coming." (Psalms 37:13 NLT) "God blesses you who are hungry now, for you will be satisfied. God blesses you who weep now, for in due time you will laugh." (Luke 6:21 NLT)

Now that we have covered and are in an understanding, shall we have some more laughter at the expense of my brothers here with me? Yes! I can hear you all screaming at me from here.

Last year when I wrote a letter to my older and only sister, I shared with her about what happened to me in the middle of one night. Most nights I lay down after the 11 p.m. count, which is when they shut the lights off on the sections. This will stop most light from entering the cage when I also shut off my night light and I'm able to get some serious sleep. It was hot so I had turned my fans on before laying down. Sometime in the middle of the night, I had this sickening thought/feeling that someone or something was looking at me. As I opened my eyes looking from under my covers to the door, there was nobody there and the lights were still off. Looking then at my radio/clock I saw that it was 1:30 a.m. Closing my eyes, I tried to get back to sleep, but as I did so I got that feeling again that someone or something was looking at me.

 I couldn't turn over as I was now facing my back wall without giving myself away, so slowly opening my eyes while facing my back wall thinking to myself I would slowly turn over after I opened my eyes, as my eyes opened and focused on the back wall which was no less than six inches away, I found myself not looking at a wall but this up-close and personal spider! Without thinking I lunged backward, in turn about knocking myself cold when my head hit the desk before the rest of my body fell off my bunk down onto the cold, hard concrete with my sheets and blanket. I cannot stand spiders, and this was no little spider as they don't have little spiders in Texas!

 As I jumped up, the first thing I did was grab my Rhino boots and put them on my feet 'cause my plan was stomping this thing into mush, but first I needed to make sure he wasn't in my bed coverings that had fallen on the floor with me. Turning on my light, I lifted each sheet and the blanket and shook each out before placing them back on my bed and reaching up and turning off my fan because I already had the willies and the fan just made me feel like that thing was crawling on my back. Once my fan was off and I started to shake off that creepy feeling, as I was turning one way to get something, I noticed something in my mirror out of the corner of my eye on my back. Not too sure what I had seen, I turn around so my back is facing the mirror that I have set on my top shelf and take a look in the mirror.

 It goes without saying that I tried to get somewhere but forgetting that I was standing with my back to my mirror the only thing to prevent me from fleeing was a solid concrete wall which about knocked me out. Sitting there on the concrete floor of my cage in my boxers and Rhino boots trying to shake off the headache that I could feel coming on, that spider that had started it all was right next to me on the floor now. I swear this thing looked right at me with its numerous eyes, and shook its head before strutting out under my cage door like it was wondering what was I thinking. He was just trying to sleep, but this big dummy had to wake him up, and then when he tried to catch a ride I got spooked. Sorry, but I don't do spiders that are the size of a quarter let alone a silver dollar! It's safe to say that I was awake the rest of the night.

There was another time and night with my best friend and homie Big Tai (Tai'Chin Preyor, R.I.P.). He and I had been up freestyling and eating tacos and playing Hangman. Yes, I said Hangman. I know, I know, what are two grown men on Death Row doing playing Hangman? We have to pass the time somehow and it was even funnier because he was this giant black guy and I was this mixed-white guy. But as we had been playing while standing at our cage doors and looking out the side as we spoke to one another asking for letters or making the noose and head on the paper, I noticed a wolf spider running from the dayroom ceiling towards Big Tai's cage. I didn't say anything 'cause I figured I would wait and see if Big Tai saw it first and then when he didn't, I started laughing to myself saying, yeah, I was gonna get the big homie. Just as I was fixing to say something to him the wolf spider ran into his cell through the crack on the top of the door and right then because I knew Big Tai was looking up as he writes, all you hear is this gigantic yell from Big Tai and his hands slapping the door and walls as he keeps missing as he's no doubt trying to kill this wolf spider.

As this is going on next door in Big Tai's cage, he can now hear me laughing my butt off and starts to put two and two together that I knew and saw this thing enter into his cage. While you can hear him smacking his hands and throwing things around trying to get at this speedy little demon, Big Tai is yelling at me, "You ain't right, Slim! I'mma get you back, Slim!" I cannot help but laugh all the harder at my friend and brother.

When he tells me it's under his bed, I try my hardest to stop laughing and remind him; "Big Tai, what about all our studies together and you telling me how you don't kill any of God's creations? You sure trying to do it now!" He yells back at me this ain't his creation this is the devil, and I cannot stand spiders this big! My big homie and I stayed awake throughout the rest of the night and half the following day until he was able to find that spider and squash it under his boot.

Hold a place for me in heaven, Big Tai, as we'll see one another again, my friend and brother. Big Tai was taken from this life through State-sanctioned execution on July 27th, 2017 at a little after 6 p.m. May he rest in peace with our heavenly Father, but when I catch up to him, it's on again, lol!

Not all laughs came from me or my big homie Tai. There are others that I had been friends with, one whom many disliked because he was a part of the Texas 7. At least those in society didn't like him and even some officers because he never let them get away with violating their own rules and policies. His name was Donald Keith Newbury, but to his friends here on The Row we called him Lizard.

You have to understand something about prisons and the life lived on this side of the walls. When something happens like an inmate jacks the food slot and refuses to give it up without getting what he wants or speaking to rank, when rank shows up they can order the prisoner to give up the slot before they speak, and in most cases the prisoner will refuse to do so. This can and will result in what is called a failure to follow a direct order, and at this point the ranking officer can and does get on the radio (walkie-talkie) ordering that a seven-man use-of-force team be suited up.

What this is, is exactly like it sounds, seven men in what most would call riot gear. The only difference is that there is no pistol or baton. That doesn't mean that they come with nothing. They do have a shield that the #1 man carries as he will be the first to enter either the cell where the prisoner is or the outside rec yard or in the dayroom and grabbing hold onto his protective vest running in a chain of sorts are six other grown men behind him.

While such a team is getting situated, the ranking officer along with maybe a captain or higher will be at the cage now with their gas mask and different kinds of chemical agents. Some of these agents can come in anything from small cans or a bigger canister that looks like a fire extinguisher, to an air gun that fires chemical agent balls that break on impact, to a canister that you pull the pin and throw onto the yard. The officers each have their own gas masks when chemical agents are utilized against prisoners.

We, of course, have nothing of the sort. That doesn't mean that we cannot make something to either protect ourselves or something that we can place to protect our eyes and face from the chemical agents, but most of us, myself as well, are not bothered by the chemical agents used regardless of the strength. I guess you can say that I and others could eat the chemical agents for breakfast or as a means to spice up our food. It doesn't bother us because over time we have been hit with everything that the Texas Department of Criminal Justice can throw at us. Over time you become immune to it all.

Now there was a day when Lizard was upset at the officers continuing to mess him over, so on their Friday just before shift change was going to happen, he refused to come off the outside rec yard here on A-Pod. The ranking officer that he had an issue with was LT. Worthy who at one point in time had also been the U.G.I. (Unit Grievance Investigator) before going to shift and thus being the lieutenant on shift. LT. Worthy and his officers tried everything they could to get him to come off the yard peacefully, but he refused and told them to suit it up!

Lizard was not very big, but he had a good size to him. He was mixed with white and Native American, loved to drink coffee and munch on peppermint sticks with each cup, but one thing he loved more was making these people bend to him and running the team. He could also be violent when he wanted to be, but on this day just before shift change on a Friday evening, he just wanted to have some fun. This I knew because he had told me that he was going to run the team before the shift change on LT. Worthy. when the officers escorted him outside to the rec yard (note: we are only allowed to rec outside by ourselves, which means that one prisoner per rec yard, and there are two such fenced-in yards right next to each other so the prisoners can talk while outside but in their own yard).

Like I was saying, Lizard on his way out was wearing his boxers with a pair of gym shorts over them and his D.R. jumper hanging off his shoulder along with a towel and a couple of pairs of socks, and on his feet were his Rhino boots. Anyone who knew him would know from seeing him walking out with all of this that something was going to take place, or in the case of these officers, they were probably just turning a blind eye to what he was walking out in because they didn't want any part of what was going to happen. As shift change is fixing to happen in about 45 minutes, Lizard is refusing to come off the yard even when LT. Worthy shows up and tells this lieutenant to suit it up!

While the Use of Major Force Team is getting ready, LT. Worthy walks off and returns about five minutes later now carrying his gas mask and holding a canister of chemical agents. Walking outside he asks Lizard to come off the yard and Lizard tells him NO! LT. Worthy pulls the pin on the canister and throws it into the yard with Lizard before turning around and coming inside while closing the outside rec yard door behind him.

Now, this isn't what policy states should have happened. What LT. Worthy should have done was wait for the team to show up along with an officer who would record everything on the video camera. When the officer with the camera was on hand as well as the seven-man team, LT. Worthy should have told the officer with the camera to start filming, at which point he would explain who he was and his rank as well as the camera officer by name and then they together would turn to the outside rec yard where Lizard was, stating: "Offender Newbury, you are being given a direct order to strip out and place your hands through the slot. Failure to follow this order will result in chemical agents being utilized against you and a seven-man Use of Force Team to come and remove you. Offender Newbury, do you understand these orders?" But none of this was done nor said, instead LT. Worthy just tossed in the canister of chemical agents after pulling the pin.

As the chemical agents start spitting out of the can (grenade), from my cage up on 2-Row #14 at the time I can see outside and Lizard is over in the corner in a squatted down position, only now he is fully clothed in everything he took out with him, and he has a piece of clear plastic over his eyes so he can see through the gas and a folded sock covering his mouth and nose tied off with another sock so that he can breathe without worrying about the gas (though it wouldn't have bothered him).

As the chemical agents are spilling out of the grenade now, it's turning the whole outside rec yard at first a white fog color which quickly turns into a deep, dark orange color that is so thick nobody on the inside looking out the window can see through to where Lizard is now. The wait is about five minutes before LT. Worthy opens the door and walks out into this orange cloud, and now under the video camera says, "Offender Newbury, you are being given a direct order to strip out for a proper strip search and place your hands through the slot, otherwise more chemical agents will be used against you and a seven-man team will be utilized. Offender Newbury, will you comply with this order?"

The next thing you hear is LT. Worthy popping the pin on another grenade before throwing it into the yard, only this time there is a difference. As LT. Worthy is pulling off his gas mask and walking back into the inside of A-Pod, as if in slow motion in comes sailing over his shoulder the same exact grenade he just pulled the pin on and threw out into the yard with my friend Lizard. Only, nobody can understand what just happened until all the officers on the inside are now choking with snot hanging out their noses. They hadn't all had their gas masks on because he was on the outside rec yard.

While LT. Worthy was trying to overly-gas Lizard, Lizard had invited everyone inside to the party with him to enjoy those lovely chemical agents! This had never happened to anyone before but to this day I still laugh when I share this story with everyone. In the end, it came down to the second shift escorting Lizard off the rec yard as he came willingly after LT. Worthy walked off after being hit with his own grenade.

Back on February 4th, 2016, my friend and the friend of many here was taken from this life by a State sanctioned execution at a little after 6 p.m. May he too rest in peace!

There are so many other stories that I could share with you about my friends and brothers here with me and the ones we have lost to executions, but if I told you everything now, what would I write about years later or share with those who reached out to me after reading this book?

Know this: just because I'm able to share with you something that we here found funny or were able to laugh about, prison is no laughing matter, and it can and often does turn violent. However, this prison in the last three years has been getting what women call a makeover. Things here on the Polunsky Unit/Texas Death Row have changed and they have done so for the better. We owe this change to the prisoners who are taking the right steps to change their lives around for the better and to the prison radio station called The Tank which can be found at 106.5 FM on the radio dial, and most of all we owe our thanks to God Almighty and Warden Daniel Dickerson and the numerous volunteers and Chaplains Gay (pronounced Guy) and Martin because, without each of these souls, nothing could get done.

More about all of that later. But before I close out this chapter, let me share one with you about our brother and Field Minister Troup. Known to the officers as Field Minister Foster, his brothers and friends call him Troup. Troup is one of the field ministers that is called by the rank throughout the days and nights to talk with the ad-seg inmates housed on E-Pod and F-Pod. These guys are always having a tough time with doing their time/sentence in isolation or because they cannot help themselves and keep messing up and getting disciplinary cases for Code 20s which is another name within TDCJ-ID for a masturbation case. This never made sense to me as I've been locked up for 18 years and I never saw the point in doing this, let alone in prison and looking at some of these women… AAAAHHHH!

Like I was saying, Troup was talking to me one afternoon about having to talk to the fools down on F-Pod, and this one inmate he was talking to, he was at his wit's end with dealing with this guy because he just kept doing the same stupid thing over and over and over again. Troup tells me that he went down there and tells this dude, look. When the guy looks out his cage at Troup, Troup is standing there holding this colored printout of the new tablets from Securus Technologies that we're getting here on the Polunsky Unit/Texas Death Row, which is a JP6S tablet. As the guy is looking at this as Troup holds it up, Troup goes, "YOOOUUU ARE NEVER GETTING ONE OF THEEEESE!"

The guy says to Brother Troup, why not Troup? To which Troup responds, because you keep screwing up and doing stupid things. You cannot get a tablet if you are on level-3! You have to be level-1 to get the tablet which has everything on it from TV/movies to law library access and telephone, e-messaging, everything, but yyyyoooouuuu aaaarrrreeee nnooooootttt geeettting one! before walking away laughing.

When he came around and told me this and how he said it I couldn't help but laugh aloud hard as heck because watching Brother Troup, he looks like someone's old-school grandpa with his white beard and bald white hair that has gone gray when he doesn't have it shaved off. His facial expressions are priceless. He's like that guy you would watch on TV on America's Funniest Videos, the guy is being pulled over for drinking and when they get him to the police station he takes off running only to run right into the glass doors! This is Brother Troup back in the day, but now he's our brother in Christ Jesus and we love him as we would love family because all of us within these prison walls from the prisoners to the wardens and officers, we've become one giant family through our Lord and Savior Jesus Christ!

To keep ourselves from dying of boredom we do our best to entertain ourselves during lockdowns as each day seems to get longer and longer even though it's the same amount of time that is passing each day. This morning an officer came on the pod announcing who had a visit for the day and what round it was via the time. Yelling at Brother Billy in #3 cage he told him that he had a visit at 3:30 pm then walked off to the other sections to yell out the others in B and C sections. This is done to help speed up the process when the escort teams come around to escort someone to visit. Not having to wait for a prisoner to get ready because he doesn't know he has a visit saves time so that when the officers show up at the prisoner's door, all he has to do is get butt-naked! Hey, hey! None of that, get your minds out of the gutter, this isn't that kind of book, people!

We have to get butt-naked before we exit our cages because the escorting team needs to do a strip search to make sure a prisoner isn't coming out of his cage with something that we shouldn't be coming out with.

But now that I've told you that, about three minutes pass before you can hear Brother RG yelling down to Billy, "Hey, Billy! You got a visit?"

Billy replies, "Yep."

RG says, "Put me in your pocket and take me with you!"

The three of us laugh a little at this. See you have to understand, Billy is this blind ol' white guy about 47 years old and stands about 5'10" and 170 pounds. When I say blind, I mean he has to wear glasses everywhere he goes, he's literally blind without them. Now our Brother RG, who is down in the #7 cage, is this little Mexican guy covered in tattoos and stands no taller than 5'2", and weighs about 140 pounds soaking wet.

A few hours pass as I've been under my headphones listening to the music on my radio and when not listening to music I'm listening to the news on NPR and the war in Ukraine as my friends live there. The whole time I'm under the headphones though I'm on this typewriter working on this book and these pages you are now holding in your hands. So, when I pull my headphones off a few hours later to check something I hear RG tell Billy, "Check!" Before hearing Billy about one minute later move his piece out of check and RG calling out his move and again yelling at Billy, "Check!" At which time I pipe in with that old "Cops" TV series theme song, but change it a bit, "Bad boys, bad boys, whatcha gonna do, whatcha gonna do when RRRGGG comes for you!" All three of us are laughing then Billy says, you're next, Tabler!

For those of you who have no idea what I mean when I said they were calling out check and out of check, they were playing a game of chess. The way this is done is we have a chess board in our cages that we either bought from the commissary years ago or we drew one on an illustration board and made our own pieces. Where you out there in society have a board and pieces and are sitting across from one another, we have to number our boards 1 through 64 as there are 64 squares on a board. That is how we play; each player has his board in his cage and the player that goes first calls out his move and the other player in his cage moves the first player's piece upon his board while also moving his own piece when he calls it out. This is how a game of chess is played between two brothers here on The Row.

CHAPTER EIGHT

Before We Went, We Had One Last Word of Advice for You

After reaching out to a few of my friends and brothers whom I have known for over 10 years, the first to get back to me during this lockdown is my friend and brother, Juju. The following are his words, retyped by me in my cage, just for you.

"Dear Beloved,

I was asked to share my story in hopes to help the youth outside these prison walls. Youths, I am sure, who are a product of a fractured past. Whose environment they feel has let them down. Ones who might have a problem learning general things in academics. Ones who did not have much growing up. Who hoped for better days, that had friends whose parents gave them what they wanted. Who never had to feel stigmatized because they were a single-parent child. Maybe one of the parents were incarcerated, one abandoned the other parent. There are many causes of this psychological "feeling" of not being cared for or loved. It actually tends to impair us in our first-person world. Just to clarify…our first-person world is the place each of us spend all of our lives. It's the place we do all our thinking, self-talk and all our planning. We typically believe only we know our own thoughts until we're duped into believing that

God and Satan know how we think and feel only. That is farthest from the truth. You must understand that our thoughts are ALWAYS specific. The condition of our internal world is always predicated upon a person's place and certain circumstances that it is possible we cannot handle that gains the worst of us. According to Mario Beauregard and Denyse O'Leary in their book, "The Spiritual Brain," our mind (the first-person world) is as if it were a telephone exchange.

If it is for mind that we are searching the brain, then we are supposing the brain to be much more than a telephone exchange. We are supposing it to be a telephone exchange along with subscribers as well.

There is a study that was conducted that enabled the neuroscientists to better understand the conditions of our internalized systems for reasoning. As they have stated and clarified.

To interpret the results of these studies, we need a hypothesis that accounts for the relationships between mental activity and brain activity. The psychoneural translation hypothesis (PTH) is such a hypothesis. It posits that the mind, the psychological world, the first-person perspective and the brain which is part of the so-called "material" world, the third-person perspective represents two different domains that can interact because they are complementary aspects of the same transcendental reality.

The PTH recognizes that mental process (e.g., volitions, goals, emotions, desires, beliefs) are neurally instantiated in the brain, but it argues that these mental processes cannot be reduced to and are not identical with neuroelectrical neurochemical process.

The gist of it all is this: we have come from a world of physical things. They represent to us what we are required or expected to believe is true. Until we take the time to ask questions it is safe to say we will gain all the wrong messages. We are sensory beings. We sense or attempt to sense every motive without properly addressing or researching things for the correct answer. I say this because I have been incarcerated for 25 years on Texas Death Row and over the years I have fallen into harmful mental patterns due to the people in my life that considered my "environment." These are family and friends outside of these prison walls. And the Administration and those I consider my friends within these prison walls. Just to be a bit more forthright, I grew up without a father figure so I tended to run rampant. I never finished school—it was hard for me to focus. Plus, I could never get settled in any school I went to because I knew we would not stay where we were for long. So, it kept me thinking ahead. I grew up with three siblings and all of us have children though I am the only one that never finished school or got a GED. My baby sister has served time, but my oldest brother and sister never have. Like most kids I started drinking and smoking drugs around 15 years old. Heck, that is when I really got buckwild. I dropped out of school in the 8th grade. I was selling weed and crack, stealing cars just to joy ride and got my girlfriend pregnant at 16 though my daughter was born when I turned 17. I never really stayed at home though at times I did come home. I stayed out as long as I wanted to. I can safely say I wish I would have taken all the opportunities to do the right thing because we ALL have them.

My mother never raised us to turn out as we had. We just judged her for being raised as she had and never being able to give us the finer things. So, my major concern is that the youth would learn to rise up from the internal voices that lie to them and make them feel unfit. All that is, is psychological trips. It's being unrealistic based on how we think people perceive us. So, for everyone who reads this, keep in mind you not only have the potential to be and do better than those who raised you. But you have the ability to accomplish all you desire if you just give yourself a chance. With that I close in the hopes that all who read this learn that a true education and a proper understanding of who they are is how greatness is born.

Respectfully Yours,
Julius Murphy, #999279
March 27th, 2022"

The Attestation of Godly Aspiration
"There is therefore now no
Condemnation to those who are
In Christ Jesus, who do
Not walk according to the flesh
But according to the Spirit."
Romans 8:1

"From an early age, I've always held a belief in God. This was due to the fact that my mother was a god-fearing woman, so she placed in my heart a revered fear for God. I even spent time in prayer as a child, seeking God to honor my request. There were even occasions in my youth where Bible reading was conducted, particularly on Sundays. Yet, I didn't have a genuine relationship with Jesus Christ. Certainly, I knew about

Jesus Christ. Every Easter my parents would have us watch movies about Jesus such as "King of Kings," "The Nativity," "Jesus of Nazareth," and "Barabbas." But we also watched the old Charlton Heston version of Moses in the movie called "The Ten Commandments." I really enjoyed the movies. Even now I still have a love for them…

But like I stated, I didn't have a genuine relationship with Jesus. I truly did not understand anything about salvation. The true knowledge of the revelation regarding salvation didn't occur until the age of 17.

It was the year of 1988 and my mother-in-law at the time invited me to attend a John Osteen sermon at Lakewood Church in Houston. I was really reluctant about attending that service. At the time, I wasn't going to church, so I didn't feel a need to go to one. thankful I did!

At that service John Osteen preached a sermon about a 17-year-old who lived a life that was the exact same reflection of mine, and Jesus called that kid to repent of his sins and dedicate his life to Christ. It turned out that John Osteen was that 17-year-old kid he was preaching about.

So, when the altar call was made to come forward to confess Christ Jesus as my savior, I did so along with at least 100 other 17-year-olds! After my confession of faith, I was happily received into the body of Christ at Lakewood Church; and was arranged to be baptized later that evening…

Once I came out of the water of baptism, I had a holy fire of passion to preach about the good news of the gospel of Jesus! And two weeks after the occurrence of all of that, I experienced a powerful spiritual prayer session at the home of my mother-in-law's sister. We all were praying for the anointing of the Holy Spirit to provide me with the gift and presence of power to speak in tongues. That living room I tell you was empowered with the Holy Spirit! One after another the five people in that room began to speak in tongues to prophesy as my mother-in-law's sister gave us their interpretations.

Then that was when the anointing fell upon me!

I issued out the utterance of tongues which was interpreted as words of praises to glorify God. So, after that day, speaking in tongues became a part of my prayer life. Where I went, I not only had a Bible in hand, but Jesus was in my mouth, so I was sharing the gospel with everyone.

One of the proudest moments in my spiritual journey at that time was to have my father come to church with me and give his life to Christ after I witnessed to him about my relationship with Jesus. That year was

1989, shortly after I married my high school sweetheart and mother of my daughter. She and I had two more children; the boys were born two years apart. The Lord had blessed us with some nice middle-class living. I was working at the security company of American Protective Services while my wife worked at this mailing service department.

All with us was going great.

But we unfortunately slowly ceased our serving of God. And my job had me working on Sundays so our church attendance fell off. Then Satan slipped into our family with sin and temptation in his hand with a determination to destroy my household. And I allowed that to occur by having an affair…

In 1992 my wife divorced me and took full custody of my kids. I was completely devastated! My state of depression was overwhelming to say the least. My family was gone, I'd lost my job, and I was back living at home with my mother. I felt like a complete failure! But instead of taking responsibility for my actions, I blamed God!

So, in my rebellious state against God, I accepted my brother-in-law's offer to sell crack cocaine in Brookshire, Texas. That lifestyle led to my having a daily relationship with sin! I made fast money, bought and drove fast cars, and slept with fast women. But none of it brought to me any true fulfillment…

During the year of 1993 I got involved in the record company of Reilly Production and performed as a hype man with the hip-hop group The Job Out Boyz. We did various concerts around Houston, and some within other cities. I really felt proud being able to open up the show as the opening act for the rapper Too $hort at Club Strawberry in Louisiana. We did that show in 1994. But my favorite show was in Austin, where we rocked the house at Club Medusa. And even though times were enjoyable, they were not fulfilling! I needed God in my life, but I still blamed Him for my divorce. So, I kept living a sinful lifestyle. Even after I got shot and had to be life-flighted to the hospital in order to be saved…

After that incident, I had to learn how to walk again. It was during that rehabilitation period that I got an encounter from God that I ignored! My ex-father-in-law who was a Metro bus driver for the City of Houston was suddenly given another bus route to drive. Since nothing like that had happened to him in 20 years, he felt God was leading him to witness to someone he had to pick up on his new route. Well, it turned out to be me! He witnessed that something worse would happen to me if I didn't turn back to my service to Christ Jesus.

Well, roughly two years later something worse transpired. On January 18th, 1996 I was arrested and falsely convicted of a capital murder crime and sent to Death Row. The circumstances involving my trial are not only complicated, but the details of it is a tale for another time since it would take a duration here to elucidate upon. But I will share that, despite the fact that my alibi witness was intimidated into not testifying, the murder weapon was not found in my possession, and a key defense witness was forced to plead his rights to not testify (he knew the real murderer was), the prosecution relentlessly pursued a conviction…

It was a devastating experience being sentenced to death. This was my first time being in prison, and I was expecting Death Row to be a place where I would have to kill or be killed! No doubt there would be a daily full-fledge battle royal that I would be forced to be a part of. So, I prepared myself to fight at the drop of a dime! But to my surprise, the men on Ellis One Unit were acting like normal human beings who were trying to live life despite their situation. Now I made a recommitment to follow Jesus Christ before my arrest and got serious with my worshipping God while in the county jail. But I hated the injustice of my incarceration, so I tried to escape from prison in 1998. This infamous incident occurred on Thanksgiving night of that year. It was seven of us who tried it, and sadly one of them men, Martin Gurule, ended up getting killed after jumping over the prison fence…

The occurrence of this escape attempt resulted in the entire Death Row being relocated from the Ellis One Unit to the Polunsky Unit. This escape attempt is an episode in my life I regretted getting involved in, especially since my friend Martin lost his life, but also due to the fact of the extreme isolation of being on the Polunsky Unit. None of us truly understood the profound psychological effects that long-term confinement in solitary could produce. And when you compound that with the fact friends are being executed, appeals are being denied, prison oppression is being highly orchestrated, and family and friends on the outside are turning away because it's too difficult to handle, this can all cause a person to question their faith.

So, for many years I became a seeker of truth! I went on a search through other religions, philosophies, political science, and any avenue I felt would help me to cope with the mental and emotional struggles that were assaulting me. And nothing brought me the comfort and fulfillment I needed. That is when I realized only Jesus Christ can truly do that. And I had Him with me all along; but I had to experience that in order to fully accept the truth of that fact. And when God came through in my life on November 18th, 2009 when I was given an execution date and came four hours away from being executed, it only gave confirmation to the fact that Christ was the way, the truth, and the life that I needed to live…

Since then, I have faithfully followed Jesus. Along the way I've made some human errors, but God be praised! I continue to pick myself up and travel forward with my walk with Christ…

Today I am now a graduate of Global University, which is a school of evangelism and discipleship. The achievement of that three-year educational endeavor was a proud accomplishment for me. At this present time, I am a participant in the Polunsky Unit's first faith-based program on Death Row. I recently graduated from its first quarter of curriculums which were "The Bridges to Life" and "Overcomers." These were some very positive and transformative initiatives that have facilitated spiritual growth and assisted me to be an overall better person…

I am in pursuit to fulfill the purpose that has sent out for me to preach His Word and share the Gospel of Jesus Christ. I know that Satan will make attempts to ruin my Godly testimony, but I am faithful in my belief that the good work that God has begun in my life will be completed for God's honor and glory.

Written By,
Eric Dewayne Cathey, #999228
April 4th, 2022"

There were a couple of other guys that at first said that they would write their own testimony to share with you readers within these pages, but for some reason or another they have decided not to because they worry that what they share can affect the outcome of their capital appeals. This is a good point, but I don't agree, though I do understand. I guess it's because I don't care if I remain in this life because I know I have a place in the Kingdom of Heaven with Jesus Christ my Lord and Savior where others are not so sure about their own lives. However, when I asked Billy Tracy #999607 what he would like to say to those of you outside these walls about why you shouldn't screw your lives up and end up in prison, Billy asked me to tell you this…you don't want to throw your life away and land in prison because if you do, then big, bad Billy will be waiting for you! This was told to me on Easter Sunday, April 17th, 2022.

CHAPTER NINE

BEING A CUTTER DOESN'T MEAN YOU'RE SUICIDAL

During the first few pages of this writing (book) you'll find some pictures of me and the aftermath of my actions that I took out on myself. A few of the pictures you see are of me covered in my own blood and even a couple of me being held down under the restraints of the officers even though I'm not moving and in handcuffs behind my back. Why am I talking about this now?

It's simple really, I just want others out there to know that they are not alone and that just because you at one point in time or another were a cutter or continue to do so to this day, doesn't mean you're suicidal or sick or mental. Sure, it makes us different, but there is nothing wrong with being different from the person next to you or your classmates. When God created each of us in our mother's womb, He did so knowing that each and every one of us would be different from the next.

For the longest time throughout my life and even before I came to prison the first time out in California, I used to cut myself because it allowed me to release the anger and pain that I was holding inside myself. I felt like people didn't understand me and that they never would nor could. All I would ever hear from others were that I could see about being placed on medication or seek out someone to talk to, but to me this was a waste of time because nobody could ever understand what I was going through or how I was feeling.

The feelings of loneliness or heartache from not feeling like I was ever good enough or accepted by family and friends who said they were friends but when you weren't around, they spoke about you behind your back just as family would do.

No one could understand that when I would cut on myself it was a way to release everything that I had allowed to build up inside myself. Seeing myself bleed made things better. It's not like I would feel the pain that most people would feel when I did something like this to myself because the emotional pain was much worse to me than the physical pain. Only a few times did I ever honestly feel like I was wanting to end my life and that is the cut you see my bone in. That was also explained in my first book which is a raw and hard reading for most.

I had been given an execution date for May 20th, 2010 after I had waived my rights to further appeals in the courts and asked that I be allowed to volunteer for execution. This was granted to me at the time back then by the 264th District Court of Bell County's Honorable Martha J. Trudo which was my trial judge and the county I was out of when I caught this capital case and sentence of death. I was taking the full responsibility for my actions and had accepted my fate which was my own death for the lives that I had taken. Without my knowing so, some lawyers had filed a motion with the court in another county under a district judge in Waco, Texas named Walter S. Smith Jr. (who was later found out to be a dirty judge with his own drug problem).

One hearing was held for me before Judge Martha J. Trudo for me to get my first execution date, where about two months afterwards I received a legal letter from said court in the form of an Execution Warrant explaining that upon such and such date and time I would be executed with a lethal dose of drugs until I was dead. I knew that this was going to come to me in the mail because everyone that gets his/her execution date is issued an Execution Warrant but knowing it's coming and reading about your own up-and-coming execution are two very real different things!

Out there some of you know and understand that one day you'll die but you don't know when or the time and date, so not knowing you go about your daily lives as if nothing else matters, but I tell you, you should not look at life in this way any longer because Jesus Christ is coming back and He's as real as you are or your loved ones are.

Not to get off track though, could you imagine reading about your own death in the newspaper? You're seeing this paper that says you're dead or will be killed at this date and time in the future and it what… totally shocks your mentalness to the point you have butterflies in your stomach like when you hit the top part of the rollercoaster before plunging down the other side. That is what it's like to read about your own death, thus you have no choice now but to make the best of what is before you now, to get everything in your life in some kind of order so that your loves ones that have stuck by your side throughout this whole ordeal aren't stuck with also having to make the proper arrangements for your cremation or claiming your remains from the funeral home.

There is so much to deal with besides the fact that you're going to be dead in a matter of weeks/months. What's more is after reading about your own execution warrant, after the butterflies have passed, this calm before the storm comes and now you've accepted your future fate and you know that when it's over you'll leave all of this behind and everyone you knew or knew you will be left behind until their own time comes and they meet back up with you, God willing, in the Kingdom of Heaven after Jesus' second coming.

Then out of nowhere everything you had started planning for is taken away from you without thought or word. Everything you thought was in your control is yanked away because some idiotic lawyers took it upon themselves to put their noses into your butt and do what they want with your life and file a motion with the court saying that you're unfit to decide what to do with your own life because simply put what you're doing is suicide by State. It doesn't matter to the lawyers of capital cases that you are a killer or monster so named by the District Attorney's office and most in society. Your victims' lives don't matter and possible closure for their families doesn't matter because the lawyers don't care, all they care about is that you don't die by lethal injection because they're against it.

So was what happened to me that very first time I had been granted to waive my rights to further appeals in the courts and volunteer for execution. Now I was being forced to continue living because of some lawyers that don't understand, all they understand is their own lives and what they want or feel is right and correct. So, when my execution date was taken away, I tried and almost did end my life by way of suicide and that is the picture you see of my arm slit wide open and the bone showing. I was saved after flat-lining three times and given 18 staples.

Does this make me a bad person who suffers from mental issues because I feel the need to self-harm? NO! And it doesn't make you that kind of person either. It just goes to show that God created in His own special way, and He loves you no matter what.

Throughout my time here on Texas Death Row I have met people who have suffered from serious bouts of depression and not all of these people are prisoners but also officers that work within these prison walls. One thing that we all share in life besides the fact that we were created in our mother's womb by the creator Himself, is that no matter the color of your skin or birth defects you may or may not have, each and every one of us has a heart that beats within our bodies, and that single organ shows that we are human beings and that we are loved.

So, no matter what you're going through or facing in life, always know that you are special and that you are loved! If those around you cannot understand why you self-harm yourself, then try sitting them down and explaining to them what it makes you feel when you do this or that to yourself, and then maybe together you can come up with a better way of doing things when you start to feel this way because it took me years and years to finally figure out and fully understand that when I hurt myself, I'm also hurting the One who created me and who resides within me... God Himself and His one and only Son Jesus Christ who freely gave His life for my sins and faults just as he did for you.

We, and I say we because it's true, we owe Him more than we owe anyone of this earth anything in our lives, we owe Jesus Christ more than we owe our own parents. We must first love Jesus Christ and learn to fully love and forgive ourselves before we can fully love anyone else as God would have us love one another. If I can see this and come to learn this truth, then so can you. All the answers that you need can be found in the Holy Bible and God's word. All you need to do is take the time to look up these answers and read them for yourself, and I promise you that once you do so, your life will be changed for the better as long as you live.

That doesn't mean that everything will become easy in your life or that you won't have difficult days and nights because you will but know that this isn't God nor His Son Jesus Christ placing these things in front of you and making things tough, but it's the world of the devil also known as Satan.

There have been days where I could go without having a single thought about doing self-harm, and then there would be days where something would upset me and I would have thoughts of just cutting like it was no big deal, as if someone decided that they wanted and needed to take the trash out. It would just happen for no reason other than I had the urge to do so. Being inside prison though, not many people understand these urges and some of the prisoners look down on this as a sign of weakness when it's not. Officers and ranking staff look at it as another reason for them to write you up a disciplinary case for self-mutilation, further punishing you when you're already feeling bad for one reason or another.

There have been days where I got bad news or just dealt with having to watch a friend and brother be escorted off of this section to take a walk, one that will be his last ever on this earth. Let me share with you just such a case that took place this past Thursday, April 21st, 2022. Really, I would like to take you back to the day before the 21st which would be April 20th, 2022, also known to you weedheads as 420.

I was laying back on my bunk and had just finished speaking up in my air vent to my Brother Billy Tracy downstairs on 1-Row #3 cage. By standing up on my toilet with my left foot on my toilet and my right foot on my desk, I'm able to stand up and talk into my air vent and hold a conversation with the person down on 1-Row using the same vent as myself. In this case that would be my friend and Brother Billy Tracy. I forget what we were talking about but I do know it was another one of our talks about God's word. So, as I was laying back on my bunk thinking about everything going on and what the next 24 hours would bring for myself and those around me, one of the officers working had been given the okay from her ranking officer to pass some things around for this fella we all know and call "CB".

Unbeknownst to any of the other five (5) of us housed on this section that is also known as Death Watch, CB had put together five commissary mesh bags filled with commissary items that he wouldn't be able to use or eat and he didn't want it to go to waste. So, being the kind of person he was, he decided to bless us with these things, thus the officer was able to open all five of our food slots and hand through these five bags from CB to each of us. Each of us over here knew what this meant, but neither one of us wanted to say it aloud. We each yelled down to CB and told him thanks and that we would hold onto these bags until we all knew what the final outcome would be. CB told each of us God bless, brother.

After looking at this commissary mesh bag from my friend and brother CB, I pushed it back and underneath my bunk to try and not think about what was coming in less than 24 hours now, turning my thoughts to my own lawyers and wondering how much more they will make me wait and go through this pain and suffering that they will never be able to fully understand nor ever come close to knowing what it feels like.

Before I knew it, it was shift change and the officers were coming around delivering the mail and JPays to each of us that had mail from family or friends. I had a JPay from my friend Sigrid and her friend Elodie, smiling over what they both had to say and feeling like I had something that I could contribute back to them because I knew what they were going through (Sigrid), I pulled out my typewriter and wrote back to her doing my best to explain to her that everything was going to be okay and how she should deal with everything and be there for her husband who was also having a difficult time with things going on in his life. Before I knew it, it was after 11 p.m. and I had to get some sleep because the next day, Thursday, was going to be a long and difficult day for all of us and our friend and brother CB.

Now, as I sit here typing this to you so that you may have something to read and pass your days and nights with or to just assist you with a better understanding of things in my world and life; I have to wonder how best to speak about it and if I should talk about CB or the day of first... Seeing as the media and even the victim's family members believe that the person that they were going to be witnessing being cold-bloodedly murdered was going to give them a sense of closure, which is a false hope in itself, is sad.

Taking someone's life for any reason is never a good enough reason, nor does it make us feel any better about the situation we are in or about ourselves. If anything, it just makes us into more of a monster or a person filled with a sick and twisted sense of life and living. I got where I'm at on April 5th, 2007 and have been held in total isolation ever since that day I stepped out of the van that transported me here from Bell County, Texas.

After spending a few months on level-3 for simply coming here and being found guilty of my crime of capital murder, after gaining my level-1 and being moved to B-Pod, I met this man named CB. He was this older guy and had just been baptized. I think it was around October of 2007 and he was talking about Jesus Christ and how he wished he'd known him before he caught his own case that landed him in the same place as myself and many others. CB had been found guilty of capital murder of a Houston, Texas police officer back in 1991 and was sentenced to death for his crime.

Any time someone ends the life of another person is wrong and the reason doesn't matter, we shouldn't be going around killing any and all who upset us. So, CB was sentenced to death and now 32 years after the fact he was going to be put to death for his crime. What is so depressing and sad was that for one thing, he would be the first and oldest living Texas Death Row prisoner being put to death in the State of Texas. Second, and I cannot stress this enough, the man that society convicted of capital murder of a Houston, Texas police officer was NOT the same man that the State of Texas was executing now some 32 years later! How could it be the same person?

When you are 10 years old, are you the same 10-year-old you were when you're 21 years old? Then how can you say that the man we all know and came to love as CB was the same man he was when he was in his 40s and is now 78 years old? What you don't know about CB or most of my fellow brothers here on Texas Death Row just as myself is that we too are someone's loved ones, a brother, a father or husband, or son or uncle or grandpa. Just like you, we too have those out there that love and care about us, and I'm sure most if not all of them understand that what we each did was wrong and that justice must be dealt, but it should be dealt fairly and in a just and humane way. It should not be dealt 15, 20, or even 30+ years later if our sentence is death. Anything over 20 years should be an automatic life sentence with the possibility of parole because to make someone wait that long in total isolation is inhumane and wrong.

Unlike many other states in the United States of America, Texas is the only state that doesn't pay its prisoners for working and those of us on Texas Death Row society was told that we are the very worst of the worst, which is nothing more than a lie your justice system has made you believe. Sure, we're not offered work or schooling, we're not allowed contact visits, and we're not allowed TVs in our cells. We're not allowed to walk to the chow hall to eat our meals or have group rec time. That doesn't mean though that we don't write to places willing to help those in prison with further schooling or a trade of some kind because each of us here on Texas Death Row are NOT the same person we were when we committed the crimes that landed each of us on Texas Death Row with a sentence of death.

What CB did to land on Death Row was horrible, but everyone here did something just as bad if not worse than his one capital murder, but did he deserve to be put to death after spending 32 years waiting for that date with death? Here was a man that spent time on Death Row and on his own doing came to know Jesus Christ and read the word of God in his Holy Bible. A man that walked the walk and treated everyone with respect and how he would want to be treated. A man who didn't cause problems and did his own time and was respected by everyone who knew him and had that opportunity to call him their friend or brother.

But you out there on the other side of these walls don't know this because you're too ignorant of what goes on inside prison. You would sit at home and watch on TV or read off the internet and believe everything you are seeing and reading, not knowing that you are just as bad as each of us were when we first violated the law and took matters into our own hands and took someone's life. You sit at home or in your office and scream about police brutality or no-knock warrants and cops getting away with cold-blooded murder, and yet you are ignorant to the fact that you are also part of the problem. That deep down you're a cold-blooded killer too. How is this so?

When you sit there and agree with what you're watching on your TV or reading off your cellphone and believe that this man or woman should be put to death for what something the media says, you become a part of the problem. Daily, people all over the world pick up the Holy Bible and read the words of God and His Son Jesus Christ and believe every word of that book 100% and follow its commandments to the T then turn right around and curse each of us in prison whether it be on Death Row in in prison somewhere else in the United States or around the world failing to understand that every one of the Lord and Savior Jesus Christ's followers were themselves in jail or prison at one point in their lives, and yet you, YES YOU, criticize myself and my brothers and friends here on Texas Death Row and in prisons all over the place. You're nothing more than a hypocrite and even Jesus says this is true of you. No? Read in the Book of Luke 13:15 or better yet read 1 Timothy 4:2. "These people are hypocrites and liars, and their conscience is dead!"

You would scream and chant about one of us being executed knowing nothing about us or the people we become because we want, WANT to change for the better, and though you don't want to believe that we can change, Jesus Christ does and knows that with Him all things are possible even to those of us condemned to death by those in society such as yourself. The society that you live in and want to believe in is filled with nothing but a twisted sense of right and wrong and what justice should be.

When you have over 200+ police officers showing up outside the Walls Unit Prison in Huntsville, Texas where the condemned are taken to so that their executions can be carried out by the State of Texas, they are showing their support they say for the family of the police officer that CB killed 32 years ago, an officer many of them knew nothing about and many that say they are religious and believe in Jesus Christ, and yet there they stand outside the Death Chamber in Texas cheering on a man being put to death for a crime 32 years ago. Have they nothing better to do, like protecting you in society from people like us or followers and believers of the law of Jesus Christ?

When is it right to push an old man in his wheelchair into the Death Chamber and lifted up to and strapped down to a gurney to end his life because you don't understand that you and the rest of society are not killing the same man that you found guilty 32 years ago? If that is not bad enough, then we must listen on our radios to these other ignorant people on FM 94.5 The Buzz talking about how an evil man was put to death the night before or about how they're going to be playing the song Jelly-roll, Dead Man Walking. This is the society you live in and believe in and yet you call us evil and that we should be put to death.

No doubt you find it ironic that the inside of the Texas Death Chamber and every Death Row in the United States, the gurney and how we are strapped down to it was and is in the form of a cross flat on our back, legs straight out in front of us strapped down with our arms stretched out and strapped down in the form of a T or cross, just as each and every one of you crucified Jesus Christ on the cross you want to relive that day by laying each of us condemned out in the same fashion as if we shall be put to death in a style that fits your twisted sense of humor because the murder of Jesus Christ just wasn't enough for you and your kind. You would sit and watch the movie directed by Mel Gibson called "The Passion of the Christ" and yet turn around and murder one of His followers and children to satisfy yourselves and needs when you should seek to forgive us as we have asked for forgiveness from Him.

Before you know it, you too will be facing death, the only difference being that CB and the rest of us here will know when that date and time is coming, but you will always wonder when your day will come and you fear that day and you should, but you should fear the Lord Jesus Christ even more!

I cannot keep giving you all the scriptures because sooner or later when you decide to pick up and read your own Holy Bible, you'll have to find your own way along in God's word, but for now, you might want to read: "You must fear the Lord your God and serve Him. When you take an oath, you must use His name only." (Deuteronomy 6:13)

The days after CB's execution are always a bit rough on myself and I'm sure some of the other fellas here, but their mindset is to never allow others to see them feeling weak or emotional. I don't have that issue anymore. Why should I be afraid to show my emotions for friends and family? Jesus Christ showed emotions and cried also. In fact, you can find it where He cried in the Book of John. Read in the Book of John 11:35; "Then Jesus wept." If the One who dies for my sins can show His emotions, then how much more can I in doing so further prove that I was created in His image?

Billy Tracy was banging on my floor to get my attention last night as I couldn't hear him because I had my speaker blasting music. So, when I turned it down and hollered, yeah, he called me to the air vent and told me that he could tell something was bothering me and to remind me that if I needed or wanted to talk about it to get up in the vent and let him know. I told him I was good and that I knew how to get him up, simply pounding on the steel screaming BIIIILLLLY IIIIII NEEEEED TOOOOO TAAAALLLLKKK!!! He just started laughing and said yeah, if I needed to talk wake him up and he'd climb up and speak with me.

This is what is called brotherly love between one another here in prison. Billy and I hadn't always been close like this and at one point in time we had stopped talking and wanted to murder one another, but through the grace of God and some faith-based courses that have been offered to those of us on Texas Death Row for the very first time ever thanks to God and the chaplaincy and Warden Dickerson, we've been allowed to participate in faith-based programs here on Texas Death Row.

There was a first time ever Kairo's walk done on Death Row back in December of 2021, and then after three months' time both Billy and I graduated from two courses called "Bridges to Life" and "Overcomers

Life-Controlling Problems." Both of us along with 31 other prisoners who were sentenced to death here in Texas received Certificates of Completion signed by the chaplain and a field minister. This goes to show you that change is possible and that anything and everything is possible when you have God in your life and on your side!

Society and the justice system sentenced us each to death, but God and His Son Jesus Christ overcame death and through Him we have been set free, even though we are here in the flesh on Texas Death Row. I know that one day probably before I turn 50 years old I'll go home to the Kingdom of Heaven to live with my Father God and my Lord and Savior Jesus Christ, and you know what? I cannot wait until that day arrives for me because when my ticket is being punched, I'll leave this world strapped down to a cold gurney and a lethal dose of drugs flowing through my corpse with a huge smile upon my face!

Because there is nothing in this life and world that man can do to me that God and His Son who paid the ultimate price for my sins and yours with His life cannot handle nor overcome for one of His. Please understand that you may or may not be one of those people out in society who think that I and most of my brothers and sisters in prison deserve whatever misery we experience inside prison as a just punishment for our crimes, but God loves all of us no matter how far we have fallen in life. He wants to reach us with His love and dispel our fears of loneliness and despair (Matthew 25:34-36).

Throughout the world people are imprisoned for their crimes and some even for their faiths, while others suffer some form or another of injustice, but God wants you to know that you can help make a change if you really want to. You can do so by simply praying for His followers and those who bring His message to those of us within prisons all over the world if you are afraid to get your own hands dirty or reach out to us on your own.

"Some sat in darkness and deepest gloom, imprisoned in iron chains of misery. They rebelled against the Words of God, scorning counsel of the Most High. That is why He broke them with hard labor; they fell, and no one was there to help them. 'Lord, help!' they cried in their trouble, and He saved them from their distress. He led them from darkness and deepest gloom; He snapped their chains. Let them praise the Lord for His great love and of the wonderful things He has done for them. For

He broke down their prison gates of bronze; He cut apart their bars of iron." (Psalm 107:10-16).

Just know this one thing if you never listen to anything else in this book or your own life and those who try to tell you something you just don't want to listen to. If I can do it in here, then you can make it out there. If I, a killer in the eyes of the system and society, can change for the better, then you can too and you're not a killer nor anything worse than the person standing right next to you. Jesus loves you too, my friend.

Before I end this chapter, let me leave you with some words from CB that were prerecorded from a media interview he gave and that was played to those of us listening as he was being killed by the State of Texas at the Walls Unit Prison in Huntsville, Texas on Thursday night at a little after 6 p.m. April 21st, 2022. "If you own a gun and you're planning on going out with friends or alone, leave your gun at home. Just leave it at home. If I had left my gun at home 32 years ago, I wouldn't be here this night being executed and nobody else would have lost their life. So, please leave your gun at home. God bless!"

Those were the last recorded words to society from CB while he was being executed. May our friend and brother in Christ Jesus rest in peace.

CHAPTER TEN

BEING TESTED BY FOOLS STILL

It never seems to ever fail that when we're doing good in our lives or at work or play that sooner or later there is always, and I mean ALWAYS, some idiot out there that wishes to test one's patience. I could never understand this, why would you knowingly go out of your way to act tough: or purposely anger someone you knew could cause you serious bodily harm? It's like you know that if you were going to a gun fight or a battle with automatic weapons, you wouldn't enter into such with a pocketknife, would you, and expect to walk away the king of all, right?

If you were getting ready to race your car or truck either on street or dirt, you wouldn't show up with a Pinto would you? Well, maybe you would, but no sane person would! Have you ever had days like this in your life? Everything is going great and then out of nowhere, WHAM! You've been struck in the face while riding your motorcycle down the highway by none other than a bug.

If that's not bad enough, right at the time you reach up to wipe his bug guts out of your face or off your helmet visor, if you're smart enough to be wearing a helmet in the first place, this bug is in your face at 80 mph on the highway and your reaching up to wipe it away causes you to twitch the bars just enough to send you into another lane, and though this lane is clear, the cop coming up behind you thinks you're drinking and thus pulls you over. Doesn't matter that you're on a motorcycle!

So, you pull to the side of the highway and turn your bike off, the cop comes up and makes a big deal of everything, and before you know it, you're in a heated conversation with the police officer. He runs your name and bam! What do you know, moron, you have an outstanding warrant for your arrest. If you had just shut your mouth and learned how to talk, you more or less could have talked your way out of the ticket and not worried about a thing.

As it is, you now have to pay a fine and pay the fine for your bike that is sitting in an impound yard and the damage done to it from being towed by that cornfed fool, and let's not forget all the lawyer fees and court costs you're going to have to pay for now, all because you couldn't keep your mouth shut.

You know this has happened to you numerous times though it may not have been while you were on a motorcycle but in your fancy car or truck. The only people that I know that can get away with such tickets or even speeding is those with money, lawyers (they can lie their way out of anything, that's why they are so good in the courtroom, just look at the District Attorneys), and politicians and the idiot and racist prick Donald Trump. If you believe in such fruitcakes as this idiot, you deserve everything you got coming to you. But you get my drift about what I'm saying.

Things can be going great and then they don't, and everything seems like it's nothing but a downhill battle now with no hope. Nobody can understand what you're going through or why someone would continuously test you because they underestimate you because of your size or the way you look and carry yourself.

When I was doing time in lockup in Florida, I had someone take me under his wing and teach me how to fight. I'm not a big guy nor am I a tough guy, I'm just a simple guy of about 6'2" and 200 pounds with a slim build, an easy smile, and willing to make a fool of himself if it will make another person laugh or even smile. I don't have a testosterone problem like most men do out there in society and some inside prison walls have. I don't workout 24/7 to bulk up, I sit back and do my time the best that I can with a laugh here and there.

Before, doing time in lockup for petty crimes in Florida I was running loose on the streets and doing what I had to do to survive. One day I made a small mistake breaking into someone's home while they were home, and in the end, I ended up working for this person. He taught me how to drive as if my life depended on it and how to fire and clean numerous weapons from semiautomatics to combat shotguns and AR-15s with extended tube magazines. I learned things that I'm not proud of, but I did so I could survive.

Taking what I learned in lockup in Florida, I applied it to prison in California numerous times, some with great outcomes and others with outcomes that cost me more time and even time in Pelican Bay State Prison and freezing my butt off while being held inside of an animal-like enclosure on the outside yard of the prison while it was snowing in nothing but a pair of boxers. Did I deserve it? Maybe, but who can really say what one person deserves to the next?

Fast forward to the present. I'm in my cage here on Texas Death Row and it's a little after 1 p.m. on Friday, April 22nd, 2022. I was finishing up work on my typewriter when this chubby sergeant named Shawn Dorman knocks on my cage door. As I look at my door and see him, I say, what's up? He tells me that I have a legal telephone call for 1:30 p.m. and that he was escorting me down to the legal booth ahead of time because they are so short-handed (no staff). I tell him to give me a minute so I can get my things together such as my legal work and a pen and such because I had no clue that I had a legal telephone call that day. Usually, my lawyers will let me know via a JPay that they have set up a call or legal visit. This way I can always be ready and don't have to waste time getting ready or get caught with things out in my cage that shouldn't be out like minor contraband. For some reason or another I didn't get notice about this legal call and for a split second I thought it might be fishy because in the past, officers would come and tell us we had a legal visit or legal call and would escort us down to the legal booth before uncuffing us and locking the slot in the door before returning to our cages to shake them down looking for contraband.

This, thankfully, was not the case. After I cuff up and exit my cage under the escort of Sgt. Dorman, we walk off the pod and are going down the hallway of 12-Building where Texas Death Row prisoners are housed along with Ad-Seg. As we're walking down the hallway towards the legal booths down by the lieutenant's office, another officer is walking towards us. This officer, seeing who the prisoner is (me) walking towards her and Sgt. Dorman purposely changes her course to walk directly toward me in a straight line now. Me being me, I refuse to change my course, but not so with this chubby dude holding onto my elbow who outweighs me by a good 100 pounds of chunkiness with no muscle build though he might think so, pulls me forcefully to the right side of where we're walking. Though it's not so easy for him to do so, I do allow it to happen.

The officer, Priscilla Montoya, is this over-the-hill cougar who preys on the younger men that find themselves working here at the prison because they need jobs. She is in her 50s and the last guy she ran off from working here was only 22 years old. As we walk by her, she says something smart to me and I say, "Yeah, sure, I see you got even this turd trained to bow down to our oldness." The look she gave was one of those looks to kill and then she was gone with her lemon scent on overkill!

Don't get me wrong, she's not a bad-looking older woman, but you would think she would stay in her lane instead of deciding to get into it this way with me, thus causing chunkiness Sgt. Dorman to run his mouth off out of her earshot and only after I was locked into the legal booth with the cuffs off. I'll get to that in just a second.

The thing about Officer Priscilla Montoya is she drinks too much and then she goes driving. This was one of the main reasons she would and continues to prey on younger men, men not in her age group. I'm guessing this is the best she can do, and she also needs them to drive her to work and everywhere else because she had her license taken away for a while for a DUI and she has the very bad habit of wearing way too much lemon-scented crap to the point I want to toss her old butt into the shower and lock her in there until her scent is no longer looming all around me! But that is just me and I felt like Priscilla wanted everyone to know about her scent, lol!

So, as Sgt. Shawn Dorman removes the handcuffs from my hands while I'm in the legal booth, before walking away he tells me this, "Hey, Tabler. Don't take this personal, but if you ever say something like that again, I'll have to knock one of your teeth out." Looking at Sgt. Shawn Dorman, I tell him right back that he would try and that it would more or less be his last time trying to.

The problem is that he along with too many other people gets secure in wearing the uniform of a correctional officer, a uniform that is lower than that of a security guard's uniform or a cop's uniform. I tell him this and I further let him know that it's been done before that someone underestimated me because of my skin tone (looking white). Furthermore Sgt. Dorman, how come it's always officers such as yourself that only talk crap to a prisoner after you have him in either handcuffs or locked on the other side of a steel door that is inches thick? You wouldn't speak to me like this if I was out in the general population, nor would you speak to anyone else like that, unless of course it was in knowing that it would have the effect that you were trying to get out of me now but failed. Where you could justify calling in for a Use of Force Team suited up in their riot gear with chemical agents to be used against me here in this little booth where I have nothing to use to defend myself and nowhere to move out of the way from such a use of force against my body. Why would you want to go there with anyone either housed in this building or myself? Do you so easily forget where you work and who is housed in this building? I hate to say the truth Sgt. Dorman, but remember that everyone in this building is a convicted killer, but you have nothing to worry about from me Sgt. Shawn Dorman, or anyone else on Texas Death Row that I know of, and you know why this is? Because I and my brothers no longer walk that path but the path of Jesus Christ, so please skip rocks and be blessed, Sgt. Dorman!

"You have tested us, O'God; you have purified us like silver." (Psalm 66:10).

Just because I walk in my faith in Jesus Christ doesn't mean that I'll never be tested in life because everywhere I go is a test, especially within prison walls. These trials though will refine my character while bringing me into a deeper wisdom and understanding, helping to discern truth from falsehood and giving us discipline to do what we and I know is right. Above all though, such trials and tests allow me to realize that my life is a gift from God, and it should always be cherished and not ever be taken for granted.

My legal telephone call was with my friend and lawsuit lawyer David Lane of Killmer, Lane & Newman, LLP of Denver, Colorado. This fella is a true friend and one-of-a-kind person and soul. What started as a legal binding/contract back on October 3rd, 2018 has since turned into one of trust and friendship, though he's still my lawyer, he's my lawyer second and my friend and brother first. I think that David is also the first lawyer I have taken on in trying to get him to stop cursing or pay the fine of five bucks into the curse word jar. He is also the one and only lawyer and friend that is pushing me to write this second book and share with you all out there in society about myself and us within prison walls and how God is working in my life.

David has gone so far as to share my first book by ordering it and sending it to the author Kevin Salwen, which I find funny and a touch crazy that Kevin would even read such a book that is way below his writing style no doubt. If it wasn't for David, I more or less would have ended my capital appeals a long time ago and in doing so I never would have gotten the chance to have such an awesome and profound relationship with my Lord and Savior Jesus Christ, nor would I have had the chance to be a part of the first-ever faith-based courses offered to Texas Death Row.

Not only have I become a published author from within these prison walls, but I have also become a graduate of two faith-based courses and am currently taking two more courses as well, one of them being a college course called "The Truth Project" and the other being "The Quest for Authentic Manhood." Those of you wondering what "The Truth Project" is can find out by going to www.focusonthefamily.com and clicking on The Truth Project. I thank David Lane and his law firm of Killmer, Lane & Newman for their support and for David believing in me enough that he would push me to write this second book and be that voice you need to hear. I also thank his wife and mother because without them in his life, David would just be another simple-minded lawyer whereas it stands his wife wears the pants in the house and his mother keeps him on his toes, and I just add more gray hair to his already-graying head as only a friend can do so.

Speaking with him on the phone about CB's execution and everything being said negatively about him on the news after the fact, David explained to me that he was outside walking while talking to me on the phone. I should mention that he was in Hawaii and as he was walking and we were talking, he tells me he was looking at this woman pushing a baby stroller that has this tiny dog sitting in it like a baby. I'm laughing and he's like, these people are out of their minds. I said, if you see him reach behind him and grab a cellphone and start talking, you know the end is here! We both started laughing, then things got serious as he could tell that the execution of CB was bothering me just a bit, but before we could really get into our talk, we were told that my time was up, and I needed to hang up.

David said that he'll get another legal call set up for next week sometime and we'd talk. We gave one another our love like family and said our goodbyes because though we started in a legal binding, we have become family and brothers through our faith as Jews.

To be correct, I was baptized by an outside rabbi as a Messianic Jew and David's family is fully Jewish, though his loving wife is Christian. My personal belief is it doesn't matter what your faith is because in the end, we are all serving the same God, we just call Him by different names and it's not my place nor yours to say one faith is wrong while another is right. These are my thoughts alone though, and you may or may not agree with me, but honestly, ask me if I care.

You'll notice at the beginning of this chapter that it's called "Being Tested by Fools Still." This book isn't just about my life and walk, but also about those around me and in my life. Though I see many officers and medical staff working within these prison walls, they are unable to speak to me most of the time, but there are a few who still do. They are not allowed to have a part in this book because their job title will not let them. That does not mean that I cannot speak up about what I see and hear every day.

It's not only I who is constantly being tested within these walls by fools, nor is it always another prisoner, because I know for a fact staff is constantly tested by the prisoners and other staff members. Last night as I was listening to Eve and Jeremy Coe of Real Life Ministries (Saturday night) and how this woman doesn't hold anything back when she and her husband speak about God's word and His love for all people, not just those in society, but the prisoners too! It's touching and real, but as I was listening to her speak, the pill tech who used to be an officer back here years ago came by to deliver medication. As she passed by my cage door, she came back and asked me the name of my book that was out there in all the major book retailers. So, I told her; "Within the Shadows of Life -By, Richard Tabler." She said okay and then walked away.

Her name is Grace Burks, and back in the day, she was a wild woman working back here. In fact, I can tell you about the day she cost me my level-1 and over $2,000 in damages to the prison, though it was never fixed and the parts only added up to around $100 total! This was back in 2009 and I was housed on A-Pod, B-Section in #26 cage on 2-Row, and my friend back then who I was close to but not as close as my homie Big Tai (Tai'Chin Preyor) was housed directly beneath me on 1-Row in #19 cage. We were the only two housed in this 14-man section. I was housed over there alone for around a year before he was moved over there with me.

We were moved over to that section as a means of punishment, I for being busted with a cellphone that was used to contact a state senator who just so happened to also be a member of the TDJC Board (didn't know this!) and Lizard (Donald K. Newbury) for numerous assaults against staff while having a Major Use of Force ran on him. For some reason or another, we had a falling out with each other. While he was housed under me in cage #19, he was doing something to constantly anger me to the point I couldn't sleep. So, one day while he was sleeping, I took my stack of New York Times newspapers and the Austin American Statesmen newspapers that I was getting through the mail delivery and tore them up into strips of shredded paper.

Back then there was this hole in the stainless steel that our sink and toilet are built and welded to. This stainless steel also housed our lights, and the hole was right where the outlets were leading down and into the pipe chase. So, sitting on my bunk in nothing but my boxers as that was the only article of clothing I was allowed besides getting my newspapers, some mail, and some writing material, I sat there tearing up a stack of papers. Then after Officer Burks (pill tech Grace Burks) made her rounds for the security check (30 minutes), I started shoving the shredded newspaper down into the pipe through the hole in the stainless steel, allowing it to fall onto the 1-Row flooring inside and thus against the stainless steel of Lizard's cage while he was sleeping.

After I had all the paper I wanted to shove into there down there, I started pushing papers out the side of my cage door onto the run until I had a good pile about 3-1/2 feet high and about seven to eight feet long and stretched out to the railing.

Next, I soaked everything down with baby oil that they sold back then that was a little flammable. I put this into the pipe too. The next step was to twist some toilet paper around a piece of a paper clip so I had a U-shape like a prong that while holding the toilet paper I could use to stick into my outlet socket to get a spark, thus lighting another piece of toilet paper on fire.

Once I had this done, I lit a piece of paper outside my cage door on fire and then dropped the remaining wick into the pipe to light Lizard's butt on fire downstairs! That sucker was burning something fierce and it was burning high. The ceiling is about 9-1/2 to 10 feet from the floor outside my cage door, and as I'm watching for Officer Burks to see the flames and call it in on either the phone in the control picket or on her handheld walkie-talkie (radio), I see the smoke alarm start melting on the ceiling! Oh well, things never worked anyway, so what did I care?

Right about that time I notice this burning, Officer Burks starts screaming, Tabler! Tabler! You little s---! I'm gonna write you up for this Tabler!

Right after she is screaming at me for what she can see on the run outside my cage door, I hear Lizard down on 1-Row screaming at me, "F--- you, Blue! You f---ing a--hole, Blue!" And he's down there now kicking his cage door screaming for the firehose and Officer Burks has no idea that he's screaming 'cause it's hotter than hell down in his cage 'cause of the fire burning in the pipe, and yells at Lizard, "you go to hell too, Newbury!"

I'm in my cage laughing my butt off at both of them because I couldn't care less what they were yelling at me about. After calling it in to her rank, they came running down to the pod and unlocked the door to where the firehose was and came onto the section and up the stairs to put the fire out that was still burning because of the baby oil, at which time they noticed that there was smoke coming out of the pipe on 1-Row.

Long story short, I was written up a disciplinary case by Officer Burks for setting a fire on the run, and in doing so I created a security threat and also for said fire destroying TDCJ property by burning the smoke alarm and the pipe wiring, etc... I was downgraded to a level-3 for 90 days and had to pay over $2,000 in damages that were never repaired, and that stupid fire alarm is still up there melted to this very day some 13 years later.

Now, Officer Burks is a pill tech with medical and when she came around asking about my book last night, I remembered what all she cost me out of pocket. I still get a laugh out of this incident though as I look back on it and think also of my friend Lizard. We had a falling out, but long before he too was executed a day before my 36th birthday on February 4th, 2016. We had made up as only real friends can do within prison walls. May he and the many other brothers and friends I have seen walk out of this section for the last time to make that trip inside of a van for the last time, may they all rest in peace!

Though Lizard had tested my patience that day and I knew I did his and Officer Burks, he was loved like a brother by myself and many others within these walls.

There was another time, while I'm on the topic, that Lizard and I were again housed in the same section. In fact, it's the section I'm currently housed in now also, known to those on Texas Death Row as Death Watch. (This section is mainly for the guys with set execution dates and for high-security prisoners such as myself and right now Billy Tracy). Lizard didn't have a date yet but was housed now in this section because every cage over in this section has a built-in video camera inside the cage right above the doors after you enter into them. These video cameras can be viewed by numerous people with the right access codes from wherever they're at by computer. Plus, Lizard had just had a major use of force where he had stabbed two of the Use of Force Team members when they ran into his cage on F-Pod. So, he was housed in the #3 cage that has a box attached to the front of his door. This is to prevent someone such as Lizard from jacking the slot when it's open but doesn't always work as there are ways to still jack the box and slot. It's supposed to be an extra security measure but is really useless and a further waste of time. He also had an extra sheet of hard, clear plastic on the front of his cage door back then.

The year was 2014. He was in cage #3 and I was on 2-Row in cage #14 right next to the shower. Note, when they would feed us breakfast it was always early in the morning around 3 a.m. They would get the chow cart (food cart) and a tray carrier that you would place the food trays onto and then carry onto the sections to feed each prisoner in his cage. There was also a pitcher for such drinks as juice, milk, or coffee at the time. In the mornings then they were giving us both milk and coffee that was drained from a container for such into the pitchers. One of the major issues/problems back then was that some of the male officers would be jerks and take down the container for coffee from the chow cart and place it on top of one of the garbage cans. This would then become a major factor because now you're contaminating the fluids coming out of the container into the pitcher. They would do this and expect us to accept it as if we were nothing more than animals to be fed.

One of the officers that was really bad about doing this and often did so on purpose knowing that those of us awake could see him do it, was this officer we all called Sweathog. Before I go on further, you have to understand that when an officer is feeding, he/she is always supposed to close one of the food slots before going onto the next cage to open that food slot to feed the next prisoner. This was to make sure everything was secured and thus no problems could happen if one prisoner jacked his food slot for some reason or another. They were also to feed with two officers back then and not alone, as further security measures.

One morning this officer is feeding A-Pod alone as the other officer that was on the floor with him went to use the restroom and the other officer in the control picket wasn't paying any attention to everything. I just happened to be awake this morning for breakfast, when usually I'm asleep and skip breakfast because they are always serving us pancakes day in and day out every week. This would get old after a while unless you had a continuing jar of peanut butter which we would slather onto our pancakes.

So, I saw when Officer Sweathog took down the container from the chow cart and placed it on top of the garbage can. I wasn't the only set of eyes that saw this either, but I didn't know this. In my mind, I was upset that this fool would do this when of all mornings I was up and was going to eat breakfast.

As he enters onto A-Section and started feeding on 1-row, I hear him open the food slot/box on Lizard's door, then I hear Lizard cursing him out and him turning right back around and cursing Lizard out. Then I hear more slots being opened and closed but nobody is saying anything about the coffee container. It's as if they don't mind being treated like an animal, but then I think to myself, maybe they didn't see what he did, or they aren't looking at where the coffee container is sitting because you can see it from where we are on A-Section.

Sweathog comes up to 2-row and is feeding one or two others that are housed up here with me. When he gets to my cage and opens the food slot, I accept my breakfast and turning around set it on my desk before letting him know also that I would like some coffee so don't close the food slot, please. Waiting for me as I knew he would, I act like I'm grabbing my coffee cup but am actually grabbing my face towel to place on the food slot 'cause I know it's going to be a long wait for some fresh coffee.

Back by my cage door, I immediately place my arm out of my food slot thus jacking the slot telling him to go to the kitchen and get a new container of coffee or call some rank, 'cause I'm not giving up the slot until one of those things happens! Now he's cursing me a blue streak because what I didn't know was that Lizard down on 1-Row had also jacked his box! Instead of fixing this problem by calling down to the kitchen for another thing of coffee, he notifies the rank which then was Sgt. Shupack, this tall, leggy blond with attitude and an overbite.

When she came down to the pod behind the jacked slot on my cage door, he left out that Lizard had jacked his box. This was a game-changer for all involved. Lizard had no problem with making them suit up a team and having a Use of Force behind his coffee, as this was his means of rec, but I have no doubt that they assumed it would require two Use of Forces even though I have not faded the Use of Force Team since being on Texas Death Row. That's not to say that I haven't had chemical agents used against me because I have on numerous accounts. But seeing both my food slot and his box jacked, the sergeant bowed out and called over her radio for a container or fresh coffee, and in turn Lizard and I both gave back the slots/box.

The next morning as he's in the dayroom he's laughing it up because neither one of us knew that the other had jacked the slot/box behind Sweathog placing the coffee container on the garbage can until after the fact! Neither Lizard nor I were written up for a disciplinary case, but Officer Sweathog did get written up for failing to secure Lizard's box then continuing to feed, having a second slot jacked in the same feeding, and placing the coffee container on the garbage can.

Trials don't always have to be about myself or anyone here on Texas Death Row as we forget that it's not only prisoners that are tested but the staff and medical staff too. Nor is it always prisoner against officer attitudes that are the issue at hand. I have been doing time now for about 22 years. That doesn't count for only my time here in Texas but in total, and here in Texas I have seen female officers put up with more crap and disrespect from males than anyone. Here in Texas, they have this disciplinary code called Code 20. This is a masturbation case that prisoners are always being written up for against a female officer or medical person who is constantly walking around.

I cannot understand how guys can get off on doing something like this. I mean, I get it, but I don't see the point nor the purpose in doing so; when if you stop to think about it, how would you react if someone started disrespecting your loved ones, such as your mother or sister, little niece, or your girlfriend or wife? Guys just stand up and start knocking off the women in your life because they are female the guy just wants to get some release? Yeah, that is what I thought, you'd want to beat the dude up for doing so, and it makes you sick just thinking about it. So, in knowing this and how it makes you feel, think about how it makes the women feel who have to deal with it every day they enter into this prison or any other prison. Why do it to them knowing that this woman is not only created by God Himself but is also someone else's loved one and is simply coming here to do a job so she can place food on the table for her family or herself and her kids? To pay the bills and put gas in her car or truck.

They come into the prison and others around the world not only for a job but to make sure you, yes YOU, have the proper medication or are being fed and showered and are remaining secure in your cell. You have no right to become upset with these women doing their jobs because they didn't put you in prison, you and your stupidity and poor choices placed you right where you are if you're in prison and reading this. I have seen numerous times how prisoners in Ad-Seg and even some on Death Row have mistreated and straight out disrespected this one female ranking officer named LT. H. Watson as well as Nurse Clinician J. Smitherman or Officer M. Watson when she comes around passing out laundry.

These are just a few of the officers that not only do their jobs for us, and how do you repay them when they treat you like a human being and refuse to see you for what you're currently doing time for? You repay them with your lack of respect and forcing them to write you up a disciplinary case for a Code 20!

Then when you don't like the food you are getting from the kitchen you try and get the officers working the pods to contact the kitchen officer to complain about the food or that you're peanut butter-free or pork-free or meat-free, but the next day when there is something good on the tray that is edible you take the freaking tray without complaint!

Back when I was constantly being escorted out of my cage for legal telephone calls, I would pass the kitchen here on 12-Building, and in doing so I would walk right past Officer R. Davis who runs this kitchen. Not one time have I ever heard her become rude or disrespectful towards me nor I to her, and yet I hear daily about how because you're not getting your way that this woman is doing you wrong or is a bad person. Why is she bad? Because she's doing her job or because you cannot get what you want from her or any of the other honest and God-fearing women that work in prison?!

Don't get me wrong fellas, as I wasn't always this way where I could point out to you these things because long before I came to Texas, I was a really bad person, but over time and the prayers of loved ones and friends and my own prayers to God, I have been able to change and overcome those things that would hold me back or cause me to think and do wrong. It's not easy and you will have trials and you will be tested daily, but with God you can overcome all of these things in your life because God overcame the world!

My fellow brothers down on 1-Row who have set execution dates and one of them up here on 2-Row with me who has a set execution date for later on this year (2022) are constantly tested by some of the officers working the pod daily and from other prisoners who are housed on B-Section and are a part of the faith-based programs being offered back here for the first time ever.

The guys on B-Section are always screaming (maybe we should say singing) but it doesn't come across as such for the guys over on this section (Death Watch) as they are trying to sleep or work on something that will assist their lawyers in getting them a stay of execution. They cannot stand it when they're trying to make a telephone call on Sundays to their loved ones and the guys who mean well (some of them, not all) start singing and praising God and His Son Jesus Christ. To us on A-Section it may not sound great or even good, but to God in Heaven it sounds great.

The guys in C-Section if you were not reading it here in this book and were just listening to them singing on the radio, you wouldn't know it but these guys are all housed in single-man cages right next to one another and yet they sound great from this section because they talk with one another and point out each other's weaknesses and spots that need lifting up or change of voice to fit the song and praises they are giving to God. I myself drown out B-Section by listening to my radio or cranking up my speaker to listen to either country music or Air1 which is a Christian radio station until they are done singing which is NEVER, lol!

I think that the reason some of the fellas over here on A-Section (Death Watch) become upset with their singing on B-Section is because they do it without asking if anyone on this section is speaking on the telephone or holding our own conversations with one another. A lack of respect can cause major issues all around. God even tells us to show respect to all equally, but most people in prison don't do that. Don't believe me? In the Old Testament of the Bible, you can find where God instructs you to show kindness and respect to all those you meet. Show others not only respect but treat them with dignity no matter how insignificant they may seem. You never know how God might use these very same people to change your own situation in life. Read through the Book of 1-Samuel 30:11-15.

An old Swahili proverb that I like is this: "Liandikwalo ndiyo liwalo" which means in English: "That which is written by God is what is." And another one is, "Lila na fila hazitangamani" which also means in English, "Good and evil will never mix."

Let me back up for a minute or two, please. I don't want this book to be a sole book of one-sidedness where it only talks about the good going on by myself or others because that wouldn't be right. There are a lot of officers inside prison walls and at this unit that bring certain things upon themselves for how they take the initiative or step to first disrespect a prisoner. A few such officers that would do this are Sharilla Gray, who no longer works here because she retired; current Officer T. Pech, who has a foul mouth and is always trash talking the male population with such words as, you're a f---ing b--ch! Sgt. J. Schaffer has a bad habit of also disrespecting prisoners in both Ad-Seg, Death Row, and out in the general population.

These are just a few of the female officers that would take the steps to show or talk disrespect to a prisoner, thus causing the prisoners to do what they knew these females would take as disrespect. When they were on a pod, some prisoners would purposely be standing in their cells butt-naked and holding their piece in their hands to start masturbating on them when they walked by their cells. This in turn would cause the offended officer who first showed disrespect to have to turn around and write up a disciplinary case for a Code-20 on the prisoner.

This was and is only one such cause of disrespect. There have been officers here that have purposely placed a cockroach in a prisoner's food, which in turn caused the offended prisoner to take his time in his own personal revenge against the officer after months went by that she forgot about. Then one day she was working the pod and the prisoner was in the dayroom as she walked by the dayroom as she had her back turned to the prisoner she disrespected by placing a live cockroach in his food. Thus, forgetting what she did and where she was, this one prisoner reached out the dayroom bars and grabbed her up by her hair before slamming her head back into the bars as he tried to get a better grip on her. She is screaming in terror now and her coworker, another female officer who was always disrespectful, pulled out her can of chemical agents and started spraying not only the prisoner but her coworker in the face in an attempt to get the prisoner to let her go, which he did, but it just goes to show that it's not always the prisoners who are at fault or the cause of such issues, but the female officers, and believe it or not, it's the females that are always causing such problems in prison more than the male staff. I'm not saying that this is right and that with disrespect actions should be taken because that is the wrong attitude and not what I'm wanting this book to be about, and yet at the same time, I want this book to be a real book of facts and truths, and most importantly, about God and His Word.

There is one officer here who acts like she hates all male prisoners and is always talking trash about their mothers knowing that she'll get someone to pop off on her sooner or later. Her name is Officer Effie Venson. She is this black woman and I say black because she is always spewing some racist words towards anyone who is white or Latino and in the worst ways possible, and what is even sadder is she is able to get away with it most of the time.

Never assume that people will know and understand what you're going through when you're doing time in prison. I gave lawyers on my appeals the benefit of the doubt in assuming that they as they were always saying they could understand when I would ask that they please drop me a JPay letter or FedEx me a letter for the days and times that they were wanting to come visit or schedule a legal telephone call with me. I didn't think I needed to get into the detail why I was asking them to do this without just popping up for a legal visit nor a legal telephone call. Proper respect would go without saying that they would just let me know.

A prime example of why lawyers will NEVER UNDERSTAND prison policies or why we ask to be given a heads up is last week I was sitting in my cage in #10 cell doing my thing on this here typewriter, but to the side and a little bit behind me I had a homemade speaker bumping some music. At the bottom of my sink, I had my eyedrop bottle of glue and some tape and a little blade I use to cut illustration boards with. Everything that was contraband was sitting out in my cage as I was typing out a fast kite (note) to my friend and brother Spook. Lo and behold here comes this moron of a sergeant that I do NOT get along with. Nope, he wasn't just making his rounds as they sometimes do but was on a mission straight to my cage to knock upon my door. At first, I couldn't hear him because of my speaker and the music I was jamming out to, plus I was intent on responding to what Spook had said to me in his kite that had me laughing. When he hit my cage door with the riot baton escorting officers are to carry at all times, I looked up and if you could see the look under my skin that was on the inside of my face you would have seen this, "Oh, --it!"

Turning down the music, I ask him what's up? He tells me that I have a legal telephone call. I said no I don't, as none of my lawyers let me know anything about this. That's when he said, your name is Richard L. Tabler #999523? I said, you know it is. Well then, you have a legal call in 10 minutes. Are you going or not? Yeah, can I have five minutes to put my cage in order? Nope, let's go. When he said that, I knew what time it was. By the time I would make it back to my cage I knew my stuff would be taken and my cage searched/trashed.

As I'm waiting out in the legal booth here on 12-Building for my legal call, the time for my call that I was told about comes and goes until finally I ask the officer passing by the booth to please pick it up (the phone) and call central and ask them what's up with this so-called legal call I have. The officer does so and central tells her that my call hasn't called yet.

It's now been 20 minutes and just when I am getting ready to ask them to take me back to my cage, the phone rings and it's one of my appeal lawyers. I'm pissed and let her know and ask why she didn't send me a JPay letting me know about this call? She starts telling me she's sorry and I tell her, David Lane as well, as I have constantly told everyone, to please drop me a JPay letting me know what time and day they are setting up calls or visits so that I can be ready. Again, she says she's sorry, and then she blows my head when she said that they told her that I was going to call her collect!

This isn't the first time she's set up calls with me while I was in prison here on Texas Death Row and she knows that she is to call into the prison, not me calling her collect on something that she has set up. By this point I'm too pissed to even speak and instead I tell her that I'm done. I'm done with the no respect. I'm done with my own lawyers not listening to me. I'm done with my lawyers not speaking to me talking things over in regards to my appeals and motions they are wanting to file. I'm done with my appeal lawyers not responding when I hit them up with legal letters. And I'm done with this drama, and I'm done with someone who once said she was also my friend but continues to remain silent and cold and unforgiving because she cannot possibly understand anything going on with me, and in all honesty I also want to be done with my appeals because I'm sick and tired of waiting in this oversized coffin for them to come to me one day and say, Tabler, the warden wants to speak with you, only to get down to his office and him to tell me that the State of Texas has issued me another execution date, or to get news that someone in my family had died, or anything else that could possibly screw up one's life inside these walls! All this became too much while talking on this phone with this one lawyer, thus instead of shouting her down and losing control, I did the only thing I could do that was in my control—I hung up the telephone!

Sure enough, when I get back to my cage that day, all my stuff had been confiscated as well as some things that I had gotten from my big homie Big Tai (Tai'Chin Preyer, executed July 27th, 2017). Most everything could have been replaced at some point down the road, but the things that Big Tai left me can never be replaced because they were things he made and had left to me. Now, not only did I lose these things, but now I face the possibility of being served a disciplinary case for contraband which would bring my level down from a level-1 to a level-3 which if I get I would be removed from the faith-based classes I'm in and all my level-1 property would be removed from my cage for three months (90 days) and I would no longer get to make my weekly telephone calls to my mom, nor would I be approved for a tablet that the prisoners in the Texas Department of Criminal Justice and here on Texas Death Row are getting in the next month or so. And why? Because a lawyer couldn't do as I have asked by letting me know via a JPay about a telephone call or visit, thus giving me the heads up to place my things up and be ready without being caught, as we would say in prison in California, slippin'.

Then just the other night I get a JPay from this same lawyer telling me again how sorry she is for not letting me know about the call and for making me wait and that she is planning on coming for a visit on May 27th, 2022 and she hopes that I will visit with her. Seriously? This is the thought running through my head, as the only reason she is now sending me a JPay is because my lawsuit lawyer David Lane emailed every one of my appeal lawyers explaining for the thousandth time about the JPays, and because when he and I spoke I let him know what I had lost and then not as badly lit into his butt too about not sending me a JPay letting me know about this legal call he had set up with me, and then I explained what happened earlier with my appeal lawyer and how I had hung up on her. It was then that it also clicked with him why I would always ask that everyone let me know ahead of time.

Prison is NOT like living your life out there in society. I cannot just walk down or drive to the store to replace something that is lost or broken. I cannot leave this cage unless I'm being escorted in some handcuffs behind my back and have two officers walking along with me, and that's only after they first did a complete strip search of my body in their poor attempt to degrade me of my dignity under a video camera both inside my cage that watches me 24/7 as well as outside my cage before they ask me to place my hands behind my back out the slot in my cage door so that they can place these steel-cold cuffs on my wrist, then and only then will the officer inside of the control picket open my cage door to allow me out to be escorted to wherever it is I'm going.

Then as I'm talking to David, he too apologized and with him I accepted this right away 'cause for the most part his office always lets me know when he has a call set up with me, but this one time the person in his office didn't do it and when she did write to me, she explained to me why and I understood. Though as David and I were talking I said to him, "So, they cried to you already (meaning my appeal lawyers)? He said, you know they did, now they are scared to death that you're really going to end things and though unlike them, I know that if you go this route you'll take your own life before allowing the State to take it for you.

Though I didn't correct David at the time of his saying this, he was correct, but that was before I had changed and that change is what this whole book is all about and why I'm sharing my life and everything going on with you. Had I never gotten right with the Man Above God and His Son Jesus Christ, I honestly don't know if I would still be here right now. But even though I get really upset more often than not at my capital appeal lawyers because they never listen, nor ever do what they give their word to me they'll do (yeah, I'm talking to you, Luis! Where are my pictures of Tiana and Tyler's wedding, amigo?!)

I care about my lawyers and their faith, and I just need to make sure that before I leave this life that they too, even though they're lawyers and investigators, that they too are saved and have come to know Jesus

Christ. It's hard to stay upset at them but the one that I'm still upset with, and she has hurt me deeper than all the rest by her silence, is Cassandra who I nicknamed years ago Scooter. I miss speaking with her and visiting with her and her laughter and just shootin' it during a legal visit. The gap between us isn't her fault alone, as it's mine too, but I have repeatedly reached out to her and she has done nothing to fix things between us.

No doubt you're asking how I came to name her this. During one of my legal visits with her she was asking questions and I to her when we came to the subject of motorcycles. She shared with me how she dated this guy that rode a scooter, though the dufus she was dating called it a motorcycle. Long story short, they crashed, she wasn't hurt but maybe her pride as I busted out laughing so hard. I mean, how do you crash on a scooter/Vespa?!

I told her maybe he should put some training wheels on it next time, though she did say that she is no longer with him. I gave her the name then and there and it has stuck, but I did shorten it to Scoots, but now she is no more in my life, but the memory will always be there though there is no longer the friendship. What can I say other than life can suck at times?

Back to my call with David though. I told him that I had had another lawyer order me the two books by Kevin Salwen who is David's friend and who happens to be reading my first book. He asked me what I thought about them, and I told him that I hadn't got the chance to read them yet but was going to. He then told me, well let me rephrase that, he gave me the guilt trip talk. You know that one where you say something to someone about what you're going to do and put your word on it, but then go back or walk borderline on what you said?

Yeah, like that. Well, David was giving me the poop over something I had told him I would do, and now because I was so upset with my lawyers, on the other end of things I started to lose sight of what I had given my word to David on. He tells me, "Come on Richard, you told me that you would write this next book, dude. People need to hear what you are saying because nobody else is going to be that voice for the guys on Texas Death Row that have been executed or what it's like to live in the same section as the guys waiting to die. You can and are that voice, Richard! People need to hear what you have to say, and you told me that you would do this and now your other lawyers are saying that you're telling them you're done. Come on man, you're my friend and brother, Richard, and I care about and love you man, don't do this."

Sounds pretty gay, huh? No worries to David's wife and friends, he's not gay and neither am I, but he's correct in calling me his brother 'cause we're both Jewish though his wife is Christian, and I thought I had it hard!

I have a legal call scheduled with David for tomorrow and plan on letting him know that I'm not going to go back on what we agreed on, but he's paying for this book to get published! People have no idea how hard it is to remain here in this section that is called Death Watch of Texas Death Row, and though I cannot leave this section or ask to be removed to another section because my being housed in this section is a means of cruel and unusual punishment by some directors and a state senator ordered for past actions that they are still holding grudges against me for some decade and change later.

I find that I'm at a loss of how to explain the pain and turmoil of getting to know each and every man that comes to this section after being given an execution date, only to later on sit here in my cage and watch as he is escorted off this section to his last day of visits with loved ones and friends and his supporters. Then around 6 p.m. on this radio station called The Execution Show that broadcasts live what is going on over in Huntsville, Texas and how when the time comes, they explain to all of us here on Texas Death Row that they know are listening in on our radios to this live broadcasting, that the witnesses have just crossed the road. This right here let's all of us know that the execution is going to take place. That our friend and our brother is now being strapped down to an ice-cold metal gurney so that another human being (doctor) that is taking money for doing this though the State says it's legal, will kill our friend and brother and call it justice. Is it really justice? And if it is, then who is it for?

There is a scripture in the Bible that I think everyone should take to heart and at some point in their lives read for themselves and think about if they are believers in God and His Son Jesus Christ, or even if you have thoughts about the Bible or someone in prison, don't be so fast to judge…

"Let brotherly love continue. Do not neglect to show hospitality to strangers for thereby some have entertained angels unawares. Remember those who are in prison, as though in prison with them, and those who are mistreated. Since you also are in the body." (Hebrews 13:1-3).

RICHARD L. TABLER

CHAPTER ELEVEN

THE NASTY CAGE AND ITS ATTACKING TENANTS

For a while two of the field ministers that are serving their time here at the Polunsky Unit and serve Him and share God's word or just be there for those of us on 12-Building are Field Minister Foster, also known as Brother Troup, and Brother Terry Solley, also known as Brother Solley. About three weeks ago they both started new faith-based classes here on Texas Death Row, also renamed by those of us Texas Death Row as Texas Life row.

Brother Troup is this white old guy that someone said looks like Moses from the Bible. He comes around giving a class that is on video and he shows us on the two big screen TVs he brings with him on Wednesdays and is on what is called "The Truth Project" which is an eight-week course. Now we find out that it will be shown on some other days than Wednesdays because Brother Troup has some other things he needs to take care of.

Brother Solley gives the class that is also on video and shown on two TVs on Fridays but will now be on Thursday nights called "Men's Fraternity the Quest for Authentic Manhood" that is also a few months long, though this class is done by Robert M. Lewis.

Being housed on 2-Row made things really difficult for me because when both Brothers Troup and Solley would come around to show their classes and then when Brother Troup would use a wireless mic to hold talks with us about what we watched and learned, it would take me a bit of time to process everything because I was having trouble reading the words from up on 2-Row. I could hear everything fine but reading the words that were also on the screen I was having trouble doing and not because I'm getting old!

Finally, this got to be too much, and I didn't want to drop out of the classes because I couldn't see, so I did the next best thing. I sent a letter of request in the truck mail within the prison to Brother Dickerson, also known to most as Warden Dickerson, because anything having to do with me has to first go through his office and if it's something that isn't so simple a solution to, then he gets the okay from his bosses in Huntsville, Texas (i.e., directors and senator).

I explained to him what my issues were and asked if he would please approve to have me moved from 2-Row #10 cage to 1-Row #1 cage at the soonest possible time, please. I sent that to Brother Dickerson on Thursday the 5th of May 2022 and on Monday evening after shift change, I was told to pack my things because I would be moving down to #1 cage.

Taking about 1-1/2 hours to pack all my property up, I informed one of the officers that I was ready to move and was told by Officer Loveday that he would let the sergeant know that I was ready to move. About 20 minutes later here comes Sgt. Hardin and Officer Loveday are coming up the stairs to my door. I do the monkey dance of stripping out butt-naked and then after getting dressed and turning around and placing my hands out the slot behind me to be cuffed, I'm escorted downstairs to 1-Row and #1 cage along with my property.

As Sgt. Hardin is standing with me outside the cage as Officer Loveday places my bagged property on the bunk and floor, I cannot help but look into this new place of living for myself that I had requested to be moved into all in the name of remaining in these two classes that I was taking to become closer to Jesus Christ and fully know myself. For a split second I thought about saying suit it up, I'm not going in that! But then I thought to myself, I asked Brother Dickerson for this help/move and he did this for me, so I would go in and do what I did best…hook it up!

I always keep some gloves (rubber kind) for cleaning when I make my own style cleaning solution because they don't really give us cleaning supplies here and commissary doesn't sell us anything other than soap and shampoo. So, I usually make my own with what I am able to get ahold of some way or another. So, as I'm getting out my gloves and cleaning products along with some old rags, the first thing I see is this… this HUUUUGE dead cockroach about the size of a 50-cent piece on his back at the head of the bunk on the floor. I'm like dude, did you really have to die on Death Row on your back like that? Well, at least you went out on your own terms you lucky roach!

As I'm getting ready to start scrubbing this cage from top to bottom before unpacking anything other than my cleaning supplies, something tells me to take a closer look at Mr. Dead Roach, so placing the gloves on I bend down and look at him only to take notice that he was murdered! Following upon closer inspection I see the fine line leading from his dead corpse under the bunk, so leaning down to study this line and look under the bunk, I not only forget that directly above me is the desk and the toilet right behind me, but the knot on the back top of my head and the bruises between my shoulder blades sure reminded me of my surroundings as I forgot to yell out as I rushed back from dead dude about killing myself in the process.

Once I was able to get myself under a little control and ask God for courage to continue cleaning, knowing that sooner or later I would have to get under the bunk and clean…but for now, for now I needed to clear my mind of what was hidden under there and that ate and killed Mr. Cockroach and the numerous other dead things that I saw under the bunk. They always said that women can be deadly, but the ladies under this bunk are not only deadly, but after they are done screwing you over they'll eat you too!

Just think about that for a bit while I walk you through my cleaning, staying far away from the bunk area for now. I turn to cleaning the stainless-steel sink/toilet and walls and light area. Grabbing my super-soaker (ketchup bottle) turned into my own squirt bottle that holds a mixture of bleach/shampoo with water, I give the stainless steel a good solid squirt all over it and down into the toilet to let it soak.

That is when I notice that there is a big gap between the toilet and the stainless-steel wall it's bolted to. The gap goes all the way around on both sides of the toilet and I can see the pipe inside the pipe chase. I see that the guy that was in this cage before me did what he could to kind of fill the gap with some papers and toilet paper, but it would take me a bit of time to fill this properly. First, I would clean everything because my butt ain't touching nothing in this cage until you could eat off it or you could see your own reflection like looking into the mirror or checking out the rims on your car or truck.

Grabbing some rags, I had and locking on the hot water button only to find it only comes out in a little trickle, I was like, you have got to be freaking kidding me! I try the cold water and it's not much better, but the water comes out more, so I lock it on and wet my rags and get to scrubbing the stainless steel and wiping it down. I pull out my scrub brush (palm brush) and little toothbrush and work the grime off the stainless steel and use the toothbrush to get in between the light grill and scrub there. Scrub around in the sink and the faucet and the buttons, then I double my gloves and start scrubbing the inside of the toilet that is black on the inside and the water is brown even after being flushed because the toilet is so freaking dirty. Scrub and let the bleach/shampoo soak some more, only to see that it's only working a little bit and needs something stronger, so I grab the good stuff I have (sorry, I cannot tell you what it is because at some point in time prison officials will read this book).

Grabbing the good stuff, I coat the toilet inside and out in foam and let that soak for a bit while I clean and scrub some more on the rest of the toilet/sink combo and lighting area. By this time my little pile of rags is laying used by the door and are black. Once again, I hit the toilet with my scrub brush and this time it's starting to become clean and I can see that it's still an actual toilet. Before long it's shining just like the rest of the stainless steel.

I then move to cleaning the desk and shelf that is right above the desk, scrubbing both really good before wiping down and drying with an extra towel.

Once this is done, I start cleaning the wall that my desk and shelf are attached to. Soon I see that there is white paint under it all and that too begins to show clean. When this is done, I take a minute to look at my watch and see that I have been cleaning since they moved me into this cage at 6:45 p.m. on Monday, May 9th, 2022 and it's now Tuesday morning early…2:30 a.m., and I'm nowhere near finished cleaning enough so that I can unpack my property and start placing everything where I want it to make it livable because truth is, even though this isn't my home, it's the place my actions got me and where I shall remain until my death or day of execution.

One thing I do pull out though and hook up because the area I'll have it is now clean is my radio and yes, another speaker! Cranking up the tunes, thumping out jams, I lose myself in the cleaning as I attack the walls and ceiling before turning around and soaking the door and letting the chemicals I'm using work their magic before I start scrubbing with brush and rags really good.

While the door is soaking, I sweep the best I can around on the floor so that I can place my property down upon it still bagged up so that I can clean the top of the bunk and the back wall and up by the little slit of a window. Officers came around with a breakfast tray and I refused it to continue cleaning. It was 4 a.m. now. Changing my gloves and grabbing another rag I squirt some bleach/shampoo into the lockers that are attached to the bunk and scrub those three clean and then dry them.

Now, the last thing for me to deal with is under the bunk, well second to last thing, as the very last I cannot do until my stuff is unpacked and that's clean the floor which is black. It is so black that I'm not even sure if there is cement under it!

Grabbing another clean extra towel and another pair of rubber gloves and an old sock and shoelace, I place a water bottle into the sock and tie the shoelace onto the end, sealing the water bottle inside, but also allowing me to throw the socked water bottle and pull it back to me. Backing up by my toilet and looking further underneath the bunk to take in the full length of it, I can see that these killer ladies are more than just by Mr. Cockroach that they murdered along with the other creatures under there, but there is around four of them and some others but not as big all over under this bunk and right where it's dark, but the thing that stands out and marks them as so deadly is the bright red hourglass shape that is the mark of the black widow spider!

Starting with the two fat broads right underneath my bunk by the desk, I slam the socked water bottle into the first one coming from under her and letting her go without pain before pulling the socked water bottle back over to me to soak her guts and legs off in the toilet that is now shining with clear water inside it.

Once she has been removed, I turn back to her friend and smash her too. As soon as the socked bottle hits the floor and I'm pulling her into being wiped off in the toilet and flushed down with her twin, I use the socked bottle to toss further under the bunk by the back wall to pull all the dust and grime out the best I can until I deal with these other broads that are going to be harder to get as they are surrounded with soldiers.

Laying down yet another towel on the dirty floor so that I can lay down upon it on my back to get a look under the bunk by where the shelves are built into it, I'm able to see that these two are right against the weld in the middle of the bunk at the end and too far for me to reach with my hands, thus I'll have to throw the bottle from my left hand coming from my desk area and do my best at hitting them as if I were throwing the disk.

Nailing the first one though I was aiming for the closest one, as I'm pulling her in, out of the corner of my eye I see something running towards me. With my heart in my chest and the yell frozen there, I all but forget about the damn water bottle-sock combo as I try to get somewhere, only for this thing to continue chasing after me from under the bunk and the dark, and I'm by this time waaay back by my cage door now and standing up with my boots ready to come flying down in the STOMP!

But when this thing running after me comes into the light and I see what it is and that it's not the other black widow spider but bigger and must have been stuck in one of their webs, is just the family member of Mr. Dead Cockroach because this sucker is bigger and is moving at a fast clip, no doubt screaming in his cocky little mind, "Blue! Thank you so much for saving my life from them dirty women!" only as my heart rate slows down and he's thankful, and now thinking he safe. I'm sure those were the last thoughts he had before my right boot did the STOMP on him for scaring the crap out of me!

Cleaning him off my boot so I didn't have to deal with him later, I gave him the goldfish solute and burial with two flushes down the toilet instead of one, then got back to work of killing the last remaining black widow spider and her associates so that I could finish cleaning this cage and the floor enough to make my bed and sleep.

By this time, it's now Tuesday morning and the new shift has come on and been here for an hour or so because it was now almost 7 a.m. on May 10th, 2022. By 10:30 a.m. I was able to have everything unpacked and my bed made and crashed for maybe an hour at the most before I was up and back to cleaning everything more thoroughly and to pull out a jar of bippy (prison Ajax). This I would end up pouring a little off into another little bowl and adding about two tablespoons of water making a thick paste of sorts. Once I had this done, I put on a pair of gloves and removed everything from between the gap around the sink and stainless steel before placing my own gap filler inside it and then using the thick paste substance, in this case bippy, to make a thicker like caulking, which I was able to do, then went on to continue caulking up all around the edge of my light and the angle iron on the back wall. This will prevent bugs such as ants, spiders, and roaches from finding their way in from either outside or from within the pipe chase.

Once this was done, I was able to climb further under my bunk close to the back wall to scrub and clean along the wall and floor where the two connect. After I had this cleaned, I used the remainder of my caulking to caulk up the crack that runs the length of the back wall and floor.

From the day I moved into this cage on Monday, May 9th, 2022 to today's date of Wednesday, May 11th, 2022, I did nothing but scrub and clean thoroughly and more, then half that time was spent on first scrubbing the floor and then using my own floor solution to strip the whole cement flooring inside my cage so that now when anyone stops by to look inside my cage, namely officers or rank or even the wardens or anyone that they are walking around showing a tour to, they will not only see a clean cage, but a white and clean cement floor.

When I was able to finally relax and get some sleep, I crashed as if I were dead, and then this afternoon just before I was getting ready to start working some more on this book, an officer came to my cage with a roll of tape and this little green card. He looked at me looking at him and we both started laughing because I knew what he held in his hand, and he knew that it would remain where he was taping it for long. I asked him, "Where are you taping that to?" He said, above your door. I said, why above my door? He said that the captain told him to put it above my door because every time they have placed them on my door directly when they are walking around they notice that I don't have one on my door but the shower sheet (paperwork) shows that I should have one of them on my door so that officers are able to show the proper precaution.

I said, why should they be cautioned by that, I don't want to let those coming to work here or on tour know about my past history, and besides, that green tag and all its markings are for things that took place inside a prison in Texas, not for actions done in prison in California. He just laughed and finished taping it above my door but wouldn't tell me where exactly he taped it when I asked.

The green tag is what TDCJ-ID calls its designator precaution tag. It's to give warning to those working around this prisoner that he has a history of not only violence but escape and escape from security restraints. So, on this bright green tag there are three boxes marked out of four. SA, which means that I have a staff assault beyond first aid treatment meaning that I sent someone to the hospital's emergency room; ES which stands for escape, as I have escape history on my record from California too; and the last one marked on my tag is SR which lets everyone know that just because you have placed me into either handcuffs or leg irons, I'm only allowing you to walk around with me and that push comes to shove I can come out of these restraints at any time I want them off my hands or legs. The last one which I do not have is HS which stands for hostage situation, meaning when I was a prisoner somewhere I took an officer or someone working at the prison or somewhere hostage. Three out of four isn't bad though, lol!

No worries though, you will all see what this green tag is that I'm talking about when this book makes it into publishing because in the next chapter of this book I'm going to share with you about how I'm NOT the same person I was 18 years ago when I first got locked up here in Texas for the crime of capital murder and this new green tag will be in this book and I have someone remove it from above my door like I have every time they have it placed on my door or above it. Why favoritize my past when it's not me? Before I close this chapter out, I'd like to leave it with this joke to all my ndugus (brothers) and anyone wanting a good laugh.

For Laughter Only

"There was a black man, a white man, a Native American man and a Latino man who were on top of a cliff discussing the difficulties their people had undergone. The Native American man said, 'My people have suffered the most. In honor of what they have endured, I will fling myself over this cliff in the hopes that my blood will change things.' So, he yelled, 'THIS IS FOR MY PEOPLE!' and jumped off the cliff. The Latino, not wanting to be outdone, quickly looked at the other two and followed yelling, 'THIS IS FOR MY PEOPLE!' and jumped off the cliff as well. The black man was touched by all this and decided it was his turn; so, he yelled, 'THIS IS FOR MY PEOPLE!' and pushed the white man off the cliff!"

CHAPTER TWELVE

"RESPECT FOR AUTHORITY"

On Thursday afternoon, May 12th, 2022, Warden Dickerson, who is also our brother in Christ Jesus, was walking on A-Pod Death Watch with some people from society and looking into the pipe chases for some reason outside my knowledge. As he came to my cage to check on me and ask me how I was doing, I told him thanks for approving the move for me into this cage. That's when he told me that he was watching the cameras for the last few days and saw me scrubbing and cleaning for days straight and jokingly said he was thinking about moving me from cage to cage just to get each of them cleaned as my cage and Billy's cage is because between the two of us that's all he ever sees us doing…constantly cleaning our cages among other things.

    I laughingly told him I wouldn't mind being placed into another cage each day so long as I was returned to my cage to sleep and eat once I finished cleaning the said cages I was placed in.

    Why would I do this, you're asking? Simple. I've not been allowed to work or have a job since I came to Texas Death Row because they do not offer nor allow us jobs here at the Polunsky Unit where the condemned are housed in Livingston, Texas. Unlike the general population prisoners who are allowed such jobs and are called SSIs (support service inmates) and I see constantly complaining about having to work in prison. I would enjoy being allowed to do this if Warden/Brother Dickerson ever decided to give me the chance to work, I would jump at any such job no matter what it was.

After he and the people he had with him left, I went back to doing whatever it was I was doing in my cage.

Then around 3 p.m. we are told that we're on lockdown. Aren't we already on lockdown? I mean, we don't get rec every day and we're not given showers every day, so aren't we on lockdown already? If that's not lockdown, being told that now we are on lockdown makes it what? More official? So, now we're on lockdown on top of our knowing we're on lockdown because officials are saying it so, so it's so.

Word started to trickle down to us from out there. Another prisoner that was being transported along with about 50 other prisoners in a prison bus somewhere north of us here in Livingston, Texas in Leon County was able to remove his restraints while this bus of prisoners was transporting them from one prison to another in Huntsville, Texas for medical reasons. Only after removing his restraints, he then broke through the meshed metal gate securing the prisoners from the driver up front where he then started to fight with the prison bus driver in an attempt to take the officer's gun, but being unable to do so, he then stabbed the officer in the chest and left hand with a shank before the driver crashed the prison bus.

The prisoner was then able to escape from the custody of the prison bus, but not before the second prison guard who was secured in the back of the prison bus was able to get off several shots from his own weapon at the escaping prisoner. From my understanding, this prisoner was serving a life sentence for capital murder. Thus, because of this now prison break from a prison transport bus all surrounding prisons in the area have been placed on a lockdown as they send officers from this prison and numerous others to begin a major manhunt for this prisoner along with some 300+ other law enforcement officers.

The news is telling those living in the area of the escape that they are not to approach the prisoner if they see him and are to report sighting of him to the police. They are to lock their doors and cars and trucks. Even as the hours tick by without finding him, the news is saying that local schools have been shut down and parents are picking up their kids.

Thursday has turned into Friday, May 13th, 2022 and still they have not been able to capture the escaped prisoner.

Coming to my cage door and talking with my Brother Billy Tracy in #3 cage, we start talking about his escape. I'm telling Billy I hope he gets away, but then again, I feel that it was wrong for him to stab the prison bus driver to make his escape. Billy explains to me that he is currently reading in the Bible from Romans 13 and it's difficult for him because he's served so long in prison where he also happened to catch his own capital murder charge some five years ago and sentenced to death four years ago and arriving here on Texas Death Row's Death Watch section in a custom cage built just for him.

His cage not only had all the shelving removed and cut from his bunk, but his air vent was welded over so barely any air comes through to him from the vent, either cool or heat when it's cold. His cage door doesn't have a slot for his food to pass through like the rest of us, but he has a metal box with two (2) padlocks on it and these locks must be removed each time he's fed or taken to the shower or rec and he can only rec outside alone every time he's allowed rec while a sergeant watches him everywhere he goes.

He has been housed like this and treated like this for the whole time he's been housed on this section with me for four years now. However, regardless of what he did in prison at another prison here in Texas, he like myself and everyone else has changed. This change didn't happen overnight for him just like it didn't for myself or anyone else, but change he did and to show that he has changed and become a believer in Jesus Christ, he was baptized in March of 2022.

He is also a writer for the Minutes Before Six and is always writing farewells after the guys that he's gotten to know since being housed on Death Watch these four years he's been here. You can read what he and many other prisoners have written about at www.minutesbeforesix.com though I have never written this place and don't plan to start anytime soon if ever.

I know that Billy has a powerful way about his writing and in a very positive light. So, we're talking about this guy escaping, and Billy takes me to Romans 13 where it talks about respect for authority, something that both of us deal with. Billy is telling me that for me to think about this guy getting away I'm going against God's law and what Romans 13 is saying. He too though is rooting for the guy to escape, thus our discussion.

Thinking for a minute before speaking again to Billy, I explain that yeah, I can see and understand what the Bible is saying in Romans 13, and yet at the same time this gives new definition to the fighting we each have within ourselves, between doing what is right in the eyes of God and His Son Jesus Christ and doing what we feel is right from our own experiences. The reason I want the guy to get away is because I know just like many others know that if they find him, there is more than a 99.9% change they'll shoot him on sight no matter what because he stabbed that prison bus driver. I'd rather him escape their search than be killed by their hands even though he may or may not deserve it, it's not my place nor anyone else's to decide such fate for someone.

As I'm explaining this to my Brother Billy, somehow our talking turns to other issues and I bring up the movie The Shack. Billy said he hated that book and I know why because at first, I didn't like what the beginning of the book and movie was about as it started off. The story is about how a small child is kidnapped and before being murdered by her kidnapper, she's molested. Neither Billy nor I like or want anything to do with sick people/prisoners. This is just something that was engraved on us as convicts/people.

After this incident takes place, the story turns to the dad's walk and faith in God and His Son Jesus Christ. A letter is found by this man called Mac in his mailbox while his wife and their kids are away. Long story short, Mac is led to this shack in the mountains and there he spends time talking with God (Mama) Jesus and the Holy Spirit, but he doesn't really believe it all after some time.

There comes a time where Jesus is taking Mac across the lake and into the mountains towards his cave, and as He leads Mac up into the cave, he explains that He cannot go any further, but Mac must go ahead on his own. Once he gets in there, he's told to have a seat on this rock and is given the chance to see what it's like to be God for a minute. Before his eyes comes two of his children and he must decide which one of the two must die and which one should remain alive, only Mac cannot decide because he loves both of his children so much. He's crying because he cannot do this because it hurts too much.

Well, my question to each and every one of you reading these words right now, could you be just like God? Could you decide the fate between two of your loved ones? Yeah, I didn't think so, neither could I. But how do you think God feels having to decide everyday of our lives which ones are to live and who is to die knowing that each and every one of us are His children and He loves us each just as much and maybe even more than we love our own!

I told Billy this and I further told him that I don't agree with what the escaped prisoner did to escape by stabbing the prison bus driver and I pray the officer is okay, but I only wish that he had gone about it differently if he had to do it at all.

Then we spoke some more about prison authority, and this led us back to Romans 13. It's a very hard read for those of us in prison but think about it. God created everything and everyone in this life was placed into their situations for one reason or another, just as we each have choices to make. Some make the right choice and some make wrong choices and when we make the wrong choices and end up in prison or even on Death Row somewhere. No matter how much it feels like it goes against everything that we believe in, we must and need to respect those who have been placed into the authority above us, such as here in prison you have officers and wardens and even directors that run everything. It's not our place to question it all, but to abide by what they say because we each broke the law of both the law of man in society and God's law and now we pay that price.

I remember when I was younger and at my best friend Adam's house that sat way out in the country. Adam was teaching me to play the game of chess on this marble set his parents had. After all those years ago when life as I knew it was okay and I was having fun with my friend. The game of chess would become a game that was played throughout my time and years in prison just as it is played in prisons all over the world by grown men and women. Most times I would lose my queen and rooks right at the beginning of the game. Once they were gone, I would act as if the game was already over and all was lost because all I had left were some pawns and a knight or bishop. But over time I learned to greatly enjoy the game though maybe I'm not as serious at it as some of my fellow brothers are and friends in life now, but it made the time go by faster.

Do you have any idea why I'm speaking to you about a game of chess? Because you all need to realize something if you are to succeed at that game. And what you need to realize is this: the game is never over until it's over. It's not over if a pawn remains on the board, if the other side has only the king and two pawns and you have most of the pieces. It's not over, or if the table is turned and it's you with less pieces and the other player with all of them. A pawn is a very powerful piece even though it looks like a tiny thing; it really isn't. A pawn is never just a pawn, but a pawn can turn into a queen at the right time.

Like life, all you need to do is keep moving forward on the board. One square one step at a time, and once you make it to the other side all kinds of things can and will happen.

Take a look at a chess board, look at how everything looks safe and in order kind of like life. It's wonderful, isn't it? Everything and piece is right where it should be, but it's boring and not fun just sitting there looking at it, huh? But at the first move, things start to take off and become chaotic, and that chaos builds with each and every move you make. It's a great game but a difficult one to master. Each and every move opens another possible outcome and possibility, just like when one door in your life closes another door opens. At the beginning of each game as in life there is only one way to set up a board. After the first few moves, thousands more variations will open up as new positions are taken.

Like life, there are thousands if not millions of ways to move forward and each with a different outcome from the first. Each possibility is an amazing thing, but it can become messy too and there is no right way to play each game because there are so many ways. In chess, and in life, the possibility is the basis for everything. Every dream, every hope, every prayer, every living moment, if only you'll continue to move forward one day at a time.

Know something else? Everything doesn't have to be taken so seriously all the time. Just because I'm in prison doesn't mean that I can't and don't play a joke on someone every now and then because I do and sometimes it was pure accident and just timing. Like this morning. It's Saturday, May 15th, 2022, and I had overslept for the first time if ever past by usual 5 a.m. or earlier wakeup time. It was 8:33 a.m. and my cage is blocked out (meaning no light is inside my cage from either outside or from the run coming in through my cage door). I had just rolled out of my bunk and was standing at my cage door trying to see who was working.

With my eyes too fuzzy trying to wake up, I notice this female officer walking towards my cage after entering onto the section. My thoughts register who it is and so I back up just a little more into the darkness of my cage thinking this officer is going by to take a look into my cage from the wire mesh on my door from the side she's closer to, but instead she goes to the farther side, and I decide to have a little fun.

She is this tiny thing maybe 5'6" soaking wet with white-blond hair and this perky little nose she's always bunching up at someone or another. And she's always talking trash but in a funny way. Months ago, I gave her the nickname of Tinkerbell. So, squatting down just about to her height, I move into and towards my cage door coming out of the darkness and we meet right at the door at the same time, and I say, boo!

Not only did she jump and scream, but she spilled her cup of coffee that I didn't see that she was holding until after the fact. Yeah, I was fair game then and she let me have it with both guns, and I couldn't help but laugh my butt off all the more 'cause she is so freaking tiny that when she's trying to look serious it doesn't work and she looks like a little girl not getting her way when her parents tell her no, lol!

As she is walking back toward leaving the section, I cannot help but look out my cage door towards her and she is walking as if she is purposely throwing/swinging her little butt more than usual and her head is held so high she has to be talking with God up there. Later on, when I apologize for scaring the crap out of her, she said it was the perfect cup of coffee and still gives me the stink eye but in a way that her eyes are now twinkling too and full of laughter. Thanks for the laugher and the way you always treat each of us as human beings back here on Texas Death Row while also not holding grudges over a cup of coffee, Officer T. Beck!

When is it okay for those in a position of authority to lie to the public through the media or any other source? That's a serious question is it not? Society is made to believe that those of us on Texas Death Row are the worst of the worst and that there is no help for us in changing but everything you have read in this book so far shows, I would think, that we and I can change and if you could hear and see what all Warden Dickerson and his bosses have allowed to take place back here through the doors that he opened and God entered through, you would know firsthand that change is possible for even those you have tossed into the trash pile as unrehabilitatable.

We are entering into the fourth day of lockdown systemwide behind the prisoner that escaped from a transport bus here in Texas and the lies spilling forth from the Texas Department of Justice is something out of a movie made in Hollywood! A prison bus is to always have three

(3) officers on it at all times. You have the driver and another officer up front with the driver in the front area and in the very back of the bus in a separate booth is what is known as a shotgunner. This officer is hidden behind tinted glass but is able to see everything that is going on through the bus from the back to the front, and he/she is able to exit the bus from their own door in the back of the bus. All officers are armed with weapons at all times while outside the prison walls with sidearms and shotguns. Each prisoner is chained from his/her waist through the hands with handcuffs and over the handcuffs is what's called a black box that is also secured with a padlock that faces into the prisoner instead of out so that it could be picked open. Higher security prisoners are also chained this way, but their legs are also in what is called leg irons and from these leg irons runs another chain to the waist/handcuffs/black box setup.

Now, I'm not saying that some prisoner couldn't remove all of this because I know for a fact I could do it and I know numerous other guys locked up with me now and in other states that could do so as well. Besides the chains and the officers and their guns, a prison bus is set up into three sections. The driver and the front officer are in one area as one first enters the bus up the steps. Taking a left, you must walk through a gated area of mesh and plexiglass that is secured to the outside of the mesh gate on the driver's side. Going through this gate you walk through maybe 15 feet tops before passing through another gate of the same kind. Each of these gates are welded to the bus flooring and run from one side of the bus to the other (in other words, there is no getting through without a key to the padlocks). The very back of the bus that is about 20-25 feet in length is seating for medium security prisoners. This spot is for those chained up without leg irons and seated two to a seat facing the front of the bus.

After this is filled with prisoners then that second gate is not only secured but it's also locked by an officer that is the second officer that should be on the bus and sitting up by the driver in the front of the bus, as it's his/her job to make sure that the prisoners remain secure throughout the transport.

Then the second section of the bus is filled with high security prisoners that have the whole setup of chains as well as the leg irons. These guys/gals are then sealed off by that gate that was locked and then the first gate upon entering into the bus with another padlock. Then the driver starts the bus and they move off to arm themselves up under a gun tower in the back of the prison. Once this is done, they start their trip to God knows where.

Now, as I said earlier, it's possible to escape from your chains and leg irons, but what doesn't make sense to any of us that have ridden on these buses or been doing serious time in prison is that they are saying to the public and media around them that this escaped prisoner not only got out of his restraints, but everyone is being told that he then cut through the security gate! This is in no way possible to do so because though there are ways to escape through such a gate, the plexiglass siding is on the side with the driver as are the locks if they were to say he opened the padlock to escape. Anyway, if he tried to cut through this gate to where the driver was it would have made tons of noise.

Now, here it gets more confusing because now the word is that all of a sudden the bus is on the side of the road pulled over and the driver and the prisoner are fighting outside of the bus before the prisoner reenters the bus and drives away, but not before the shotgunner officer had exited the bus from the back and shot out the bus's wheels, thus causing the prisoner to crash the bus a mile down the road where he fled on foot and now we're here on day four.

Yesterday they say they found a prison officer's uniform near the field. Things don't add up. We could go back and forth with ideas of how he got away, but I have one serious question myself. Why did TDCJ-ID only have two (2) officers working a transport bus filled with about 50 prisoners instead of the three policy states they're to have at all times?

One other thing to think about, could you imagine the lawsuit TDCJ-ID will face if this escaped prisoner kills other innocent people while he's on the run out there? I pray to God nobody gets in this dude's way because this guy hasn't changed or tried to change his ways while he's been in prison, and if he's willing to stab an officer (the driver) then he's still a violent individual. As it stands, he's already killed before and that's why he was in prison to start with. And while the prison uses sources that it doesn't have in this manhunt for this killer along with hundreds of other law enforcement agencies, they search in the wrong area because if this man could get out of that bus the way he did and the way we inside know he did, then he had outside help and is long gone from where they're searching. And yet, the rest of the Texas prisons across the state are on full lockdown, thus closing down even legal visits with lawyers of those of us on Texas Death Row and stopping legal telephone calls with lawyers as well. But if any one of us tried to explain this to the courts we have deadlines in, they don't care because with the condemned…time is not on our side.

Knowing this and knowing that it's the authority that allowed only two officers to be on that transport bus, thus allowing this escape to happen in the first place and those in society to be placed in jeopardy by this escaped killer who has killed before, how do we as believers respect this authority without judging them as they do of us? Because what this one escapee does doesn't or shouldn't represent us as a whole but that won't stop the media or those of you in society from calling us all the same because we're not anything like one another. In my own opinion I'm praying they catch this guy before he's able to hurt someone else just to get away. What if he hurts a kid? Think about the pain and suffering that family is going to go through, and why? Because TDCJ-ID cut corners in their security and yet they say we are the worst of the worst because we're on Texas Death Row.

Take a fast flight over to the East Coast with me now and let's think about what just took place over there. A young, white neo-Nazi wannabe went into a Tops Grocery Store and shot and killed ten (10) African Americans for no other reason than hate. And what is the first thing the District Attorney's office lays on the table? Well, I can tell you that they won't seek the death penalty when he goes to court, and why not? Is not all life equal to the next? Why should one person because of his/her skin color not be sought after in the same way as my African American brothers and sisters?

We sit back and read all over the USA and on our radios and watch on TV about how whites are going all over the place and killing people in cold blood and each State and District Attorney's office is calling them hate crimes but don't seek the death penalty in any of these cases. Now, if these were African Americans walking into a white grocery store of any kind and killing white people, you are swift to want to hang them and place the death penalty on the countertop. How twisted is that?

It makes me sick to call myself an American and I'm only that because I was born here, but you best believe if I could claim some other country as my own, I would do so in a heartbeat because this country is filled with hate and its politicians and even its president doesn't trust those in office. How can America become what it once was if there is no trust among one another?

If I were a man of violence still, I would say that if anyone has the right to return the violence against others it's my African brothers and sisters because everywhere you turn it's them on the receiving end of a pistol, it's their loved ones being shot and killed by some punk kid who was raised wrong and has a twisted sense of what is right in this world and what is not. It's cops and their no-knock warrants and getting away with cold-blooded murder, and who is it other than the white man in office letting it happen?

But when has violence been the solution to peace and happiness? How are those that are hurt from losing a loved one or a friend to violence or to cops getting away with murder, how are they to respect the same authority that is responsible for their loved one's death?

To the young white man reading this and not liking what I'm writing, let me further upset you about some cold-hearted truth. First, I'm not a racist and cannot stand those who are racist, but as much as I don't care for them, I would still nowadays offer them my shirt if they needed it. I would offer them food and a helping hand if they needed it because without love, this cycle of hate will continue to go around and around with no end.

Furthermore, to those of you who think you'll get away with doing something stupid, let me give you some solid advice. Throughout the United States and its prisons, you might think by not getting the death penalty in some cases that you're getting lucky, and that prison is going to be like what you see on your TVs or on a DVD that Hollywood made. If you believe this is how it will be and that you'll make it, I got news for you--you don't know nothing! The truth, and though it stinks it's still the truth, is 90% of the prison population is African Americans and Latinos, and if you think you'll be safe inside these walls wherever you end up behind a hate crime, the brothers and sisters inside are going to welcome you with open arms and I promise you, you'll be screaming for your mother before the first day is over if you land somewhere in prison in California or Florida.

I've seen some of the biggest and toughest men get their butts beat by the smallest, and I've seen the ones that are supposed to keep you secured do worse than anything you could have ever imagined. I've been inside prisons in California and jails and camps in Florida and down south of the border in Mexico City, Mexico. I've been locked up in Michigan and my final spot in more ways than one…Texas.

Prison is not fun and it's not cool, so do your best to change your ways so you don't end up inside one of them.

Before I close out this chapter, I'd like to give a little humor as laughter is the best medicine for all of us. If you lose your sense of humor, well then, you've pretty much lost everything and though I don't recommend it, you might as well go ahead and throw in the towel.

Yesterday afternoon a new commissary worker came onto the section here on Death Watch of A-Pod 12-Buiding. Myself, Billy, and RG were standing at our doors talking. At first it was just Billy and I speaking about 1-Corinthians 12 and the Gifts of the Spirit (Holy Spirit). Then somehow RG got into the conversation, and then the gate to the section pops open and this dude none of us have seen before comes into the section.

He's around 5'9" and 160 pounds with closely shaved hair that was black, and his eyes are like those in a pug dog where they are popping out of your head a bit. At first neither of us knows who it is and then I see the words COMM on the stab-resistant vest, meaning he works in Commissary. So, I yell out to him, "Hey, what's your name?" He tells me something that sounded like Shovan but pronounced like (Show-van). Then I ask him, "Where you from?" (meaning what prison did you work at before or are you from the general population).

His response was, "This is my first time in prison." Before I could say something smart, RG says, well hey, if you get out of here don't come back! To which the poor guy just about runs off the section to the three of us laughing.

CHAPTER THIRTEEN

WHY COULDN'T IT BE DONE?

D o you ever just stop and wonder about things in life and how everything got to this very point in time? Or thought about what dream you would like to see come to fruition in your life or for those you love and care about, or just about anything else that comes to mind?

Being in prison I have read thousands upon thousands of books, both fiction and nonfiction. Books authored by Lee Child, Ralph Compton, David Baldacci, and books on Michelangelo, Malcolm X, Nelson Mandela, The Holy Bible, the philosopher Kierkagaard just to name a few. Then most recently my friend and brother who happens to also be my lawsuit lawyer David A. Lane told me about his friend who is also an author along with his daughter, Kevin and Hannah Salwen. So, being a curious sort of person, I had someone order both of his books for me to read over and see what all the hype was about this guy and his daughter.

His second book is what I read first and this book he wrote with former U.S. Attorney for the Northern District of Georgia, Kent Alexander. Kevin Salwen was a long-time Wall Street Journal reporter before he became a writer in his first book with his daughter Hannah Salwen. His and her first book is called "The Power of Half," which is probably one of if not the best book I have read since being locked up in prison, as well as when I was not in prison. This book not only stopped me in my tracks but made me think about some very serious things in life and how I might become something or someone better than my old self and the way I used to think. If you've not heard of nor read any books by Kevin Salwen and Hannah, I strongly suggest that you start with their first book "The Power of Half (ISBN 978-0-547-39454).

His second book is called "The Suspect" and is also a very moving and powerful book because he and Kent Alexander show how easy it is for the media to condemn an innocent man as well as the FBI and other law enforcement officials as they share with you the story of Richard Jewell and The Olympics bombing.

Throughout the book "The Power of Half" Kevin and Hannah share more than any other family I have read about, but what they end up doing from one point in their lives is just mind boggling!

As you get closer to the end of their story (true story) on page 171 you have Hannah's take and here she writes about something on the man Zell Kravinsky and how he sees everyone in the world as well as himself as equal. It goes on to talk about how thousands upon thousands of Americans are in need of a kidney donation and that so many other thousands die because they don't get one. This stopped me in my tracks cold.

Before I came to prison, I was what is called an organ donor marked on my motorcycle license as well as my driver license. If I got into a wreck and ended up in the emergency room and was not going to survive, then my organs could be donated to someone that was in need of them and on the waiting list, and so long as I was a match for whoever was in need then, my organ would be removed from my body, cleaned, and placed by a surgical team of doctors into the other person. However, that has never happened because as you know I'm in prison and have been for the last 18 years and counting.

Now, hold all of this in mind as I share with you something else. The last few months I have read in my USA Today newspaper and heard on NPR about people out there volunteering to have a transplant done, but the organs they were receiving weren't that of another human being but of a pig's heart.

The surgery took around 20 hours to do and the man lived for about a week or so with this pig's heart. If God wanted you to have such a heart in you, he would have made us look more like animals. I cannot understand how a doctor would nor could approve of doing such an animalistic deed no matter the reason or cause.

That brings me to this. I don't have the means to give out money or anything else because most of the time I have to depend on others to help me with things to survive inside these prison walls, such as money or books or newspapers ordered from outside. This is something that is beyond difficult for me to do because I don't feel that it's right to ask others to spend their hard-earned money on me when it was my own actions that landed me in prison in the first place. Nobody that is in nor a part of my life are responsible for where I'm at but I alone. I understand that the few who do help and that are family do so because they care about me as a person or because I have managed to become a true friend from within these prison walls and they help out of love and kindness and even compassion. But what I can do and do have the power to do, is seek out to help those in need through my letters in return and maybe even get the attention of someone in a more powerful position outside these walls to help bring about such a change.

There is no question about it that I'm currently housed on Texas Death Row and that I have been sentenced to death for my crimes back in 2004 in Killeen, Texas. But why couldn't it be done, or a new law made, that gave the condemned the choice to donate one of their organs or all of them to someone in need of a life-saving gift? We are to love one another just as Christ Jesus loved each and every one of us, and yeah, I made a horrible mistake that cost the lives of others, but two wrongs don't make a right and if I'm willing to donate my organs upon the set date and time that the State of Court has ordered my execution, then why couldn't I be taken to a hospital and my organs removed, and then once done, it would be just as simple as taking me off of life support and my life would be no more, but someone else's family member could continue to live out the rest of his/her life?

Why must I die when I have the means to save a life? I have two healthy kidneys, I have a healthy heart, two healthy lungs, among other healthy parts within my body and lots of O-positive blood to give. So, I sincerely ask, if you're reading this book and have the power to assist in bringing this about, then help me do so because I don't know the first thing to do or who to write to bring about such a life-saving change. I'm not asking to be recognized for this if it were to be done because it wouldn't be right nor fair to the people who lost loved ones by my hand, but it sure beats placing the organ of some animal into your loved ones or friends waiting on an organ donor list.

I thank both Hannah and her dad Kevin for their book "The Power of Half" because without reading their story and all they have done and continue to do for society as a whole, and when I say whole I mean the world as a whole, they along with David Lane and good old Yeshua, for without Him neither their story nor David's support would have been possible.

I have read somewhere once that there is a great deal of pain in life and perhaps the only pain that can be avoided is the pain that comes from trying to avoid pain. If you can stop looking at me for my crime and the actions that landed me here, then maybe you can save your loves one's life by accepting one of my many organs that I freely offer to someone in need. Through teamwork and lawyers and God, anything is possible.

I know this is the shortest chapter in this book so far, and before I close it out, I would like to leave you all with this Jewish quote: "You save one life, you save the world."

CHAPTER FOURTEEN

JUST ANOTHER DAY, OR IS IT?

These last few weeks have been somewhat different for me than usual in the sense that lately I have been getting letters from some women asking questions about what my daily life is like and some that ask if I'm religious or not and one or two that don't really talk about anything, but no doubt are trying to find out more about me so they can sell what they learn on the internet, as this has been done before.

But one of these young women by the name of Katie truly touched me with her question: "What do you feel that you took for granted before you came to prison?" I sat around a couple of days before responding back to her on this answer and told her…life. So many things that I'm now missing out in life outside these walls that I'll never get to see nor do or taste because of some very stupid actions on my part. Only time will tell if this young lady responds to my letters or not. If she does, then great, and if not, I hope and pray that she learned something from what I wrote to her and shared with her.

My mornings usually start right around 4:30 a.m. when the alarm in my head goes off and I wake up, though I don't get out of bed then. I usually lay there a few more minutes then get up in the dark and make my bed up by folding the sheets and blanket, then stepping to my sink where I wash my face, brush my teeth, then plug my Hot-Pot in to heat some water for a shot of my morning coffee. While the water is heating, I'll sit at my desk and read my Daily Bread and then do my devotional for the day before talking to God for a few minutes.

Once this is done, I'll cross the day off my Puppy Dog Dreaming Calendar, then I'll put a spoonful of instant coffee into my coffee mug and add the now-hot water, stirring, and then taking my first sip of the day. I'll turn my night light back off and just think about everything that I would like to do and plan to do this day, from writing my letters to family and friends and lawyers, reading my word, and fellowshipping with Billy Tracy and RG (Ramiro Gonzales) some days, to listening to some music on the radio and then working at some point in time on this manuscript.

So, what was different about today? Well, as of this day which is May 19th, 2022 and day seven of this TDCJ-ID system lockdown behind that escaped prisoner who is by now somewhere in Mexico, this day also marks for me 240,000 hours that I have been locked down inside of prison throughout my life. Crazy, huh? Could you imagine being locked away somewhere for that many hours not being able to do just anything that you wanted to do?

Have a girlfriend or wife? Well, not no more you don't. I assure you that you'll go crazy not having them in your life after the first 72 hours of your time away from them. Think I'm wrong? Well, you won't have your cellphone so you cannot text them or your friends to explain to them where you've gotten off to, so yeah, I'm willing to bet if you're a man you'll be crying from not being able to be with your Queen, whoever she may be.

You know what has been on the news on my radio here in Texas lately that is just about to drive me completely nuts? This whole critical race theory and how states are banning it. How stupid is that, really? God knows how many times I've had to sit here and listen to news outlets talk about critical race theory as if it's the new bogeyman for society because they are unwilling to acknowledge the country's racist history and how it impacts the present.

To understand why critical race theory has become such a flashpoint in our culture, it is important to understand what it is and what it is not. People fear that critical race theory admonishes all white people for being oppressors while classifying all black people as hopelessly oppressed victims. These fears have spurred schools and state legislation from Tennessee to Idaho to ban teachings about racism in classrooms. However, there is a fundamental problem: these narratives about critical race theory are gross exaggerations of the theoretical framework. The broad brush that is being applied to critical race theory is puzzling to academics, including some of the scholars who coined and advanced the framework.

Critical race theory does not attribute racism to white people as individuals or even to entire groups of people. Simply put, critical race theory states that U.S. social institutions (i.e., the criminal justice system, education system, labor market, housing market, and healthcare system) are laced with racism embedded in laws, regulations, rules, and the procedures that lead to differential outcomes by race. Sociologists and other scholars have noted that racism can exist without racists.

However, many Americans are not able to separate their individual identity as an American from the social institutions that govern us, and these people perceive themselves as the system. Consequently, they interpret calling social institutions racist as calling them racist personally. It speaks to how normative racial ideology is to American identity that some people just cannot separate the two.

There are also people who may recognize America's racist past but have bought into the false narrative that the U.S. is now an equitable Democracy. They are simply unwilling to remove the blind spot obscuring the fact that America is not great for everyone.

Scholars and activists who discuss critical race theory are not arguing that white people living now are to blame for what people did in the past. They are saying that white people living now have a moral responsibility to do something about how racism still impacts all of our lives today. Policies attempting to suffocate this much-needed national conversation are an obstacle to the pursuit of an equitable Democracy.

Supporters of critical race theory bans often quote Martin Luther King, Jr.'s proclamation that individuals should be viewed by the content of their character instead of the color of their skin, ignoring the context of the quote and the true meaning behind it!

One other thing that I would like to say that allowed me and my brothers in Christ to close out the day over here last night, Field Minister T. Solley came around with the two TVs that the people of Texas Prison Outreach have supplied our chaplaincy here at the Polunsky Unit/Death Row and showed us the movie "The Hulk" from 2008. I couldn't believe the graphics and how things have changed so much in the last few decades that I have been locked up in prison.

But when Bruce was with his girlfriend and they were on the run in New York City and that cab driver was driving all crazy, I'm like, hey! He's driving like the women I know out there in society right now, lol! You ever see my sister on the road, be sure to pull waaaay over to the side of the road on the next street!

Speaking of which, I was just talking the other day with my brothers over here on Death Watch about how my sister when we were all younger, though even then I was the outcast, our mom had this big screen TV that she had left behind while she was searching for a place to live down in Southern California. Two of my older siblings, Sean and Kristina (brother and sister) and I were home alone at their dad's house in Turlock, California at 1340 Darlarna Way. I had been playing that Nintendo game Duck Hunt with the game's gun and then my sister Kristina started playing for a bit and her brother Sean.

For some reason or another, Kristina left and returned with her pellet gun that she started pumping, and before you knew it, she was aiming it at the TV as her brother Sean played Duck Hunt. Thinking to herself that the gun was empty, she took aim and fired at the TV Duck Hunt game, and wouldn't you know it, a pellet came flying out and there is Kristina in all her glory scared to death about the hole she just shot in our mom's big screen TV.

She and her brother Sean did their best to try and cover it up. Boy, was I laughing my butt off at everything. She never got into much trouble if any, but what did I expect? Neither of my siblings could nor would get into trouble by their parents—that was passed down unto me…the black sheep of the family.

Even to this day you'll notice that I speak as though Sean is her sibling and not mine. That's because though I have forgiven my brother for turning his back on me for this whole time that I have been locked up in Texas and on Texas Death Row, he has also become dead to me, just as his and Kristina's older brother Greg. The only time either of them have thought to reach out to me was when I was first given that execution date back in 2010, and it was because they wanted to see me killed, though that isn't what they said. What they said was that they didn't want me to be alone when I was executed.

Crazy, isn't it, that they would say this and yet when that execution date was taken away without my knowledge or say so, they went on with their lives without so much as asking me one time if I needed anything or if they could do anything to help me while I'm here. Eighteen years and counting and not one word to me through a letter explaining or saying anything to me. I understand that they each have their own lives, but couldn't I at least hear something from them and maybe they could share with me about my nephews? Nope, nothing. I'm as dead to them as they are to me and though, like I said, I have forgiven them for turning their backs on me, I'll never seek them out ever again. Where they once had a place in my heart, now my Lord and Savior Jesus Christ fills that spot and many other places as the first love of my life while my mom is second then others fill places in my life.

My sister's siblings are just ignorant to things and they're afraid of themselves and the Lord, but I still pray that one day they both and their families come to honestly seek Him out and know Him before it's too late just as I pray for many other people daily and nightly in my life.

Today though, May 20th, 2022, started like all the rest, but those of us on Texas Death Row were in for a HUGE surprise! The people from the Texas Prison Outreach came through with fellowshipping with those of us on the faith-based sections of Texas Death Row which just happens to be sections B and C on A-Pod, though every one of us on A-Section, also known as Death Watch, are currently enrolled in the faith-based courses.

So, along with them and Chaplain Gay (pronounced Guy) and all the field ministers and the prison choir, they held for us all on these three sections a mini church service with singing and then we took a break as they passed out box lunches to all 33 of us prisoners that was provided by the Texas Prison Outreach brothers and sisters, along with a bottle of ice-cold water. Inside each box lunch was two chicken breasts, a biscuit so fluffy you thought it came straight from Heaven, a dish of coleslaw, and a cup of mashed potatoes with gravy.

After we all ate then we had more church service and some of the brothers from the Texas Prison Outreach shared testimony with us and the word of God, then we all sang some more and also sang the song "Way Maker." For those of you that don't know that song, here is how it goes:

"Way Maker"
You are here, moving in our midst.
I worship You. I worship You.
You are here, working in this place.
I worship You, I worship You.
Way maker. Miracle worker. Promise keeper.
Light in the darkness. My God, that is who You are.
Even when I can't see it, You're working.
Even when I can't feel it, You're working.
You never stop. You never stop (x2).
Way Maker. Miracle worker. Promise keeper.
Light in the darkness. My God, that is who You are.

Now, can you imagine that song being sung by 33 Texas Death Row prisoners who have renamed Texas Death Row to Texas Life Row because it is through Jesus Christ that each of us have found life! Oh yeah, I almost forget, in each of the box lunches there was also a Grandma's Cookies!

Nowhere else will you find prisoners that have come together as we have as a whole and worshipping the Lord and Savior from within the walls of prison, let alone those that society has condemned to Death. Warden Dickerson opened the doors and God walked through, and once He came inside, He's been working from the inside out in each and every one of us.

Before I end my writing for today, as it's been a super long day though a great one that I'm beyond thankful for, I'd like to leave you with these words: Time is against you. Gravity is against you. The system is against you. But if God be for you, He is more than the whole world against you!

In the book by Kevin and Hannah Salwen, Hannah pens one from Martin Luther King, Jr. that I would like to add in these pages too because I feel it's a good question by the King and that you should ask yourselves: "Every man must decide whether he will walk in the creative light of altruism or the darkness of destructive selfishness. This is the judgment. Life's persistent and most urgent question is, what are you doing for others?" – Martin Luther King, Jr.

You know, when I started writing this second book, I thought that I was doing so for myself as much as for each of you that now hold it in your hands reading these words, but the more I sit and think about it each day and night, I'm not so sure. I feel more and more like this is just something that God wants me to share with each of you, whether it be about how the Lord is and has worked in my life or how screwed up my life became before I came to fully know Him and understand His words and the Bible.

Deep down I feel this…urge…to clear the air about something that had to do with something from the past that was semi brought to my attention by my little niece. One of my family members was dating this man that had a history in his old life. This was when I was just starting to really understand God's law and the Holy Bible. But when I first found out that this person in my family was dating this man, I did what anyone who has a loved one they care about would do if they had the opportunity to do so. Before my little niece brought it to my attention and that of her mother too. No, they didn't tell me anything, but it was what they were hinting at that I already knew.

I had a full background check run on this individual and knew that he had a really messed up history and it was for something that in my old life and prisoners all around the United States and other countries more or less would have taken it upon themselves to cause great harm to this person just because he had it on his jacket (jail/prison records). When I found out about it, I had a choice to make. I could go about it as if I were my old self and still doing time in prison out in California, even though I was locked up in Texas here, or I could respect my loved one's life and give it to God to deal with.

I did the latter and in return I got crap from my niece and her mother, and it was then that because I did something that I normally would NOT have done, my relationship with both my niece and her mother have become like a gorge between the three of us to this very day. I stood up for the man because I felt that it was something done in his past and he did some jail time for it and had his own regrets about everything, plus it wasn't my place to judge him for his actions nor past, nor was it my little niece's and her mother's.

Stating as much to the two of them caused me to also in many ways lose them, though I think and feel that was just an excuse on their part because they were already starting to withdraw themselves from having as much to do with me while I sit here awaiting news from a court someday and whether or not that news will come with another execution date, one that I'm no longer looking for at this time, and yet, if I were to get one, I would accept it with a smile on my face.

Back to what my little niece and her mother did and how I felt. In their own way I felt that they were trying to get me to not like the guy or judge him or in some aspect turn against the family member that was dating him, and when I tried to point out that they shouldn't worry about the man's past because in truth they should look in the mirror; or if they really wanted to judge someone, why didn't they judge me? After all, am I not a convicted killer and in the eyes of society a monster that was not only convicted but sentenced to DEATH?

The problem is that when we accept Jesus or Yeshua into our lives we are to obey God's law to the T and not just try and explain things to others when what they are trying to explain is wrong. How much easier is it to explain to others than to put the law of God into practice? How are you doing in obeying God's law? Yeah, that's what I thought. It's not easy, is it? But you know something? I came super close to giving into my old self and the way I was taught in prison in California and lockup in Florida, but I'm thankful that I didn't because in the end the person in question couldn't keep to the path of good and ended up losing the relationship with one of my loved ones, and in turn he turned right around and acted like an ignorant child by toilet-papering their cars early in the morning.

When I heard about this, two things happened: I laughed aloud, and the flesh became weak because I started to see RED at this act against my loved ones. But through the grace of God, I was able to let it go and give it to Him, and this is what each of you must do in order to better yourselves to the point where you can have your own sense of peace of mind.

It's like my friend…she knows that life can be very difficult and people in our lives that are blood can be even downright rude and cold because they cannot understand how and why someone would fall in love with someone that was in prison or on Death Row in another state. Because I don't have her say so nor permission to talk and share about her own life, we'll call her Mrs. S.

Mrs. S. fell in love with someone in prison who was also on Death Row. At first their friendship was just that of pen-pals, but soon things heated up and they fell in love. Nothing wrong with that because God created us all in His image in the first place and the human heart wants to love and be loved, but when she made the announcement that she was going to be getting married to this man on Death Row, that loving family of hers split in all directions, even though they had been dating for a couple of years.

I feel deeply for my friend and her husband, who also happen to have a son together (wish that I was in the state 'cause I'd have me a kid or two too)! But it's just like family to judge others because they either don't approve or are ignorant of things. People in general are fast to judge others regardless of the fact that they should first judge themselves and stop.

Stop right there for a second. How many of you reading this book are religious and have your own relationship with God and His Son Jesus Christ or believe in Yeshua? Man, that's a lot, lol! Being the believers that you are, do you also believe everything that you read in the Bible, and do you follow it to the T and obey everything within its pages? Then you know that it's a fact that EVERY ONE OF THE LORD'S FOLLOWERS WAS AT ONE POINT IN TIME OR ANOTHER IN JAIL OR PRISON? THAT EACH AND EVERY ONE OF THEM WAS IN TROUBLE WITH THE LAW?

And yet, here we are over 2,000 years later and you're still following the Bible. So then, my question is to all those out there that are judging their loved ones for dating or marrying someone in prison or on Death Row because they're in prison for breaking the law of man.

Each and every person in society and even those inside prison walls should examine his/her self and their own motives instead of judging others. We often feel a perverse pleasure when we're able to bring someone else down, but often what the problem is, is that the very faults of others that we dislike are the very traits we dislike about ourselves. Our bad habits and behaviors are the very ones that we want to point out in others.

What about you? Do you find it easy to catalog other's faults while excusing your own? Criticism of others will lead to disdain for them and eventually will make you feel contempt for another person also created in God's image. If you're ready to criticize someone, you should go check and see if you deserve the same criticism. Always judge yourself first, and then after you've done this, then forgive the other person just as Christ Jesus forgave you!

Today is a new day for me just as it is a new day for many of you out there. For some it's a day of death and sadness, but we don't know about it because we're caught up in our own lives.

I laid in my bed last night and thought long and hard about something very few know about within these prison walls. I thought to myself, should I share with you something that happened years ago in the hopes that it will grab some of the younger crowd's attention to show them that just because you are reading within these pages about how I now have a deep love for the Lord and other people that I don't even know, like you out there reading this right now? Yes, even though I don't know you I have love for you.

Years ago, I lost someone very close to me, though he was locked up inside these walls with me. He and I were best friends and as close as two grown men can get and still call one another brother. He was housed/caged in the #14 cage, and I was at the time in the #13 cage. His name was Big Tai. Both of us were housed on 2-Row of this section called Death Watch. It's where those that have a set execution date are housed before they're driven to the Walls Unit in Huntsville, Texas to be killed in cold blood.

Each single-man cage has a built-in video camera that watches our every move 24/7 in numerous places. Only two of us that are housed on this section do NOT have set executions and are currently housed on this section under video camera because we're deemed a threat to the security and general population, though that is untrue and just gives them an excuse to house on this section, which also happens to be the section that all the big wigs walk around on when the directors from other units (prisons) and those that they are giving a tour to, to show what this place looks like and how we all act within its walls. We've had people from other countries do a walkthrough with the wardens and directors of the Texas Department of Criminal Justice, as well as politicians and their staff, and senators and their staff. This section is more or less the show-off section. Sometimes I feel as though I'm in a zoo and people are coming to see the animals within its holding cages.

The other day Billy Tracy called himself the Vanilla Gorilla and called Ramiro Gonzales a Little Baboon, while I've taken on the form and name of a Chimpanzee. If we could get the head warden or the directors to start charging a fee before entering, we could all make some serious money, but that is wishful thinking, lol!

Back to what I was saying about my friend/brother Big Tai and I. The year was 2017 and it was the month of April. Down on 1-Row directly below the two of us was this other prisoner named Steven Long. He is this white dude covered in tattoos and with no teeth whatsoever. When I first met Steve some 10 years earlier, he was always assaulting the female officers by throwing excrement and urine on them that he would place into a bottle and let sit for days before chunking it on them because he had a past where his own mother did things to him and gave him to her boyfriends to do sexual acts upon. Thus, as he grew older he came to hate women because they represented his mother. Which, when you stop and think about it, you could kind of understand why he was doing so but not always. Back then there were decent women that worked here, and he would chunk on them, and it wasn't only the disrespect he was doing upon them by hitting them in their faces and upper body with poop and urine that would not only get into their faces and eyes but their mouths too, but the smell was overpowering and would stink up the whole section and everyone that was living in their own cages on that section.

His other bad habit was that he would become intoxicated on prison wine (hooch). Back in April of 2017, he had an execution date along with my ndugu (Swahili for brother) Big Tai. Big Tai and I knew that it was a good possibility that the State was going to execute him this time around, so we had planned on celebrating his birthday early because he wouldn't be around for it. We cooked some food that we bought from the prison commissary, made a couple of our own bottles of drink to sip on and kick it while listening to some R&B music on the speaker of our radio and laugh and play a few games of Battleship and Hangman and we smoked one (joint). This was to be a great day between two friends to take into the memory. Only it didn't pan out the way we were wanting it to throughout the night. I mean, we laughed and did what we set out to do, but there is always someone around to screw things up, and this night would be no different from any other, or would it?

Steven Long, who was directly below us housed in #7 cage, is 100% white and is also only around 5'9-1/2" but his mouth is bigger than the rest of him. He had the bad habit, like I said, of becoming intoxicated on prison drink (hooch) and his way of thinking was that when he became this way it gave him the right to speak and get away with everything that he said to people, regardless of who they were or if he was in the wrong.

To have a full understanding you should know that Big Tai is 100% black and I am mixed with Jamaican and white. Big Tai was around 6'5-1/4" and 230 pounds and I am only around 6'2" and 190 pounds. Big Tai is from Brooklyn, New York and I'm from Northern California.

So, as we're enjoying this night between two friends/ndugus, Big Tai was the only person to know and call me by my street name in Florida which was Slim before I became known as Blue. It must have been around 2:45 in the morning when all of a sudden out of nowhere Steven Long screams up at the two of us from his cage on 1-Row #7 cage, "F--- you Big Tai, you f---ing nigger! And f--- you Blue! You half-a--, b--ch-a--nigger!"

If either one of us had any right to go smooth off on him for saying this, it was my ndugu Big Tai, and yet it wasn't him, it was I that went off. I have never been one for the racist crowd and I wouldn't ever be one that supported those who are so ignorant that they can walk around with a swastika tattoo somewhere on their bodies and not know the history of that very tattoo. You could have heard a pin drop on that side of the pod, it became so silent other than Steve still screaming obscenities at both Big Tai and myself because as we would later find out, though we already knew, Steve was drunk from the prison drink he made and had been drinking. Just because you have become intoxicated does NOT give you the right nor the okay to do as you please, nor does it give you a pass or excuse. NOTHING CAN EXCUSE YOU FOR BEING DISRESPECTFUL AND RACIST!

Remember that nobody likes an ugly person, and I mean the ugliness that flows forth from within your being. That ugliness that you speak comes directly from the heart and when someone is intoxicated or under the influence of anything, they cannot help themselves but show their true colors to come out and most of the time that will happen at the worst possible times. If you just have to drink something for whatever reason, please make sure that you do so with the sole intent of drinking to enjoy and not become overly drunk and mean.

Big Tai and I had drunk ourselves that night/morning but we had been doing so to enjoy and laugh and keep the volume down between the two of us in cages that were side by side. Right away, Big Tai told Steven Long that he could say that behind these steel doors, but then he turned right around and told him that that was his opinion and that he needed to shut his mouth now. I wish that I could have remained so calm like my ndugu, but I went off.

The next morning, or should I say that a few hours later, it was time for rec and the first round to the dayroom was Big Tai because they came around asking who was going to rec on 2-Row and Big Tai wanted to go first as he and I were the only ones on 2-Row as everyone else was on 1-Row. So, when the officers asked me first, I told them that Big Tai was asking to go first because he had a legal visit later that afternoon. Thus, Big Tai was the first round in A-Dayroom which is directly in front of all of our cages here on Death Watch.

It's a little after 6 a.m. and I get up and start talking to Big Tai while he's in the dayroom and then once again out of nowhere-ville, Steven Long tries to talk to Big Tai and Big Tai tells him to shut his mouth because he's not trying to hear anything he has to say. Steven walks away from his cage door to the back of his cage I assume because I can no longer hear him trying to talk to Big Tai. 'Bout time he took someone's advice.

After two hours in the dayroom, they switched Big Tai and me out in the dayroom. Big Tai can tell that I'm about to go off on someone, so he allows me to walk around for a while in the dayroom without the two of us speaking. I cannot help as I'm walking in this big cage thinking about how everything played out last night/this morning in the early morning hours, at which point I look over at cage #7 and Steven Long's cage.

Like some sixth sense, this fool comes to his door, and don't you know it…he tries talking to me to apologize but is falling over his own words because he's still drinking. Nope, I was nowhere close to being as calm as my ndugu. I told Steven to shut his mouth and don't say anything, not even to speak my freaking name ever again for nothing!

I can feel the beast inside of me and that animalistic desire wanting to come forth; and yet I fight it. As I'm battling within myself, the two officers that I had no idea were on the section because I was in another zone in my head, were asking guys starting in the cage I'm currently in #1 on down to #7 cage if they were going to take a shower. Every one of them until they got to #7 cage VR'd (verbally refused).

Cage #7 sits directly in front of the dayroom and though there is wire meshing on the bars directly in front of #7 cage, the bars to the side are open and someone could reach through them if they wanted to. Every time a prisoner comes out of his cage he is ordered to strip out by the officers before being allowed to get dressed and then place his hands through the food slot to be handcuffed behind his back. Once this is done, he is ordered to step out backwards when the cage door is opened and step into his shower shoes. The shower for 1-Row is right next to cage #7.

When the two officers who were what is also called OJTs (Officer Junior Training) asked Steven if he wanted a shower, Steven said no, but that he needed a razor to shave with. The only way to get a razor was to get one when you went to the shower, so he was told this even though he knew it.

In the end because he couldn't get them to give him a razor to shave in his cage, he stripped out and cuffed up behind his back. Getting ready to exit his cage by stepping backwards into his shower shoes that the two OJTs had placed outside his cage door for this purpose, the two officers and even Steven Long failed to pay attention to their surroundings. I was standing directly behind the two officers and directly in front of Steven Long's cage, though he couldn't see me because the two officers were blocking his view to the dayroom.

As the two officers holler for the control picket to open #7 cage's door, I'm now right up on the dayroom bars with my left arm outside of the bars hanging down loose. Once Steven's door is rolled open, he goes to step into his shower shoes backwards and what I was expecting him to do, this fool does. He stumbles back after missing his shoes because he's so drunk and it was so bad you could smell the drinking coming out of his pores. When he stumbled back, it brought him within reach and I wasted no time in snaking my left arm around his throat and pulling him to the bars, enough that I could snake my right arm, my dominant arm, through the bars and around his throat, thus letting go of him with my left.

As soon as I had him like this, I was able to lock my right arm's forearm flush against the underside of his throat and enough that I was able to also lock my hand onto the dayroom bars, thus getting him into a somewhat arm-bar hold. Wasting no time, I am now choking him to death while my legs are locked standing on the bars, thus lifting Steven Long off the ground as he is being choked for calling me and Big Tai a nigger.

The two OJTs are screaming at me to let him go but have yet to pull their cans of C.O.P. (Carry On Persons) chemical agents and use them against me. It wouldn't have bothered me because I could eat that stuff like it was hot sauce though it would burn a little if it got in my eyes.

Steven is now no longer struggling but started to look like my nickname, blue, lol! The only voice that was able to get through to me was Big Tai up on 2-Row screaming at me to let him go, Slim! Sliiim! Let him go, ndugu! Let him go, Slim! Think about your mom, Slim, and what it would do to her! Come on Slim, let him go, man!

Dropping my hold on him, he fell to the ground like a wet bag of cement before he was able to crawl away from the bars back into his cage. I had walked away from the bars myself and was now standing by the opposite side of the dayroom. Rank came onto the pod because the control picket officer called them to let everyone know that I was choking this fool to death from the dayroom.

When they showed up, I was removed from the dayroom and placed back into my cage on 2-Row. Disciplinary actions were talked about but would never come because security should have had two officers working the floor with both OJTs because the OJTs were alone which is against policy. They screwed up just as much as I screwed up but not as much as Steven Long screwed up.

Later on in the evening, Big Tai told me that I needed to forgive Steven Long and let God deal with it, otherwise He would not forgive me. Big Tai had me turn to the Book of Matthew 6:14; "If you forgive those who sin against you, your Heavenly Father will forgive you. But if you refuse to forgive others, your Father will not forgive your sins." (Matthew 6:14)

That night, even though I could hear what my ndugu was sharing with me, it just wasn't sinking into my heart because I was still upset at everything. Two weeks later, Steven Long would be granted a stay of execution and moved off this section called Death Watch and over to B-Section into #15 cage. This made me enraged even more because why would God give this disrespecting fool a stay of execution but not my friend?

So, I decided that Steven Long should feel the wrath that I was feeling at him using that N word and for him being given a stay of execution and thus moved from this section when I thought and felt that my friend should have been given a stay and moved instead of Steven Long.

A female officer that I got along with really well and the night shift lieutenant at the time that I was also friends with, would become my own personal tool. I could hear Steven Long over in B-Section once again intoxicated and screaming at others over there because he couldn't handle his drink and was shouting his true colors from his heart and out that foul mouth of his. So, when the female officer was making her rounds doing a security check and stopped at my cage on 2-Row A-Section, I asked her to do me a favor. I had her go into the control picket and contact the night shift lieutenant and explain to him that #15 cage was threatening her and that he should run a seven-man use of Force Team into #7 cage behind these threats. It was the only way I could have something done to this fool for what he said and how he was able to get away from his own date with death.

A little over an hour later here came the night shift lieutenant along with seven men suited up in their use of force gear. As the lieutenant made it over in front of #15 cage you could hear him falsely telling prisoner Steven Long to put down the blade or chemical agents would be used against him. Without waiting to hear him respond to this bogus order, the lieutenant released a full bottle of LE-10 chemical agents into Steven Long's cage and all over Steven Long.

Everyone could hear right away as Steven Long started screaming and asking them to stop the burning! It burns, please STOOOOP!! Did it stop? Oh, it stopped alright, just long enough for the control officer to roll open his cage door, thus allowing in the seven-man use of Force Team that ran right over Steven Long. That was about 1,000 pounds give or take against 140 pounds of racist, intoxicated fool. Steven Long was taken out of that section and off the pod on a gurney down to F-Pod.

Years later when Steven Long and I would once again cross paths, he would apologize to me and I would also apologize to him, and though we have both forgiven one another, we do not speak to one another, not even in passing for any reason. It wouldn't be until many years after the execution of my friend/ndugu Big Tai (may he rest in peace, Tai'Chin Preyor, executed July 27th, 2017) that I finally understood all those years before why he asked me to read Matthew 6:14. If we refuse to forgive others, God will refuse to forgive us. Why, you might be asking? The reason is that if we don't forgive others, we deny our common ground as a sinner in need of our Father's forgiveness and thus we break the family relationship with our Father God that He wants us to have with everyone in life.

Salvation of our sins is not based on forgiving others, but we will not receive God's own forgiveness until we realize what forgiveness really means. We can constantly ask God to forgive ourselves and the anger we hold against others who have sinned or we feel wronged us or someone we love and cared about or just our friends, but when we do ask Him for forgiveness for our own faults/sins, we need to first ask ourselves if we have forgiven those who have angered us or sinned against us.

Food for thought from me to each of you who finds him/herself struggling with things in general…" The ultimate purpose of life is to develop character. The more you depend on outside assistance to develop your character, the weaker you become. Strength of character comes from within…"

In the next chapter of this…book, I'm going to share with you many quotes made to me by officers, medical staff, and even the mailroom supervisor herself. Before we get there though, I'd like to ask that you think about something.

Do you believe that prisons are safe for the prisoners and those that work within them? I ask that question because I feel that some of you that are currently reading this believe that I have become a passive prisoner as well as those around me that I write about, and deeper down inside of ourselves there's need or tiny hunger for violence, though you don't want to admit this to yourself or those around you and those who know you. You think that my sitting here and typing all of this out to you is a sign of weakness.

Don't think you have any anger issues? What about that driver that cut you off the other day and you went off cursing him/her a blue streak or even, dare I say, gave them the middle finger? What would you call that if not anger issues? Now that I have pointed this out to you, stop mumbling under your breath about my writing. Stop acting like a hypocrite. I promise that before this book/writing is finished, I'll share with you some violence that will make you cringe. This I know because though I have done some serious things to others, I did so because I was ignorant and a dumb kid/adult at that time.

In truth, there is no excuse to cause another person to hurt in any way, shape, or form for any reason. I cannot stress that enough, and yet I don't want you to misunderstand anything I'm saying and think that by my saying it that it excuses the actions of those who did them because it does NOT!

As I end this chapter here, think on this: June 25th, 2021 marked the 60th anniversary of prayer being removed from schools. Since then, society now memorializes anniversaries of the killings taking place in the schools.

CHAPTER FIFTEEN

"VOICES FROM THE MEN AND WOMEN WHO WORK INSIDE THESE WALLS..."

For this next chapter, I have decided to ask some of the prison staff, such as the officers, medical staff, and even the mailroom supervisor what would be something that they would like to tell you about prison and why it's not the place to come to, though you will find one or two who shocked me with what they want you to know. For their own security, I have decided to only identify them through their initials. This way, whenever the head honchos that run the Texas Department of Criminal Justice read it (trust me, they will if I'm writing it) these officers and staff that trusted me to quote them will remain somewhat protected. I don't want them or anyone else to get into any kind of trouble for speaking with me.

So, with that said, allow me to share with you what some of them have said. Think of this part as being a voice from the other side, being that it's not from the animals but the keepers of the animals!

"What is something that you want society to know about prison and why you don't want to come to this place ever?"

"The food sucks and it's always cold and yucky." – C.L.

"It's not my place to judge you or anyone else in here. That is God's place, so I just try and treat each of you the same way or how I would want to be treated. For whatever reasons, you each did what you did and now you're paying for those actions. Other than that, this place, nor any prison, is not a place of fun and games. It's not a place to come to because your friends or you think it's cool, because it's not." – H.W.

"If I had to do prison time the way you guys have to do it, constantly locked down 23/7 and eating food that is often filled with roaches or other bugs in it and is cold instead of hot, there is NO WAY I would be able to last as long as you all have. Not being allowed to visit your family and friends except through glass. That is just plain crazy, I couldn't do this time like you guys on Texas Death Row." – J.L.

"This prison is only one out of many here in Texas. Texas has over 100 prisons throughout the state. That said, this is the only prison that I have seen change as a whole; however, other prisons are not like this one. You have to always be on point around both officers and inmates because either one or both can cause you to be shanked, regardless of the fact that officers working out in the general population of the prison also wear a little device in the shape of a white box with a button on their body somewhere. This is what's known as a 'panic button' which sends out a signal that an officer is in need of emergency assistance (being attacked). But that isn't going to save your life in prison and it's a false safe. Prison is not a good place to come to." – J.T.

This morning I asked an officer that I get along with really well what he would say to those in society about why prison is not the place to come to. And he shocked the heck out of me with this answer...

"Prison is changing, but if you want to screw your life up, then by all means come, come to prison, because by you coming here, I'll always have a job and a paycheck in my pocket. So, if you want to come to prison and put money in my pocket, then come!" – J.J.

As I was sitting here typing this all out, an officer was talking to my Brother Billy Tracy in #3 cage about his making a telephone call. He was being told that this sergeant that I speak about for running his mouth like a tough guy has been made an unofficial lieutenant! That is just plain crazy, like find-a-cockroach-in-your-food crazy! I asked the officer because I just couldn't help myself, what shift is he going to? Don't know, but it's going to be one of the night shifts and if he's on my shift, I'll stop working before I work for him as my lieutenant.

After the officer left, I told Billy that he wouldn't last one year as a lieutenant before they either took it from him or he gave it up. Yes, I'm speaking about you, LT.S. Dorman!

So, one thing I have been asked to bring to everyone's attention both inside these walls and outside of them is that the Polunsky Unit houses around 3,000 prisoners give or take. So, if each of us within its walls were getting a single letter or even a JPay letter printed out every day Monday through Friday, the days that mail runs inside prisons here in Texas, that is a LOT of work for the mailroom staff to do, not counting the numerous packages of books and other things coming into the prison from outside vendors.

When I first entered into Texas Death Row, the mailbag that was being delivered to each pod on 12-Building was huge! There are 84 single-man cages on each pod on 12-Building. This building houses Texas Death Row and now over the years as we started to be executed cages were becoming open, so TDCJ-ID started housing Ad-Seg prisoners on this building instead of just Death Row. But back then everyone was getting no less than between three to six letters plus magazines and newspapers and pictures from family and friends. So, do the math, people. Could you imagine the work that would be involved in sorting it out every day for 3,000 prisoners and how tiring it would become after a week of this?

Hey, hey, I'm not making this up and until recently you would never hear me siding with the mailroom, but you know what? God has not only worked in my life and continues to work in my life and through me and my fellow brothers, but I have come to seek and receive the mailroom's forgiveness and I even apologized to the mailroom supervisor, Mrs. Sumner. I get that her job is difficult and is at times beyond stressful. She understands too that we each would like our mail on time and our JPays from family or friends and whatever else we've been approved to have come in from an outside vendor, but fellas, and gals at the women's prisons, we as a whole need to be more understanding of the mailroom's jobs and what they go through each and every day to assist us.

Mrs. Sumner doesn't enjoy it when she has to come down here and deliver a denial form to us for books or certain pictures that you know might come across as offensive. She understands more than you think as I'm sure other mailroom staff throughout TDCJ-ID or in other states do but let us be less demanding and more understanding and patient, showing more appreciation and compassion towards those in the mailroom, knowing that in doing this we are helping to make things all around us run just that much smoother inside these walls and for those whose job it is to work here.

Do the math as there are less than a dozen people working in the mailroom at the Polunsky Unit, even though Mrs. Sumner has asked for three more people to be hired on and approved to work in the mailroom months ago, she's not been given the approval. Let's be patient, my brothers and sisters, and in time everything will turn out better.

Well, well, well, what do you know? A couple of officers working came around saying that Sgt. Dorman became a lieutenant and that is why I said what I did a few pages back. However, these officers not only lied once but twice because they just didn't want to give my Brother Billy his due telephone call.

So, after Sgt. S. Dorman came down here and hooked Billy up on his telephone call, I called him down to my cage to speak with him for a minute. I explained to him that I had written about him in previous chapters of this book about the time he was escorting me to the legal booth and running his mouth, but for some reason I wanted to see what he would say and if he would say anything about wanting to answer my questions about why you don't want to come to prison.

To say that he shocked me with his answer would be an understatement! However, as much as I would like to tell you what he said I cannot, but I will share with you what someone very close to him told me, and that is this…

"Life is a lot bigger than what you see and hear about that is going on around you right now. If you're a teen reading this book and the pages within that Tabler is writing, then you're thinking about the small things in your life and what is going on at school more than what is going on all around you. These guys in prison have no choices and the few that they do have don't really count. Right now, out there in society you have the freedom of choice. Inside prison you don't have this, you cannot even change the temp on your sink or shower water. You cannot decide what you want to eat for breakfast, lunch or dinner. You cannot go to a store and buy whatever it is you want. Sure, the guys here in prison might be able to order items through the prison commissary, but that is the extent to what they can decide and pick on their own. Life is so much bigger than what you're seeing and understanding. If you make one mistake, your life as you know it can be taken from you, and you could end up in prison. Life is so much more than what you know, so please think about things before acting on them because prison isn't a place to come to for any reason." – S.D.

Before I close out this chapter, some words to you… The more you fail, the greater your chance of succeeding. Failure is often the first necessary step toward success. And if you don't take the risk of failing, you don't get the chance to succeed. When you are trying, you are winning.

CHAPTER SIXTEEN

THE PRANKSTER AND THOSE WHO DO VIOLENCE

Do you know someone that is always playing pranks on another person, or maybe you're that person doing the pranks on those around you? Either way, just because I'm in prison that doesn't mean that everyone can get a free pass, nor the fact that I have a deeper and loving relationship with God means that I too cannot have some fun at the other's expense.

Though I'm not alone in thinking this, as many of the fellas here with me on Texas Death Row/Texas Life Row have played a prank or two on someone else, most of the times though, and I say most of the times, but you need to understand that sometimes it will backfire on you if you read the other person wrong. Oh yeah, just because I've been sentence to death also doesn't mean that the officers and other prison staff that works here gets a free pass either. What? They're not special! It's a dog-eat-dog world, people, lol!

So, I have some seriously funny stories to share with you in this chapter and one of them just took place this evening, May 22nd, 2022 at 5:45 p.m.; but I'll save that one for last because I'm still laughing inside as are RG and the male officer in the control picket. I guess he would laugh because years ago I got him about the same way, and he said he nearly pissed himself because he wasn't expecting it.

And while it's all fun and games, sometimes it doesn't pan out how I thought it would nor the way anyone else that has done something like this and when I get closer to the part about those who do violence, this I speak about to raise your awareness and to show you my point that prison can be a deadly place for those sent here and those who work within prison walls.

Life out there is like in here, how you treat someone is how you'll be treated in return, though nowadays out there in society if you mistreat someone or anger someone, you're liable to find yourself shot, at which point you may never have to worry about anything ever again. So, always think before you act, and if you can just allow whatever someone said to roll off your back like it's no big deal, then that is all the better. Just because you're young doesn't mean you're the only ones that can be scared. Even adults that have some serious years under their belts can be scared to the point they need to check their underwear!

Back around the year 2017 and right before the execution of my best friend Big Tai, Texas had a major thunderstorm that ended up causing the power to blow out here at the prison right around shift change at 5:30 a.m. When the power went out this time, for some reason nobody knows the backup generators didn't kick in and turn the lights on inside the prison. So, all of the lights in the cells and on the pods were out and it was pitch black inside the prison 12-Building.

This was right before Big Tai moved onto A-Section with his execution date and I hadn't yet moved to #13 cage but was still in #14 cage. Officer Littleton was working on the run while some officer whose name I cannot remember was working in the control picket. I could see Officer Littleton, who is a young black woman, walking around with her flashlight and trying to talk to herself in a brave voice while she was walking around telling everyone that it was special count due to the power being out.

As soon as the power went out, I had woken up from a dead sleep and as I came to my cage door, I could see Officer Littleton walking up the stairs to 2-Row. My cage is blacked out with the back window also covered up, so it's extra dark with no light coming in from the outside security lights surrounding the prison, though they were out too.

When Officer Littleton was about 10 feet from my door, I ducked down below my cage door's mesh windows until I could see by looking up that Officer Littleton was right at my door. Just as she started to shine her flashlight into my cage and knock on my door, I popped up from below and smacked my steel door yelling out BOOO! Everyone was at the door when they heard Officer Littleton scream sooo freaking loud and drop her flashlight! I'm laughing so hard I'm now back on the floor of my cage holding my sides as tears run down my face. As she's trying to put on a brave face, I couldn't help but tell her that she screamed like a white girl! To this very day she talks crap to me, and I always remind her that she is an undercover white girl inside.
   When that happened all those years ago, guys that were housed on the other side of this pod said that they could hear her scream, it was that loud. Oh no, I didn't just go after women like this once I felt they were relaxed enough. I got some of the men and even some of the ranking officers and I got one male officer so bad that after he was done yelling he turned right around and emptied his can of chemical agents into my face and I laughed all the harder, which just made this dude start laughing because after he gassed me it finally dawned on him who had scared the crap out of him (friends).
   He started apologizing and I said don't worry about it. He's no longer here but his name was Officer Spencer. This fool was funny as hell, and he was also one of the most laid-back officers working Death Row back then. Last I heard he was working at the Dunkin Unit.
   Another time I was still being isolated alone on B-Section of this pod and they had decided that they would start allowing me to rec in the dayroom alone on B-Section only, but nobody else could use that section for rec.
   While I was in the dayroom they moved my friend Lizard into #19 cage on the section with me, thus making us the only two housed on that section. He had just had a major use of force about a week before and they decided to move him and isolate him on the section with me now. Both of our cages over there had video cameras built into the stainless steel above our toilets that could view the whole cage, so they no longer felt the need to have me on one-on-one anymore as it had been two years and some change that I had been isolated alone on a 14-man section with video camera and officer sitting on me 24 hours a day.

While I was in the dayroom, they started feeding the whole pod as the chow cart was now on the pod. When the chow carts come onto the pod, they come with this metal tray carrier that holds seven trays that the officers then carry to each section to feed the prisoners. This carrier weighs about 10 pounds give or take without all of the trays. Just before they start feeding C-Section they rack me up and ask Lizard if he wants to eat first or go out now to the dayroom? He told them to put him out now that he didn't want a tray.

Lizard and I had been friends for a long time and just like friends we had our own falling out before hooking back up into the friendship mode. While he's in the dayroom he is bringing me up to speed on everything that he's been doing lately, at which point I say, well you're here now so why don't we have some fun?

Looking around as we're talking, me up on 2-Row in #26 cage and he down in the dayroom some 30 feet or so from me, I tell him hey, why don't you grab the tray carrier and hang it from the bars at the top since they're done feeding now and not around?

The top of the dayroom bars goes up to the ceiling about 30 feet or so up. Lizard says, shoot me something to tie it off up there with. Getting my fishing line out and my pole I shoot my line out to the dayroom with some more line on it for him to take off and use. Climbing down off the bars he goes over to the other side of the dayroom by where the chow cart is and reaches out and grabs hold of the tray carrier. I playing lookout, I tell him, GO!

Climbing one-handed is no easy task while carrying this thing up the bars, but he makes it and sure enough he's able to tie this tray carrier off by its handle at the top of the bars. Days turn into weeks and nobody notices this thing hanging from the top of the bars like that until they do and it couldn't have been the more wrong person.

Three weeks had gone by when a tour is walking around the pod with wardens and directors and people from State offices and their staff. Lizard and I had been standing at the door talking when they came through the crossover door from C-Section on 2-Row. You could hear them talking until all you hear is," What the hell is that thing doing up there? What the hell is that? Is that a freaking tray carrier? Tabler! Tabler, I know you're up here on 2-Row, what the hell is that thing hanging from the bars up there?!"

"Where at, Warden? I don't see nothing, you know I'm blind right, Warden? Where you lookin' at, sir."

"Cut the crap, Tabler. I'm talking about that tray carrier up at the top of the bars, Tabler!"

"But, sir, I thought you said you didn't know what it was?"

"And Tabler, I thought you said you were blind! Busted."

Next thing you know here comes a sergeant to climb the bars and cut this thing down, and when he does, it drops straight down and pancakes upon itself. Lizard and I split the cost of that one, $78.50 out of our inmate accounts for property damage. But it was worth it now that I look back on the memory, and I'm laughing like crazy now too!

So you can have a better understanding of what I mean when I say that I sent my fishing line to the dayroom or someone shot their line to me down the run, a fishing line is made from either spun/twisted/or braided line that is strong enough to lift a six-pack off the ground and into the air and over a railing if need be. The poles or sliders are made from rolled up magazine paper so tight that they feel like a fishing pole. These lines and poles can be shot out one's prison door from 2-Row and down onto 1-Row by shooting out over the railing. Once your line is down and over the railing, if you know how to shoot it out far enough, then you can pop it back and it'll slide into one of the cages down on 1-Row or into a spot so your friend can shoot his line over your line and pull your line in with the hooks he has on either his pole or the ones you have on yours.

By using these lines, we are able to traffic and trade things such as books, magazines, bagged up food such as tacos that we cook for one another, and we can play pranks on others and even the officers that go out of their way to make it hard on us. Oooohhh yeah, those are some of the best ones to prank.

One day back in 2007 on F-Pod both Lizard and I were housed on F-Section, it must have been a good six or so months after I got here and had started to relax and learn things. Lizard was in F-dayroom, and I was housed up in #82 cage on 2-Row. Someone from over in Ad-Seg had shot me a kite (note) under the doors from the other side of the pod. Back then Ad-Seg was mixed on the same pods with Death Row though on separate sections.

One such Ad-Seg inmate who is like a little brother to me and has some 100+ years to serve in prison was housed down on F-Pod at the time. His name is Terry M. He's this short little white dude with glasses and loves to paint elephants of all things, but he hasn't always been so mellow and used to always be into trouble for one thing or another. So, he's the one that was sending me a kite, and when it got over to the section, Lizard hollered at me, "Blue! You have one time in the dayroom. Shoot your line!"

So, I get my line out and kick it down the run to the dayroom and Lizard gets it and ties the kite on and I pull it in. Just as I get the line in, what does Lizard do? He ties my damn line off onto the dayroom bars so I cannot pull it back! Come on, Lizard! Let go my line, fool! Sure enough, he does so too late and the officer doing his security check walks through and cuts my line before pulling it in from the dayroom along with my pole! Lizard is laughing and I tell him it's on now!

Lizard used to braid his lines out of the Red Chain bags that officers give us to pack our property in when we're moving. These lines are super strong and take a really looooong time to braid together.

A few months go by and I'm in E-Dayroom and Lizard is over in his cage in #79 on F-Section 2-Row, but nobody is in the dayroom in F-Section. So, he yells over to me in E-dayroom letting me know he's got one time going to Billy Mason in D-Section #55 cage and he's coming under the door. I yell back, shoot it!

Climbing up the bars in E-Section dayroom by the pullup bar, I stand on the pullup bar waiting for him to shoot his line under the door so I can pull it to me and the kite that he's sending. He yells, go ahead. I said, did you just call me a goat head? He said, pull, idiot! I said, go ahead (we would clown like this). Pulling his line and grabbing the kite off, I climb down off the bars but not before tying his line off at the bottom of the bars in the dayroom! That fool was pissed 'cause he had to cut his own line, but I told him it was on when he tied mine!

There was another day when we were both housed here on A-Section Death Watch because he had been given an execution date for February 4th, 2015. I was housed at this time in #14 cage and Lizard was in #3 cage at this time. The officers were serving lunch trays and it was pizza which they hardly ever serve us here. I yelled down to Lizard and said, hey Lizard! You want an extra tray?! He yells back at me, shoot it! I said, okey-dokey.

When the officer came to my door to feed me, I reached out and took the tray and gave him back an empty tray from breakfast and asked him to give this to Lizard in #3 cage! The officer is trying to keep the grin off his face as he takes this tray down to Lizard, placing it in his box. Lizard grabs it thinking he's got an extra pizza tray only to find out he has NOTHING BUT AN EXTRA TRAY, lol! Ever since then he would always make sure if I asked him if he wanted another tray if there was food on it. The pranks were great back then and always back and forth. May my friend rest in peace! (Donald Keith Newbury, executed February 4th, 2015).

Years before I got here, the guys here on Texas Death Row took things further with the officers that would get out there with them, as told to me by many. There have been times when an officer was working the pods that they would come through slamming the crossover doors throughout the days and nights, or when the guys were running line (fishing lines) the officer would come through and cut it or grab it up, even going as far as running to catch a line and whatever was tied onto it, then turning around and writing them up a disciplinary case for traffic and trading and for contraband (the lines). So, as told to me after I got here in 2007 by Lizard and Billy Mason and even Big Tai and Sarge (Cleve Foster, executed September 25th, 2012).

One day Lizard was in the dayroom down on F-Pod and Billy Mason at this time was housed somewhere on E-Section 2-Row. They were planning on getting the male officer that was always going out of his way to write guys up for anything. This day though would be a different one for him and costly.

Billy had shot his line over the railing and towards the dayroom, enough so that Lizard could grab it up. When the crossover doors had popped open letting them know he was walking around, Lizard tied onto Billy's line a brown paper bag that was old and barely hanging together. Had one looked closer though they would have noticed that the line was also old and grayed. Inside the paper bag was a plastic bag with something inside it.

Billy's pulling the line up until Lizard tells him to hold it right there and pop it a little so it's swinging back and forth. Everyone is in on what is fixing to happen. As Billy is popping the line about 6-1/2 feet off the ground, the officer walks through the crossover door, sees the bag, and runs to grab it. Lizard being a good actor yells at Billy, "Hurry up, Billy, he's running after it, pull it up!" Billy screams back the line is stuck on the railing!

Next thing you hear is the officer screaming, "I got you, you motherfu---!" before grabbing the paper bag off the line and part of the line. Walking off the section with his prize, they watch as this fool tosses the bag like a great prize up in the air to catch it, but when he goes to catch it on the downfall, he smacks the bag in a tight grip, thus busting the bag and what it holds inside.

There is a moment of dead silence and then the officer is screaming bloody murder and throwing up 'cause he has excrement running all over his chest and face area! Word was after that incident that officer never rushed to grab another line or cause any problems on the Death Row pod when he was working.

When that story was told to me, I laughed so hard tears were coming down my face because I couldn't help myself at thinking the officer deserved it 'cause he brought it upon himself. That brings me to another subject and one that many officers working within prison begin to forget or simply put, don't think about because they no longer care until after the fact. I'm not saying that everyone in prison is bad or evil because nobody here is the same as the next man or woman standing next to them, just like no two people were created the same. Each person, whether inside these walls or outside there in society, always brings things upon themselves. If something happened to them, it was more or less because they said something to the wrong person or offended someone that they shouldn't have. Someone else was having a bad day and you cut them off while driving. Next thing you know, you're in the middle of some serious road rage that you never saw coming, etc.

Well, inside prison you have all kinds of people, and you have what some call the two kinds of prey or pray, meaning that some of the people inside prison walls are the kind that fight and take serious action while others are not that kind but because they lack the courage to do anything for themselves, they become the prey that those with the mentality of a predator will seek out. It matters not if you're a prisoner or an officer in some cases.

Officers have the tendency, though not all of them are like this, but they have the tendency to talk crap to a prisoner that is locked behind a steel door or is out of his/her cage and is being escorted somewhere in handcuffs and/or leg irons. Some will go so far out of their way to even write up a bogus disciplinary case to get the prisoner into trouble.

Whenever someone is written up a disciplinary case, most times it's a major case which can cause the prisoner to lose his level-1 property (i.e., his electronics; hardback books; commissary; and also be placed on no visitation for the ninety days (90) he's on level but once a month. No rec except for once a week), so things can become extreme and all behind an officer writing up a bogus case because they don't like prisoners, or they think it's funny. Also, some of them don't realize that a lot of the prisoners in the general population have an out date, so any infraction such as a disciplinary case can cause their date of release to be pushed back further.

Yesterday, I was asked if I wanted a haircut, which was the first time for around five months because things have been so messed up with COVID-19, plus we have been on lockdown behind that escaped prisoner who they still have not found. When I told Sgt. Grisby that I wanted a haircut, he and another officer pulled me out and escorted me to the dayroom where the barber was set up to cut hair (another prisoner) that his job is cutting hair out in the general population.

As I take a seat on the chair that has been provided for this, the barber asks what I want done and I tell him to do whatever he wants to do. As he's cutting my hair, the sergeant and I are talking about how much things have changed around here in the last five or six years. Both the barber and the other female officer are listening to us speak. When I say that it used to be rock and roll around here, the female officer looked at the sergeant with a doubtful look that I caught. I told her seriously, it used to be bad here, in fact I can name an officer or four that no longer work here but one that stands out is this female officer that did property and would go out of her way to write bogus disciplinary cases on everyone. Heck, she wrote me up a bogus case and though I beat it, I still got screwed over for it.

After I told the officer this, I looked at Sgt. Grisby and said, tell her about ol' property officer Whitesel. When I said her name, he said to me, that was what, about five, six years ago? I said, something around there, but tell her so she knows what I'm talking about, please.

He goes to tell this young officer about Officer Whitesel, who was a dirty-blond, white woman about 46 years old and a little overweight. She had the bad habit of writing bogus cases against prisoners. One day she was out in the general population working and showing some OJTs (Officer Junior Training) around when two prisoners entered into the building she was in. Seeing the two prisoners, she got this sense that something was wrong but didn't know what it was. However, she had enough sense to tell the two OJTs to go enter into that empty cell and close the door. As soon as the two OJTs did this, the two prisoners were on Officer Whitesel and they beat the living hell out of her, to within an inch of her life!

When they life-flighted her to the emergency room from the prison and removed her clothing to save her life, she had boot prints and treads from those boots on her face and chest area. Come to find out these two prisoners had been written up a bogus disciplinary case by Officer Whitesel which caused their release dates to be pushed back by years.

After Whitesel got out of the ICU many months later, she never returned to work here at the prison because she was scared for her life.

Now, I don't condone someone beating up a woman for any reason, nor laying their hands on one, but a lot of prisoners here don't believe the same things as I do, and yet I understand why they did what they did to her, and she cannot blame anyone other than herself for what happened because she was a dirty officer that screwed prisoners over. But did she deserve to be beaten like this? No. Officers forget sometimes where they're working or they get it in their heads that because they are now wearing a uniform that nothing will happen to them, but they couldn't be more wrong. By wearing the uniform, they're placing a HUGE TARGET ON THEIR BACKS!

A lot of prisoners in other prisons cannot stand officers just like many people cannot stand the police. They come back onto Death Row and Ad-Seg and talk crap to us because they think they can get away with it because we're all locked up behind steel doors, then they turn around and are ordered to work out in the general population, and here they forget that these prisoners are not locked up but walking freely among all the staff and officers that are working inside the prison. Here they say something that they got away with back here on 12-Building but find out they have nowhere to run out there in general population!

It's not always prisoners against officers or vice versa either, but prisoner against prisoner even here on 12-Building. There have been numerous Death Row prisoners shooting spears out their cage doors and into another Death Row prisoner. I myself have tried to spear another prisoner, only to miss him and take a chip of concrete wall. But these last five years a lot has changed, and things have cooled down greatly. Most if not all prisoners have decided that they don't want this kid of life and want to go home or want to become something better than what they were when they came to prison, and most of us have finally found God and He is working from the inside out.

Like I said, not all officers are bad apples. There was this one lieutenant that worked here back in 2009-10 though he worked as an officer longer than that. He was one of the few back then that was a man of God, but he didn't shove the Bible and God's word down anyone's throat.

When I was in total isolation over in B-Section #26 cage, this one lieutenant who when he was working on shift would be the one to come and feed me either a hot try (cold) or a food-loaf because I was once again being punished for something. His name was LT. Hiens. He would come into the section and tell his officers that were assigned to sit in front of my cage 24/7 that he would watch me and for them to go take their breaks each day.

After they left, he would tell me to cuff up which I would do and then he would have my cage door opened by himself. I would sit on my bunk with my legs crossed over at the ankles and he would sit on my toilet, and we would talk as two human beings would talk. He would teach me a little about the word of God and his own faith and would let me know that he knew that everything that was going on with my being isolated wasn't entirely true and that the way they were doing me was wrong.

Here was a man in the uniform of a correctional officer and a lieutenant and he was treating me as if I was a friend or brother or his own kid with…compassion. Every day he worked he would do this with me before he was transferred to the Hightower Unit and made captain, but by now I don't know what rank he holds, but I know last time I checked he was a major and he has since moved up from that position by now. Wherever he is, I wish him the very best in life always and may his family be richly blessed by God Himself.

Before I end this chapter as well, let me share with you what happened last night on May 22nd, 2022 at 5:45 p.m. Officer C. Price and Officer Fisher were working on this pod. I had just finished working on this manuscript and put away my typewriter when I heard the gate coming into the section pop. Getting up from sitting on my bunk I walked to my door to see who was working this coming shift and who was entering to make a security check around the whole pod. I saw that it was this 21-year-old female officer named Fisher.

As soon as I saw her I thought to myself, Tabler, it's time to get her like all the rest. So, before she saw me at my door, I squatted down below my door until I could make out that she was directly in front of my door and getting ready to shine her flashlight into my cage to check on me. The timing couldn't have been any better as I popped up and slapped my door and yelled BOOOO! The look on her face was that of a deer in the headlights and the scream she let rip was out of a horror film. She not only screamed but jumped a good foot into the air and her flashlight she kept hold of, but the light was shaking all over the freaking place.

After she stopped screaming and shaking, I asked her, you okay, lol? She couldn't speak and slowly walked away down to the crossover door, but I heard RG ask her, "Did you pee yourself?!" as he continued to laugh along with the others on this section. Fisher's response to him about peeing herself was, "I don't know but I'm going to check later!"

About 45 minutes later she and I were talking again, and she was now smiling because she found out from Officer C. Price in the picket that I used to get everyone this way, kind of like an initiation process, and after he said that he too laughed at her being scared like that. She was a real Trouper about it and when her boyfriend came down to the pod to let her know he was going home early, I told him about it, and he too laughed all the harder.

CHAPTER SEVENTEEN

FAMILY

What do you think of when someone asks you about family? In the dictionary the word family falls under many definitions. Here is what my Webster Dictionary says about the word family: 1) a group of individuals living under one roof and under one household, 2) a group of persons of common ancestry; clan, 3) a group of things having common characteristics, a group of related plants or animals ranking in biological classification above a genus and below an order, 3) a social unit consisting of one or two parents and their children. This is what the word family means in the dictionary.

When someone is in prison or on Death Row and he/she is writing about their family inside these walls, one would never think that he could be talking about those he's doing time with as being his family. And before a few months ago I never would have told you that the guys housed in this section with me right now are my family, that I love and care about each one of them, and until recently I didn't realize that this is how I thought of my best friend Big Tai and how he thought of me.

You may or may not have family members that are a part of your life right now. It could be that you only have yourself and a friend or two and to you these people are your family. Family doesn't have to be those that are born into your life from the same parents as you can read in the dictionary. Thus, they don't have to be your blood, and yet you can have a strong bond with them and this need and strong feeling to want something better for them and for yourself.

This morning I woke up with this sense of such strong bonding with my brothers here on Texas Death Row's Death Watch Section that I started thinking what could I do to help them or make sure that when the time comes for them to take their own walk, a walk they won't return from, to make sure that you and others out there in society stop looking inside the box and start looking outside of it too.

You people have no idea the pain that I have endured at having to watch so many men walk from this section, knowing there wasn't a single thing I could do to change what the end results would be or how to stop the pain.

Some of the staff that work here at the Polunsky Unit prison in Livingston, Texas in the medical department feel that I suffer from what is known as survivor's guilt, but I think it's much more than that, only I don't know how to explain it in the right words or thoughts that reside deep inside myself.

Before I get into why I brought this subject up and the title of this chapter, I would like to ask that you sit and think about something for a few minutes, please.

Imagine being in a cage that is no bigger than that of a dog run/kennel that is enclosed all the way around it so that you receive no fresh air and that the only means of air is an air vent that can be shut off at the flick of a switch. Can you picture this in your head? Now picture yourself or someone you love and care about with snot running out of their nose and tears pouring down their face that they are unable to control.

What would you do to help someone you knew that was going through this or they had come into contact with something that would cause their pain receptors in their bodies to redline in their mouth, nose, stomach, and mucus membrane, but it could also incapacitate the esophagus, trachea, respiratory tract, and eye muscles?

Could you imagine this either happening to someone you know or someone you love and there was nothing you could do to stop their pain? Could you go through it? Yeah, I didn't think so, it takes someone that is able to completely shut off their feelings of everything to take being gassed with chemical agents inside of the Texas prisons and where Texas Death Row is.

This chemical agent is also known as an OC which stands for oleoresin capsicum. This is a blend of about 300 varieties of pepper plants and is only one of many chemical agents that can be and often are utilized against prisoners on Texas Death Row and Texas prisons and many prisons throughout the United States of America.

What about this, do you have a family pet that has been with your family for years upon years that you've grown attached to? You notice that your pet is becoming sicker and sicker or is pooping on his/herself or can no longer see and you know it's now time to have it put down. So, you get the family ready to say goodbye to Fido. Your kids and other family members are crying because this is painful for them just as it is for you, no doubt.

Then it's time to take that final drive to the veterinarian, and you think while you're driving there that this family member, even though it's a pet, it's also become a part of the family, you think that it's not going to feel anything because the veterinarian knows what they're doing, right? It's just a needle and a cocktail and he/she will go to sleep and that will be the end of it, right? Or will it? Is that it? I mean, what about all the memories that you have and that your family members and children have?

This is how you feel about a pet. It's a great feeling, right, to know that this animal loved you and your family members just so much, and it really sucked having to let go and have the animal put down so it would no longer be suffering, correct?

So, let's step it up another level. We know what you would do for a family pet as I have been there before too and many families throughout the world have been there and it sucks, no question about that, but it's a part of life, right?

Now you have before you a human being, something that was created in God's image, and yet is smart enough to know between right and wrong. We as human beings have intelligence, and we are able to evolve and grow and learn more so than an animal. Now, I ask you to picture this. Are you ready for this? Are you sure? Let's see…

Texas Death Row prisoners are now taken for their own drive in a van for about 60 miles from the Polunsky Unit Prison in Livingston, Texas to the Walls Unit in Huntsville, Texas. This is where the execution chamber is and this is where my friends and brothers have been driven to walk on their own strength and lay upon a cold metal gurney or bed, allowing correctional officers to strap them down and some hidden doctor to place an IV into their arms so that a drug called pentobarbital will be pumped throughout their bodies until they too are DEAD. People say that you don't feel anything, but how do they know unless we test it out first on the doctors? I mean, this sounds like a great idea, right? Everything should be tested before given the green light to use and what better way than to test it on those who say it not only works but it's not painful either?

It used to be that we would be killed with a three-drug cocktail that was designed to sedate us and render us unconscious, theoretically reducing the pain, but how did they know it would work? These drugs were sodium thiopental, pancuronium bromide, and potassium chloride. Now, I can seriously understand why society feels the need to kill/murder, or as they like to call it, execute someone for breaking the laws and taking the life of another. This is in their eyes a just punishment, right? If there is enough evidence to show that someone is guilty of such a crime and a jury decides that someone should be sentenced to death, thus a life for a life.

But why should the condemned have to wait decades before their punishment is carried out? Waiting this long changes thing because you're no longer killing the man/woman that you were sentenced to death a decade or two decades earlier for. How can it be the same person? Are you still with me?

Now, think about this. What should be done when an innocent human being is killed by this so-called system? Isn't the life of one innocent one life too much? How many hundreds of lives have been executed throughout the United States of America because District Attorneys and later on Attorney Generals withheld evidence that should and proved without a doubt that the man/woman that was before the court and the jury really was NOT the one and this person was NOT guilty, but the District Attorney and later the Attorney General continued to hide this evidence by breaking the same laws they were to uphold in that courtroom with people such as yourself?

The cap on money to be paid to innocent people is at $250,000 per year, but what about the guys and gals that were put to death and later found to be innocent? How do you pay the dead? Can either one of you bring someone back to life after you have killed them through this so-called legal system? After you pumped this cocktail through their bloodstream and into their heart? Would this not consist of what is known as the Color of Law? This is conduct based upon what appears to be a legal right or enforcement of statute, but in reality is a violation of law.

    This morning as I was thinking about bringing this topic up to you and everyone else, I came to my cage door and asked my Brother Billy Tracy two cages over from me what the statute of limitations was on murder. I knew what it I was, but each state is different, and I wanted to doublecheck. Know what he told me? There is NO state in the United States of America that has a statute of limitations on murder. This means that if you kill someone, there is no set amount of time that charges may be brought against you once enough evidence is found and can show without a doubt that this person is responsible for the death of so-and-so.

    So, knowing this, I bet if the District Attorneys and the Attorney Generals of society and every state in the United States of America decided to place into effect a new law that would hold those who purposely set out to withhold evidence in a capital murder trial from the court and jury and those in society, that cost in the end the life or lives of men and women that were found guilty under the holding of such evidence, that those individuals should be charged with capital murder instead of just being given a slap on the hands as they are now doing!

    In my eyes this is also known as premeditated murder because they not only withheld evidence, but they took the steps and planned such a violation of law out and then they carried it out in a way that was controlling.

    The system is broken and will always remain broken because society and the courts have lost sight of what it means to be tried fair and just. When you place into authority those who are willing to do what they can to get a conviction by any means necessary, especially in a trial that has capital punishment on the table and a human life on the line, then you become the problem and you should be held accountable for those actions just as those of us in prison and on Death Row should be held accountable, and not with only a slap on the hand or the loss of your job.

    After all, the person or persons that they are responsible for getting the State to kill knowing that they were innocent cannot get a second chance at life because there is no do-over when it comes to capital punishment and the murder chamber of Texas also known as Texas Death

Row. Friedrich Nietzsche said it best… "If you gaze long enough into an abyss, the abyss will gaze back into you."

Prison can do things to one's mind because of the things that one is sometimes forced to be a part of and do. Your family and friends outside prison walls cannot begin to understand something that they have never had to deal with on their own. Thus, because of their lack of wanting to understand the horrors that can take place in prison, they choose to believe things about prison from what stories they see on shows on their TVs or maybe some movie, thinking that it cannot be that bad. This in some ways allows them to continue to go on with their lives and forget about you and what you are going through with the mindset that is out of sight, out of mind.

You cannot blame them for doing this even when it's so hard to accept. You need to let go and let that family, the family you were born into by birth, you need to let them go and live their lives and pray for them and hope that they have a great life. You need to be understanding in the ways that they were not able to be for you.

When you're inside and looking at serious time such as a life sentence without the possibility of parole or in such cases as my own, you got to cut that tie somehow, someway because it's not fair to them. That's why it was so hard on me recently to cut the ties of my little friend and lawyer/investigator Cassandra.

It no longer matters if the bridge between she and I can be rebuilt because she's shown me that I cannot trust her and as she doesn't respect me, I will never respect her like I had at one time. This is just a fact of life. Being inside, you come to depend more than you should on those who step into your life from outside. People that you allow under your skin to become friends are the ones that can and will hurt you the most in the end when they decide to. It doesn't matter at this point who was in the wrong or what started it because I had tried over and over to make amends only to receive silence in return.

One thing that I have never shared with anyone other than my brother and friend Mac in California, also known as Carl Skinner who's serving life without for murder 1, is that when you're in prison you want to find something or someone that can help anchor you to something good and positive out there in society.

When I was locked up in California, I did things not because I wanted to, well not really, lol, but because I wanted to survive/live. Prison isn't a nice place regardless of what some lawyers and other people think or say. CDC (California Department of Corrections) has some seriously HARD PRISONS! Prisons that can and often do break even the toughest, and it's not always the prisoners that are at one another's throats but the officers.

So, after living through violence that your favorite TV show or DVD movie might show which has nothing close to what it's really like in places such as Pelican Bay State Prison, Correctional Training Facility Soledad State Prison, Duel Vocational Institution (Gladiator School), Old Folsom State Prison, CMC-East, CMC-West, Salinas State Prison, these are just to give you an idea of the hard prisons I have been in in my time inside prisons in California among others.

When I came to Texas and became convicted and locked up for my actions/crimes, I had nobody other than my sister, niece, and mom for a bit, and over time and the years my sister and niece would separate themselves further and further because they have their own lives to live. My mom is still riding with her baby boy, but I know it's not easy for her and it hurts her knowing that her youngest son is on Texas Death Row.

At some point in time, I started to crack up and I thought I was going to end up losing my sanity. I had finally had enough of prison, so in a moment of weakness I allowed myself to anchor myself to my legal team even though I knew they were speaking falsely to me on what they would say. However, I still allowed myself to become attached to some of them and this would be my downfall. Just look at what took place between Cassandra and I. A friendship of almost seven years thrown away over B.S. on my end and her lack of respect.

By having these anchors, I was able to keep myself in line and do right not only for them but for myself. When I was doing my time in prison in California, I had no family support whatsoever and without those kinds of anchors in my life, I did what I had to do without question. I fought numerous other prisoners and even officers. I shanked numerous prisoners and have been stuck twice myself. I have witnessed both prisoners and officers get stomped to death and even prisoners shot point blank with no warning shot fired on the yard. I have watched an old 50-gallon steel mop bucket filled with water be dropped over the third-floor tier on purpose where it landed on the unsuspecting correctional officer on the ground floor, killing him instantly as his head was forced down into his chest area. I've witnessed numerous prisoners thrown from such places as well as officers. I have watched, and sad to say even been a part of, another prisoner being shanked only to hand off the shank to another prisoner to be used on another person before disappearing before the responding officers showed up on the scene. I've seen a guy in California standing in line to receive a 50-pound package that one of his girlfriends sent to him from the free world, only to get up to the receiving desk and the officer to get him to sign his name and CDC number before handing him a big box, only to open it and find inside a note with cruel words and a 50-pound bag of dog food!

My point is in sharing all of this is to let you see and try to understand that prison is not what everyone wants you to believe (meaning your homeboys/fellow gang members, etc.). You cannot depend on anyone else other than yourself, and maybe along the way you'll find a handful of people that will ride with you for who you are regardless of you being inside or on Texas Death Row or any other Death Row, but you should always be ready to be screwed over by these very people.

However, those that do show you that they are willing to ride with you if you find yourself in such a sad situation as I and my fellow brothers instead of learning from our mistakes and getting your life right and staying out of prison, you should always be honest with them every step of the way and explain to them what their friendship or their continuing to be with you all these years later means to you because if you don't say anything they will never know and they might decide to move on because they too don't feel appreciated.

But sometimes even that may not be good enough. I have a few such friends that are down with me and I with them. One such young woman calls me her grandpa because I always write her and tell her something along the lines as this old man. So, she told me I should act in the role of grandpa or old uncle. So, I decided that I am already an uncle and an old one to my niece, so I would adopt this young lady who's my dear friend in Italy and I would become through our letters as her grandpa!

She is a very special person and I give her crap for thinking she is aggressive, but I did ask her if I could include a picture of her when I publish this book and if she had anything that she would like to share with society and young women/men who may or may not read this? Instead of coming on as her so-called aggressive self, she came over as her shy side instead! One thing she did share though that I wanted to share with my readers is this—as she was telling me something I found myself moved by such a beautiful young woman and the words she could speak about herself and what she would like to become more of over time, and see others become:

"I'm trying to learn and think that I could become useful to all people, in that our imperfections are the things that make us human and beautiful. That our contradictions are a treasure, and we need to accept ourselves the way we are: accepting doesn't mean we don't have to improve ourselves to become the best version of ourselves, but it means not being too severe or too judgmental with ourselves and others." – Margherita Ravizza

I never realized until most recently that we can have those we would call family other than those we were born into. Now that I do, I think you should know that if you're in a bad place in your life that isn't working or is one of the abusive households, you should do what you can to get away from it all.

A few years ago, Billy Tracy and I wanted to kill one another and now we couldn't be closer as both friends and brothers through our Lord and Savior Jesus Christ. Billy is not my blood brother, he and I didn't know one another before coming to Death Row, but through the blood of Jesus we've seen the errors of our ways and it hasn't been a change that happened in a day or even in weeks. This relationship between my friend and brother took months to build into, just as it did with RG (Ramiro Gonzales). But you have to want to make the changes in your life that are both good for you and positive and that down the road can help those around you do the same.

My family no longer consists of just my mom, sister, and niece, nor that of my cousin Damon. It now consists of thousands instead of only three that I love and deeply care for. Now I love and care for all my brothers and sisters around the world, and if they needed my help with something and I could assist them I would without question, if I could do so from where I'm currently at. This doesn't mean that everything you do needs to be serious all the time, but you can have laughter and fun times without cursing or getting angry with those around you if you constantly ask the good Lord to help you stop doing things that you know to be wrong and negative.

Each of us on this section, Death Watch, have stopped cursing and using any kind of foul language or remarks that could bring down our brothers or friends. Our attitudes have even changed towards each and every one of the officers working and the medical staff and other workers here in the prison. This is going to sound funny as heck to you but know that it's true and it even works.

About five months ago I started this invisible curse/other words jar. If someone walked around me on this section and passed by my cage, I would stop them and tell them as kindly as could be that they now owed $5 to the curse word jar! They would stop and look at me like I was crazy and ask me what did I just say to them? I said, you cursed, and this is a curse-free zone and now you owe $5 to the jar!

I would get officers and SSIs (Support Service Inmates) as well as medical that came around. I mean after all, this pod is also known now as the faith-based pod and even though this section isn't a part of that section because it's called Death Watch, each of my brothers on this section with me are religious and are a part of the faith-based classes that are being offered, and each of us are graduates of previous classes such as Bridges to Life and Overcomers.

Just because three of them have a set execution date and Billy and I are high security and have to be under direct observation of a video camera inside our cages to watch us doesn't mean that we are not religious or allowed to take the faith-based classes. Though I might have run into a situation even though I have graduated from such faith-based programs because of my housing/restrictions placed upon me by the previous director of Texas Department of Criminal Justice and State Senator John Whitmire refusing to forgive me for past actions and mistakes. Though he claims to be a Christian, he continues to keep his foot upon my throat so that I cannot do certain things like a normal prisoner of Texas Death Row would be able to do.

On this past Monday the prison radio station announced that prisoners on Texas Death Row could send in their I-60s (Inmate Request Forms) to the unit chaplain's office requesting to be placed on the list if they were approved for the coming religious service also known as Kairo's Walk for July 2022. So, I turned in my own Request Form to the chaplain's office and yesterday Field Minister Troup (H. Foster) came by my cage in the afternoon and let me know that Chaplain Gay has approved my Inmate Request Form and placed me on the approved list for the Kairo's Walk in July 2022, which is one month away.

The only problem? My security and housing. So far, it doesn't matter to those who hold offices in Huntsville, Texas (i.e., directors, state senators, etc.) that I've shown I can change and have also been able to show that I can and am rehabilitated and that I can follow the rules and guidelines of a condemned prisoner who for the last 14 years has been in total isolation from normal Death Row prisoners.

The only thing that matters to them is that I remain in this isolation/punishment until my own date with the death chamber in Huntsville, Texas at the Walls Unit or I die from natural causes and am taken out of this cage in a body bag, all behind being busted with a cellphone back in 2008. They have done everything they possibly could to break me mentally and at times I even thought they did and when I realized they have not, I again think that some days they come really close to doing so.

However, today, June 2nd, 2022, after speaking with both my Brother Billy Tracy first and then with the UGI Losoya (Unit Grievance Investigator), I took their advice to write a letter/request to Captain Nyland first explaining my situation in the hopes that she and maybe the unit administration can assist me in being able to participate in the July Kairo's Walk 2022.

So, that is just what I did this morning. I explained that I'm a graduate of some classes already and am currently taking others, and that I have been placed on the approved list by the chaplain's office, and would like to ask that, if possible, she please assist me in this. I thought that maybe each day that Kairo's Walk is taking place over on D-Section of this pod (A) that I could be escorted out of my cage here on Death Watch and taken to a cage over on that section for the day while the service is taking place, along with my Bible and something to drink and writing materials, and then at the end of each day simply returned to my cage on Death Watch. It would be no different than if I were going out to visit or out for a legal telephone call with one of my many lawyers and/or to rec, and on these days that Kairo's Walk is taking place the unit's warden and other ranking officers will be on hand as well as Regional Chaplaincy Director Hazelwood.

So, I don't understand why this couldn't happen, and this way by my seeking out the captain's assistance now, nobody can say that I waited until the last minute before trying to get something done, thus losing my approved place to attend myself. God willing, she will be able to help or at the very least take my letter of request to her bosses and maybe they can get it done for me. I have faith in Jesus Christ that He will either allow this to take place or He has something else planned for me that I don't know about. Either way I will be content in knowing that I have tried my best to make it happen.

Oh yeah, I forgot that we were talking about the curse word jar. So, I had started this thing and telling everyone that passed my cage and what do you know, after a while it started seriously working! Officers walking by my cage or into this section no longer cursed, and then I started telling Billy and RG and anyone else when I went to rec or was talking to them and they cursed that they owed five bucks to the curse word jar, and for every time they said things like shut up or stupid it would cost $2.50!

Every time I talk to my brother and friend David Lane and other lawyers and investigators, I tell them the same thing and they have slowed down on their bad language too. I mean, would you curse if Jesus was standing directly in front of you and you and He were having a serious conversation?

That brings me to something I read in one of my free-world newsletters. Let me pose it to you and may you too think it over, and while reading it once you finish, seriously think it over and ask yourself, what would you really do?

"If Jesus Came to Your House"
If Jesus came to your house to spend a day or two
If He came unexpectedly, I wonder what you'd do
Oh, I know you'd give your nicest room to such an honored guest
And all the food you'd serve Him would be the very best
And you would keep assuring Him you're glad to have Him there
That serving Him in your own home is a joy beyond compare
But when you saw Him coming, would you meet Him at the door
With arms outstretched in welcome to your heav'ly visitor?
Or would you have to change some things before you let Him in?
Like hide some magazines and put the Bible where they'd been?
Would you turn off the radio and hope He hadn't heard?
And wish you hadn't uttered that last loud, hasty word?
Would you hide your worldly music and put some hymn books out?
Could you let Jesus walk right in, or would you rush about?
And I wonder if the Savior spent a day or two with you

Would you go on doing all the things you always do?
Would you keep right on saying all the things you always say?
Would life for you continue as it does from day to day?
Would your family conversation keep up its usual pace?
And would you find it hard each meal to say table grace?
Would you sing the songs you always sing and read the books you read?
And let Him know the things on which your mind and spirit feed?
Would you take Jesus with you everywhere you'd planned to go?
Or would you change your plans for just a day or so?
Would you be glad to have Him meet your very closest friends?
Or would you hope they'd stay away until His visit ends?
Would you be glad to have Him stay forever on and on?
Or would you sigh with great relief when He at last was gone?
It might be interesting to know the things that you would do
If Jesus Christ in person came to spend time with you…

Now, I would like for you to think about something else and what I say next may or may not concern you, but if you're going down the wrong path in life and someone got you this book to read or you got it yourself, I ask that you think about this with the mindset that it could be you and your family or someone you know if you're gang affiliated.

Back on May 12th, 2022 around 4 p.m. a Texas Department of Criminal Justice bus was transporting prisoners from one unit to another unit with a hospital for reasons unknown to me. There was a total of 16 prisoners and only two prison officers (the driver and the one hidden in the back of the bus). By prison policy there should always be three correctional officers on such a bus, but this day there were only two. In the third part of the bus, which is the back, there were 15 prisoners chained up with black boxes over their cuffs and leg irons on. In the middle section of the bus there was only one prisoner, prisoner Lopez. This individual was chained up like the rest and while in this section of the bus there are two gates that are both padlocked. Then in the front section you have the bus driver and normally there would be another officer standing up front with the driver, but nobody can explain why there was not one this day.

The story is that prisoner Lopez was able to remove his chains and leg irons then cut through the gate/mesh and plexiglass on the other side of the gate, then he got into a fight with the bus driver. Next thing you know, the bus is on the side of the road and the driver along with Lopez are fighting and prisoner Lopez is trying to get the officer's weapon.

Next thing we're told is the officer in the back had exited the bus as Lopez climbs back in and begins to drive the bus away. At this point the officer that exited the bus uses the shotgun to blow the tires out on the bus. Lopez drives the bus one mile down the road before crashing and there escapes into the woods on foot. However, if that's not enough, the two officers were able to run the mile and fire shots off at prisoner Lopez.

Now, let me poke some holes in this false story provided by officers on the scene. There is no way in hell that he could have cut through the gate/mesh without making noise, nor could he have broken through it or bent it upwards enough to crawl under without the driver noticing what was going on and reacting to it.

Next, let's just say somehow he was able to get out and the driver decides to hit the brakes and swerve to the side of the road. How is it that both of them are now out of the bus fighting and the back officer is nowhere around until after Lopez is already climbing back into the bus in time for him to shoot the wheels out on the bus with his shotgun. And I don't know if you've ever taken a look at prison bus drivers, but they are not the type nor are any of them in shape enough to chase a bus on foot for one mile and catch it in time to give chase and fire shots at Lopez.

After three weeks of searching with over 300 law enforcement officers and corrections officers, know what they found? His clothes folded on the side of the road. The only way this guy could have gotten off that bus the way he did was if he had help from the inside, that is the ONLY WAY. Now, why were there only two officers on the bus when there should have been three? Want to know why I'm speaking of this? That's easy because somebody on the inside wanted to get paid. I mean after all; prisoner Lopez was connected to the drug cartels and had already killed someone else while on parole with a pick axe.

Not only does he escape custody and all the chains and leg irons and get out of a locked gate that is locked with a padlock that only the officers on the bus have the key to, as they do with the chains and black boxes, but after three weeks on the run he has time to go somewhere to get clothing and an AR-15 and then instead of fleeing the State of Texas, he does what? He travels north to a specific house, a house he was looking for, where he enters into the house of this grandfather and his grandkids who were vacationing there and kills the four little kids and then the grandfather before escaping in a white Chevy Silverado truck that was at his farm and running south now about four hours away where police throw road spikes before his truck, thus flattening all four tires.

Prisoner Lopez continues to flee before crashing the truck and getting out with the same AR-15 and engaging the police, where he is then shot and killed on Thursday night, June 2nd, 2022. Know what's even crazier? This killer escapes on a Thursday and is killed after he kills this innocent family, only to be killed on another Thursday.

Had someone inside the Texas department of Criminal Justice not become money hungry or had there been three officers working on the bus, these little kids and their grandpa would still be alive this day enjoying life and playing with their friends and other family members, but now that's no longer possible, and why? Because some stupid cartel member who was just another gang member and a corrupt correctional officer(s).

Imagine those of you who are gang affiliated if while you were in prison because you're too stuck on yourself and trying to fit in with something that you're not, instead of walking the right path in life and being there for your own loved ones, this could just as easily happen to you just as it does to anyone else. I'm not saying that all prisoners are bad because there are lots that do change their ways and become rehabilitated, just as not all officers are bad, but it only takes one to screw everyone's life up.

Please think again before coming to prison because it's not what everyone wants you to think that it is. It's not a place of fun and games. Just the other day a friend of mine was shanked to death in prison. Is this really the kind of life you want for yourself or someone you know?

I don't know about either of you out there reading this, but if someone was taking the time to share all of this with you, I would listen to reason instead of ignoring it. God knows that I and any one of my brothers here with me on Texas Death Row would jump at a second chance in life. To be able to be out there and helping our loved ones and to hold down a real job and enjoy life for what it is. Instead, we are inside of here taking care of one another as we have become family to each other inside these walls where we spend 23 hours a day locked down three days out of seven and the other four days we spend it locked down 24 hours a day.

Every once in a while we shoot one another kites (notes) and my homie/amigo/Brother Spook (Fabian Hernandez) shot me just such a kite the other day telling me: Blue, what's up Bro I mean fatso…haha I guess we are both fat, huh? Anyways thank you so much for the piece of chicken that you sent over here. (Note: I had received a box lunch that had two chicken breasts, coleslaw, biscuit, and mashed potatoes in it for the faith-based programs, so I sent half that box lunch to my friend and Brother Spook because it's not about me, me, me. It should be about us or how you can help someone else because change takes place from within and just because I'm in prison doesn't mean that I don't know how to be kind to another person or show love to my brother and friend Fabian.) It was good. And yes, I'll get some stuff for a spread. I'll buy some taco meat, brisket, chili with beans and chicken chili. You get some pork skins or chips…Also, I'll send a pack of flour tortillas. (By the way, don't you know I'm also the cook and baker, so this fatso sends me everything to hook up! Talk about lazy!) Oh, and the cheesecake you sent the other day was so good that when I put my spoon inside the bag for another piece, it was empty, damn it was good.

One thing about Spook is that he's not only a great friend to have and person to know, but he's also a good artist, not as good as me, but good enough, lol! His only fault is that he's a Boston Red Sox fan. This I cannot understand. I mean, how does a Latino who is from El Paso, Texas become a Boston Red Sox fan? You should see him; he looks like that bald-headed dude from the Mr. Clean ads only drop him down in size to about 5'10" and add about 100 pounds! Regardless of what he looks like or how we kid one another, we both love one another like family because we are. Fabian Hernandez is my brother and friend and I pray that one day he and I both are off Death Row along with many of my other brothers here with me.

Funny thing took place the other day. Billy Tracy was talking with me at our cage doors. and he goes, hey Blue, bet you 100 pushups I beat RG (Ramiro Gonzales) in chess, what's up? I said, heck no, do you know when the last time I worked out was? When my big homie Big Tai was still alive back in 2017. Besides, if RG heard you and I talking about this, he would lose on purpose. Then after saying that I told Billy, okay bet! One hundred pushups that you don't beat him. Next thing you know, Billy calls RG out for a game of chess and RG kicks his butt!

Laughing down here in #1 cage I holler down to RG in #7 cage and tell him thanks. He says to me, thanks for what? Billy bet me 100 pushups that he'd beat you in a game of chess, and he lost so now he owes me the 100 pushups.

RG tells me that if he had known that he would have lost the game! I yelled at Billy then and said, see! I told you he would have lost had he known we were betting 100 pushups! Truth is I'm not fat and am 6'1-1/4" and 200 pounds with hazel eyes that turn blue and short blondish/brown hair and many tattoos.

Those of you who think prison is the place to be or continue to travel down the wrong path in life, the path that will either end in your own death or the death of others who were only living their lives the best way they could until you entered into their lives with your own intentions.

Here on Texas Death Row across the hall on B-Pod (I'm on A-Pod) there is/was an inmate named Stone (this is a nickname) who was housed in #68 cage. At some point during the night of May 31st and June 1st, 2022 this idiot decided to take some drugs that were brought to him. Instead of taking just a little bit he took three grams of meth (methamphetamine). Only he knew that he had done this, as he didn't share with anyone else around him this bit of information.

Then around 5:50 a.m. on June 1st, 2022, one Sgt. Legg was trying to speak with him while standing to the side of Stone's cell door, and before you know it, because of the drugs he took, Stone attempted to spear Sgt. Legg, only being as high as he was on dope, the spear flew across Sgt. Legg's chest area missing him completely.

This would be Stone's second mistake. His first mistake was taking the drugs in the first place and bringing unwanted attention to the building (Death Row). After trying and missing his target, Sgt. Legg, two other sergeants try to talk to him to find out what the heck is going on because for those who know Stone, he's usually either quiet or I hate to say this, but he may also be drunk on prison wine (hooch). Now Sgt. Dorman and Sgt. Schwartz are talking to him also standing to the side of his door. Things seem to be calming down until inmate Stone hands the sergeant a kite (note) which says upon it: "Hey, there's a cellphone in #68 cage."

As the two sergeants read over this kite, it's then they realize something is wrong because Stone is in cage #68. Now, however, it's gotten taken out of their hands as Captain J. Sliger has to come up the stairs to

2-Row #68 cage dismissing the two sergeants who have things somewhat calmed down.

Nobody said that this captain was smart because those of you that have read my first book know that this individual is not only cocky but full of himself from when he waws a lieutenant and got into it with me as well as the others all the time.

Once Captain J. Sliger is standing at Stone's cage door and not to the side but directly in front of his cage, it's as if something inside Stone's head that wasn't yet fried said, "Hey stupid, you have the perfect target standing in front of your cage, go for it! You cannot possibly miss at this close of a range, come on Stone, do it!"

And Captain J. Sliger, being cocky as he is and thinking he's untouchable because he wears a uniform of a correctional officer with the rank of captain with a tiny brain that has already forgotten how many prisoners at the Polunsky Unit and Texas Death Row he has made enemies of, starts mouthing off to Stone. Don't you know it took only 30 seconds for Captain J. Sliger to find out the errors of his ways?

Yep, you guessed it, Stone listened to the stupid voice in his head and the drugs running through his system and Captain J. Sliger was speared, but because Stone was so high and Captain J. Sliger was just so dumb lucky, Stone's aim was off and instead of spearing Captain J. Sliger directly in his throat he hit him on the side of his neck.

Had Stone not been on drugs and had Captain J. Sliger not been so lucky he would have been dead from being speared directly in his throat. As it was, he was able to run off the section and call for a five-man use of Force Team to be suited up and instead of using a regular team he called up all sergeants loyal to him. (Note: LE-10 is a mini fire extinguisher of a chemical agent that lights your whole body on fire, snot comes out of your nose and mouth, and your eyes tear up unless you know how to overcome this.)

After utilizing these chemical agents on Stone, his cage door was rolled open and the five-man Use of Force Team (all sergeants) went inside Stone's cage and beat the living crap out of him because as everyone knows and rank will tell you; when you take a shot at rank with a spear or anything else, you don't get a free pass. Though Stone is still alive, he now sports two black eyes, a busted lip, and bruises all over his face and head and body. He spent about 72 hours in the prison hospital where he was cleaned up by the medical staff and given two bags of intravenous fluids before being released back onto 12-Building Texas Death Row and placed on C-Pod where all level-3 prisoners are housed.

The word now is that many heads are going to roll and possibly the jobs of many including Captain J. Sliger for the way things were handled. As for Stone, in my own opinion he got what he deserved because he never should have taken the drugs in the first place. Nothing good could have come from doing so, but we each must learn things the hard way and many of us here on Texas Death Row and in prison have slid backwards since being here and those of us who have said we'd never do it have in fact done it. Though we may not have been beat up like Stone was, we did in fact lose something we held dear.

I myself lost a very dear and close friendship with Cassandra Belter, but when I tried to make my wrongs right and apologize, she refused to fully understand how badly I felt and in turn gave back silence, thus sealing anything further friendship-wise between the two of us. It took me a hot minute to let go and now that I have, I'm choosing to share with you everything so that you too don't throw away good things or good people in your lives because let me tell you, it's not worth it and it can become hurtful to you and those around you. So, please think before you act and learn from my mistakes in life and the mistakes of my friends and brothers.

Before I close out this chapter, let me give you some food for thought: I am convinced that only one person in a thousand really knows how to live in the present. Most of us spend 59 minutes an hour living in the past with regret for lost joys or shame for things badly done (both utterly useless and weakening), or in the future which we long for or dread.

There is only one world, the world pressing against you at this very minute. And there is only one minute in which you are alive, this minute here and now, so learn how to live it as though it were your last. One day it will be your last!

Also, though we often have genuine disagreements with one another, substantial differences we often can't ignore, there are far deeper realities that bind us together. We're all created by God and bound together in one beloved human family. God has created each of us, regardless of gender, social class, ethnic identity, or political persuasion "in His own image" (Genesis 1:27).

Whatever else might be true, God is reflected in both you and I. Further, He's given us a shared purpose to "fill" and "rule" God's world with wisdom and care. Whenever we forget how we're bound together in God, we do damage to ourselves and to others. But whenever we come together in His grace and truth, we participate in His desire to make a good and flourishing world.

CHAPTER EIGHTEEN

SPECIAL SECTION

For some reason or another that I'm unable to understand, thoughts of my older sibling Sean and his family keep popping into my head. I know that I said I would no longer have anything to do with him because that side of my life and family have since died away and I have moved on. But as is the case in life, nothing we plan nor say we're going to do happens because God has other plans for each of our lives.

As Sgt. M. Ruble came down here to shower Billy, Captain Neyland showed up behind him about six minutes later to speak with me about my letter to her and if I'm picked for the Kairo's Walk in July. I explained that I had also spoken with and to Warden Dickerson on Friday the 3rd about it briefly and he said that if I'm picked he'll get it taken care of, though speaking with Captain Neyland, she also thought that something could be done for me.

It's rank like Captain Neyland and Warden Dickerson and LT. Watson that make things around here run smoothly and in line with how God would like. I even heard something about LT. Watson the other day and how she would charge her officers and sergeants 25-cents for every time they cursed out there. I laughed so hard when I heard this because it's like me and this curse word jar I have and charge everyone with. Could she collect a quarter for every time an officer cursed and used foul language she could retire already, but as it is she should be making the rank of captain in September and I wish her the very best wherever she goes but God willing she'll remain right where she is here at the Polunsky Unit and 12-Building Texas Death Row.

These three people are special and I feel God is going to use each of them to do some very important things in their lives and the lives of those they're placed in charge of, such as I and everyone here at the unit and maybe other units too.

My older sibling Sean has his own son and wife and I find myself often wondering how they're doing even though I know nothing about either of them other than a few things about Sean. One thing I knew about him growing up was that he enjoyed Spider-Man the superhero who could shoot webs out of his hand and swing from building to building as he saved damsels in distress. Sean was quite the Spider-Man fan as well as The Hulk, and from everything that I have heard, he does what he can to take care of his wife and son and self, but that is it.

I feel that if Sean would apply himself to God's word he could do even better and greater things in his life, but what do I, a little brother, know about anything, right? If you ever decide to pick up this book and share it with your other brother Greg and your dad Bob and each of your loved ones, then this is dedicated to you and our older sister Kristina and her daughter and your family and Greg's.

If only our lives could be like that of Joseph in the Holy Bible. Joseph covers what it truly means to be a faithful servant of the Lord. I won't go into great detail because I want each of you reading this to decide on your own and go and pick up the Bible and read it for yourselves. You can find this amazing story in chapters 37 through 50 in the Book of Genesis in the Bible.

Here are a few points that I would like to share:

Joseph served faithfully even though he was falsely accused of a crime he didn't commit. If you've read the story, and I highly suggest that you do, you'll notice that even when he was incarcerated, he wasted no time licking his wounds. I'm positive he felt bad about his situation, and who wouldn't? But he didn't allow self-pity of any form of victimization to dominate his life. Joseph served faithfully even while under the chains of a foreign nation.

He served faithfully even though he was incarcerated. Closely tied to the previous point, this one cannot be understated. The fact is Joseph was sold into slavery and ultimately served a total of 11 years in prison (note here, one of Jesus' followers is in prison and yet society condemns all in prison now). Throughout his incarceration, he served well. He used his gifts and talents not to benefit himself, but to serve others, and while doing so, eventually became the hero of the story. The point here is that he didn't serve faithfully to be a hero; he served faithfully because it was the right thing to do.

He never repaid evil for evil. After he was elevated to second in command in the land of Egypt, he had the opportunity to punish those who sold him into slavery. He could have used his position of power to repay those who hurt him. But he didn't. instead, he forgave them and welcomed them into his home. He told them what they meant for evil, God had meant for good.

Here's the thing for me. God's plan was not altered by evil and misfortune but was actually advanced by it. In some inscrutable way, evil was not allowed to overcome, not only the plan of God, but also not overcome the will of a man who chose to do good even when his circumstances were tortuous. Misfortune and tragedy were not greater than the power of choice.

In my own life, I have seen the same principles at work during my 18 years of incarceration. Though I'm not innocent like Joseph, I've come to take his same attitude. I have begun to make the most of every opportunity I've had to become the person God created me to be. Plenty of bad things have happened since I've been in prison and numerous mistakes have been made, and though I have come very close to giving up, I have not. I have studied, prayed, read many books, and written numerous letters to help others and educate them about prison life and going down the wrong road in life. Setbacks have become comebacks because I haven't allowed my incarceration to overtake my power to choose, and the payoff is being seen in many ways out there right now and in this book you hold in your hands.

The moral of my sharing this with each of you? Never squander an opportunity to improve yourself, even when you think your circumstances are tragic. As moral beings, you and I have a germinating power. We are resilient. We have major comeback abilities, and we don't bury easily. Instead, we plant. And when you are planted, you develop roots. You cultivate and eventually you sprout. But you first must remain in the soil of your circumstances. You have to dig deep roots wherever you are, then you must nourish the seeds of your situations; and when you do this, stability occurs, security ensues, and success blossoms. Trust me my dear readers, it's possible.

I'm no hero nor am I a saint, but maybe just a little bit of Joseph is inside of me, and I sincerely thank God for that. You can have a little Joseph in you too. But first you must make a decision. Nobody can do it for you and your family cannot do it either. Will you choose to view yourself buried in misfortune, or will you see yourself planted in fertile ground? The choice is yours…

Furthermore, as I look back and see that I have spoken more and more about everything else but the Word and how God would like to see you positively invest in your life instead of how you've been doing things, I'm trying to remember something that I read recently about the word challenge. How about this, what is the meaning of challenge? The first is a literal context, for which if we have a good dictionary we shall find an entry that reads something like this:

Challenge: [from L. calumniary to accuse falsely] 1) test, trial, contest, difficulty; 2) to arouse or stimulate by presenting with difficulties; 3) a sentry's command to halt and prove identity.

If properly mined, this definition supplies us with various approaches we can synthesize in the effort of answering the question in terms of its deeper, philosophical context: challenge consists of those situations and circumstances in life that call us out, confront us, and seek to test our ability to cope.

Challenges are designed by the Creator to try our ability to exercise patience and restraint or to take decisive action on short notice. Challenge is the command of the sentry guarding the immediate ascending echelon of our progressive personal evolution, demanding we prove our identity. Challenge insists we demonstrate that we are the confident, capable adults that we say we are. Challenge is what keeps us on our toes, sharp and ready to deal with the inevitable difficulties that arise merely as the result of living as imperfect beings amidst other imperfect beings in an imperfect world.

The meaning of challenge is show and prove. The nature of challenge is described in ancient scripture. In the Qur'an there is an ayah (verse) that reads: "Did they (believers) think they could say they believe and not be tested?" This means that what we profess is merely vain, empty babbling unless backed up by action, specifically in the form of rising to the challenges designed to test one's dedication to the professed belief.

In the Bible there's a verse that says simply: "Many are called but few are chosen." This can be interpreted many ways, one of which is that while many may be inclined or called to a given vocation or field of endeavor, only a relative handful will be able to meet the challenges that come with pursuing the calling. This ties in with another Biblical scripture which says, "Be not weary in well doing." Essentially, there is an inherent challenge in there being no rewards, accolades, or kudos for doing the right thing, meaning we've got to rise to the challenge of "try" doing right, of reliably doing what we are supposed to do without any expectation of reward.

None of what has been expressed up to this point sounds especially enjoyable. Frankly, there's nothing pleasant about being tested, being tried, and not even getting a word of praise for our good deeds. Based on this, a very valid question emerges: why should we embrace challenge, particularly in light of that word embrace with all of its connotations of closeness and intimacy? There are five (5) reasons why you should embrace challenge.

The first reason is that challenge is a part of everyday life. Rest assured, each day that we are blessed by the Creator to see will bring with it in some form or fashion a challenge from someone or some circumstance. Some challenges are small ones that we are more or less accustomed to. Others are quite significant, perhaps even more than we ever had to contend with before. There are challenges that lie within us and those that reach us by way of external routes. Nonetheless, if we look back over our lives for just the past three days, it is easy to observe the truth of this observation.

The second reason we should embrace challenges is that without them, we cannot come into our full strength. A powerful illustration is the butterfly trapped in the chrysalis. The life of the caterpillar is vastly dissimilar from the life of the butterfly. So, while the chrysalis constitutes a protected stage of growth for the caterpillar, it is not meant to house the butterfly it transforms into. The transformation brings it to the threshold of a radically new stage of growth and development. To cross that threshold and embark upon this next stage, the butterfly must surmount its first great challenge: breaking free of the chrysalis.

This is no small feat, as emerging from the chrysalis requires all the strength that the butterfly can muster. It must struggle, then rest, struggle, then rest, for some time until it has freed itself. If one were to happen by while this struggle was taking place and filled with sympathy, decided to help the butterfly by breaking open the chrysalis for it, this well-meaning but wrong-headed gesture would doom the butterfly to a quick death. The reason is because it is the very struggle that one "saved" the butterfly from that builds within its wings the strength it must have to fly. The challenges and struggles in our lives have the same effect; they build within us the strength required to run and not get weary.

The third reason we should embrace challenge is because it is one of the most profound ways to establish the truth of who we are. Remember the sentry's challenge? In old war movies they say something like, "Halt! Who goes there?" This is a demand to prove who we are. Mere words are not good enough. Who we are must be demonstrated in the crucible of challenge. Coward or hero, villain or saint, challenges will cause us to reveal our real identity.

The fourth reason we should embrace challenge is because it is proof of our evolutionary progress. Progressive evolution is essentially personal growth that occurs gradually but continuously from coarse to refined, reactive to responsive, and immature to mature. The proof of whether or not such growth is occurring can only be determined by how we handle challenges. To face and effectively overcome a challenge tells us that we have learned, and more importantly, successfully applied the lessons of our past struggles. Challenge management is the report card that exhibits our positive development. Attempting to live free of challenge denies us the opportunity to gauge our progress. In truth, evading challenge in itself is an action that tells us quite a bit about our progress, or lack thereof.

The fifth and final reason that we should embrace challenge is because it is inevitable. Like death and taxes, challenges are an integral part of the human experience. Seeking to somehow evade the inevitable can be considered a form of insanity. Because of the inevitability of challenge, evading it in one form or context only leads to encountering it in another. The person who seeks to evade the challenges of obtaining a college degree must then face the challenges of trying to navigate the workforce without one. The person who seeks to evade the challenges of a relationship must then face the challenge of being lonely. Therefore, the issue is not how do we get out of a challenge, but how we overcome it. A large part of overcoming is to embrace the significance of challenge and rising to meet it.

As I was going back over and through this first half of this manuscript, I was informed that the DRC (Director's Review Committee) had lied about the reasons they decided to deny my first book "Within the Shadows of Life" as they marked down saying it was behind security concerns but was in fact denied behind gang affiliation information.

So, now that I have sat down and typed out this much, I think it's as good place as any to stop the first half of the book (manuscript) here at just shy of 300 pages. Once it's been edited and retyped it will no doubt be less, but it is what it is. The second part that you'll read will be about all the questions I have about myself and the what-ifs and wondering what it would have been like. One thing I know for sure is that if any dance could distract us from the boredom of living, it would be the dance of the dead, and that there is why I titled this book "Advice from A Dead Man."

Human beings enjoy talking about DEATH and watching movies about such things, but if you dig deeper, you'll see that every one of Jesus' followers were at one point in time or another in jail or prison and to this very day and age millions of people in society hold onto His teachings and what those prisoners had to say thousands of years ago. They love hearing what our Only Creator had to say when He created man in His image, and what His Son did for each of us; and now another of Jesus' followers is speaking from a place of death. Question is…will you listen as He uses me to teach you about mistakes made and how it's not too late to change your own life or help someone else?

"Storytime for a Trip"

Now the trip has come my little friends—
time for a trip where there are only dead ends,
this trip is called addiction at its best.
You can do what you want,
but it's gonna put you to the test.
It will push you and prod you all around.
It will pick you up and throw you to the ground.
Just when you think you have control,
here comes the devil, always on patrol.
You will taste a little here and taste a little there;
you will be hooked before you know it.
I can see it in your glare.
It always seems like it's all fun and games,
but who do you think you are?
He has all of our names!
Don't push that needle; don't smoke that pipe;
don't snort that powder; don't fall for the hype!
It's gonna take you places;
It's gonna take control.
Just when you think you hit rock bottom,
it's gonna take its toll.
So…listen here and listen well;
walk away now-
or you're gonna go straight to hell!

By Eli Lucero

Advice from a Dead Man

"Canvas of Time"

I took a look at my lifespan,
A picture portrayed by
God's divine hand.
I'm on a journey across a canvas of time.
God is the artist; He draws the line.
The brush is His providences,
He holds the time.
My life is the ink,
He spreads it so sublime,
I'm on a journey,
With the Heavenly Divine!
I think about the path I'm on,
About the choices I've made,
And the seeds I've sown.
Since I gave my life to Christ
I'll find a beautiful picture of me,
On God's canvas of time!
God is the artist, He draws the line,
The brush is His providences,
He holds the time.
Yes, my life is the ink, so nice and kind,
He spreads…
I'm on a mission with the Divine!

By Tone F. Jones

Testimony of Alan Wade

(The following is by my friend Alan Wade of Florida. Please note that this was written while he was still on Death Row in Florida but was recently resentenced to life.)

My perception and personal experience with the stigma that is imminent in the majority of prison relationships. Even if you are in prison for minor violations and you are still relatively early in a relationship and especially if the relationship begins while someone is incarcerated…the free world person will come under heavy criticism, possible abandonment by family and friends, and various unforeseeable negative effects.

It is rare to see support from both family and friends. Starting a prison relationship will bring any unknown fissures in your familial bonds and exacerbate them, serving as perfect springboards to jump out of ties with you. I am not an advocate for or against prison relationships, but I do know really good-intentioned people and really bad-intentioned people. Not to mention how hard it is for the poor souls who are actually in love to be separated by prison, whether it only be a year or a day or a life sentence.

If you are uncertain about the authenticity of the people you rely on or people you care about, whenever the people close to you are not happy about your happiness, it is good to know, and should you ever be unlucky (or lucky to have found great love, depending on your philosophical bent) enough to find yourself in a prison relationship, it will put all the flaw ass people in your life clearly on the radar!

I am personally hated (and rightfully so) for what I have done. Besides being sentenced to the worse possible sentence, I do not encounter the general hatred that people harbor for me. I think mainly because people are smart and, after their initial disgust with what I have done, they also feel some tiny level of the same compassion for me that they feel for the victims.

This is another conversation entirely, but it does bring me to my next point. Whenever we look at a prison couple and then the crime, we immediately judge not only the convicted but also the person or persons associated with them. Unless you are God or something or if you like to pretend to be on some type of nonsense like this, "How can anyone love someone who has done this or that," or "How can someone think so little of themselves to love that," and so on.

I think mostly it is an impulsive response whenever people attack or misappropriate the hatred for criminals onto the people in their life and later, they see the contradiction. No one likes to be a hypocrite, but we all are at some point, if not constantly, and if you think this does not apply to you, then I am talking specifically about you and probably closer to the "constant" side of the spectrum rather than the "some point side!"

You hate me for hurting innocent people and yet you hurt the innocent people I know, along with my being sentenced to die in prison. Somehow, it seems like my wife is more hated than I am because of the frequency of threats and hatred that she receives, which is absurd because she is one of the sweetest people alive and certainly does not deserve any negative attention.

I suppose that if your life is reduced to hurling threats and insults online, I should feel sorry for you, but I am prejudiced. It is my wife, and she is certainly more innocent and undeserving of stigmatization and attacks so…fill in the blanks. The hypocrisy seems apparent but mysteriously it still seems to elude people. Either those people are too stupid to see the contradiction, or they are too sadistic to care.

If you are currently hurting innocent people (I am talking specifically about the people who have loved ones in prison) then you are more dangerous than you think I am currently. It is not too late for you. If I can change, then I am sure that you might be able to as well. You can still contribute to humanity rather than being a troll on the internet. If this were a rare or isolated occurrence, then there would not be a reason to write about this, but the reality is, this is so common that it is basically an accepted evil.

I have been on Death Row for 15 years and I have seen the extreme examples along with the minute, neither of which should ever be accepted nor tolerated. Prisoners are doing time for their crimes, and time should be given to those who stigmatize and attack the family and friends of prisoners. I am not a religious man, but I think that the golden rule is a good place to start, and if not, the Department of Justice is eager to make your acquaintance. It is impossible for me to be unbiased, however, this is my best attempt.

Richard L. Tabler

MORE TO LIFE

TESTIMONY OF JIMMY D. SMITH

I was born in Dallas, Texas, and was raised in a small town called Duncanville. My parents did have a nice piece of land and we had chickens and a garden. But I don't ever recall being considered ranchers or farmers. Mom always said we were just poor country folks. Comin' up it was pretty rough. My dad was never around much and when I did see him, he was drunk.

He and my mother spent most of their time together cussin' and screamin' at each other. My father never could hold a job because of his drinkin' and because he never learned to read or write, so this put most of the work on my mother. My mother, at times would work two jobs; cook, clean, help with my homework and see to it that I got to school.

But no matter how much my mom did to please my father, it never seemed to be enough. Never was church or God mentioned in our house as a kid. I loved my father, but he never to let me and my mother down. He constantly cussed and screamed at both of us. As a young boy, wanting so badly for his father's love, I clung to any male figure that would spend time with me. My cousin and his wife lived just down the street and would occasionally come over to the house to visit.

I remember them coming to the house and my cousin would play ball and take me places. I also remembered how he and his wife would sexually abuse me time after time. I remember how they threatened, that if I told anyone how I would get in trouble. I also remember my cousin made fun of me after he would sexually assault me. The sexual abuse went on from the time I was six years old until the time I was nine years old, and then they just stopped abusing me and stopped coming to visit.

I guess they thought that I would finally tell if they kept abusing me. I was too scared of getting in trouble and too ashamed to ever tell anyone. After the abuse stopped, I had so much anger and fear inside of me that I couldn't or wouldn't trust anyone. By the age of twelve, I was sniffing gasoline and glue and smoking marijuana.

I became a kleptomaniac and a bully by the time I was 13 and started using cocaine, acid, crystal, and any other drug I could get my hands on. I tried to commit suicide at the age of fourteen by taking 150 extra strength Tylenol with codeine but this just caused me more pain and several hours in the hospital with a tube up my nose and down my throat to pump my stomach.

By the age of sixteen, I had been in jail half a dozen times for shoplifting. At eighteen years old, I received a ten year sentence for robbery and was on my way to a Texas prison because of my habit of crack cocaine. At 22 years old, I was released from prison. Upon my release, I got a job, got married and had two beautiful children, but I was still living a life of hurt, pain, anger, and distrust. Eventually, my marriage ended, my drug addictions increased, and I became a total monster, not only in my own eyes, but in everyone's eyes that knew me. I was literally trying to kill myself with drugs.

In the summer of 1996, that would all change, and my life would take a much needed dramatic turn. While sitting in a hotel room waiting on a drug connection to bring me more drugs, I decided that I didn't want to live another day the way that I was living and that I was gonna blow my brains out with a Ruger 9mm. I remember looking in the mirror and hating the man that I had become. At that point, I remember putting the gun in my mouth and putting my finger on the trigger.

I began to cry, and I asked God to help me end it. I squeezed that trigger with all the strength that I had, but the gun wouldn't fire. You see, He already helped me end it, but, He didn't do it that summer in 1996 with a bullet. He did it in the form of His Son on the Cross over 2,000 years ago (John 3:16). I carried the anger and hurt of being abused around with me for 30 years. Not, at 37 years old, as I sit in a Texas prison, with a life sentence for yet another robbery, I can honestly say that all the pain from a life of physical, mental, sexual, and drug abuse is gone.

You see, God is a father to the fatherless (Psalm 68:5). He is a light in a dark place (Romans 2:19). He is the only One who can end your life the way it is now. He can end the hurt and the pain and replace it with His peace and joy (John 14:27; Psalm 30:5). Don't spend the rest of your life running from your past, because if you don't have a past, you won't have a future, and if you don't have a future, then you will eventually return to your past.

God says in His word that He has plans and a future for us (Jeremiah 29:11-14). He says that He came to set the prisoners free (Psalm 146:7). That means you! Today, I am no longer a thief and a drug addict, but for the rest of my life, I am a child of God. I thank God for the things He has done in me and I thank Him in advance for the things that He will do for you if you will just ask for His help.

I can finally breathe easy, think logically and have peace of mind. (Note, this part of my Testimony was written in July of 2006).

Update:

One upon a time, I was a shy little boy who was used and abused and too scared to speak. But, today, I am a man on a mission. In 2021, I was sent to the Wynn Unit in Huntsville, Texas to go through Life Coach training. Today, I am proud to say that I went from a life sentence to a Life Coach, and that I spend my days helping incarcerated men learn how to make better decisions in their lives. Richard Tabler and many other men who live on the Polunsky Unit's Notorious Death Row have changed my life forever, and it's for me like these that I do what I do. It's for men like these that I traded my life sentence to be a life Coach.

By Jimmy D. Smith, Life Coach
August 2022

BONUS BOOK

Within the Shadows of Life

Richard Tabler

The character of our society, our commitment to the rule of Law, fairness and equality cannot be measured by how we treat the rich, the powerful, the privileged, and the respected among us. The true measure of our character is how we treat people, the disfavored, the accused, the incarcerated and people like myself… the condemned.

We are all implicated when we allow other people to be mistreated. An absence of compassion can corrupt the decency of a community, a state, a nation. Fear and anger can make us vindictive and abusive, unjust and unfair. Until we all suffer from the absence of mercy and we condemn ourselves as much as we victimize others. The closer we get to mass incarceration and extreme levels of punishment like it is today, the more I feel it's necessary to recognize that we all need mercy, we all need justice and most of all we all need a measure of grace.

Chapter One

I was born on Monday February 5th, 1979, at 9:20am in the Visalia Community Hospital in Visalia, California. My parents are Lorraine C. Lee of Kingston, Jamaica and Robert W. Tabler of Glendale, California.

I have three older siblings named Greg, Sean and Kristina, throughout my whole family I only know about my older sister Kristina and my mom. Robert and my two older brothers and I have nothing to do with each other nor do we really know anything about one another's life. I never felt any kind of love from Robert or my brothers. It just was never there nor the feeling of being accepted when I was younger. Around the age of 12 my parents got divorced in the superior court of Modesto, California on August, 6th, 1991. From that point on I would start to bounce back and forth between the two of them. When I was living in California, I would go to both Turlock JR. High and Turlock High School's, though I would never finish school there. Instead, I ended up getting mixed-up with the wrong crowd and doing drugs at a very young age. It's at this point in my life I would blame my parents for not giving me the love I needed nor the proper direction in life. Robert was always doing things for both Sean and Kristina while they were living under his roof. My oldest brother Greg, I didn't start to know about until years later because when he was born, he was placed for adoption, which would be luck on his part though he would never know it. It was always Sean and Kristina who had Robert's full love. Kristina was bought a little red car and Sean got, not one, but two motorcycles.

    Let's talk about that right there, so you can see what I'm talking about. Sean was given by his dad (I call Robert his dad because he never acted in any way shape or form like a father to me) a red and black with white 1989 Kawasaki Ninja 600R Motorcycle. I remember this one well because one night while staying over at my best friend's house way out in the country named Adam Enos. His mom had driven me home and when I went to go into my bedroom my brother Sean was asleep in my bed. I woke him up when I came in and took notice that he was wearing a sling around his left arm area. That's when I found out that he had tried to run from the police out in the country, and while going around a bend in the road had lost control and wrecked. He totaled his bike and when the cops caught up to him, they slowed down to ask him if he saw a guy on a motorcycle fly past this way. He told them it was him and that he was hurt. Did he go to jail? Nope. Went to the hospital then his dad came and got him and that's how he got to be in my bed. Two days later a tow truck showed up at our house to drop off what remained of the motorcycle. Sean totaled that bike and was lucky to walk away from the wreck. Not three months later though, his dad bought him another 1989 Ninja 600R this one white and black. Whenever my brother or his dad would ride this bike in and around town, they thought they were the crap. I just wanted to feel that same love some time in my life, that wantedness from others. It didn't really matter that I wasn't getting the material things because at the time that wasn't important to me. I was just a kid. When Robert got tired of having me stay with him and my siblings, he sent me to stay with my mom, who was living in Fort Myers, Florida. While I was there, I attended for a short time Fort Myers Middle School. Before she too would get tired of having me and send me back to Robert. This isn't how any child should feel while growing up, and it's sad to think about how many kids are still going through this same thing in their young lives even now. After being sent back to California, I started doing whatever the hell I wanted to do. I had no direction and nobody cared about me so why should I care about myself and what I was doing. There was only one time that Robert did anything for me that was something I really wanted. When I was 16 years old, he drove me to Sacramento, California so I could attend the motorcycle training course. This is something you have to do in order to get your motorcycle license, also known as your M1. Throughout the course they train you on Kawasaki's little bikes. You learn that 70% of your stopping power is done by the front brake and the rest by your back brake. A motorcycle is nothing like a bicycle. Where your brakes are up by the handle bars. There are so many parts to riding a motorcycle. Once you start the bike after placing it in neutral, you'll notice when your there when a green light shows by your gauges. Once there sitting on your bike, your left hand controls the clutch and your left foot controls you're shifting down by the left peg. Your right hand controls your front brake, your throttle and your right foot down by the peg can relax! Back brake is down by the right foot peg. Of course, you have turn signals and everything, but learning to ride a motorcycle right is one of the greatest things. Once I had learned these things and how to control my bike and ride safely and had passed the schooling, I was given my certificate and I took that back to Turlock and went to the local DMV to take my driving course for my car license. Passing both I now had my M1 and my driver's license at 16 years old. The one thing Robert never knew about me though, was that I had been racing dirt bikes with friends, so I knew how to ride long before that.

 As for learning how to drive a car, I knew the basics, but it was my sister Kristina who took me out one day and taught me how to drive a stick shift. Who would know that her teaching would come in handy to her little brother and his life of crime as a driver? Not much longer after I had my M1 my older brother Sean and I got into a fight. I had been doing some things I knew I shouldn't be, like stealing from my brother and his dad (money) and using it for drugs and to buy things I wanted. Sean had come home and caught me and instead of telling his dad, he made me go outside on this rainy day and start digging a hole in the ground while getting rained on. At first, I was okay with it because I had got caught. But after he had made me dig it and fill it in over and over and over again. I thought he was just being a dick and told him to kick rocks. Mistake. I saw my brother snap in front of me and he changed. See, Sean was bigger than his little brother, I was just this skinny kid and he was this football player and the guy screwing all the girls kind of dude. He didn't put his hands on me so much as he started choking me. I didn't fight back, I just let him do it cause one I didn't really want to live anyhow, and two what would be the point? Once he saw that I was about to lose consciousness though, he let me go. I got up and looked at my brother in a way that spoke volumes without having to say anything to him. He knew that that ended the two of us being called brothers. I vowed I would never love my brother after that nor would I ever do anything with him or for him. (Years later, that would change only one time).

The next day while Sean was at school CSUS (California State University Stanislaus) and his dad was at work. I left school from Turlock High early and went home. Stole money from both Sean's bedroom and his dad's, then walked out and into the garage. Took the key for Sean's Ninja off the hook, placed the bike on its center stand then placed it in neutral and started it up. Letting it warm up, I opened the garage door then went inside and put on my jacket and grabbed the tank bag for the bike. Went back out to the bike and placed the tank bag on it then took it off its center stand. While sitting on it, I put on my gloves and helmet, put it in first gear and left. My first stop was the local gas station to fill the tank. While at the gas station and getting gas I also bought myself something to drink and some snacks for my trip. Caught the freeway which is known as Highway 99 and went south down to around Bakersfield, California before catching and cutting over onto Highway 15 and into Mojave and through the desert of South Eastern part of California and into the end of the Sierra Nevada desert before going into Las Vegas, where I found out that my mom was now living. She had moved a few months before after getting an offer from a friend of hers to become a part owner of a restaurant called Flame and BBQ, located at 1770 S. Rainbow Blvd. While staying with my mom after showing up on her door step with a stolen motorcycle and nowhere to go as a runaway at 16 years old. My life got worse if that was even possible. My mom was dating this guy named Terry Brotherton, who was a rent-a-cop working at one of the casino's there in Las Vegas. He was a big dude that enjoyed drinking and cheating on my mom. My mom you need to understand is a tiny thing at only about 5'4. She has always had a great heart, but she knew deep in her heart and soul that she couldn't take care of me and that is why she left me early on to live with Robert and my older siblings. She too had a hard life growing up when she was younger and living back home in Kingston, Jamaica. I just didn't know this until I got older. Terry would soon come to introduce my mom into a new way of living that would take serious effect on her way of living and would have devastating effects on my own life. During my first two weeks in Las Vegas, I did nothing but ride the bike around and take in the sights of Las Vegas. I met a lot of guys and girls who would meet down on Las Vegas Blvd on Friday nights and talk shop about their bikes. They would also meet up at Red Rock and do their illegal races against other bikes and sometimes against cars, each of which were souped up just for racing. I started hanging out with this group of people, some who were cops and some that also worked and were stationed at Nellis Air Force Base and others that worked at the casinos. A couple of the cops and the fella's from Nellis taught me how to do standup wheelies on the Ninja. One of the girls that would be there all the time and racing the guys and sometimes their cars had a Kawasaki ZX10 and taught me how to race and shift properly. One day when she was to meet me and she knew I was a runaway, she gave me a leather jacket, pants and boots. She explained to me that if I was going to ride right, I should wear what would protect me should I crash. She said I owed her nothing but to remember her and she said that she too went through a rough life like I was going through before she joined the Air Force. Her name was Amber.

After a couple of weeks staying with my mom and her boyfriend, Terry. I was told that I would need to start going to school if I wanted to continue living with my mom and Terry. I ended up being enrolled at Sunset High School West over at 2832 E. Flamingo Road there in Las Vegas. What a lot of people didn't know was that Sunset High was a school for troubled kids like myself. There were as many guns, knives and drugs at this school as any other. The thing is it didn't matter where I was going to school, it never took long for me to leave it. School just wasn't my thing. Next thing I knew I was doing illegal racing and then getting into trouble with the cops in Las Vegas. One night while riding with friends and on our way to downtown Las Vegas, we stopped at the local Honda Dealership. It was while we were all there that I got to talking with one of their mechanics in the back. As the two of us were talking he said that he had another bike that he was selling or was willing to take a trade for. He had been looking for a 1989 Ninja and I explained to him that I had one of these sitting out front. We walked to the front of the dealership and I showed him the Ninja. He asked what I wanted for it and I said let's take a look at the bike he was talking to me about. We walked back to the back where we were and he motioned me to the side. Around the corner was this bright yellow and chrome 1992 Suzuki

Katana 600. Upon a closer look and talking with the mechanic I learned that he had just placed a 1989 GSXR 750 motor within the frame of this Katana 600. It bolted and lined up perfectly. Everything about this bike screamed racing. There were so many illegal parts that wouldn't pass a DMV testing for riding it on the streets. I told him that I would trade him if he wanted to do so right now. The only thing was that the bike was in my older brother's name back in California but I'm sure we could figure a way out to get this done. He said no problem and we walked inside and before leaving the dealership I was the proud owner of this new bike and he was the owner of the Ninja!

(2 months later)

After being downtown, we decided to take a ride up to Red Rock in an evening race to the loop that comes out at Blue Diamond. As we were racing up the straight away towards Red Rock outlook, we were all running pretty much side by side up the street. Just as we were passing the last parts of the city and getting ready to start into the mountains and parts of Red Rock, I noticed that everyone was slowing down. That's when I looked over my shoulder and saw the cops! I started to slow down by down shifting, but then I got the great idea of trying to out run them up into the mountains. I had been in 4th gear and was slowing when this thought overcame me and I down-shifted once more into 3rd, before rolling the throttle and taking off. Shifting up through my gears and making it to 5th gear before having to down-shift for a slow sweeping left turn up into the mountains, coming out of the turn, shifting up into 4th then down to 3rd again before catching another straight that allowed me to reach 5th gear before a tight right had me dragging my right knee-puck of my leathers. Only to come screaming around that turn and have to apply my brakes while forcing myself into the upright position because the cops cheated. Right in front of me was the Las Vegas Police Department Helicopter sitting in the middle of the road. I pulled to the side of the road where when the cops behind me caught up decided to slam me against the hood of one of their cars and scream at me how stupid it was for me to try and run from them up through these mountains as just last week, they had another try the same thing only to run right into a jackass (donkey) crossing the road in front of him. They spent hours picking up parts of his body and his bike from the crash site, while the jackass got up and walked away!

Once the officers cooled down and they found out that I didn't mean any serious harm as everyone once in their life tries to run from the cops, they decided to let me go, but not before calling my mom at her work and explaining to her what had happened. Before they hung up from talking with her, they handed the phone to me and she went off on me, before calming down and explaining that the cops were going to give me the chance I had wanted by running; but if I lost my bike would be impounded and I would be taken to jail. When I asked her what she was talking about, she said the cops would explain it to me as it was their idea, then hung up on me. I gave the cop back his phone and asked what he and my mom had been talking about. I was told that since I wanted to race that they would escort me back down the road and at the straight away that they had first took notice of all of us coming up. We would stop. From the turn down into the city we would set up side by side and race to the first light where the rest of the cops would be sitting and waiting for us. The deal was if I beat him to the light, they would let me go, but if I lost, I would go to jail and my bike impounded. This was only because they had just gotten the new chevy Camaros in that they were using as their cop cars for chasing drivers/riders that ran from them and they haven't had the chance to test them out yet. I was thinking to myself yeah right, you guys are full of crap and I'm going to jail. Once we were all back down by the said straight away, the cop's pulled to the side of the road, and while looking way down towards the end I could see that they were serious. The road was free of all cars and bikes to the first light! That crap was crazy as I was only 17 years old now! There was one thing on my bike that I too had never tried out because there was never any real place to try it other than the drag strip. This was one of the reasons that the mechanic had also traded me and why he had a better motor placed into the Katana frame. Under my seat was a valve that was connected to a bright blue canister that was mounted on my right back swing-arm (under my seat, yet on the outside not directly under). On this canister are the letters NOS. The mechanic had been building my bike before I came along, just so he too could race it (illegally). I couldn't run it on normal fuel and had to pay more for the higher/costly JP fuel that came in a blue can. Please note that while the cops had been explaining to me what would take place, they had never stopped to really look over my bike and were always on my left side, even when I was up in the mountains and pulled to the side. Thus, they never saw the NOS canister. As I'm sitting on my bike

I had been debating if I should use the NOS or not. I decided to use it and set about reaching back and down to open the valve on the canister. Once this was done, I told myself to relax as best I could. Right next to my left hand by where I grab my clutch was another button that would give me my hit of NOS when the time was right. Placing my helmet back on and making sure it was snug, I waited for the cops and the one cop I would be racing down. Once he and I were both ready, another officer down the road flashed his lights, this was for us to get ready. I placed my bike into 1st gear and smoked my tire, while the cop did the same. Then we were both ready. The cop down the way flashed his lights again and we both took off. From 1st gear through to my 3rd gear the cop and I were neck and neck, as our speeds are hitting into high 90's. I start to pull away after hitting 4th and then 5th gears, just after shifting into 6th gear my speed is showing 140mph. It's now or never as the cop is about two and half lengths behind me. I hit my NOS button. To say that I smoked the cop would be an understatement. I won hands down no questions asked, but I lost more than I won. At the end of the road and at the light there's a gas station and it was there that my friends had been waiting for me. When I got off my bike and placed it on its center stand, I was shaking like a leaf and refused to get back on it to ride it home. My friends and I loaded it up into one of their trucks and we drove to a friend's. That thing scared the crap out of me! It would be weeks before I got back on it. While I wasn't riding or going to school, I had gotten a job at All Air Systems which was this place that installed air conditioners on huge homes and at casinos. I was taught how to drive and work a crane and lift, but again for reasons back then I couldn't sit still or hold a job for long. I left and through a friend that worked at this one casino started working at New York, New York Hotel and Casino in the gamming room for the kids. It was around this time that my friends made the offer to me to go up to the State line and the casino there for some fun and maybe a race. So, I went with them. For reasons unknown to me at the time, once we got to the State Line and casino, I called my mom. At the time we were living at 1836 Winners Cup.

Chapter Two

Things Become Worse

We were having a blast on our way to the State Line and Casino, just messing around and poppin' wheelies and goofing off with one another. When we were there, I made the telephone call home to my mom to check in with her, something I didn't do often. Instead of my mom answering her phone or her boyfriend Terry, her best friend Sheila answered, and the first thing out of her mouth was, "Richard, your mom is alright. " I had stepped away from my friends in the parking lot to make this call home, and now I could hear myself raise my voice as I asked Sheila what she meant my mom was alright. In fact, I remember telling her to put my mom on the phone, only for her to say that my mom couldn't come to the phone. What the heck?! I hung up on Sheila and walked over to my friend's and told them that I needed to get home as fast as possible because something had happened at home with my mom but nobody would tell me what. I just knew that it was something bad and needed to get there. As I was walking away one of my friends that was stationed at Nellis Air Force Base ran to catch up with me and told me to take his bike. I asked him if he was sure and he said yes. We traded keys, and I told him to go ahead and race my bike if he wanted. It's got a full canister of NOS and the tank is almost full itself. His name was Chris and his bike was a 1992 Honda CBR 900RR that was red and black. Placing my helmet on tight and shifting into first gear I left my friends to get back on the freeway and ride as fast as I dared back into the city of Las Vegas. Hitting speeds of over 100+ mph I was able to make it back into Las Vegas and to my mom's house in time to see the cops leaving and some still standing around. It took me about 50 minutes. Getting off the bike and walking into the house I noticed two things right away. One, my mom wasn't in the living room nor kitchen like she always is, and two, Sheila met me when I was coming inside and she was stone cold sober. Thinking that she was in her bedroom with Terry I went that way only to find out that I was in for one of the biggest shocks of my young life. My mom was in her room but Terry wasn't with her nor was he anywhere in the house or anywhere around to be found. That's why the cops had been there and they too wanted to talk to Terry. My mom was laying in her bed with tears running down her face as soon as she saw me and I saw what had happened. While my mom was sleeping or taking a nap, Terry had come home drunk and thought to try and beat my mom and suffocate her while she was sleeping. Only he failed (thank God) and then he took off and my mom called the police and then her friend Sheila. To see my pride and gold beaten like that with both her eyes black and blue and hand marks around her throat, that crap broke something deep within my core as a youngster. My mom seeing that this was messing me up, did the one thing she could but to her it meant everything. She begged me to not tell my older brothers and sister. I never told anyone in our family, but I did call my friends up at the State Line and Casino, because two of them were cops there at the Las Vegas Police Department and the other three were stationed at Nellis Air Force Base. I explained to them what had happened and they told me to meet them at Chris's place on Base. I told them okay and hung up then went and told my mom that I was going to a friend's on Nellis Air Force Base and would be back later, and if she was going to be okay with Sheila. She told me that she would be okay and to keep in touch. I gave her a lite hug and kiss on the cheek and then left. When I got to Nellis Air Force Base which is northwest of Vegas. One of Chris's friends were waiting for me in Chris's truck at the gate to escort me onto the base after I signed in as a visitor. I followed him way over to the other side of the Base and to the barracks that they were assigned to. Once there we didn't wait inside for very long before Chris showed up on my bike and with everyone else. I explained to everyone what had happened and that Terry Brotherton was missing (hiding). We agreed to leave all the bikes there at Chris's barracks and take his truck and two others, but first they wanted to make stop at the armory because as Chris said he wanted to sign out his guns (Chris worked as Nellis Military Police). Once this was done, we all drove around looking for Terry. We drove over to his daughter's house, where she was married to some fat dude; though she didn't know where her dad was. He was not inside because she let me go inside to have a look around. We drove over to his work at Circus Circus, Casino and Hotel, and nobody there had seen him since he left work six hours before. We drove to Danny's II over off of S. Rainbow Blvd. The parking lot was full but he wasn't there either. Chris and some of the other fellas along with Amber made some calls to their friends, asking that they please let them know if they see someone matching the description I had given them and that they had also given from seeing Terry before. As it turned out, and it was a good thing for Terry; we never found him nor caught up to him anywhere that night nor the following couple of days after.

After that night though and the following few days, my mom and I never spoke about what all had happened. I think she knew though and could see that something in her young son had been broken. About one month later Terry showed back up and was once again in my mom's life and they were back into their relationship as if nothing had happened. I couldn't understand how she could do this, and yet at the same time I thought to myself that if he beat her again it was her own fault. Would I do anything about it on her behalf without her ever knowing? Who knows, we may never know. Sure enough, not much later they got into it over Terry cheating on my mom. In her own way when she found out, she went into his closet and cut off one arm of each shirt and one pant leg of each of his pants. To me this was childish, but to each his/her own right? It was also my pushing point, because when I tried to stand up my mom even thought she was a fool for getting back into the relationship. My own flesh and blood went off on me and told me to mind my own business and to get out. I wasn't yet 18 years old and had just sold the Katana after scaring the crap out of myself trying out the can of NOS, again. I made up my mind earlier that night that since she wanted to get beat up on and stay with that jerk who would keep doing that until someone beat him up or put him in the ground, that I would steal her brand-new Chevy Camaro and drive back to Modesto, California. That's just what I did and though I wouldn't know it she would call the cops and report her car stolen. It was around one week later while I was in Modesto, that the cops would catch up to me and arrest me for GTA (Grand Theft Auto). When the cops searched the car, they also found drugs that I had been selling. After being placed into the cop car and transported to the juvenile hall because I wasn't yet an adult. The cop was relaxed as he was taking me out of the backseat, he failed to realize and understand that I had removed the cuffs and took off running. He gave chase, we ran for what seemed like forever and I had just made it to the highway (99) which sits just about half a mile from the juvenile hall center in Modesto, California. When another cop car and other officers showed up to give assistance to their partner. As the officers were trying to take me into their custody, I started fighting them. Thus, I was given more charges on top of my GTA and drugs. I was charged with obstructing/resisting and assault on a peace officer. I was sentenced to five and a half months in the juvenile hall center better known as CYA (California Youth Authority) being that it was my first time in trouble. The sentencing Judge was easy on me. What was worse was the only person to show any kind of support for me when I got into trouble wasn't either one of my parents. Nope. It was my one and only sister, Kristina.

When I finally got out of CYA, I was an adult as I had just turned 18 years old. I had nowhere to go and nobody that would take me in. I was to report to a parole office for probation but that never happened. I ended up going to the only place where I know people and that was to and into parts of Deep east Oakland, California and also San Francisco, California. While in both these cities I did what I could to survive because I had no family that wanted anything to do with me. I started out small and working for a dealer in the Bay Area's mostly in San Francisco. Selling crack, weed and cocaine. Before I knew it, I was shooting the stuff up myself. It was the only way to escape all the pain I was feeling at a life I didn't understand. The rush of taking a hit for your first time is something that one cannot honestly explain, though I can tell you one drug I started selling when I got into doing sales deeper for my supplier. While I was a young homeless person was black tar heroin. This drug I can tell you scared me straight into getting the heck out of the Bay. When I tried it, I thought I was going to die from the rush alone, while others around me were throwing their guts up after injecting it. It was around this time that I was making my way back to where I was staying while selling, that I passed my older brother Sean and his then girlfriend (who is now his wife). They were going to eat inside of a restaurant. My brother saw that I noticed him, notice me. But neither of us said anything to the other. I had a feeling deep inside that once he went inside, he would come back out and try to talk to me. So as soon as they were inside, I took off running up the street to hide behind a dumpster. Sure enough, when I looked back down the road, my brother was outside looking up and down the street for me. After that day I never saw my brother again, until years later, and it would be the first time we would speak face to face as well as being the last time. When I got back to where I was staying, I explained to the guy's that I had decided to leave and go back into the valley of Turlock and Modesto. One of them told me he was ready to go to and asked if he could skip out with me. I said yeah, let's go. We left the condo and walked down to market street where we boosted a car. Once we were through the hills and on our way down into the valley, we stopped off in the city of Tracy, California. Here we decided it would be best to get another car because we had been in this one long enough and someone would have by now reported it stolen. Stopping in an all-night shopping center, we got out and walked the lot before finding a black Infiniti. I busted the back window, reached around to the driver's door and popped the lock up and opened the door. No alarm went off so we did our thing and about 90 seconds later had the car started and were driving off catching the freeway. Stopping off in Modesto at first my friend Aaron's house and then his friend's house, where we both obtained a mixture of drugs and guns. My mind went into a hate level and I thought to drive us to Turlock where we ended up at Robert's place of business in the middle of the night. Going to his office, I went around to the back door and busted his glass door, thus leaving it open to anyone who wanted to enter his office in the middle of the night to steal everything. All throughout my young life I would have many run ins with the law along with some serious escapes from them too. I had even tried suicide by cop once and I did in fact get shot by them but not a killing shot. They shot me with their bean bag slug from their shotgun. That crap seriously hurt like hell!

CHAPTER THREE

GOING TO JAIL AND LEARNING HOW TO FIGHT

Around the end of 1999, I ended up in Florida again and as usual was running wild. My mom was also living back there in Cape Coral and dating this guy named Doug Reiter. Doug, for the most part, was good to my mom and not abusive physically but mentally he was to her. I was told flat out that I couldn't stay with them and honestly, I wasn't looking to stay with them. I ended up in Florida because I was mixed up with some bad crap. I was still doing my own wild thing and now I was stealing crap from buildings, houses and other places, but on a much bigger scale. I had even started taking guns and turning around and selling them. I wasn't breaking into places in or around Cape Coral, but in cities like Fort Myers and down south in Miami and the Keys. It was while breaking into a place in Key West that I met someone named Danny. You know you're in serious crap when you break into someone's house and find out they're still inside and that they've been watching you on their home security cameras that you failed to see or notice. The outside of this home looked like crap, and that's why I had decided to break into it, but the inside looked nothing like the outside did. It was while I was walking out of the master bedroom that I was met with a sawed-off shotgun in my face. There is no place to run from something like that without getting your butt handed to you. The rush of breaking into places is one thing, but the fear and adrenaline that is running through your body as your looking down the barrel of a shotgun in your face cannot be described. At the time, I didn't know his name was Danny, this would come after he and I spoke for a while. Before we got to this point though, he was asking or yelling at me why the hell and what the heck I was thinking breaking into his house!? I explained to him that I was just trying to make some money and that I was always on the run. I started to apologize, but he didn't want to hear any of that crap he said and told me to stop. I stopped. I mean what else was I to do with a shotgun in my face. Pointing with the gun he told me to walk into his living room and have a seat so that we could talk.

 I did as I was told. Once he saw that I wasn't going to try and make a run for it, he placed the shotgun down and had a seat himself. He said that his name was Danny and that instead of taking me out back he would offer me a job running for him. I accepted. He started laughing and said that I shouldn't be in such a rush to accept his offer before understanding what I would be doing. Being young I thought that he was talking about running things around for him at an office, not so. What Danny meant as he explained to me was driving for him all over the place, mainly up and down the East Coast. This he said would place money into my pocket and give me a place to sleep without having to break into anyone's house nor sleep on the streets. He asked me what my name was and I told him it was "Blue". He said not my nickname, but my real name. I told him it was Richard. He said that I was to call him Danny at all times and he would call me Blue. He got up and asked me to follow him into the kitchen, leaving the shotgun in the living room. Once we were in the kitchen, he made us both something to eat, and told me that I had some guts breaking into his house. Then he started laughing his ass off. After he got his laugh, he asked me if I knew how to drive and I stated that yes, I knew how to drive and ride a motorcycle. To show him that I could he had me once again get up and follow him into the garage where he tossed me the keys to his SUV. Inside he instructed me to drive him anywhere, to show him that I could handle an SUV of that size. After driving in the city and up to Fort Myers, he had me drive him back to Key West and to his house. Seems pretty simple right? Wrong. What I didn't know at that time was that Danny would have me moving his narcotics and vehicles. Nobody in my family ever would know this, nor anything close about what kind of crap I was doing when I wasn't around them and acting like a bum. The only thing they ever knew was that I was always getting into trouble for stealing things and writing bad checks. I ended up driving from the Keys all the way up to places in Michigan and over to cities and places around Boston and New York; and places that had funny names out in the middle of nowhere like Parsippany and Egg Harbor Township, New Jersey. It was cool driving for Danny and I learned many things about the narcotic industry and of the vehicles being moved/chopped. Danny had ways about welding onto the underbody of a vehicle so that you could hide either a body or cocaine as well as bales of money. But as always, all good things must come to an end some time, and some of the people that Danny worked for and ran with were serious about the crap they did. One late night as I was returning to Danny's home in the Keys and walking in through the backdoor like I always did, I found Danny sitting next to his kitchen table doing his best to hold his intestines inside of himself. I froze up until he told me to take what I could find left from the safe in the bedroom behind his dresser, then to get out and don't tell nobody anything. Coming back into the kitchen I tried to get Danny to let me call him some help but he wasn't trying to hear any of that. He told me to go on and get out of there and to take his SUV as far as I needed. That was around I want to say April of 2000 down in Key West, Florida. Danny and I became friend's and he taught me tons of crap. Sure, it wasn't all good things to the way someone in society thinks, but to someone always on the run or doing illegal things in his/her life, it would be golden. He was one of the only people to give me such lessons about things. I ended up drifting back into Cape Coral and Fort Myers, Florida. Not for long though I was stealing a truck from a dealership and fleeing in it to parts of Michigan. I made it all the way up to Detroit, Michigan. Here is where I dumped the truck and boosted another car and drove to Lansing, Michigan, where I met a young girl named Tonya S. Wilson. At the time, my life was nothing but always being on the run from the cops for something and for doing drugs. After leaving Danny behind at his house, which would never sit right with me even to this day. I still knew where to get a hold of some of his people and the drugs they delt with and cars that needed moving from point A to point B. Most of the people that Danny worked for and was a part of himself was a gang that wasn't heard of so much back then like it is now a days, MS 13.

    Tonya and I hooked up. She was a good girl who had one older brother named Chester and her mom, though both of them drank and did their own share of drugs. Tonya wanted something better, thus when I told her that I was done freezing my ass off in Michigan, she said that she wanted to go with me. She knew that I didn't have a place to stay and that I was on the run from the cops, but she still wanted to go with me and even offered to use her car for our return trip together to Cape Coral, Florida. I don't know to this day how it happened but we ended up being allowed to stay and live with my mom and Doug. She didn't like Florida that much and decided to return to Michigan on her own. We parted ways, and not long after she left, I was picked up by the cops and being busted for an outstanding warrant for GTA (Grand Theft Auto) along with assault on a peace officer, forgery, terrorist threats, transporting narcotics and commercial burglary. I was taken downtown to the jail and booked and processed. My thumbprint and fingerprints were taken along with my mug shot. Then I was transported to the camp where inmates waiting to go to court are housed for the time being. This is still in parts of Lee County, Florida, though it's way out in the middle of swamp land. Aside from your initial processing upon being received at camp, you're on your own once you're placed into a dorm. In other words, if you didn't know how to fight, you were going to learn really fast how to do so. Camp is just what they called the place. It wasn't really a camp of sorts, but dorms that were all connected together through an electronic steel door between each one. The front of each dorm was entered through a steel door that was opened by a control booth and the officers about 50 yards from the dorms. There is a chain-link fence running all the way around the place. At each entry, the steel door would roll open and you would step inside to another small cage-like area. Once you stepped inside, the outer door behind you would close and the inner steel door would open into the eating area of the dorm you were being housed in. At that place there is usually six tables that seats four inmates, and above the tables are two TV's mounted high up on the walls. Beyond this area you'll see two rows of bunks (double beds) on each side of the main run down the center of it all. Following the walkway through the sleeping area all the way to the back and you'll find the showers and toilet areas. Each dorm holds between 25 and 30 inmates of all race and size. The inmates control their own dorm, not the law or the correctional staff. Meals are brought to us three times each day on a small cart that is placed into the entry area that you first enter through. Other than that, we're left to our own devices. My bunkmate was this guy named Anthony Q. He was this big black dude that was awaiting trial for murdering two cops. One of which he ran over with his truck and the other he shot in the head when they raided his home after fleeing there. Not everyone who is in jail or prison was always a criminal. Anthony Q was a law-abiding citizen of Florida who taught Jujitsu and Kempo Karate. He held a 3rd Dan Blackbelt in both. Mixed throughout our dorm was every kind of street gang you could think of. From Folk Nation and Latin Kings, to Damu's and Crips and KKK, BGF, Mexican Mafia and your blue-collar criminals and plan old white guys scared to death. For recreation we were allowed outside into the fenced in area for a couple of hours weather permitting. Usually, the weather was going full blast rain and thunder and would be knocking out the power which would allow the steel doors that separated the dorms to open. This is how all kinds of fights would break out between each of the dorms. Inmates would come in from another dorm and try to steal crap from us. This caused us all to stand together, though at other times and many at that we would be fighting amongst one another. I myself had numerous fights, along with many broken noses and ribs. Nobody taught me how to fight when I was growing up, but after getting my butt kicked by three of the KKK members after they tried to get me to side with them and some of the other whites in the dorm, and I in turn calling them the Ku Klux Klowns, instead of the Ku Klux Klan. They didn't think I was funny and went about showing me what they thought. I lasted about five minutes and was able to break at least one of their noses before getting knocked to the floor. Nobody stepped in to help me because I look like a white guy, though I'm not 100% white. I'm mixed. The thing that caught my bunky's attention though was that I had heart and didn't think about backing down (just stupid). This caused him to take me under his wing as he said. From that point forward he taught me what he could about fighting and how best to defend myself against an attack of any kind other than with someone holding a gun some distance from me. Throughout my lessons with Anthony, he would have me always call him Sensei Q. Everything that he taught me was hard to learn and understand. Anyone can throw a punch and kick someone, but doing so, so that you mess somebody up is another thing all together. Everyone in the dorm would laugh at me when he was giving me these lessons because I was calling him Sensei Q. He would take both of our mattresses and roll them up and tie them to the end of the bunk, so we would be standing in the middle of the run that went down the center of the two rows. When the mattresses were rolled this way and wrapped with a sheet around them, they took on the shape and form of a heavy punchbag. I never saw anyone fight the way Q did. When he showed me how he went after this heavy punchbag, hitting and kicking it. The man's hands were a blur. I tried counting his punches but could never keep up. His demonstrations were so smooth and always looked practiced. After four months into my stay in this dorm and being taught by Sensei Q. He told me to take five minutes and show him what all I had learned from him, as he would be leaving for the start of his sentence. I remember it like yesterday… staring at the bag with a practiced intensity. My workout started long before I threw my first punch. I could feel the aggression levels build rapidly inside. In my mind, an attacker rushed towards me, intent on doing me serious harm. Just when I felt the moment was right, I exploded into the bag. I worked a series of punches first, my arms pumping like pistons, fists diving deep. My body snapped from side to side as I sent punch after punch into the mattresses. My feet moved in short crab-like steps. I then began to incorporate knees and elbows into my combinations, opening up with punches then crowding close to slam home short-range blows. When I finished, Q was laughing his butt off and telling me that I wouldn't win any prizes for my form, but would seriously mess someone up because I did fight and move like a Pitbull. I ended up serving a little over one year in the dorms, and Q left about one week after my show to start serving his two life sentences for killing those cops. When I got released, I was to report to a parole officer in downtown Fort Myers, Florida. My parole officers name was Carol Romer #11664. I had reported to her from around September of 2000, she worked in the downtown central part of Fort Myers, and was a real ball buster. When I reported to her, she was told that I was gang affiliated with Folk Nation, and that people had seen me with numerous guns and drugs, which would be a violation of my parole. I told her that none of this was true and that I wasn't gang affiliated with Folk Nation. She didn't care and said the first time I mess up she was sending me back inside. That was the last and only time I saw that chick before I absconded and was again on the run. I did a fast lick and stole a street bike from a local motorcycle shop. Stopping at my mom's place to let her know that I was leaving again, in my sprint to be gone I broke the speed limit and was pulled over by the police. Thank god for full faced helmets and it being night time and for fake ID's. I didn't have a driver's license for Florida, so I was using one under another name. I was written a ticket for speeding and then let go. The bike was stolen but I figured that it wasn't in the computer system yet; but either way it was time for me to find new wheels and to get out of Florida for a while. I went down to the Keys and hooked up with one of Danny's old friend's I knew he trusted. I was tasked with a Chevy Blazer along with five pounds of marijuana and two kilos of cocaine, that was to be dropped off in Egg Harbor Township of New Jersey. After that I was driving another stolen SUV back into California and it was there I was busted for my outstanding warrants.

Chapter Four

Gladiator School

It was just after the new year of 2001 and I was sentenced to almost four years in prison. I was picked up along with about thirty others from the jail in Modesto, California, and driven to Tracy, California, where I would get my first taste of prison. I was twenty-two years old and had been living a fast and highly illegal life style, and now I would be entering a place known as Gladiator School. The Duel Vocational Institution, better known to all who enter it as DVI. DVI is where you go once you've been sentenced and are entering the CDC system (California Department of Corrections). While here you're processed and asked numerous questions about your life and schooling along with work if any. You're asked your age and if any at the time gang affiliation, and ethnic. Once they have all this done, you're given a cell to live in until they decide where they're going to ship you to. This is somewhere up or down the coast of California and depending on the amount of time that you have and the nature of your crime, they decide whether or not to send you to a serious prison or a minor one with light security. While I was housed there awaiting to be transported to another prison, I would spend time in the following cells/dorms: HW-208, EH-340, WK-331, B-233 and K-123. Most of the prison is ran by nothing but racist jerks who hate all blacks with a vengeance and most of the Mexicans. These are the white supremacist that can be found in all of society's prisons today. The first cell I was housed in had one around my own age, who had been awaiting transport to another prison as well. The windows of the cell were broken out and there was a single light bulb for us to see by during the night time. During the winter time we were freezing our asses off. Once each day we were allowed out of the cell to walk down the stairs from the third tier to tier one for a shower. The shower area is one of a giant open space with around thirty showers nozzle, just before entering this part of the showers though there is a place for you to remove your clothing, then you walk into this area butt naked, and shower with everyone else in a butt to nuts fashion. You get in and wash and then get out and walk back to your housing. The only other time we're allowed out of the cell is to walk to breakfast, at which time we're given a paper sack with a lunch inside and then we come back down for dinner. The individual I was housed with had the problem of always talking like a tough guy. He spoke about how he and his friends beat the crap out of this black kid and his girlfriend, and that when I got to whatever prison they decided to ship me off to, that I should go directly to the Wood-Pile (prison talk for where the whites hang out and group together). Once there I should show them my paperwork, etc... He just never shut the hell up. I was never one that spoke much in prison in California, but I do remember my first fight, if that's what you call beating the crap out of your celly. I was going on my third month being housed in that cell with him and hearing him talk about this and that and all this crap that didn't meant crap to anyone. Then one morning when he woke up, I was already up and had washed my face and drank a cup of coffee. The second his feet touched the cell floor, I threw a punch directly into his throat, which almost crushed his trachea. By not hitting him hard enough though it didn't do this. But it still choked him, causing him to grab at his throat while going to the floor. Once he was on the floor, without saying anything to him, I started to stomp on his face and body. Once he was unconscious the cell door was opened for us to go to breakfast and it was then I dragged his sorry ass out of the cell and down the metal stairs to tier one. Once there the officer's slammed me to the ground and placed handcuffs on me behind my back, before asking or screaming at me what the hell was going on. I calmly explained that my celly fell down the stairs. They didn't think that was funny nor were they trying to buy that crap I was selling, because he had a boot print on his left cheek. I explained that he wouldn't shut the hell up about beating up some black kid and his girlfriend, and that was when I got pissed and told them I WASN'T A STINKING RACIST! I was written up for assault on an inmate with bodily injury and a note was stuck in my file that you couldn't house me with a white prisoner, even though I looked white myself.

One week later I was shipped off to CMC-West (California Men's Colony) in San Luis Obispo, where I would get written up for an article 115 for getting a tattoo and then I would be again shipped across the street to CMC-East because they received word that I was planning an escape. Snitches deserve stitches, and child molesters deserve ditches. Upon being received at CMC-East I was told to report to D-Quad for my housing. Once I reported to the officers of the building on D-Quad, I was given a key to 7 Building cell #D-7173. For the first 72 hours I would be locked down (unable to leave the cell). I could however see and talk with the inmates that were passing underneath my cell window as I was assigned a cell on the first floor, which was even with the yard. Once I was finally allowed out of the cell, I found myself walking the yard and getting a feel for everything and where everyone was. Over at the weight pile is where all the so-called peckerwoods/whites hung out and got together. The Mexicans were over by the handball courts and the tables along the back wall beneath tower #5. The Damu's hung out around the bleachers under tower #7 and the Crip's got together by the telephones under tower #8. The Black Panthers and the BGF (Black Gorilla Family) got together in the middle of the yard and around the horseshoe area. Your other odds and ends walked the yard. These were guys that didn't belong to any set of family, such as myself. While you're in CDC (California Department of Corrections) you're given a pair of blue jeans, a buttoned down blue long sleeve shirt, white socks, white boxers, a pair of black boots and a blue jacket. Throughout your stay within CDC, you can have 50-pound package sent to you from your loved ones or friends once every 60 to 90 days. This can have canned goods and clothing and CDs for your CD player, everything that you can think of along with tobacco products of any kind and lighters. (I don't know how it is today though.) You could also order a TV from an outside vendor along with once in a while they would allow you to order things like pizza when they were doing a run like that. The yard there consists of a yard with a soccer field, handball courts, basketball courts, horseshoe area, bleachers and tables. In the middle of the yard is a little store that they allow you to purchase all kinds of commissary items from foods to canned goods to ice cream with this paper money they would sell you. This was due to the number of prisoners that were not allowed to get away from work to purchase their own commissary. Plus, if you got the urge to eat an ice cream before the start of a movie that was coming on later that night, you could walk out to the yard before it was closed down for the night and get whatever you wanted while watching the movie or TV show that was coming on. On the far side away from both buildings there on D-Quad was the kitchen and medical area. All your meals from breakfast to dinner were taken in the chow hall (kitchen). The chow hall sat above the yard, so to get there you had to walk around the yard to and then climb a set of steps and show your ID to the officer at the door. Once you show your ID, you can grab a tray, which is this thin silver-metal thing that is supposed to be a plate for prisoners. After grabbing your tray, you go through the food serving line like you were back at school somewhere. Then you take a seat. Most of the tables are assigned to the ethnic you're a part of and running with while in prison. The cells themselves are either two-man or single-celled. The two-man cells have a very small living area to them. Once you enter a cell there is a bunkbed shoulder high on either your left or right side. On the opposite side is another bunkbed, but this one is on a chain that allows it to fold up and sit along with the wall and out of the way. Straight back to the back of the cells are a single window that is wired with mesh but does allow you to open to get fresh air inside your cell. Right beneath the window is your toilet/sink and a mirror. Right next to this is a single desk. Up along the wall from the front of your cell is a shelving area made from wood that hangs down from chains allowing you to store your commissary and clothing. The bunkbed that doesn't fold up along the wall has a shelf at the foot of it but out of the way so that you could set your TV. You and your cell mate would take turns each day cleaning the cell so that it was always clean. While using the restroom during the night, the rule was if you're doing the #2 you flushed every time you dropped one. You also wiped the rim of the toilet after using it, then washed your hands. Also, your celly would rotate with you on cooking for each other if neither of you were going to the chow hall for your meals. Only after 11:00pm did the yard close down and you had to be inside your cells. At this time, the officer assigned to that floor you were living on would come around for count time and when he or she got. to your cell door you would have to show your ID card and state your name and number. Like my name and number back then were: Richard L. Tabler, #T-07607. Once count was finished the officer would throw the bar which would lock down all cells preventing you from opening your cell from the inside like you were able to do throughout the whole day. When you were not inside your cell and you left it, you could lock it with the key you had. This was to make sure that neither you nor your celly lost anything, nor could anyone just enter your cell and steal whatever they wanted to. Prisoners also were allowed to hold jobs in CDC, unlike say the state of Texas. Where they still believe in slavery and not paying the prisoners. In CDC, you could work in food service, auto repair, metal shop, clothing, garbage, you could clerk for rank and there was maintenance and yard work as well. Also, if you were at a prison that allowed it, you also got paid as a firefighter. The pay started for jobs from anywhere at 0.50 to $1.80 an hour. Also, please note that back when I was telling you all about the cells, note that they are not big cells and that you could not stretch out your hands without hitting the walls. Only from front to back were they long around 11 feet. So, the cells are around 11 X 3 1/4 feet.

Your friends and family members could send money to your Inmate Account. The amount can range from $1.00 to $1,000.00 anytime they wanted. There was no set amount they could or could not send to you. Money just like in any prison in America helps the inmates survive, because the foods that we are served does nothing to fill a grown man, let alone a dog if he were locked within a prison of the American people.

Things within the prison system were anything but kosher. There were always fights breaking out between one or two inmates every day, and sometimes it was between officers and inmates, but these were very few of. Only when the fight was serious did the officers do any paperwork and file a written report. Most of the times everything was ran by the inmates, such as the whites. This, in turn, is what would cause the fights to break out amongst one another. Just like out there in society, there is nothing but racism. I had my fair share of fights and only one of them ever started out one-on-one. Most of the times when I was assaulted it was two or three on one to try and teach me a lesson and to click up with some set. When I was moved from 7 Building to that of 8 Building

#8307, I was housed with a big black youngster named Poo Bear. He and I would also walk the yard together. He was doing time for GTA and DWI. When he got caught, it cost him his scholarship at UCLA. The fight that was my first major one took place about two months after I had gotten to the prison and was in the chow hall. I had gotten my tray and was sitting down at a table with my celly on my left and Mac across from me and Smurf on my right. Each of these men are black, and I'm the only looking white inmate sitting at their table. The rule of prison was that you sat at your own color table. If you were black you sat with the blacks, and if you were Mexican you sat with the Mexicans/Latinos and so on so on. You never mixed races with one another. Sitting there as I was, I was breaking every rule you could find within prison, but I didn't care. I was going to do my time how I wanted to do my time. I had just finished eating the main course on my tray and was taking a drink of milk, when my celly told me that one of the main peckerwoods was walking my way fixed on me. I kept eating and drinking, but took notice of how it became quiet within the chow hall. Not five seconds after Poo Bear said this to me, I felt a tap on my left shoulder, and these words, "Look out Wood! Come have a seat at the Wood table." I continued to eat as if I hadn't heard him say anything. Mac across the way from me and the other two at our table had stopped eating and were waiting to see what would happen. Again, the peckerwood tapped me on my left shoulder but a little harder this time and said, "Look out Wood, you're not to be sitting at this Nigger table! Come sit at the Wood table!" Instead of continuing to eat, I took another drink of my milk, but this time I was thinking about what to do as I was drinking. Once again, he tapped my left shoulder and went to say something but never got the chance to do so. I was in motion before anyone could understand it. I had picked up my metal tray and was coming around in a half circle and crashing the metal tray into and across his face, which in turn slit open his face from the jaw up to his ear. This also in turn caused everyone within the chow hall to break out into fighting, or I guess I should say rioting. All I can say is that it lasted for a while before it was broken up by the correctional officers and their riot teams. Once everything was said and done and we were all allowed to walk back to our cells. I did so with a busted lip and a black eye along with a large bump on the backside of my head. Nobody left that chow hall that day without shedding some of their own blood.

It was amazing that nobody was brought up on disciplinary charges that day. On the way back to our buildings all of us were laughing about what had happened, but most were shocked that I had did what I did without giving any kind of warning to anyone. It was good to be able to laugh with one another, but things aren't always able to be laughed at or about. Payback against me for what I did would be short in coming to find me. While walking the yard one evening, I found myself on the receiving end of a violent attack. Understand that the only reason the blacks backed me in the chow hall fight was because my celly was black and I was sitting at the blacks' table. Had none of these things been so, I would have ended up fighting on my own against who knows how many peckerwoods (whites). Coming from under Tower 6 one evening I was attacked by two skinheads with socks packed with batteries. This made for a crude weapon. Before I knew that they were behind me I was being struck down with one of these packed socks with the first hit striking me in the back of the head and neck area. While the first attacker was hitting me in the head and neck area the other one was hitting me in the stomach and legs. It was after that first blow to the back of my head that caused me to go to the ground stunned. That is the worse place you ever want to go in prison during a fight. You never want to be the fool on the ground because now they can stomp you and kick you and there is nothing that you can do other than curl into a ball and do your best to protect your head and face. They beat the crap out of me. In the end I took either a boot or a sock of batteries to my face which broke my nose. Right after it happened my celly and a few others showed up trying to take me to medical. I told them to take me back to our cell so I could clean up. With every step we took, it felt like my insides were on fire and I hurt all over. Once we were at the cell, I told Poo Bear to take a walk while I cleaned up. As I was washing the blood from my face in the sink and pulling off my shirt to wash, the building officer for floor 3 showed up at my cell door asking what happened. I told him that I fell down on the bleachers and was just cleaning up, and that all was good here. As I went back to washing my face, he said bullcrap and told me to come out of my cell. Outside my cell there were four other officers already waiting for me to escort me down to the Quad Captain's Office. Once there I was again asked what happened and again, I said that I fell down the bleachers. They asked who attacked me and I said I fell. They stopped me and said that someone already told them I was attacked on the yard. At that point

I stopped talking and had refused to identify my attackers, even though I knew who they were. I was escorted off the Quad to the Emergency Room over at medical. Once I was checked out and cleaned up, I was then taken over to the ASU (Administrative Segregation Unit) Building. At first, they charged me with being the victim of an attack, then they changed it to me being charged with an Article 115 for battery on an inmate. About one month or maybe two months later I was found not guilty and the charges were dropped, and I was released back onto the Quad. Once back on the Quad I was again assigned to 8 Building with Poo Bear. He brought me up to speed with everything that had taken place while I had been in the ASU Building. Soon as I had left a lot of the Brothers had gotten together and were talking about striking back and going all out into a race war on the yard, but that was shot down because I didn't belong to any set or family. I was a loner with a black celly and nothing else. While Poo Bear was bringing me up to speed on everything, there was a knock on our cell door, and then this HUGE black dude poked his head inside and said that I was wanted down on floor 2 to speak with someone. I told the big guy that I was good, and he said that it wasn't a request, that someone wanted to talk with me and if I didn't want to walk down there, he would take me down there. I looked at Poo Bear who raised his shoulders in a like what the heck?

 I got up and went out and followed this dude down to floor 2, when Poo Bear tried to follow us down the run of floor 2, the big dude stopped him and said only I was to come down there, but not to worry because nothing was going to happen to me. Guess that was enough for Poo Bear, because he didn't follow us! So many things were running through my mind at that time. I was thinking that this was a trap and I was fixing to get into it again, but way worse. Before I could decide what was going on though, we were at a cell door at the end of the run, on floor 2. Knocking on the door, I was told to enter. Thinking this was it I went in fast ready to fight. Only to realize that it was legit and there was this bald black guy sitting right beneath the window facing the door. He was only about 5'4 and he was just sitting there watching me watch him. Within his hands he held a roll of paperwork that he unrolled as he was watching me. Letting me see that my name was printed at the top, he went on to tell me to relax that he only wanted to speak with me about some things.

 He told me that he and some of his family had been watching me since I rolled up on CMC-East. When I took on a black celly, word went around that there was a white guy that could only be housed with blacks or Mexicans. That he couldn't be housed with any whites for any reason. When he heard this, he had all my paperwork pulled and then he had family outside of these prison walls do a search as well. He said that he thought I handled myself well in the chow hall the day of the riot behind that peckerwood coming at me the way he did. He also thought I had heart at the way I handled getting my ass beat by the two skinheads. But he wanted to know why I didn't say anything about who had attacked me when everyone knew that I knew. I said that I wanted to return the favor and mess them up some time. Turning a page on the papers he held he said something that to this very day, still has me wondering how the hell he found out. He asked me about the story or rumor of me and the abattoir. I looked at him like what was he talking about, but he could see that it was true. When I asked him what he really meant, he said that there is talk on the streets back in Florida about how a young kid named Blue who looked white but wasn't had pushed a pedophile through an industrial meat grinder. I said that if it was true then it must have been because he had just raped his daughter after torturing her with a lighter, and he just happened to be standing next to it laughing.

    I asked him what all this was about and why he had asked me here today. He said that he thought I might like to join up with the family that he and many others had belonged to. It was a spinoff of BGF and its founder was another Brother who was killed in prison. This individual was named George Jackson, who everyone who is about anything and is willing to look further then what one is told will know that he was killed inside his prison cell by white officers who said he was trying to escape. How could that be when he was killed inside of his cell? George Jackson was killed by white men inside San Quentin State Prison back in the 70's after founding Kumi African Nations. He said that almost everyone inside prison was with someone or another and that if I kept going about doing my time as a loner, I would always be fighting with everyone. You had the KKK, Peckerwoods, Skinheads, Aryan Circle, Aryan Brotherhood, Bloods, Crips, Latin Kings, Folk Nation, Gangster Disciples, BGF and Black Panthers plus many other off the walls set that would take a run at me, not counting the officers themselves. However, most of the blacks would leave me alone, except for the Bloods and Crips, as they're always trying to make a name for themselves. By coming into our family, you don t have to worry about any of the bullcrap. There's no jumping you into it, it's as simple as reciting an Oath spoke by each of the Family. You would have to start speaking fluent Swahili and reading and studying the Holy Qur'an. There are laws and byelaws for all Members of Kumi African Nations. I asked why me, or more importantly how can I be in this Family? I was told that they had all my paperwork and that they knew that I come from a mixed background. That my mom is full blooded Jamaican and my father is white trash (my words). That, because of this, I would be accepted as a member so long as I stayed sincere and was able to recite the full Oath. After which point, I would be offered either of the two tattoos, one of which is of a soldier holding a flag with 415 on it or the simpler one of Kumi. There was no fighting unless absolutely necessary, and then it would have to be okayed by the elders. I accepted his offer. He then told me that his name was Mac, but in the free he was known as Carl Skinner of Oakland, California. I would come to know Mac well and we would both become close friends and family. I learned to speak fluently in Swahili and also in Ibo, as well as my own language of English. I studied the Holy Qur'an and was given a tattoo on my right back arm… Kumi.

Mac is currently serving two life sentences for Murder 1. About three months after my time in the ASU Building and being attacked the two inmates that attacked me were released back onto D-Quad. Once I was given the green light to do so, my chance at retaliation came in the worst place right in front of the building I was assigned to. Simply put, as I was coming out of the building, they were coming into it. I did the only thing I could and that was to grab hold of a shovel that one of the maintenance inmates had standing by the building. Grabbing it up and swinging all in one motion I caught inmate David Salerno #J-98438 upside his head with the edge of the shovel blade. Then while everyone was in shock, I turned on his buddy, inmate John Emmons #E-30529, and caught him in the lower back before beating them both over and over until I was tackled down by officers. I was taken straight to the ASU Building and later that night I was transported to Pelican Bay State Prison in Northern California. My stay there was short, but not short enough. Pelican Bay broke my mind in ways that would break any normal person. I refuse to even speak about what I went through at that place (it's bad). After doing my stint in Pelican Bay, I was shipped to CTF Soledad (Correctional Training Facility) Soledad. This was in the beginning of 2003, and just as I was getting into being settled, I was told to pack up because I was being shipped to CSP Corcoran (Corcoran State Prison). I would only be there for a little over one month before being sent back to CTF Soledad. As usual, it didn't take long for trouble to find me there either, but not before Mac was transported from CMC-East to CTF Soledad and we became cellies. Things were crazy at CTF Soledad. I had been working as a Captain's clerk for about three months before I got into it with an officer and bought myself a one-way ticket to Ad-Seg. While housed at CTF-Soledad, I was in two cells: D-242 and O-143. CTF was bad, but their Ad-Seg was way worse, if something broke out on the yard between you and someone else or a riot broke out, you didn't have to worry about getting a fast response from the officers. They walked around with their weapons hot and gave out only one warning. That was to lay down on the ground with your arms out away from your sides. If you failed to do this you were shot on the spot. If you ever ask an officer that works at a real badass prison, where they aim to shoot inmates, they'll tell you they aim to stop the threat. Meaning they're aiming to kill you not to just injure you. They're aiming for your head.

From CTF-Soledad, I was extradited back to Florida on an outstanding warrant and violation of parole. Here is where things get interesting. When you're being extradited to another State from one State, there are numerous ways for them to transport you. If the State that wants you want you bad and fast, they'll have the US Marshals pick you up and fly you back on a plane. If they don't need you that fast, or you're not that important to them, they'll have a transportation company pick you up on the Blue Bird Bus with numerous other prisoners waiting to be transported to other States as well. From CTF-Soledad I was packed up in a van by a transportation company, along with three other inmates from parts of CTF-Soledad. Inside the van were others both of the male and female sexes chained together. From CTF-Soledad, we were transported to a point over in Palm Springs, California, at which point we all got onto a Blue Bird Bus for cross country travel. Once I was chained up to the inmate that would be chained to me throughout the trip, we were told to walk onto the bus. On the bus there is the driver and a front cage officer to watch over things from the front by said driver, and yet in between the cages that separate the women prisoners from the male prisoners. Then at the very back of the bus hidden in his/her own cage with a tinted window is another back gunner. Each of these officers is armed with his/her personal weapon on their side along with either an AR-15 or a shotgun. Each prisoner is chained to another, unless he/she is in a single cage for either further security or for their own safety. Prisoners have leg irons on, with a chain running from the leg irons to a belly chain where your hands are cuffed in the front of you. From the belly chain another chain runs to the other inmate that you are chained to. During this trip, I was chained to a loud mouth from CTF-Soledad who wouldn't shut up. If he wasn't talking to the female prisoners when he was told numerous times not to by the front-gunner (not the driver), he was talking crap to the gunner herself. She was pretty and had nice long legs, but who in their right mind wants to piss off a woman with a gun? Not I. From Palm Springs, California, we traveled across the country with stops in Arizona, New Mexico, Colorado, and many other States. Please note, that while we were traveling across the country, the Transportation Officers did stop every morning at a fast-food joint to purchase everyone on the bus breakfast and lunch. For dinner we were taken to the city jail where we were picking someone up or dropping off to spend the night. Somewhere along the way and around the city and State of Kansas City, MO, or Nashville, TN, the idiot I was chained to and I got into it. I don't remember what caused it other than he wouldn't shut up and it was early in the morning as we were getting ready to stop for our daily breakfast. All I do remember was the bus was already slowing down when I turned to him and told him to just shut the hell up. He looked at me like I had grown horns, before telling me to shut the hell up or do something about it. When we had got onto the bus back in Palm Springs, I had taken a paperclip that I found on the van, and had been working it into shape every time that we stopped somewhere, before once again having to hide it. That morning I had been working at the padlock on my belly chain and handcuffs. Without him or anyone else knowing it, I had already picked the lock and my hands were separate from the belly chain. When he told me to do something about it I did just that. I snapped and had him in a choke hold, because there wasn't any room to fight on a bus and in those seats. The only thing one could really do was choke someone's ass out, and that is just what I set to do. The only thing I could hear was the screaming from everyone. That crap was loud as hell as all the prisoners were screaming for me to kill him, with the female gunner screaming for me to let him go. Talk about mixed signals! What seemed like forever was really only a few minutes, but I had somehow carried us into the walkway between the seats. I didn't have a good solid hold on him at first because he didn't just sit there. He tried his best to get away from me, only to fail to realize that he was chained to me. Fear does that to people. You forget things when you fear for your life and you panic. Once I got a good hold on him though, it didn't last long because I had failed to pay attention to my surroundings and where the front gunner was throughout this ordeal. One minute I was choking this fool out from all my built-up anger at being stuck on this freaking bus for weeks, and for all the crap I would now miss, to being knocked smooth the heck out after being hit with the stock of the shotgun. I can honestly tell you that is the only time that I have ever in my life been knocked out cold. When I came to, I was in a county jail and awaiting special transportation. My actions caused the transportation company to have to transport me the rest of the way on my own by van. This worked out great, because I ended up in Fort Myers, Florida, within the next three days.

Once there, I was processed and sent out to the camp. I only had to do a short amount of time before being released in April of 2004. The minute my feet touched ground outside of jail, I ran.

Chapter Five

Road Trip

The first place I went to when I got out after getting laid was to say goodbye to my mom. I had this feeling that I wouldn't be seeing her again but didn't want to tell her that. I just wanted her to know that I loved her and that I was leaving. From my mom's house I walked down the road to a friend's house there in Cape Coral, Florida. From this house I caught a ride with one of his sisters into downtown and to the first car dealership. After she had dropped me off, I walked inside and asked to test drive a dark blue Chevy Silverado quad cab that was a 2004. The car sales man took a copy of my ID card that I had stashed at my mom's house, then handed me the keys and told me to be back in thirty minutes or so. I drove out of the lot to another friend's shop, where I had another set of keys made. I also had him place the truck up on the lift to remove the speed chip that these newer cars and trucks have in them. It's a computer chip that prevents them from going over a set speed. I had plans on stealing this truck later on that night. After returning the truck back to the dealership, I explained to the salesman that it was a little steep for my liking, but would think it over the next couple of days. We shook hands and I left. Walking down the street to Taco Bell, I got something to eat. While eating inside, I thought about everything that I needed to do and wanted to do. While sitting there I got a call on my cell phone, and from Taco Bell went to one more friend's house that was three blocks from where I was. (I do not say names here because these people are involved with illegal crap.) At this friend's house, I smoked a little weed and popped some ecstasy, also known as X. As I was sitting there chillin', a group of people started showing up for a party my friend was throwing. Next thing I know as I'm sitting back on his couch just in front of his big screen TV, he places in my hands two triple stack of Buddha pills. Without missing a beat, I throw them into my mouth and chew them up before swallowing them and washing the nasty ass taste down with some chick's fuzzy navel flavored wine cooler. Almost spitting that crap out, I grab a bottle of Dos Equis that I had been drinking. After about thirty minutes I'm starting to feel the effects of the X. This girl I don't know climbs onto my lap and starts blowing into my face with a Vicks inhaler. The thing is she had reversed the insides of it so that she could blow into my face while also giving me a massage on my upper body and neck area. The effect this had on me was one of a super high and rush that had me wanting to bang, and that's what this chick and I were doing right then and there on the couch. She had pulled out my cock and was riding me right there while blowing me up with that Vicks inhaler. That was one of the best bangs I ever had. I guess the mixture of the drugs and what she was doing to me just mixed right. About one o' clock in the morning I left the house and walked back to the dealership while carrying a set of bolt cutters with me that I had taken from my friend's house. Once I got to the dealership, I had to cut through the padlock holding a chain across the entrance to the lot. After this was done, I walked to where the Silverado was that I had tested that afternoon. Using the keys I had copied, I let myself in and started the truck before driving out of the lot to the nearest gas station to fill the tank. Driving up the East Coast alone gave me time to think about everything. I had no set destination in mind, only to get the heck out of Florida. I drove through Atlanta, Georgia and both South and North Carolina and into Virginia before making my way over to Cincinnati and then turning a bit north and going into Detroit, Michigan. For some dumbass reason I still cannot understand, I made a stop at a gas station in Calhoun County in Michigan which is in Belding, Michigan. After going inside to pay for the gas, I was waiting inside the truck and staying warm while the tank was filling. Next thing I know, I'm surrounded by cops. They have their guns out and pointing at me in the truck screaming at me to show my hands and exit the truck. Exiting the truck with my hands held high in the air to show they're empty, I am instructed to kneel on the ground and interlock my legs over each other with my hands behind my head. Once this is being done, they run up to me grab my hands while throwing me to the ground face first, and dropping a knee into my back and pulling my hands down and behind my back to place me into handcuffs. Being placed into the back of one of the cop cars, I watched as the truck was placed onto a flatbed tow truck and taken to the impound yard (I was told). While I was driven to the jail in the next county over. Other than the truck being stolen I had no idea why I was being arrested right then. Nor did I have any idea why so many cops had shown up with their guns trained on me. Any thought I had of fleeing was out of the question as there were too many! It was while I was being booked into the Montcalm County Jail, which was in the next county over from the one I was busted in (don't know why they take me to the next county). But some female that I had had a one-night stand with and had heard stories about me afterwards from people she hung out with. Decided to go to the police and take out a PPO (Personal Protection Order) against me without me knowing. While I was inside paying her for the gas, she recognized some of my tattoos and called the cops. I sure in the hell didn't recognize her, guess that was why she was so pissed and had to call the cops, eh? So, I was arrested for violation of a PPO and two counts of FTA (whatever the hell that is). I was sentenced to a $175.00 fine and had to do 17 days in jail. I was released on, May 9th, 2004. Upon leaving the jail, I took notice that these hicks left my ass stranded way out in the middle of nowhere. The stolen truck was in the next county over and the nearest town was ten miles away. In the distance I could see some apartments and made my way in their direction. Once there, which was further than it looked, I was freezing my ass off. I made small talk with this country boy who was working on his truck and asked him if he could give me a lift into the next county over to get my truck out of the impound yard. He said he could but wanted to know what I was in their jail for. I told him that I had violated a PPO that I didn't know someone had out on me. He laughed at that and said he'd been there a time or two himself. He finished up and we got into his truck which was a Ford F150 that looked beat to hell with rust everywhere. When he dropped me in the next county at the impound yard, I thought it was going to be a yard but was a local truck shop. I went inside and asked about my truck and was told that it was in the back and covered with a tarp. I owed $100.00 to get it out. I paid the fee and got the keys and left. Tell me that's not some seriously slick crap. Knowing this truck is stolen and still going to get it and drive it away! I drove it into downtown Belding and found my way to a local carwash. Nope, I didn't get the truck washed because I didn't want anyone to get a clear shot of my plates. Sitting in the parking lot I started thinking and realized that there was someone in that town I knew and could get some serious cash from, until I found out what I wanted to do and where I wanted to go. I walked over to a telephone booth and grabbed the phone book. Looking under lawyers I found who I was looking for. Yep, there's crooked lawyers everywhere if you know where to look for the bastards at. In the case of this one he worked for a time for Danny when he was alive and his associates when they were near Michigan. I don't owe this fool one thing. His name was and is Pete Fry, Attorney at Law in Belding, Michigan. No crap, look this dude up. See, Pete had a drug problem and got into some serious debt with Danny and friends to keep his life and job he was bought and paid off. Pete had a nice house on the Lake with a new Chevy Tahoe and a car along with his old model Z240. So, I looked old Pete up and got some cash and went to catch some sleep at his house while he remained at work for a while. Pete gave me some information to some locals that were in the market for some cocaine and I went around to their place only to catch them in a party.

 Inviting myself inside, I spoke to a few people and found myself looking into the eyes of this long-legged beauty named Lisa Wagner. Lisa and I got to talking and she asked me what kind of drugs I had on me. I told her that I didn't have anything on me, but could get it within the hour if it was needed. She said she really just enjoyed smoking some weed and asked if I could get her some and we could just go off on our own and smoke and chill. I told her to come on outside with me and we got into my truck. I drove her over to Pete's house and ran inside grabbing an ounce of weed and a half ounce of cocaine. Though she didn't ask for the cocaine, I figured I would introduce her to a primo if she was willing to try one. A primo is a joint laced with cocaine. After returning to the truck, I asked her where she wanted to go. She directed me to way the heck out into the middle of the woods and onto a dirt track that led to her house. About two miles from her house in the woods, we pulled over and I rolled her some joints to smoke. I asked her if she wanted to try a primo and she said no. We climbed out and I opened the tailgate and we sat and talked. I got to know Lisa and the things she liked to do and a little bit about her family. She was a good girl and was doing small things like pot with no other drugs. She asked about myself and I told her some but not much. We started kissing and making out, but for some reason I stopped and lightly pushed back from her. She asked me why I was stopping and I told her that I didn't want to just screw in the bed of this truck as it was too freaking cold! She laughed at me and said she was use to this cold weather. I explained that I was from California and Florida and I didn't do cold, not even for some sex. She told me to get my ass in the truck and to drive her home which I did so. Thinking that this was it, I waited for her to get out but she just sat there asking me what I was waiting for. I said what do you mean? She said she wanted me to come inside with her as nobody was home, she wanted me to stay over and show her how guys from Florida and California had sex. Sorry people, but I'm not going to share the details of my sex life with Lisa with you. Even though she and I don't have contact, I still hold her in respect and know she has a family of her own now. Long story though, we hit it off and Lisa and one of her male friends ended up leaving with me from Michigan in another stolen truck, though this time I brought her friend Scot Nash into it. Made Scot take his license into a dealership and take out a new truck for a drive while Lisa and I waited across the street in my stolen truck. Once Scot brought the truck around, I changed plates and we left. I had to make some stops before leaving Michigan to pick up some guns and a few other things, then we were on our way. Somewhere in or around the states of Indiana and Kentucky we got pulled over for speeding. I pulled to the side of the road and watched the officer come up alongside of the truck. Not once did I place the truck into park or take it out of gear. I had my foot on the brake though. When the officer came up, I gave him one of my old licenses and he went back to his car to run it. When he came back, I took notice of how he had his hands on his gun now. I didn't want to get into a shooting match with Lisa and Scot in the truck, nor did I want to shoot the cop. I did the only thing that popped into my mind at the time. I took my foot off the brake and fled. I saw in my mirror that the cop was running back to his car to give chase. I told Lisa and Scot to put their seatbelts on. I drove like the wind. As the cop was coming up on us, I took notice that an 18-wheeler that was ahead of me was swerving all across the highway trying to assists the cop by getting me to slow and stop. Wasn't going to happen. I swerved onto the exit ramp and took it and raced us out into the middle of nowhere. As we came upon the woods, I got out of the truck after telling Lisa and Scot to remain inside. See, I had pulled the truck off into the woods and was now waiting for the cop to show up. He never showed, thus I started thinking that he called off the pursuit. After two hours or so I got back into the truck and made it back onto the highway. I never really thought about it much back then, but I'm sure you're all wondering if I would have shot that cop if he came up and found us. Probably, but I'm glad I never had to find out. Throughout the road trip I never allowed either Lisa or Scot to drive the truck. Not because they couldn't, but because if there was ever another incident like with the cop pulling us over, I had tons of experience with driving and evading from when I drove for Danny and friends. My plan was to drive over to California and then maybe go see my older brother Greg, who I think was living in or around Portland at the time. Right then though I was taking us to visit with my sister Kristina, who was living in some little town called Killeen in Texas. She had gotten married to her high school sweetheart, who in my rightful opinion is nothing more than an asshole, even if he did serve in the military and was stationed at Fort Hood Military base. But when we went to see my sister, I hadn't seen her in years because I had been in prison in California and then right on over into jail at Fort Myers, Florida. Once we got into Texas, I contacted my sister at her work because I didn't have any of her information like house address or numbers, but I knew where she worked, at least the name of the company. So, I looked up the number in the phone book and called her there. I explained when she got on the phone that I and two friends were there in Killeen and if she could visit for a few minutes? She gave me directions to her job and we met in the parking lot and she met both Lisa and Scot. It was the first time I had seen my older sister Kristina in over four years and some change. She told me that she got off work in a couple of hours and that if I wanted to, we could meet at her house that she gave me directions to. We did that and, in the end, she allowed us to stay with her for a couple of nights. After our short visit, we left with my sights set on California. We traveled through this big ass State of Texas for what seemed like hours and hours before coming upon and going through New Mexico and the city of Albuquerque. From there we drove onto and through the State of Arizona and onto and through the State of Nevada and into California. Along the way we made tons of stops for both rest and gas and to eat. When we got closer to Turlock, I decided to take a chance and contact my dad just for the hell of it. He agreed to meet with us at a local restaurant for lunch. After meeting in the parking lot and introducing both Lisa and Scot to my dad we all went inside and ordered lunch. I excused myself to use the restroom and while I was gone either Lisa or Scot took it upon themselves to explain to my dad that I had guns. When I came back to the table, he asked me to talk with him outside for a minute. I did this not having a clue what he wanted to talk about as I had no love for him as a dad. To me he was just another person, but I was still curious about what he wanted to talk about. When we got outside, he said that he knew I had some guns and wanted to know if I wanted to sell them to him or his friends? He wouldn't tell me which one of the people inside had told him about them, but there was a touch of fear that I would hurt someone with one of them (isn't that what guns are for!?). I told him that I didn't mind getting rid of one of them and sold him for $150.00 the Ruger 9mm, though I kept a 45mm S and W. After lunch, we all parted ways and the three of us continued on our way up the coast of California. Though I promised myself I would never have the love for my brother Sean like a sibling I decided to also contact him in the Bay area as that was where I understood him to be living with his girlfriend who would later become his wife. When we got closer to San Francisco, I got on my cell phone and called information for his telephone number. When his girlfriend picked up, I kindly asked to speak with Sean if he was there. A second later he came on the phone. I explained that for some reason or another I was coming through Frisco and wanted to know if he wanted to visit? I was shocked when he said yes and instructed me to his condo. I was told to enter the underground parking. Driving into an underground parking lot in a full-sized Chevy truck was a tight ass fit and even more so when I decided that I wasn't going to be parked nose in and instead backed into a spot on the third floor. When my brother met us at the elevator in the garage, I introduced to him both Lisa and Scot. Sean and I shook hands and he led us into the elevator and took us up to their condo. He and his girl had a really nice place and I was happy for him, but I never told him so. Sean and his girlfriend Laura asked us if we would stay for dinner and then for the night.

We accepted. Lisa and I slept on a foldout bed and Scot took the other couch. In the morning, before we left Sean asked me where I was going? I told him I didn't know (though I did). Before we left, he gave me some money that I didn't ask him for. The three of us got into the truck and left. Before leaving San Francisco, I thought to show Lisa around and to walk on Pier 51, as she had never been out of Michigan before this. We found another underground parking lot and paid the fee to enter. While I was getting ready to exit the truck, Lisa being a little slick ass called my name, and when I turned my head towards her, she took my picture! The picture found in this book is the one she took and it's the last picture anyone would ever see of me before I made the biggest mistake of my life back in Texas. We all walked around and enjoyed ourselves before it was time to leave. Back on the road and in turn the freeways. I took us to the Oregon State line and in we went on our way to find my oldest and last sibling, Greg. At the time my older brother was married and he and his wife Tabitha were living around Portland, Oregon. When we got closer to them, I called my brother up from the hotel we were staying at. He came out and we all met and talked. Greg asked me if Lisa was my girlfriend and I told him yes and that Scot was a friend of hers from Michigan. He asked me what our plans were and I told him nothing really, though I would like to find a job for a bit. He thought it over and the next night he and his wife Tabitha asked if I wanted to stay with him for a little while. Greg said he would get me a job working for his partner as they were doing concrete work. I asked about Lisa coming with and then what about Scot. They were welcome for the time being. We drove over to my brother's apartment complex and he showed us around. Tabitha met us and gave me a hug and I introduced her to Lisa and in turn Scot. She and Lisa hit it off. Scot and I ended up going to work for my brother and his partner for Maui's Construction. I had done construction work before when I was younger and not into so much crime, so this was nothing new to me, but for Scot, he didn't last long and before we knew it, it was decided that we would send Scot back to Michigan on a flight. One-week later Scot was flying home to be back with his loved ones while Lisa would remain with me for the time being. While working for my brother and his friend at Maui's Construction, I drove the heavy dump truck and the skid (Backhoe and Bobcat) for them. About two months into our stay, my brother helped me get a place for myself and Lisa, while Lisa was working with Tabitha during the days and I was working with my brother.

It was hard work but it paid cash at the end of each week around $700 to $800.00 each week. Greg talked me into leaving the truck in a parking lot with the keys in it after contacting the law in Michigan and explaining to them where I was leaving the truck for the car dealership to recover it if they still wanted it. I made sure to wipe it down really good so there were no fingerprints, as they still had no idea who took their truck. I also got rid of my gun. Things were working out great for a while and then as usual my past found me and I started making money the other way and left working for my brother and his friend. Lisa tried her best to get me to do good and leave that kind of life behind and I honestly wanted to. In the end I just couldn't do it though. Lisa and I broke up, even though our feelings for one another were really strong, we both thought it best that she returned home to Michigan (to this day from my understanding she is married with a couple of kids. I wish her the best).

After Lisa was gone for good, I started going backwards in my life again, doing drugs and mixing with the wrong crowd. I knew where to look for the things I wanted to enjoy, and while I greatly enjoyed the help of my older brother and his wife at the time, I just couldn't deal with life like that. I needed the fast life and the drugs to run. One-night while having people over to my place, my brother and his wife entered and I was caught with drugs all over the place and people enjoying themselves. The things that seriously broke me inside though was the fact that my older brother had seen his little brother messed up on dope. Had he and his wife entered a minute earlier, they would have caught me shooting up a major hit of cocaine. I was so screwed up back then that I was driving one day and while sitting at a stoplight, I was caught slipping and this fool attempted to car jack me after hitting me full in the face through my window with brass knuckles. I kept my piece of crap car but I ended up in the Emergency Room at the University Hospital South. (Please see that back of this book for medical papers and criminal papers).

After my carjacking incident, I and my brother got into it a bit, and I ended up leaving Oregon and traveling back into California and the Bay area of Oakland to a friend's place there. Once again back into this area of California, I located a friend that drives 18-wheelers for a living. I just happened to catch him at home and talked him into giving me a ride out of the State. He took me with him to Salt Lake City, Utah, where I caught a flight for Killeen, Texas. My friend tried to talk me into staying in Salt Lake City and working for the same company he drove for, but I knew there was no way I could do this with my criminal past and no CDL. Told him thanks and left. Upon landing in Killeen, Texas, I contacted my sister Kristina and asked if she could please pick me up and if I could stay with her for a few days before leaving. She came and got me and with her she brought a surprise. My mom was now living with my sister while my brother-in-law was in Iraq fighting in this stupid war when they should have just nuked that country.

Chapter Six

Teazer's Gentleman's Club

After my sister and mom came to get me from the airport and take me back to my sister's house, I was told that my mom had just moved in at my sister's request for company while my brother-in-law, Matthew Martinez, was over in Iraq. I hadn't seen my mom for almost one year now. I explained to them both that I wasn't planning on staying that long, just long enough for my face to heal from where I was sucker punched with brass knuckles in Oregon, as I was still black and blue around my left eye and cheek area and my jaw was still swollen. My sister said that she didn't mind, but that I couldn't stay longer than that. I told her I understood. Everyone knew that I wasn't one that could sit still for very long nor not get into any kinds of trouble. After about one week, I had flown back to meet and talk with my friend in Salt Lake City, Utah, the same one that had given me a ride in his 18-wheeler from Oakland, California. When he met me at the airport we drove back to his job and got into his truck. He had a big double sleeper Volvo, that was basically like a tiny house on the inside. While sitting inside and talking he asked me what I really wanted. It was then that I explained that while

I had been driving all over the place on the run from Johnny Law and saying goodbye to my siblings and even seeing my dad. I got it into my mind that I wanted him to find someone for me so I could end it. He said who? I told him to find Terry Brotherton for me. I gave him all the information that I knew about him. He said to give him about one week and then to come back here. We parted ways and I went back to Killeen, Texas. When I got back, I called my sister and asked if she could please come and pick me up? She said no, but that mom would come and get me and not to make this a habit. I explained that I would be gone shortly, though that's not what happened. While I was staying at my sisters, she was allowing me to drive her Jeep Wrangler around and do whatever I needed to do. Seems like it never fails though as I found myself at this Club called Teazer's. I thought I would go inside and see what they had going on there. It was during the afternoon hours so it wasn't very busy inside the semi-dark club. Once you enter inside there is a bar to the right and a dance floor with pole to the left. Straight back between the two is a sitting area and to the right the restrooms and next to the restrooms is a set of stairs leading to the second floor. Up here there was more seating and a pool table and the dancers changing area. Aside from the entrance that I came through in the front, there were two others that were inside and out, but were only being used for emergency exits at the time the club was open. One was back at end of the club that opened onto a parking lot that was shared with the club behind it called Dollhouse, and the other exit was through the dancers changing room on the second floor. Back behind the bar and to the left were a small office where the money and safe were being kept along with a telephone if someone needed to make a call. While I was inside, I took a seat and thought while watching one of the dancer's do her thing on the dance floor and moving on the pole. Needless to say, she sucked and her body wasn't all that. While watching her a man I'll describe as Middle Eastern with dark-black hair came walking inside and barking orders to people here and there. His name I was told was Mohamed but everyone at the club called him by his middle name, Amine. Amine was part owner of Teazer's, and weeks later I would know more about Amine and he would know lots about me. I left the club about two hours later and returned to my sister's home. My sister at the time had been working for Dynamic Designs there in Killeen and my mom got a job working on base in the children's part of the hospital. Without being asked I kind of moved into my sister's place with the two of them, but not before obtaining everything that I needed to know about the where abouts of one Terry Brotherton and the fact that he was in a little town in Indiana, but had been returning to Las Vegas a couple of times recently. I wasn't planning on staying in Texas nor with my sister and mom. I had no real destination in mind other than finding Terry so I could kill him.

That day/night when I returned to my mom's place in Las Vegas and saw her battered and bruised face and neck from Terry trying to beat and suffocate her while she was sleeping. That crap broke something within me that could never be replaced. Nobody should ever have to see their mom, their pride and gold beaten down like a dog like that. Especially no kid who had already been living a jacked-up lifestyle. What kind of piece of crap puts their hands on a woman!? I'll tell you what kind: a freaking coward and a piece of crap who should be taken out in the woods and either beat the fuck out of or shot dead! Nobody has the right to place their hands on a woman for any reason. That not only hurt me, but pissed me off more when in the end my mom got back together with this piece of crap. And in all honesty, that is what sealed Terry's fate with me. For some crazy ass reason, I kept returning to Teazer's and before long Amine and I met and talked about something. I found out for example that Amine enjoyed doing cocaine but didn't have a supplier that he could get it form anytime he wanted it. He also liked to act like he had more money than he did, though he had bought a boat that was out on one of the lakes, had a nice house that he was sharing with his sister and was screwing his choice of dancers from the club. Before long, it came to my attention that Amine also bought stolen goods and he was in the market for some stolen stereos for his car and home.

I got to thinking and looking around, but the one thing about Killeen? There are cops everywhere! Plus, I had to be on the lookout for military police that would come off base for some reason or another. By this time, I had been screwing this woman named Wendy that was a dancer at the Dollhouse, which was the club directly behind Teazer's. Her boyfriend at the time was also in Iraq, and while over there he had left Wendy the use of his lifted Dodge Ram truck. This truck was too big for Wendy to be driving, so she allowed me to use it whenever I needed to. Using my cell phone, I contacted my friend back in Salt Lake City and asked him if he knew anyone on Fort Hood Military Base. I was told yes and given a name and number to call. Once I had this information, I called the number I was given and spoke with the person on the other end. We decided to meet up at Taco Bell and discuss things. We'll call him Mike (because he's still in the military). I met up with Mike and asked him what kind of things he could help me with at the Base in exchange for some cocaine. Mike would turn out to be a gold mine. One week later, he and I met up outside the gate of Fort Hood Military Base's Airport and right next to this place called TGI Electric. A place that I would return to not far from then. Mike was doing a lot of work around ACP 9 Alpha, West Fort Hood, after work two days after we met, he brought me a set of military BDU's a pair of boots and tags along with a military ID. I was dressed as a soldier every day when I was going onto Fort Hood Military Base even thought I was not a military soldier. The reason for my being this way was I was dealing in illegal activities having to do with the property of the Department of Defense. Mike was getting me guns and military issued Kevlar along with other items of military goods that could be sold off base. While doing this, I went about my usual and bought up stolen stereos and other items with bad checks. A few times I had to drive to San Antonio, Texas, to pick up a kilo of cocaine for Mike. I ended up getting caught up with the police early and had to go downtown in Belton, Texas, to meet and talk with the district attorney. It was here that an offer was made to me to work in OCD (Organized Crime Division) as an informant to clear up my record with them and a few other places. All I was thinking was that I was stupid for showing up there and I took their offer so I could get out of there. My contact was Detective Tim Steglich assigned to the Killeen Police Departments, Criminal Investigation Division of Organized Crime. I had their numbers and they had mine. Once they let me go, I contacted Mike and my friend back in Salt Lake City, Utah.

Both of them told me I needed to leave Texas right away. After I hung up with them, I got a call from one of the dancers at the club that told me Amine was going around telling people that he could have my family killed for as little as $10.00, and that I was being kicked out of the club and no longer working for Amine. I was never really working for him in the first place like everyone had thought. As I left the parking lot of the District Attorney's Office from talking with the Defectives, I headed towards my sister's house thinking that I should go ahead and just leave, but something kept me back. I ended up staying longer than I should have, thinking that I could play the cops and find Amine for the money he owed me for the stolen stereos and the cocaine. In between everything I still went out with people to other clubs and I still did stupid crap. Screwing this chick that was a one-night stand and jacking her ex-boyfriend for his 9mm Ruger. In my mind, I needed to leave Texas, but I never made it out as I was too caught up in things and wanted to do something about Amine first.

   Near Thanksgiving Day, I had gone to Fort Hood Military Base and signed this punk out of CQ (Confined to Quarters). This caused me to have to dress in my BDU's and grab my military ID I had gotten from Mike. I went onto the Base and signed out the punk from CQ and we left the Base. The year was 2004. About two weeks before Thanksgiving Day, I showed up at OCD and had my fingerprints and past ran through the NCIC (National Crime Information Center) before being wired up to go and make a buy for over $300.00 in cocaine. The buy went smoothly and I left OCD afterwards, returning back to Teazer's even though everyone was telling me Amine didn't want me there. Just as I was leaving in the lifted Dodge Ram truck, Amine was pulling in with a friend of his in a dark green Jeep. The guy that Amine was with was named Haitham, but I was introduced to him as Blue and he as Frank. He was nothing like Amine, this guy acted like he wanted to be anywhere else than where he was that time. I paid little attention to him and asked Amine when he was going to pay me the money he owed for the stolen stereos and the cocaine. I was told that he would have the money soon and that for the cocaine he would trade me this Jeep they had just showed up in. That is when it was brought to my attention that Frank owned a car dealership of used cars in Cameron, Texas. Frank acted like he wanted to say something but he never did because Amine cut him off. Frank got back into the Jeep and came out with a title and we talked it over (Amine and I) and then Frank signed the Jeep over to me there and then. I was now the owner of a used green Jeep. They walked into the club and I left with the promise from Amine that he would have my money for the stereos by that weekend. The weekend came and went and Amine couldn't be found anywhere. I ended up taking a couple of girls to my sister's house for Thanksgiving Day, afterwards we left and went back to this chick's house to party. Two of the guys I had been doing things with and they had been buying cocaine from me were there at the house and I asked them to leave with me. One was named Chris and the other was named Tim. Chris couldn't come because he had somewhere else to be, that left

Tim riding around with me in the early morning hours of November 27th, 2004, or I guess you could say late night on November 26th, 2004, Thanksgiving night. By this time, I had taken the Jeep and traded it in for a midnight blue lowered Chevy S-10 with tinted windows and a sound system along with a bed cover. I had all kinds of drugs and weapons within this truck. Tim and I left and went looking for Amine.

We drove all over Killeen, Texas, and I called Amine on his cell phone numerous times and even went by his house where I ended up talking to his sister who was just getting home from being out with her friends. She said that she didn't know where her brother was but did try and call him with no answer. As we were leaving his house, he called my cell phone and explained that he and Frank were out at a club and they would meet me in one hour. I told them where to meet and it was set up. Tim and I raced back into Killeen and back to the party, where I traded trucks and then Tim and I went to the location that Amine was to meet us at. Now we were riding in the lifted Dodge Ram truck that belonged to Wendy and her boyfriend who was in Iraq. What Tim didn't know at the time though was that when we got into this truck, I had removed a 9mm Ruger from my lowered S-10.

Every time that I drove in any other truck or car, I would always be wearing these thin black gloves. I never took them off for any reason unless I was at my sister's house. When Amine was supposed to meet with us after one hour and he still hadn't showed, I called him on his phone. He answered and said that they would be there in another twenty minutes, that he was just picking up the money. It was now around 2:00am November 27th, 2004, and we were sitting outside the gate of Fort Hoods Military Base Airport and next to TGI Electric in a dark and secluded area with a field beyond it all. It was set back away from the main road.

When Amine showed up finally, he was with Frank in a white Mitsubishi Eclipse. They pulled into the lot and then shut off their lights, but this forced me to turn the truck around because I didn't want to have to get out of the truck for any reason unless I had no other choice. Once I got the truck turned around so that we were now parked driver window to drive window where we could talk through our open windows. I made small talk with Frank because Amine acted like he was too busy talking on his cell phone with someone. To my right, Tim is hidden in the shadows videotaping everything, even though this was not planned he was just doing it. For some unknown reason, Frank turned his head away from me and said something stupid to Amine about how Amine said he could kill my loved ones for $10.00. When he turned back around, Frank caught a slug from a 9mm Ruger straight through his head, he was dead before his head fell forward. Right after the shot was fired, Amine who was still talking on his stupid cell phone is now screaming on the phone, "What the F! What the F!" before he was able to fully finish the third what the F, he was shot with the same 9mm Ruger, but my aim caught him through his left hand which caused the bullet to go through his cell phone and out the back side of his head. Before I knew that I had said anything to Tim, he was getting out of the truck and walking over to their car. I dropped down out of the truck and opened the driver's door to make sure that Frank was dead and to have Tim pull him from the car. Once this was done, we slowly walked around to the passenger's side and opened the door to get Amine out. As I opened the door, I took notice of the floorboards and that there was a black bag along with a folded down SK-74 assault rifle. Smiling to myself, I looked at Amine who was still breathing but barely. He had his seatbelt on and I instructed Tim to cut him out and pull him out of the car, which he did so. Once Amine was out of the car and laying on his back, he tried to reach up towards the sky by pointing his finger and trying to talk or maybe it was just to gurgle like a bitch, either way I no longer cared about the money he owed or anything else, I was pissed that this fool had the nerve to show up with a rifle like he was planning to kill me. I walked over to Amine and noticed that Tim was still filming everything. Though he was also covered in Amine's blood from when he had to cut his belt off of him and pulled him from the car. He even pulled him right out of his dress shoes. I rested the .9 mm Ruger on Amine's head and told him F Allah and that he no longer held the power before blowing his brains out. After killing Amine, I looked back inside their car and grabbed the black bag along with SK-74 and threw everything into the truck before driving back to the party.

Chapter Seven

Not Finished Yet

The next 24 hours would become one giant clusterf... and things would get way out of control. After returning to the party and being idiots and showing the video to this broad I was screwing, I instructed Tim to get rid of his bloody clothing. He took off for parts unknown to dump his bloody clothes while I went to sleep. When the morning came, Tim dug a hole in the dirt to burn the tape, then we left to wash the truck and return it to Wendy. While we were doing this, I noticed that two of the shell casings from the shots fired were still inside the truck. I removed them and threw them into the trash. After the truck was clean, I drove back to the house we had stayed at and I got this girl's car and told Tim to take the truck to Wendy's place and drop it off to her and tell her I said thanks. We parted ways. I drove to my sister's house and while I was there, I was watching the news (something that I never did). While I was watching this, my sister showed up and started watching it along with me, because I guess she might have been curious as to why her little brother was watching something he never does? Who knows? Just then a breaking news story shot across the screen. Then the story of the shooting was on the news and my sister saw how I got really interested in it all. You could see footage an aircraft had taken overhead pictures of the scene. You could see footage of many different departments of police all the way from the locals to DOD (Department of Defense) along with the DOA (Department of the Army) and MP's (Military Police) along with your EMS and other police departments. I think that my sister was able to put two and two together because after she looked at the news and then at her little brother, she knew. I made the mistake of looking at her and knew it was over. She, along with my mom who she was thinking about telling, started talking and telling me I had to turn myself in to the police. I got up and left the house in my lowered truck. Went around doing some things and thinking about turning myself into the law. As I was driving around, I got two calls on my cell. One from this fool out in East Killeen, talking about how he was going to catch up with me and kick my ass for screwing his chick. I asked him who the hell he was and he said his name was Anthony from Detroit and that I was screwing his chick named Zoe who was a dancer at Teazer's. I told him I wasn't screwing his chick and that now was not the time to be screwing with me and hung up on him. The thing is, I knew who Zoe was and where she was staying and that was at this fool's house. The second call came from this other girl I was kind of seeing on the side that was also a dancer at Teazer's, named Tiffany Dotson. Tiffany started telling me about how she knew that I was the one who had shot and killed Amine last night and that everyone was talking about it and that Zoe's boyfriend was talking about giving me up to the cops. I asked her if his name was Anthony and she told me it was. I hung up with her and left for Anthony's house alone in my S-10, but not really alone. When I got over into the right neighborhood, I slowed down real slow and just kind of creeped through at first to locate the right house. Once I found it, I sat across the street for some time before finally driving around the block. When I came through on my second pass, I had my window down on my driver's side and the barrel of the SK-74 resting on it. Stopping in front of his house in the middle of the street, I unloaded everything in the clip into his house. Spraying his house from top to bottom and side to side before burning rubber out of the neighborhood. Not five minutes later my cell phone is ringing and its Anthony asking me if I was just by his house. In response I just laughed as he started screaming at me that I was a dead motherf... Leaving the neighborhood, I returned to my sisters after making a stop to rid myself of the SK-74 in a dumpster outside of Fort Hood Military Base. I dropped my truck and grabbed that chick's car I had driven over there from the party house. My plan was to go to the party house and get my stuff together and then make one other stop. On my way over there though, Tim called me and said to meet him at the McDonalds because he needed to talk to me about something that was really important. I told him that I was just up the street and would be there in a few minutes. When I pulled into the parking lot, he was there with Chris and Tiffany, my side piece. Tiffany ran over to me talking about how she and Zoe were going to be leaving to go out of the State later on that night, then started asking me all kinds of questions about the shooting. I told her that I would talk to her later before they left and we would meet up. She said okay and got back into her friends black Jeep and that's when I noticed Zoe was sitting inside too. As they left, Tim started talking to me and telling me that Chris was looking for some cocaine and that his friends were wanting half a key (kilo). I told them that I would make some calls and then get back with Tim later on tonight and he in turn would contact Chris. We all left Tim in his truck with Chris and me in this chick's little red car. I made some calls to Mike and my Salt Lake City connect. Mike already knew what had happened and told me to get the hell out. I told him I was leaving that night but had one more thing to take care of then I would be gone. In the meantime, I told him that the kids were looking for half a kilo and gave him Chris's number and then hung up. I drove to my sister's house and spoke with her and my mom and told them I would be leaving tonight, though they continued to tell me to turn myself into the police. I left telling them I loved them, and got into my lowered S-10 and drove it to a used car lot to sell. I sold it in Killeen, Texas, to this used car dealership off of the main street in Killeen for $2,500.00. He paid me in cash and then gave me a ride back to my sister's house, where I got into the little red car and left. By this time, it's already after 8:00pm on November 28th, 2004. I got in touch with Tim and told him to meet me at Fort Hood's 4th ID. We met up and he got into the car with me and we left Base, and were in route to hook up with both Zoe and Tiffany before they left the State. Tiffany called me while Tim and I were driving out to meet them at a gas station, she said that she wanted to see me before she left. I explained that Tim and I were coming out to the station to meet them but were about thirty minutes away so wait up. When we finally made contact with them, Tiffany asked me if I had any cocaine on me and I said a little bit, but that I would give it to her at the lake we were going to go to after we all got gas, I told Tiffany to drive ahead of us to Stillhouse Park which was about forty minutes from where we were at the moment. Once we get off the Highway and took the exit for Stillhouse Park/Lake, there is this road that you have to take that twist and turns way out in the middle of nowhere. It sits back from the highway and is in a wooded area some 3 miles from the highway and lots of road travel. After we rounded the last turn in the road there was the gate to the park but it was closed and locked, so we parked outside the gate. Tiffany and Zoe were in a black Jeep Wrangler. They got out and walked over to Tim and I as we were getting out of the car. It was a little chilly out and Tiffany had a large blanket wrapped around herself and Zoe had on a light jacket. They were telling us about how they were headed out to visit with Zoe's grandma in another State, but my head was nowhere near listening to what they were talking about. In fact, my head and my thoughts were already gone. I was filled inside with nothing but rage and hate towards everyone including myself. Zoe climbed back into the Jeep and Tiffany walked over to me to give me a hug and a kiss and tried to hold onto me like she knew something was going to happen. I pushed her away and told her to take care and to leave, but she didn't do it fast enough and after she was inside the Jeep and Tim was getting into the car, I stepped over to the driver's side and opened the Jeep where Tiffany was sitting. The look she gave me was one not of fear but deep sadness before I pulled the 9mm Ruger from behind my back and shot Tiffany numerous times in the head and upper body, before turning my gun on Zoe and finishing her off with the remainder of shots. When the slide locked back, I turned around and got back into the car and we left racing out of there at a little over speeds of 100 mph.

 Two hours and some change later and back in Killeen, Texas, I turned myself into the OCD even though they asked me to come in under a fake warrant. I still showed up, thinking about what I had done and that I could probably talk my way out of it all. In the end though after almost 15 straight hours of interrogation by detectives, I confessed to everything.

Chapter Eight

Bell County Jail

After my interrogation, I was escorted in handcuffs to the main part of the jail there in Belton, Texas. Instead of having me wait like everyone else being processed, I was taken right up to the booking desk and told to be processed right then and there. An officer took me into the fingerprinting and photo room, and my prints were taken along with my mugshot. Before coming out of there, I was given one telephone call and I used it to call my mom and sister. After speaking with my sister who already knew that I had been arrested as did my mom, I then spoke with my mom. She was crying the whole time, but I remember very clearly something she asked me. She said son, if you had the choice between life in prison and death which one would you take? I told her honestly that I would take a death sentence. She cried harder but told me thanks for being honest with her about that. We then had to hang up so they could finish processing me into the jail. I was not yet being charged with anything, but was placed directly into an isolation cell per the directions of the detectives. Throughout the following days, I would go through more and more interrogations by detectives before finally being taken to court for a bail hearing and to be told my charges. At the start of January 2005, I was escorted to the 27th Judicial District Court of Bell County, Texas, where I was indicted on two counts of Capital Murder and given a 2-million-dollar bond. I was then escorted in handcuffs back to my single man isolation cell on the third floor of the Jail.

    I would remain inside of the county jail for a little over two years while going to trail, but long before I started my trial I was getting into fights with the jailers and their Major. Around February of 2005, I was being escorted downstairs to talk to a bonds person because someone was willing to post my bond from the East Coast. Just as I was getting ready to be shown into the holding booth where the bonds person was, I was turned away and down a short hallway and into a small court room. Please understand that anytime I came out of my cell I was in both leg irons and handcuffs. Inside this little courtroom there were other inmates in both the orange that inmates wear and street clothes, as well as both male and female. However, I was the only one sitting inside with a three-officer escort. While sitting inside there and waiting for them to call my name for what I didn't know at the time. The Judge kept calling the names of others and setting their bonds at $500.00 here and I think one was around $1,500.00. Then my name was being called. As I stood up in front of this little turd of a hick Judge and he's saying my name, all of a sudden, my head whips around and looks right at him. He's telling me that my bond is being raised to another 2-million-dollars and that I was being charged with another two counts of Capital Murder. I totally lost my cool, and before I knew what I was doing I was both yelling at the Judge about how the hell am I to post bond on 4 million dollars while trying my best to get at him! I was tackled down to the floor by the officers and many more that came out of nowhere and from around the corner. The inside of the courtroom became a clusterf... of fighting along with me in the middle of the pile. Though I'm in cuffs and leg irons it didn't stop me from trying to fight with the officers and I did fight. After a while they were able to raise me up off the floor and get me off of two of the officers that were stuck on the bottom of all of us, before escorting me out of the courtroom (drag me). I was taken down in between the booking desk and thrown into a small holding cage with the restraints still on my body before they closed and locked the door. There was a small window that I could see out of and into the booking area, and a side from that there was nothing in the cell but a hole in the floor for someone to take a piss.

Basically, I was thrown into a rubber room/padded cell because they had nowhere to put me and try to calm me down. Now they had a problem though because I was beyond pissed off. An officer named Smith who I remember well was a real laid back black guy, but that day when he came to the little window in the door and asked me to allow them to remove the leg irons and cuffs from me, I wasn't really feeling him or anyone else and what they wanted. I did allow them to open the door and under the instructions to kneel down I allowed them to enter inside and remove the leg irons, after the irons were removed, I was told to stay down until the door was closed and then to place my hands through the slot in the door so they could remove the handcuffs. Everything was going well until this point. I still couldn't believe that they had slapped me with another 2-million-dollar bond! I was on my freaking way out of that hellhole and this sorry ass state called Texas! I decided that every day they were going to have to fight with me for everything! I refused to allow them to remove the handcuffs and instead removed them myself and showed them that I now had my own weapons and for them to come on inside and we could play. They tried to get me to come and place the cuffs on the slot for them. It just wasn't going to happen without them having to work for it. At this time, the administrator who is also the Major showed up and instructed them to suit up a 7-man team to go inside and remove the cuffs from the cell. The Major's name was Robert Patterson. He was this big ass corn-fed looking sum bitch with pink cheeks. As the team suited up to get ready to come inside and try to remove the cuffs, the area around the booking desk was shut down and the holding cells that could see everything were being secured. Everything was stopped while they were trying to deal with me. In the jail they didn't have gas (chemical agents) that were used on inmates. Nope, these people loved to use force and to hit with their batons. I got up close and personal with these things over the years I was there. Once their team was ready, the Major threw open the cell door and the 7-man team came inside. Contact was made and all anyone from the outside could see or hear was the contact from fist being made to all inside. I was finally taken down to the floor, but in doing so I had an officer underneath me, while an officer on top of me had me in a choke hold. The only way I could get him to let up so I could breathe was to do something I have never done in my life. I grabbed his nuts and squeezed as hard as I could! He let go really fast and I was able to catch my breath, then before I knew it, I was being dragged out of the cell by my legs, where everyone that was outside looking in piled on top. I stopped fighting. I mean seriously what the hell was I going to do against half a dozen assholes? The handcuffs that I had been using as a weapon were removed from my hands as I was using them like brass knuckles. Leg irons were reapplied and another set of cuffs were placed onto my hands but they were interlocked and then placed on my wrist, so that I had no give in them to work with or to remove like I had that first time. I was then escorted by the 7-man team and many of the jailers to the third floor and placed into a new isolation cell that looked out across the downtown street and right at the courthouse clock. These assholes had a sense of humor, look at the time dickhead they're saying. You're fixing to get a lot of it!

A few days later I was taken out for court, and afterwards I was allowed to use the telephone for ten minutes each day. The only thing was that every time I came out of my cell, it was with the handcuffs on and interlocked so I couldn't get out of them nor do harm to one of the staff. In the Bell County Jail, they have an inside rec room that has a ping pong table and weights along with this hanging camera that watches everything you do inside this room. There are two ways in and that is through a huge steel sliding door on each side. Once you're inside, these doors are sealed shut. Looking through one end though you find yourself looking into the control booth and through the control booth you can look into the visitation area. The visitation area is non-contact and has 8 telephone-like booths on each side, where your loved ones or friends will come up through an elevator, go to the control booth and give them their pass and tell them who they are there to visit with. Visits are for one hour only. While everyone else in there is free of handcuffs, anytime I was in there to visit with my mom and sister, I was always in handcuffs and leg irons. I remember this one time I was inside the rec room when my mom and sister showed up for our hour visit on the weekend. I watched them come up and exit the elevator, and then stand there waiting for me to be brought out to visit with them. While I was waiting for my escort team to come and cuff me up and take me out there, I watched another inmate pull his dick out and start jacking off while looking at my sister and mom. My sister turned away and my mom never noticed. Then there was my escort and I was being cuffed up and taken into the visitation area and told that I would be sitting in booth 4, so telephone #4. Just so happened that the guy that was jacking off on my loved ones was seated next to me and visiting with his either wife or girlfriend I didn't know which one.

I had a good visit with them and when they started to get ready to leave my sister told me to not do anything stupid. I just kind of laughed and told her all is good. I deeply loved and cared about my mom and sister, but inside jail a place they have never been they had no clue about how things are ran and that there are things you do and don't do within both jail and prison walls. Most inmates show respect, but this guy that didn't know I saw him jacking off on my loved ones didn't show I nor my loved ones the respect they should have been given, regardless if I saw or not. What he did is something that you should NEVER DO. As soon as my loved ones were on the elevator and had waved goodbye to me, I was in motion and standing behind the guy while he was still talking on the phone to his visitor. While I had been visiting with my mom and sister, I had been working a homemade handcuff key into the lock on the cuffs and removing them from my hands. So, when I stood up the cuffs were no longer on my hands. I did what most inmates or prisoners call stealing on another inmate. Meaning without giving this fool time to acknowledge that I was standing there behind him I hit him upside the back of his head with my fist holding onto the cuffs. When his head slumped forward on the desk of the booth, I grabbed his ass up and dragged him off the stool he was sitting on and went about beating the holy hell out of him for jacking off on my loved ones! The steel door behind me slid open and many officers jumped on top of us in their attempt to pull us apart and to stop me from killing this fool. Once we were separated, I was taken back to my single cell and later on that night the Major of the jail advised me that my visitation was being suspended until further notice. I ended up losing my visitation for like two-and-a-half months. So, while I wasn't allowed to visit, I took my frustration out in other ways, namely on Timothy Doan Payne; my co-defendant. Tim, as we all call him, ended up turning himself into the Killeen police department after his commanding officer at Fort Hood told him to.

While Tim was in the military, he was with the 4th ID located off of Old Army Tank Destroyer Road on Fort Hood Military Base. The sad thing was Tim was just about 19 years old when he messed his life up by meeting me. While sitting here typing out this story about my life and the crazy crap I did to land here, I can't help but feel sorry for screwing up his life and many. others. But back then, I guess you could seriously assume that he was on my crap-list within that jail. When I was on my way to court one day and being escorted to the elevators on the third floor by two officers that would be driving me to court. We had to pass the library which you could see into from through the control booth in front of the elevators. I had been hearing back in my isolation cell that Tim was turning states evidence against me and that he was being offered a deal in turn for testifying against me. Whenever we stepped onto the elevator, the officers would have me turn around so that I was facing out instead of in. This way they could always watch my hands to make sure I wasn't trying to remove my restraints. This was fine with me because it always allowed me to see everything that was going on around me and when we would pass the other floors and dorms. This day though as we were passing the library and they instructed me to turn around. I noticed my co-defendant Tim standing next to my friend named Vernon Walker who on the streets we all called Big V. I had no idea that he was in this jail with me, but at the same time I took notice of my co-defendant. Big V noticed me in the elevator and waved his hand at me. I leaned down as much as I could and really fast like cut my hands the best I could across my throat while then pointing towards Tim. Tim saw this happen and his eyes got really big and if we had been anywhere else, I would have been laughing my ass off. As it was, Big V Looked directly at Tim and before I or the escorting officers could warn anyone in the booth, Big V started beating the snot out of this little white boy named Timothy D. Payne! By this time the elevator doors were closing and my escorting officers were screaming for the elevator doors to open, doing this by looking at the video camera inside with us that was being watched by an officer downstairs. Throughout my two-and-a-half-years stay in that jail, my co-defendant would come to get his ass beat almost daily regardless of where the Major and his screwballs placed him. I did my best to have Tim killed within that jail before he was able to testify against me.

 After a while I started to be good because I wanted to see my mom and sister. Sometime in 2006, I was moved down stairs to the first floor and the single cells there. While being housed down here, you could see the park from the windows, you could also speak to the guys next to you on each side. Most days and nights we would be playing chess against one another or doing some kind of workout in our cells, but all together. There were about 15 of us together in those single isolation cells downstairs. After each weekend that my mom and sister would come to visit, they would drive to the park and get out of their car and walk over to this big oak tree that I could see from my cell and wave to me. I would always scream at them and they would laugh and wave more and when they wrote to me or we talked on the phones they would tell me that they could hear me. While I was in jail, I got tons of mail from people I didn't know and this one young woman wrote to me thinking she would say her peace and that would be that. Back then I was young and full of myself and I loved to talk crap. In fact, I still talk it to this day, just not as bad or as much. Her name was and is Paula Dicky from Waco, Texas, though back then she went by the last name of Brown. I knew nothing about this woman, but she wrote to me one day and didn't bother to put a return address (not many people did, writing to a killer). What she wrote though not so much as upset me nor pissed me off, but it did bother me for some reason. So, not caring about the jail staff listening in on my phone calls I contacted a friend here in Texas and asked about looking for this woman for me so that I could return a nice response. Three days later I got a letter in the mail from my friend and he came through with not an address but a telephone number and the place she worked. The next day, I was allowed out of my cell to make a telephone call and did so by calling this young woman at her place of work. When she came on the telephone, I explained to her that my name was Blue and that I had placed her onto my visitation list and that she needed to come and visit later that night. She said she didn't know anyone named Blue, and I said that I was sorry. But was this Paula Ann Brown of Waco, Texas? She said yes, and I said well in that case we do know each other. My real name is Richard Tabler and you went and sent me a letter telling me how you knew Amine from when you worked at CityLights and Teazer's, and that even though you knew Amine to be abusive you didn't have anything done to him. You talk to me about crap like this but you don't know me or why he got his ass shot do you? Like I said you're on my visitation list, be here for a visit tonight and we'll talk. I hung up and returned to my cell. Paula Brown showed up later that night for a visit and we became friends! She would return over the next few months and she would even come and visit with both my mom and sister. Then one day she showed up to visit wearing some dark sunglasses and sweats. When she removed her glasses, I about hit the roof and became pissed off. Both her eyes were black and blue from being punched by her ex-boyfriend. She had just driven home from work and was walking to her door when he came out of nowhere and started to beat her. What is it with men beating up on women? Are you assholes out there that small-minded and small in the other parts that you feel the need to abuse those that God created for us to cherish and love? Motherf...s like these make me sick. Paula started telling me that it was okay and that she had called the police and made a report. See, back then she was mixed up with this guy that was how can I say this nicely… There's no way to say it. He was a white supremacist kind of asshole who thought he was the crap because he had this huge swastika tattoo on his arm like a badge of honor or something. All this did was make it easier to identify him when someone was looking for his stupid ass. Paula left after our time was up and I was taken back to my cell. She drove to the park and got out to wave at me, but being that it was dark out now it was hard to see her, but she could see me and that was all that mattered then.

After she left the park, I spoke with the officer on duty for the first floor, Officer Smith, and asked him to please, allow me to get on the phone real fast. I told him that if he let me out, I wouldn't cause him any problems for the rest of the week. I just needed to make a fast telephone call nothing more then maybe ten minutes tops. He let me out without the handcuffs on and I got my ten minutes on the phone. I made call to another friend in Copperas Cove, Texas. I explained that I could use his and his sister's assistance in something please. I explained that I didn't want the guy killed but wanted them to carve his swastika tattoo off his body after beating him. We hung up the phones. Two weeks later after her eyes had healed and she was feeling better, Paula showed up for a visit that I was not expecting. The first thing out of her mouth was why did you do that to him? I told her at first, I didn't know what she was talking about. She told me that her ex was found in an alley in Killeen with his face a bloody mess and his tattoo cut from his arm. I said it sounds like some kind of race thing, how could I have anything to do with it? I'm stuck in jail and have more important things to worry about then some dumbass. That was the last time she came to visit with me for months. Some women just don't know how to appreciate things that are done on their behalf.

In cause number 57,382 of the State of Texas verses Richard Lee Tabler, around March 20th, 2007, I was found guilty of Capital Murder in the deaths of Haitham Zayed and Mohamed Amine Rahmouni. The time was 1:23pm.

Less than three weeks later, I would be sentenced to Death for the murders of both Haitham Zayed and Mohamed Amine Rahmouni in April of 2007.

Darkness cannot drive out darkness;
Only light can do that.
Hate cannot drive out hate;
Only love can do that.
-Martin Luther King, Jr.

Chapter Nine

Not even after 24 hours had passed since I was sentenced to death in the 264th District Court of Bell County, Texas, under the Honorable Martha J. Trudo, and I was entering the Polunsky Unit where Texas Death Row prisoners are housed. Upon exiting the van that transported me here from Huntsville, Texas, I was met with a seven-man Use of Force Team. This consisted of seven grown men in riot gear. Seems word was called ahead of my arrival that I was going to be a problem. This was totally untrue, but when someone at the Bell County Jail contacted the Texas Department of Criminal Justice explaining that I had constantly been fighting within their own jail with their staff, up until my actual day of trial, people just couldn't help themselves in assuming that I would continue to be an asshole once I got to Death Row too.

When I got here, I was met by Assistant Warden Timothy Lester, who was nicknamed "Little Hitler", and Major Nelson, who was this little blonde lesbian. So, along with a seven man team and these two, I was introduced to Texas Death Row. Where a normal inmate would be placed on a normal pod filled with single man cells from sections A-F, numbers 1 through 84, and would be allowed to go to commissary and purchase items needed to survive while being a Level-1 inmate, I was being downgraded and placed on Level-3. I would automatically be starting at the bottom and have to make my way to Level-1. All because some crackers in the Bell County Jail was caught in their feelings.

After going through the process of having all my tattoos taken pictures of in a small classification office here in 12-Building, I was then given a white jumper with the letters "DR" on the back and down the side of one leg. I was given a bed roll consisting of two sheets, one blanket, toilet paper, some tooth powder, 3 pieces of tiny green soap, and an inch long toothbrush, along with a pair of gray socks, and a pair of boxers that you had to tie on the sides like a man bikini! Tell me that's not some crap right there. I was then re-cuffed behind my back and escorted down to F-Pod where all the Level-3 prisoners were housed. On F-Pod, I was placed into Cell #74. Once the cell door was closed behind me, I was instructed to place my hands out through the food slot so the cuffs could be removed. Once this was done, the slot was closed.

One of the very first people I met was my neighbor in Cell #75 named Carlos Trevino. He had gotten together with everyone, letting them know I had just rolled up. Next thing I knew, an officer was opening my slot on my cell door to hand me a brown paper bag that was filled with a pair of shower shoes, writing tablet, pen, stamps, soap, toothpaste, a homemade stinger (to heat water), a coffee cup, along with soups and coffee and a few other things to get me started. I was thankful for this because I didn't have anything with me other than my address book and a few pictures of my loved ones. Over the next couple of days, I was also given a t-shirt and a pair of gym shorts. I was informed that I shouldn't have been placed on Level-3 and should have been placed on Level-1. Thus I and those around me figured out that I was being screwed with because of my past actions in the county jail.

Aside from meeting Trevino, I would also meet one of the Texas 7, Donald Keith Newbury, who everyone called Lizard. It would be Lizard who would take me under his wing to show me the ropes while I was there on Level-3. This was one individual who was always, and I mean always, having a major use of force, making the officers suit up so that he could run the team. It was almost like he loved doing his best to make them use chemical agents on him (though they never really bothered him.) He was a beast when it came to having a use of force. Once they had utilized as much chemical agents on him in his cell as they could (really making all of us eat gas along with him), they would have his door rolled open, and off they would go, running into his cell in an attempt to extract him from his cell while also throwing a few punches here and there where nobody could see. Since when is it right or fair to utilize chemical agents on a man inside of a cell, then use seven grown-ass men in full riot gear with a shield to do their best to beat him, with the excuse they were extracting him? How is one man who weighs around 220 pounds going to beat seven men with a combined weight of over 1500 pounds? This is how they were treating those of us on Texas Death Row. Let's be fair though, Lizard did his best every time to return the favor by striking each and every team member that entered his cell with one of his homemade shanks. One of the ones to get hit the worst was Sgt. Harlen Petty. Lizard ended up stabbing Sgt. Petty seven times. This was the same time that when the Team entered his cell on F-Pod #46 that the Number 3 man on the team, Officer Pope, did the only thing he could to get Lizard to stop fighting. He got a handful of Lizard's balls and started squeezing! Lizard stopped fighting, and they were able to place him in restraints and leg irons before removing him from the cell.

When I made my Level-2, I was moved from F-Pod F-Section Cell #74 over to D-Section Cell #43, which is right next to the shower on One Row, as well as the cross-over door that is used to go from one section to the next. I had been in this cell for about 15 days when in the middle of the night I was awakened by some dumbass screaming aloud. When I came to my cell door to find out what and who it was, I would encounter my first problem with another Death Row inmate by the name of Hank Skinner.

Skinner, as everyone calls him, is a known drunk and drug user. He's a loud-mouthed piece of crap. But hey, I'm getting ahead of myself. After figuring out who was doing all the screaming, waking everyone up in a disrespectful way, I got out there with him. I just couldn't help myself. I hadn't been on Death Row long, but after doing time in prison in both California and Florida, I knew enough that most prisoners wouldn't get out there in this way. Coming to my cell door, I yelled out to Skinner and said, "Look out, Skinner! Man, what's up with yelling and waking everyone up like this, man!?"

It got real quiet for a few seconds. Then, "Who the f... is that hollering at me about waking everyone up!? F... everyone else and you, who are you?"

I said that this was Blue down in #43 Cage. "Man, why you disrespectin' everyone like this, waking us all up?"

"Man, f... you Blue, and f... your mama, biiitch!"

I told Skinner, "You know what, we are set to go outside tomorrow on this section, Skinner, why don't you and I go outside first round and we can clean this up?"

Skinner said bet that!

That was it, it was all set up. Lizard heard this fool, and Billy Mason heard this fool. The next morning we had Officers Nickerson and White working the pod. These two officers were as laid back as could be. When C/O (Correctional Officer) White came around setting up the rec for that morning, I asked that he place me outside with Hank Skinner up in #54 Cell on Two Row. He told me that we would be going outside third round. About one hour later, my cell slot was opened, and a brown paper bag was dropped into my cell, making a loud banging noise when it did. I didn't see who had opened my slot and dropped the bag in, but once I went to see what was inside of it, I knew who had sent me the use of what was inside. Inside the bag was an 18-inch long piece of steel that had been ground down on the concrete of someone's cell floor, into the shape and sharpness of a machete. The one end was wrapped with homemade rope for a handle, with a loop hanging off so that it could be looped onto one's wrist.

When it was time to go outside, C/O Nickerson came to get me. With the machete hanging off my right shoulder and my green prison jacket to cover it up from everyone else seeing it, I placed my hands out my slot and was cuffed behind the back and escorted out to the outside rec yard. This is a big two-caged concrete yard with a basketball hoop, a pull-up bar, and a urinal and water fountain on each side. One side has glass windows so you can see inside the pod from outside. To get outside you have to go through the green outside rec yard door, then into one of the rec yards, where a steel gate is closed behind you and the handcuffs are removed. Once I stepped into the yard and C/O Nickerson closed the gate and removed the cuffs, he went back inside, closing the green outside rec yard door behind him.

Once this was done, the C/O who was up in the control picket on F-Pod opened the outside rec yard gate that I was in. I stepped out of the rec yard, closed the gate, and stood to the side where I would be behind the green rec yard door when it opened to bring Hank Skinner outside.

The machete was now hanging loosely from my right hand by the loop. Waiting to hear the green door pop, I would then raise it in a grip to use on Skinner when he came through the door.

Instead, C/O White started beating on the glass windows to get my attention, letting me know that he was not going to come outside to rec. The gate to the yard was popped open, and I stepped back inside and closed the gate behind me. Nickerson came back out, and I asked that Lizard be placed outside with me, while handing him my green jacket, asking that he please return it to Billy Mason.

After a couple of months being on Texas Death Row and down on F-Pod, where I would end up spending most of my time my first one and a half years, I would meet my court-appointed lawyers who would be handling my direct appeals. They were John Jasuta and David Schulman, out of Austin, Texas. One of my first meetings with them would be the deciding factor on not wanting to go forward with the whole appeal process. John told me right off that I had less than a one percent chance of ever getting off Texas Death Row. Knowing this, I honestly knew there would be no point in going forward when I had spent most of my life in prison anyway. I knew what the rest of my life would be like, because I knew the kind of person that I was.

Throughout my time spent in both California and Florida, I was constantly fighting with both prisoners and officers over the color of my skin. I look like a white guy, but my parents are mixed. My father was white, and my mother is full-blooded Jamaican. In prison in California, I was always being approached by the whites, also known as the wood pile or peckerwoods, to join up with them. This way I wouldn't have to constantly fight. Instead, I took a step when I first entered the CDC system in California at DVI. On my ethnicity, I put down black and was then celled after they made the mistake of housing me with a young white guy, who I ended up stomping on one morning and dragging down the stairs from Three Row. After that one time, I would always be housed with either black prisoners or Mexicans, or I was housed in dorms.

After leaving that legal visit with my lawyers and being escorted back down to F-Pod on 12-Building, which is where Death Row prisoners are housed at the Polunsky Unit, located in Livingston, Texas, I told myself that there was no way I was going to spend the rest of my life in prison nor fighting for my life through an appeal process while on Texas Death Row. I started sending legal letters to Judge Martha J. Trudo at the 264th

District Court in Bell County. This was the same courtroom and judge that my trial was held before. I explained that I was wanting to waive my rights to further appeals and volunteer for execution. I saw no point in wasting time and effort in a lost cause because I was indeed guilty of the crime of Capital Murder. The two men I was convicted of killing I did in fact kill. There was never any questions about that, nor did I ever try to say that I was innocent of my crime. The truth is, even to this day I have deep regrets for my actions as a young and immature man back then who lost control of his temper. That though is no excuse for what I did. This was around August of 2008. Then I got a response somewhere in the first week of September, letting me know that I would be escorted by the County of Bell back to the 264th District Court of Judge Martha J. Trudo for a hearing to waive my rights to further appeals. This date was for September 30th, 2008.

During this same month of September, while I was waiting for the 30th to roll around, I was in E-Dayroom on F-Pod when I witnessed Sgt. Terry Valentine, C/O Robert Peters, C/O Michael McKnight, and C/O Robert Moss escorting an Ad-Seg inmate onto the pod and over into my old cell when I was Level-2 #43. This time around though, the Administration had turned F-Pod A-Section through D-Section into Ad-Seg housing, while those of us that were on Death Row and on Level-2 or Level-3 were housed on Sections E and F. While I was in E-Dayroom, I watched the above named officers escorting a black Ad-Seg inmate over and into Cell #43. Thinking nothing of it, I started to turn away from watching over there when I heard what sounded like someone hitting a piece of ground beef with a mallet. From E-Dayroom you can see a bit into Cell #43 when the cell door is opened. I could clearly see the Ad-Seg inmate's legs with his leg irons on and hear his sounds of pain as the officers continuously beat the inmate over and over with their riot batons while this prisoner is in both hand restraints and leg irons. The whole time I'm witnessing this, I'm hearing one of the officers yelling, "You want to spit in my face, you f...!?"

When I could no longer see the prisoner moving and the officers were done beating this man, they exited the cell without removing the restraints or leg irons, then slamming the cell door closed and walking away. Not one time while I was in the dayroom did I see someone come to remove the restraints from this man nor give him any kind of medical attention. I told my friend Lizard what I had watched/witnessed, and he told me that this happens all the time but there's really nothing that we can do about it aside from fighting back. And it's the price one pays for being stupid and spitting into an officer's face while he's in any kind of restraints.

A week later, I was being escorted off of F-Pod to a holding booth out in the hallway of 12-Building to be transported by the Sheriff's office back to Bell County for my court hearing that was scheduled for 10:30am on September 30th, 2008. Once there, the Judge held her little hearing, and the District Attorney said some things, and my counsel said some things before the Judge asked me some questions about my understanding what I was asking her to grant. That once I did this, there was a very good chance that I would not be able to try and pick my appeals back up, and that I would be executed. I explained that I understood and that I felt this would allow my victims' families closure, and that I was guilty of the charges and didn't want to spend the rest of my life in prison. The Judge was told during the hearing that I was competent and understood everything that was going on, and that I would indeed be executed if she granted this motion of mine, to waive my rights to further appeals, volunteering for execution. The Judge said that she was going to grant my motion to waive and volunteer for execution. After the hearing was over, I was transported back to the Polunsky Unit in Livingston, Texas, back on 12-Building F-Pod, E-Section Cell #61.

During the first couple weeks of October 2008, I was offered the use of an illegal cellphone to use that was the property of one of my neighbors there on E-Section. Having a cellphone on Texas Death Row had been unheard of and, in all honesty, never should have happened, but this is prison, and in prison you'll always find contraband of some kind or another, including all kinds of drugs. Most of the contraband found in prisons around the world are brought in by a corrupt prison officer. In order to use this other prisoner's smuggled-in cellphone, I had to be willing to have some prepaid minutes placed on it in exchange for using it. I had no problem with doing this, because the only thing I was thinking about was contacting my loved ones. Not one time was I thinking about doing harm to someone outside these prison walls or causing some kind of mayhem. I did however start to think back on what I had seen happen to that Ad-Seg inmate before I went back to Bell County for my court hearing.

After speaking with my loved ones who would be making the proper plans to come out and visit with me near the end of October because I would be getting an execution date, I started reaching out to some people in society that I knew might be able to help me get something done about the way we were being treated in prison. Had I thought about it thoroughly and what the repercussions might have been, I more or less never would have contacted the person I did. After explaining to someone in society what I had seen happen and who I wanted to contact in regards to the treatment and confinement of Texas Death Row and Ad-Seg prisoners, I was given the cellphone number for Texas State Senator John Whitmire. The first time I contacted this man without knowing that he was also a Texas Department of Criminal Justice Board member. I told him that I had witnessed several correctional officers beat the crap out of an inmate and then left him inside his cell with the restraints on and no medical attention at any time for 24 hours. We spoke several times cellphone to cellphone before he asked me to contact his office on a landline telephone. I never seriously thought about what I was doing other than the fact that I was going to be executed soon and wanting to bring to attention the beatings inmates were taking at the hands of those who were supposed to secure us and watch over us until our own execution dates arrived. Next thing I know as the days are going by, along with Little Hitler, O.I.G., and Warden Simmons, and some Directors of the Texas Department of Criminal Justice, my cell water was shut off, and I was escorted out of the cell and placed into the shower while my cell was searched by numerous officers, at which point a single Tracphone was found on the side of my cell bunk. All hell would soon follow.

Once the cellphone was found, I was then escorted down to the Major's office in the front of 12-Building, where officers with O.I.G. started questioning me about the phone and how I got it and what I was doing with it. I was also informed that my mom was being arrested at the Austin, Texas airport for her part in buying her son prepaid minutes, though she nor my sister who O.I.G. also later placed a warrant out for her arrest (though she turned herself in.) My mom and sister, along with my grandma, were coming to visit with me because I had just ended my appeals, and we knew I would be getting an execution date soon. Throughout the day and coming following days that I was pressured into giving up the ownership of the cellphone and who brought it in and what it cost, I was told that if I worked with them that it would help my mom and sister.

The two people I love more than anything in the world had been arrested behind some stupid crap I did. Neither my mom nor my sister had ever been in trouble with the law, and their arrest would eat at me for the rest of my natural born life that I was in prison here in this hell hole state people call Texas. I couldn't give anything to O.I.G. for the simple fact I didn't know anything, but after so much of their in my face crap and the threat towards my mom and sister, I admitted that the phone belonged to Obie Weathers, who was another Death Row inmate. That was the only information I gave to O.I.G., other than stating that I saw officers beating the crap out of an Ad-Seg inmate and leave him without medical attention for over 24 hours.

Not only did my actions with contacting State Senator John Whitmire cause the Texas Department of Criminal Justice to lock down the Polunsky Unit, but also they locked down their other 102 prisons throughout the state of Texas. The media did what they did the best: tell lies about what was really going on, and how I used the telephone to contact State Senator John Whitmire to get his help in visiting with my loved ones and help with my appeals. Rumors started flowing among both inmates and officers. I was transported for security reasons to a prison hospital called Jester-4 in Richmond, Texas, where prison officials said that I had attempted to hang myself after being caught with said cellphone. This was a bold-faced lie. Throughout my life and even while in prison in both California and Florida, it was known that I was what people in society call a cutter. This means that I would take either a sharp knife or a razor blade and cut myself to release my pain or anger or just to feel something. It didn't mean that I was suicidal, only that I liked to cut on myself. Not one time in my life have I ever tried to hang myself. If I didn't see some blood then I wouldn't start to feel better.

After returning from Jester-4 one week later to the Polunsky Unit/Texas Death Row, I was escorted to A-Pod, B-Section #26, which is located on Two Row. Each section of every pod on 12-Building consists of 6 sections starting from A-F, and on each section there is two seven single-cells per row. On Row One is seven cells and a shower, and on Two Row is seven cells and a shower. Out in front of the cells is a dayroom that is just a bigger caged-in yard but inside. This is where inmates go to rec inside for sometimes 1-2 hours per day alone. There is no contact with one another on Texas Death Row. Each prisoner is celled alone in a cell. There are no T.V.'s or telephones for us to use in the dayrooms nor inside our cells. However, after my return to 12-Building Death Row, and my escort to A-Pod, B-Section #26, where I was placed into this cell, I was instructed to place my hands through the slot so the handcuffs could be removed. At which time I did this, I was then instructed to strip out and hand all my clothing through the slot to the LT standing on the other side next to Assistant Warden Timothy Lester. Once this was done, the slot was closed.

While standing there butt-naked, I was told by Assistant Warden Lester that while I was in this cell I would remain butt-naked and on a 15-minute shakedown and one on one until further notice. This meant that aside from the video camera that they had placed in the cell above my sink/toilet, that would be monitored by the officers in the control picket but also the Warden's office, I would also have an officer, either male or female, sitting in front of my cell 24/7. They were to watch me 24/7 while either standing or sitting in a chair that was provided for them. They had with them a canister of chemical agents, along with C.O.P., a flashlight, a hand-held radio, and a log book/sheet. I was to remain inside that cell butt-naked with the AC blowing full blast while it was winter time. The officers inside the control picket were instructed to leave my inside cell light on 24/7 and that nobody was to enter that section unless they were a LT or higher. Where the section would normally house 14 grown single men, it now only held one single isolated prisoner of Texas Death Row, butt-naked, who was allowed no property, clothing, or anything else within his cell until further notice.

After being deprived of sleep and only being given a food-loaf to eat and two showers a week, while also being shook down no less than 20 times through the day and night in a 24 hour period, I requested to speak with someone from O.I.G. At this point, I was not only sleep-deprived, but was also starting to lose my mind. While I was at Jester-4, I was told by O.I.G. that if I worked with them, then it would be easier on my mom and sister. At this time I hadn't been told anything that was going on with my loved ones other than that they had both been arrested and had both bonded out after a little bit. This news on top of everything that was going on with my new housing situation was enough to cause anyone to start going insane. Instead of O.I.G. coming to see me, they sent a sheet of paper for me to write down what I wanted to say, along with a pen. It was now November 6th, 2008.

I wrote like a man without sleep and going nuts without a care in the world about what might come from the letter I was writing. I went off on O.I.G., and in my rant about them and everything I said something along the lines of 'f... Senator John Whitmire and Mike Ward of the Austin American Statesman Newspaper.' That I wanted to see them put those two dicks into protective f...ing custody behind O.I.G.'s f...ing lies and their lies about why I contacted them. This letter not only brought me longer time butt-naked and isolated from everyone on Death Row, but it caused my mail to be watched even closer and for another set of charges to be placed against me for Terroristic Threats, along with the charges of a prohibited item in a correctional facility. My only interaction with anyone for the first six months I was butt-naked inside a cell was with the officers assigned to sit in front of my cell 24/7. Though it was after the first week into December 2008 that would bother me for the rest of my life on top of the trouble I caused on my mom and sister for loving me and for the trouble I ended up causing my fellow Death Row brothers.

While talking with C/O Rachel Alexander, who was this white chick with DD tits and a nice ass, with her one crooked tooth, an officer that usually always worked down on F-Pod came over to A-Pod and was allowed to enter B-Section and come up the stairs to Two Row to holler at me. His name was S.O. Woods. He was an older C/O that was really laid back and cool with all of us prisoners. It didn't matter what ethnicity you were or what your crime, he treated us all the same, and when you were on level he did his best to give you an extra tray of food or some extra rec time or pass commissary from one prisoner to another that wasn't supposed to have any commissary because he was on Level-2 or Level-3.

As he came up to my cell for just a few minutes, he said, "Tabler, I just want you to know that this has nothing to do with you or what is going on. Keep your head up and try to do your best, but know these people are going to f... you over every which way they can. Again, this has nothing to do with you." Then he left. I looked at C/O Alexander like, what the hell? I had no idea what he was talking about, as it was a little after midnight on a December night in 2008, and I was trying my best to keep my naked ass warm and not freeze to death in that cell.

Less than one hour later, LT Brown and a few other officers came up to my cell to shake me down and question me about what S.O. Woods was talking to me about. I explained that he didn't say anything to me other than to say that what was going on had nothing to do with me.

C/O Alexander supported me in everything that I had said. What happened was that S.O. Woods had gone out to the parking lot on his break after leaving my cell and being the last person he spoke to. Once in the parking lot he got into his truck, opened his glove box, took his pistol, and blew his brains out, killing himself in the parking lot of the Polunsky Unit Prison in Livingston, Texas, in December of 2008. Even though he said that I had nothing to do with why he went out that night and took his own life, I would still harbor some guilt thinking that I was in some way or another responsible for his actions. It would be years later that I would hear from his wife, who was also an officer here at the Polunsky Unit, that he was having some problems out in society with their marriage and other issues, though it wouldn't help ease my mind any.

After six months of being butt-naked and shook down every 15 minutes, they issued me some state clothing and a mattress with sheets and blanket, and I was allowed a hot meal instead of food loaf. I was still being isolated and had to have an office in front of my cell while a video camera continued to watch me from within. Around the start of month seven, in 2009, every time they came to escort me to the shower, they would shake me down. I was still not allowed mail during this time other than legal mail from lawyers or the courts. I started jacking the run every time I exited the shower. Refusing to walk back up the stairs to Two Row and my cell in #26. By sitting on the run and refusing to walk back to my cell, this would cause them to have to have a major Use of Force, because they would have to place me in leg irons and then carry me up the stairs to my cell and place me inside it, then remove the leg irons. This in turn would cause each officer that was involved in having to write up a Use of Force report while video was taken of them carrying me. My state of mind was, since they were going to continue with this shake down crap every time I came out of my cell to shower and that I was beyond any normal level and not allowed my own property, then there was no sense in me behaving and trying to do good. F... with me, and I was going to f... with them. It was the only way I could hold onto some sort of my sanity without going batcrap crazy from lack of sleep and total isolation from everyone other than the correctional officers assigned to sit in front of my cell 24/7. Texas Department of Criminal Justice prison officials had gone out of their way to devoid me of any kind of stimulation, intentionally trying their very best to drive me to the brink of mental collapse.

Once I was finally approved to go out to visitation to visit with lawyers, after months of not being allowed this, Assistant Warden Timothy Lester instructed the officers working on Death Row that I could only be escorted out to visitation by an LT or SGT, but not just the officers, and I was to be placed in leg irons because I was an escape risk. (Where the f... am I going to run to? The electric fence?) As is always the issue with prison officers and those who operate the Polunsky Unit/Texas Death Row, people mess up and just simply don't care. I had been escorted out to visit with my court-appointed lawyer, Kenneth Nash, for my charges of terroristic threats and prohibited items in a correctional facility. I was being escorted back by two OJT's (Officer Junior Training.) There was nobody with them other than myself. No LT, and certainly no SGT, nor any officer that I knew, and I knew a crapload of them cause they had been sitting in front of my cell every day for almost one year now. Walking back from visitation on the walkway that runs alongside of 11-Building from the visitation building, I had the urge to spit. So, leaning away from the officer and ahead of him, I spit in the grass on my right. Well, the dumbass on my left decided that my leaning away from his gave him the right to take his baton and strike me in the back of my legs, causing me to fall forwards into a kneeling position. This caused me to pull completely away now from both escorting officers because I was falling forward with no way to prevent myself from doing so because I was in leg irons and handcuffed behind my back. From that point on, they beat my ass on that walkway next to 11-Building with no give as if their very lives were depending on it. In the end, they didn't hit my face or head, but struck every part of my lower body and legs. A baton is made to jab a prisoner with; they are not made to beat the hell out of someone with like you're going to a baseball game. I was placed on a gurney and returned to my cell on A-Pod B-Section #26 without any medical attention. In their eyes and my fellow inmates', everything that was happening to me I deserved 110%.

Then, on September 28, 2009, I was escorted out to the 258th District Court of Polk County, Texas, under the Honorable Elizabeth E. Coker. Under a plea deal I would accept, both my mom and sister only got probation and community service, and had to pay a fine. I pled guilty to a prohibited item in a correctional facility and to terroristic threats. I was sentenced to two ten-year sentences on top of my death sentence.

Once I was returned to my cell in total isolation, and under camera and the watchful eye of the officer assigned to sit in front of my cell, I tried to figure out a way to get a telephone call to my loved ones through the Administration. On November 1st, the mailroom brought me legal mail from the 264th District Court of Bell County, Texas and the Honorable Martha J. Trudo. Before the Texas Department of Criminal Justice or my own lawyers, David Schulman and John Jasuta, knew, I was served through the mail my own Execution Warrant, explaining that on May 20th, 2010 I was to be executed by the State of Texas until I was DEAD.

Chapter Ten

I don't know what it was about reading about my own execution/death that caused me to reflect on my time in the SHU (pronounced shoe) for 16 months up north in Crescent City, California. This is where one of the toughest prisons are to be found in the United States of America: Pelican Bay State Prison. The crap I went through while in there when, by all current records, I shouldn't have been. Whenever I try to explain things to my current lawyers, they look at me as if I have three heads and am speaking in another language they don't understand. Don't get me wrong, I have a wonderful legal team, but they're just too naïve about things and how a serious prison is run. What happens inside prison walls are beyond the imaginations of most lawyers who represent those of us who break the law and never really learn any better to change our ways. They don't understand that prison officials will and do cover up and doctor paperwork if they are aware that what they're doing is breaking the law themselves. The crap I went through at Pelican Bay when I was there would mess with any normal person's head, regardless of how strong they think they are. When I first arrived there, I was left out in the snow in nothing but my boxers inside this animal cage for hours, freezing my ass off and on the edge of hypothermia, before being removed from the outside to the inside. During my time there I saw prisoners get their legs broke, fingers broke, and guys shot point blank by guards. I've had my 7th rib broke, shoulder dislocated, and my ass beat down and while down on the ground repeatedly hit with an electronic stun gun.

    The hardest thing for me in the SHU was mail time and being allowed to write and mail letters. Once a week, officers would roll a board up to my cell door with my incoming mail/letters and pictures stuck to the board with tape. They would then open the window on my cell door, allowing me to see out into the hallway where they would be standing, thus allowing me to see my property. I would be asked if I wanted to send a letter, and if I answered yes, they would hand me the letter without the envelope it came in, to read over. Once this was done I was told to hand the letter back. In return I would be given a 1 inch rubber pen and a single sheet of writing paper. I was granted one hour to write my letters in this fashion. Each time I finished a letter, I would have to hand it back to them, along with the pen, to read over. They would then in turn hand me a stamped envelope to address and hand back to them, along with the rubber pen. They would read it over, then seal it and place it in the pile to be mailed out. Once I was finished or my hour was up, whichever one came first, I would be instructed to return the pen and paper, the slot in my cell door would be closed and locked, and the window over my cell door would be closed. I was allowed to write letters and read mail only once a week, and that was only if I had been good without causing any problems that month or week, however they looked at it.

    Unlike here in Texas where prisoners wear white and can purchase clothing while on level or in Ad-Seg from the prison commissary, while you're housed in the SHU at Pelican Bay State Prison, you're dressed in an orange jumpsuit and these ugly-ass yellow slip-on shoes. Pelican Bay was built and run to break the human spirit. You can find the prison on the Oregon border with California; the place is always surrounded in fog and huge-ass redwood trees and hills. While most politicians here in Texas want the public to believe that Texas Death Row and the General Population of its prison at the Polunsky Unit is the most secure facility, with only its one electric fence going around 12-Building as well as one on the roof, other than two twelve-foot fences topped with razor-wire, Texas security is trash. That's why there's always contraband of one kind of another being brought into its facilities.

If I remember correctly, the security while I was housed in the SHU at Pelican Bay State Prison consisted of seven layers of what was considered the most high-tech security there was back then. #1 is a pressure-detection system buried under the gravel border inside the first perimeter fence. #2, an above ground microwave detection system. #3, a twelve-foot fence, topped with razor wire. #4, a deadly electrical fence, capable of zapping a prisoner with 750 milliamperes of electricity (60 will do the job.) #5, another twelve-foot fence with razor wire. #6, a roving patrol that circles the prison twenty-four hours a day, seven days a week. #7, a coaxial cable connected to the first interior fence that detects when someone is trying to climb it.

Shortly before I had arrived at Pelican Bay, a U.S. District Judge had ordered that a Psychiatric Security Unit be built into the prison as well. The prison can hold around 3,800 prisoners and is divided into four parts within its grounds. The minimum security unit, a maximum security unit, the psychiatric security unit, and the security housing unit, also known as the SHU. The SHU alone housed 1,500 prisoners, though its prisoners were not the worst to be found within its walls. This honor would be taken by the guards that got away with literally murder within its walls. During my time there, guards were being charged with various crimes against prisoners. Violence beyond one's imagination, beatings, and even arranging to have a prisoner shot.

Some information about the Polunsky Unit, which was once called the Terrell Unit. 80 percent of the guards are white, though 82 percent of the prisoners are not. Virtually all of the guards come from small towns all over Texas, places like Diboll, Point Blank, Fred, and Kingwood, just to name a few. Back when the Terrell Unit was opened, a correctional officer could make a little over $22,000 a year, plus benefits like health insurance and a meal or two. Back then, this was more money earned than most people working in Polk County. At the time of its opening, Terrell Unit was supposed to be among the most modern and sophisticated prisons in Texas, a vast 463-acre complex capable of holding 2,250 prisoners. All of its doors are electronically controlled. Each cell block/dorm is bugged with listening devices and monitored by video cameras.

When the Terrell Unit was built here in Livingston, Texas, a Baptist stronghold in the heart of Polk County, one in every six people lived in poverty, one in every five lived in a mobile home, and fifty percent never make it through high school. To the people in Polk County, getting married, having a family, and living in a trailer home, then turning around and getting a divorce and paying child-support was the life for these so-called Texans of Polk County. While Texas prisons are vast places of inhumane conditions for those of us sent to them, for those of us sentenced to death and housed in 12-Building, along with those in Ad-Seg, it's a place of cruel and unusual punishment, but an economic salvation for those in society looking for jobs. Back in 1999, a federal judge found the Ad-Seg Units (12-Building) in Texas to be virtual incubators of psychoses. They inflicted such cruel and unusual punishment, he held, that confinement in them violated the Constitution. And yet, this is where we are caged like animals on Texas Death Row.

    The thoughts running through my mind upon reading about my own execution, along with the feelings, were one of remembering and feeling what it was like to be on a roller-coaster once you reach the peak and drop down on the other side. The butterflies you feel, along with the touch of heat from a mixture of adrenaline and fear at the fact that you are now on your way to meet death face to face. Though this was something I had sought after, it still hit me hard to read about my own death. It made me think about all the times you're having a dream or nightmare while you're sleeping. You can see yourself running from something or someone, because your body is telling you to fear whatever it is that is chasing you. But when the time comes, and you know you've run into a dead end, your mind/body always wakes itself up before allowing you to see yourself dead. Isn't that crazy? Yet, here I was reading about how the state of Texas had been given the green light to kill me. That is beyond f...ing crazy just sitting here thinking about it all. After two weeks, it no longer bothered me that I was going to be executed the following year on May 20th, 2010. I was content and had accepted it. I never realized just how much it had an impact on me reading that execution warrant though.

    Not even three or four months later, the mailroom brought me some more legal mail, this time from a District Court Judge in Waco, Texas, named Walter S. Smith, Jr. It would seem that there were some lawyers out there in society that were putting pressure on my two lawyers that did what I asked, which was nothing, after I explained I wanted to waive my rights to further appeals and volunteer for execution. To this day, I still have no idea which lawyers placed pressure on them to do what they did, but I honestly wished that whoever the hell they were, they would have minded their own f...ing business. Without my authorization, nor talking to me about it, both David Schulman and John Jasuta filed an emergency motion to the judge in Waco, Texas, and this asshole judge granted their motion, which in turn gave me a stay of execution! I was served this stay of execution from Judge Walter S. Smith, Jr. in the mail. I sat my ass down and wrote out a letter to the judge, cursing his ass left and right, telling him nobody had any right to file something without talking to me about it first, and that he needs to remove the stay of execution he ordered. F... the lawyers that were placing pressure on my lawyers for doing nothing! In my mind, I couldn't understand why, why, why! Reading about my execution messed me up, and now to know that I would have to remain in this craphole and continue living with the way these people were f...ing me over was too much. I started making plans to end my life.

First I had to get one of the officers sitting one on one with me to bring me a razor or a box-cutter blade because I was still isolated on the section by myself. SSI's couldn't even come on that section to clean up, the officers had to do everything on that section. Everything I did I had to do through the officers. The first officer I tried to get to do this for me was this white girl with big ears that was named Deborah Hamilton. She was sitting on me during the day shift, and I thought, what the heck? I flat-out asked her if she would bring me a razor to shave?

"Are you out of your f...ing mind, Tabler!?"

"What's the big deal? All I'm asking for is a razor to shave with. You're sitting right there, plus I got this f...-all camera watching me inside my cell. What's up, Hamilton?"

"F... you, F... NO, TABLER!!"

See, not all officers will do just anything. I went through a crap ton of officers asking for someone to bring what I was looking for, and the person I least expected to help me with anything is the one that brought me what I needed. Sgt. Richard Hale was breaking out one of the officers that had been doing overtime and was watching me. Just shooting the crap with him, I told him that I was wanting to end my life, but some lawyers decided it was their business to pressure my lawyers into filing something without my say-so to a judge. Next thing I know, I'm being given a stay of execution I hadn't asked for. "Not like you seriously care though. If you did, you'd drop me a razor or box-cutter blade."

Twenty or so minutes later, the officer returned from her break, and Sgt. Hale left. Just before shift-change, the SGT returning with a johnny-sack for my dinner. I was supposed to be getting a hot tray but thought nothing of it cause I was in a funk still about everything and not knowing how I was going to be able to get the items needed to end my life. Sitting on my bunk, I opened the sack and started pulling things out: peanut butter sandwich, some prunes, a milk, and another sandwich. On the bottom of the bag was a brand-new box-cutter blade! I was as happy as pigs in crap, lol!

Sometime during the night, I was able to fall asleep, and when I woke up, the officer sitting in front of my cell was Officer Stanley Kimes. He opened my food slot and handed me a roast beef sandwich he had brought from home, and a Coke. In his own words, he thought it was messed up the way they were treating me and singling me out from everyone. From everything that he was hearing, I was not the one talking and giving everyone up. I told him I knew this because, for one, I hadn't been here long enough to know the people who were getting busted, nor had I known any of them. But people are going to believe what they want to believe, regardless if it's the truth or not. Inmates here in Texas and officers don't do things the way we do it in prison in California or Florida, where you only go by the black and white, also known as paperwork. "It is what it is though. Thanks for the roast beef and Coke."

Officer Kimes and I spoke about a lot of crap that day and some following days. He said he couldn't understand how we could do time in prison as long as some of us had been doing it. He would have taken his own life or tried to escape a long time ago if the tables were turned. I told him there was no way for me to get outside this building; otherwise I damn sure would try to escape. Anything is better than sitting here waiting for that day you know is going to come. Just before he left to start working at another unit here in Texas, he asked me if I needed anything. I told him if he could get me some rubber bands, I'd appreciate it. Sometime before he left for good, he came around and gave me some big rubber bands. That was the last thing on my list that I needed supply-wise for how I was planning on taking my own life.

The morning of November 13th, 2009 came around with Officer Heath Beard working on the floor of A-Pod while also working with Officer David Aguero, and Officer Crystal Nettles working in the control picket. Just after noon sometime, the officers working the pod had taken their breaks and switched places. C/O Beard went into the picket while C/O Nettles came to work on the floor with C/O Aguero, so they swap out recs and slop trays. They were short staffed, so they didn't have an officer sitting in front of my cell all day, just for the morning. They figured I was under the watchful eye of the video camera inside my cell, and that should be enough. Standing at my cell door and waiting until I could see the officers were no longer working on this side of the pod and that C/O Beard was busy watching the officers on the other side of the pod, I turned away from my cell door and grabbed the rubber band from underneath my mattress and placed it up and around my bicep on my left arm to stop the blood from flowing in my arm and to pop up my vein. Once this was done, I reached under my desk and pulled the box-cutter that I had taped there down, turned around, and sat on my toilet. I turned my arm so that my left forearm was facing up towards me and slit my arm from my left wrist up to 1 ¼ inches from my elbow joint. I then pulled the rubber band off my arm as the blood started pouring out of my arm/body like a waterfall. Before losing consciousness, I threw up and heard the gate down by the opening to this section popping over and over and over as C/O Beard tried no doubt to get the officers' attention. One minute I was sitting on the toilet, the next I was on the concrete floor with my blood all over me and C/O Aguero banging on my cell door calling my name. "Tabler! Tabler! Wake the f... up, Tabler!"

Slowly as I came around and noticed C/O Aguero, I also noticed the box-cutter still clutched in my right hand. Doing my best to stand up, I turned around, now facing the officer, and made one more attempt to finish myself off for good. This time I hit the main artery as well as the bone in my arm. C/O Aguero emptied his C.O.P. onto me, I guess in the hopes this would stop me from, what... dying? Lol. I found out later that I flat-lined twice when medical and security were able to get me out of the cell: once on the gurney on the way out of 12-Building, and once in 10-Building where the prison hospital was found.

Once I was considered stable and the on-call doctor showed up because security refused to transport me to an outside hospital, you found everyone inside the ER with me, from O.I.G. Terri Gardner, to Warden Simmons and Assistant Warden Lester, SGT. Chyrinie Youngblood, LT. Raymond Duff, and numerous other officers. The cut in my arm was 7 inches long and was closed with 15 staples. I was placed on suicide watch within the medical building for only twenty-four hours before being returned to that same cell, where I had to clean up all my own blood from the day before. This time though they made sure that I was with an officer watching me twenty-four seven now, as well as the video camera. After cleaning up the blood and my cell, I felt like there was nothing left inside of me. That my life had no meaning or purpose other than that the state of Texas would do anything to see to it that I was unable to end my own life, because they wanted the privilege of being the ones to insert the needle into my arm through lethal injection. In their eyes, they alone got this opportunity because, according to the status, by contacting that dirtball state senator John Whitmire, I caused many heads to roll onto the plate before Governor Rick Perry as he called many of them to stand before him in the Governor's Office to explain how a Death Row Prisoner was able to get his hands on a cellphone within his cell to make such a call. Furthermore, it caused the State of Texas and the Texas Department of Criminal Justice to spend more than $60.2 million dollars on all new security for its 103 prisons, starting with the Polunsky Unit and its 12-Building where Texas Death Row prisoners are housed. I was informed that I would remain under video camera till the day I died while I was a prisoner within TDCJ-ID and on Texas Death Row, and that while Warden Simmons and Assistant Warden Timothy Lester were working this prison, I would never be allowed to make a telephone call to my mother or sister or anyone in my family; it didn't matter if there was a death in my family!

Knowing all of this while I was cleaning up my cell from my suicide attempt, I rolled my mattress up so that I could stand on top of it to see outside my cell window and look at the sky and watch the sunset in the west, while looking outside and thinking about all the problems I caused everyone since I came to Texas in August of 2004. The pain I caused certain families along with my own, the ache of loneliness and pain within myself, as well as all the built up anger and rage. Thinking about how my visitation was revoked with my mom, sister, and grandma, and everyone else until further notice. I seriously saw no point in remaining alive when in all honesty, I'm guilty of the crime and charges of Capital Murder and deserved to be where I was sent, Texas Death Row. Looking outside that window and watching the sunset, just barely moving my lips, as I was watching the clouds in the sky and the sunset, I spoke to God. I asked that if He was real, to please open my eyes and let me see something. To open my ears and allow me to hear something other than the emptiness. Please just give me some reason as to why I am here, why I should remain alive. Please, God, just give me a purpose. Show me anything to make me believe that you are real, God.

As soon as I said that, as I was watching the sunset, the sky took on a different shape and appearance. It was as if I was now up in the sky, looking down onto the land, where Jesus had parted the Red Sea. The clouds were blood red and had parted to reveal a city of nothing but gold as far as my eyes could see. I saw buildings with white light shining out of their goldenness, and a golden wall all the way around the city as far as my eyes could see. As soon as I said I saw, it all disappeared in a flash, as if it was never there. The next thing I saw, it was pitch dark outside. As I turned around to get off my bunk, I took notice of LT. Brown and a bunch of officers standing at my cell door watching me. I found out that I had been standing up there looking outside for 7 hours, and the officer that had been watching me said he had been trying to get my attention, but I had refused to acknowledge him or anyone else for all these hours. To me it seemed only minutes or seconds, if that. That night I slept for the first time in one year without any bad thoughts or nightmares.

I would remain on this section in isolation from everyone else and on a one on one security watch with a video camera inside my cell and cameras on the run for another year and a half before I would be moved. On the day, I was told during a minister visit, which were the only visits I was now allowed other than legal. On a day that was supposed to be good with the meeting of my spiritual advisor, Mary Hampton, for the first time. Other than my visit with her and knowing that someone cared enough to drive four hours to come and visit a total stranger, my world would start to be challenged in ways that no human should ever have to go through, regardless of the crapstorms he may have caused. Mary explained to me that she had spoken with my mom, and that early that morning, January 2nd, 2011, my mom's sister, who is my Auntie, lost her battle with breast cancer and died in the hospital out in Florida. After being escorted out of the visitation after our visit, I was informed that the prison knew about the death of my loved one and that the warden wanted me to know that I was not going to be allowed to contact my loved ones even though there had been a death in the family. They didn't care, they said; they did, however, have a surprise for me. I was moving to a new cell after 2 ½ years of being isolated in B-Section by myself. I was now being moved over onto the section better known as Death Watch. This is the section that houses the men with a set execution date. Each cell has its own in-cell video camera that watches the prisoner twenty-four seven. There are also video cameras on each run and in the dayroom. Death Watch is the only section to have video cameras inside the prisoner's cell. These cameras are monitored by the officers in the control picket on the pod, 12-Control, the Major's office, the Warden's office, and the Directors' office in Huntsville, Texas. Moving to this section was not better for me; it has become my hell on earth, and the most severe cruel and unusual punishment and constant restrictions, and punishment by the Directors of the Texas Department of Criminal Justice and the Chairman Patrick O'Daniel, as well as State Senator John Whitmire.

"If you gaze long enough into an abyss, the abyss will gaze back into you."

-Friedrich Nietzsche

Chapter Eleven

Death Row prisoners in Texas used to be executed with a three-drug cocktail that was designed to sedate and render the condemned unconscious, theoretically reducing the pain when the final fatal dose was administered. These drugs were sodium thiopental, pancuronium bromide, and potassium chloride. Now though, the politicians in Texas feel the need to cause the condemned as much pain as possible by using a one-drug cocktail call pentobarbital. This so-called drug is a sedative that's said to slow the activity of the brain and nervous system and is often used by veterinarians to euthanize animals.

As we move on to the next part of this book and my life story, I thought it would be best to start with the herein, as opposed to the very beginning of my moving onto Death Watch, where now the pain is fresh from the recent execution of Quintin Jones, also known as "GQ" to those who knew him and were his friends. His execution took place on Wednesday night just before 7:00pm, May 19th, 2021. May GQ rest in peace. Before moving into everything going on here at the Polunsky Unit, allow me to put a little spotlight onto what an individual goes through the day of his execution by the administration and the Directors of the Texas Department of Criminal Justice. Many people out there in society have no idea what the condemned go through, nor the humiliation by those that keep us within these walls, and what about if the condemned gets a stay of execution. Won't what he went through effect him upon his return to the Polunsky Unit/Texas Death Row? Turn the page to read about what Quintin Jones went through the day of May 19th, 2021.

Once you're removed from either being out at your last visit with family and friends, or you chose to remain on the pod and spent your time in the dayroom like GQ did, you're then escorted out into the hallway by an LT and SGT. In the case of GQ, on that midmorning of May 19th, 2021, he went out to the visitation for a little bit to visit his people before asking to return to the Pod and the dayroom, where he spent his last hour before they came to escort him off the pod where he was speaking to the guys on A-Section, also known as Death Watch.

In the case of GQ, one of the most disrespectful and undercover-racist officers came to escort him off the pod, LT. James D. Sliger. This officer, if he can even be called that, walks like he owns the world, and yet he refuses to even see to it that his clothing is starched and ironed like those of his co-workers. Usually you'll find LT. Sliger with other trash of his kind. On this day though, it was a freshly new SGT that had the misfortune to be with LT. James D. Sliger. On his way off the pod, GQ hollered at many of the fellas on the other sections, some saying goodbye, and others keeping a positive attitude, saying they'll see him when he returns with a stay of execution.

GQ was escorted down to the metal cage that is out in the hallway between C-Pod and D-Pod, which is bolted to the floor. This is a heavy mesh cage approximately six feet wide and seven feet tall. Once you're locked in this cage and the handcuffs are removed, all your personal property you're wearing is taken away. You're then strip-searched by a lieutenant. Standing butt-naked in front of the head warden, assistant warden, regional directors, executive director, and many other prison officials both male and female, in a last resort to degrade and dehumanize you. You're instructed to run your fingers through your hair slowly front to back and on the sides. Turn your head to each side and run your fingers behind each ear. The lieutenant will produce a flashlight to look into your ears and even into your nose. You're instructed to open your mouth, wiggle your tongue, and pull your cheeks outward as the lieutenant looks into your mouth. Raise each arm so that he or she may inspect your underarms, then lift your penis and testicles, turn around, bend over and spread your butt-cheeks, lift each foot, wiggle your toes, run your fingers between each toe.

Then you're instructed to walk around inside of the cage, from corner to corner, butt-naked. They have this detection device outside of the cage at one corner. It's a gray plastic pole with a pyramid-like base that's nearly as tall as the cage, with small lights near the top. While you walk around butt-naked, if you touched the metal of the cage, the device will beep. After this is done, you're given a new pair of prison whites to dress in before being handcuffed. Either a Captain or a Major will explain to the condemned the way they want you to place your hands to be cuffed. Your hands are to be cuffed with the backs turned inward and the thumbs pointing downward. Once the cuffs are double-locked in front of you, you're told to rotate your right hand until your hands are stacked on top of each other with the backs still facing each other, and your fingers now pointing to the opposite elbow. They do everything out of the sight of your friends to dehumanize and degrade you on the last day of your life. Once you're out of the cage, you're then instructed to kneel down so that leg irons can be placed on your legs. After the leg irons are secured, they assist you in standing up. Then a chain leading from the leg irons is connected to the handcuffs and locked into place with a padlock. This is to keep your hands from rising above your waist while standing. Most of the time they shorten the chain so that you have to shuffle along in a hunched over/stooped position.

These restraints are then checked by four officials. The Captain, which in the case of GQ would have been Captain Jekerria R. Carter, an assistant warden, senior warden Daniel D. Dickerson, and one of the transportation officers. You're then escorted out of 12-Building, where Death Row prisoners are housed, to a waiting van. Inside the van with you are four guards. An assistant warden from the Walls Unit sits in the front passenger seat, armed with an AR-15 rifle with a fully-loaded thirty round magazine. A Captain will be driving, armed with a 357 Magnum revolver. Sitting in front of GQ, turned sideways so they can watch him, is another Captain, also armed with a 357 revolver and a speed loader with six extra rounds. The ammunition used by the guards is hydro-shock man-killers. The final guard will be a lieutenant sitting in the rear of the van, armed with a 12-Gauge shotgun loaded with magnum loads.

The sad thing about this whole situation is that the young black man known as GQ to those of us left behind wasn't the same person that he was when he was locked up by the State of Texas. After twenty years in prison, GQ was a changed person, so how can you justify killing someone after twenty years from the time of his crime, when he's not the same person? Leave it to the State of Texas to start executing prisoners again, and who cares that there's a pandemic going on, and police all over the United States of America are killing unarmed black men and women. Still, Texas wants to be in the spotlight by executing a young black man as a way of making a statement… Slavery and Execution is what Texas is all about.

Furthermore, those in society never see what a prisoner on Texas Death Row sees out in the visitation or when they are escorting a Death Row man from visitation to 12-Building to strip-search him and chain him up before placing him in the van. On the walkway outside of 11-Building, a prisoner within one of the cells inside of 11-Building or on 12-Building B-Pod can view the officers and wardens and directors and other prison officials high-fiving one another, shaking hands, congratulating one another and patting each other on the back, celebrating the execution that is going to take place a few hours from then. Society fails to understand that 99.9% of Death Row prisoners are not the same people they were when they were first locked up. You're not executing the person a jury convicted and sentenced to death. How can you be, when it's been 17 or 20+ years from the time you sentenced us? Many of the men that are housed on Texas Death Row and here on Death Watch with me are talented. We've learned to draw, paint, make dream catchers, write poetry and books. We've taken classes through the mail because Texas refuses to rehabilitate us because those in society deemed us a continuing threat to society. That right there is why we've been sentenced to death. By being placed on Texas Death Row, we're considered in the eyes of the Texas Department of Criminal Justice and the Courts to be the worst of the worst; and yet it was Jesus Christ himself who worked with the criminals throughout the Holy Bible. Most of the prisoners are also very religious, though lately I have seen many prisoners give in to temptation and turn away from their religion to drugs, such as K2 which is a synthetic marijuana, as well as fentanyl, cocaine, and pills. In my opinion, the ones that turn to these are beyond weak and have no room to even talk trash about myself or anyone else. One day they claim to be a Christian, and in the very same sentence turn around and say they're a convict. How can you be both? You're either the one or the other, but what is worse is when someone's true colors come to the surface. Under pressure, (and trust me, the pressure comes when you're housed on Death Watch) a person's real feelings come out. They get into it with others, calling them names and being straight up disrespectful, and yet see nothing wrong with their actions. Seeing this has turned me away from claiming any one set religion. If people ask me what I believe in, I tell them that I have a relationship with God and that I believe in the Son Jesus Christ, but I no longer say I'm any one sect of religion, such as Christian or Catholic or Messianic or Jewish. I claim nothing because too many people are fake and hide behind the Word of God. What I do believe in though is Capital Punishment. I believe in the Death Penalty, and I strongly feel that all child molesters and sexually violent predators should be either taken out in the field and shot point blank by the family members of the ones they assaulted, or in the very least, given a sentence of death to be carried out within five years.

Don't get this autobiography twisted thinking that this story is about how innocent I am or those around me are. Because you couldn't be further from the truth. I am not here to tell you about everyone around me, only myself and the crap I have gone through at the hands of the Texas Death Row administrators as well as its directors and the system as a whole that runs the Texas Department of Criminal Justice. Some of the crap I no doubt brought on myself, but for decades? Refusing to allow me to visit with my mother, sister, and grandma for 13 years because of my involvement with a cellphone?! Isolating me on a section that houses the men with set execution dates when I have not had an execution date myself since they placed me on this section as a means of punishment. How can they justify treating me in this way when other prisoners have been busted with cellphones numerous times and have never been charged with a free-world case? Have not lost their visitation for over a decade and counting. What about being given wrong information that my older sister died, when they knew this to be wrong. What kind of sick and twisted games are the prison officials playing at, by making me remain on Death Watch where my only contact is with men set to be killed by the State of Texas within three months to a year. Can you even fathom the pain and heartache I feel from watching guys I have gotten to know and even befriend some, to watch them walk off this section to go to their last visit knowing that in less than 10 hours they'd be executed. Over 100+ grown men have walked off this section since I have been housed on Death Watch to be executed from January 2nd, 2011, the day I was given news that my Auntie Donna Bird passed away from her loss with breast cancer. Information that was given to the wardens of this prison and who in turn refused to allow me to make a telephone call home, but moved me to Death Watch, until this very present day of 2021. I no longer fear what they can do to me or that more men I know will be taken from this section to be executed as much as I fear losing my sanity and my state of mind. I no longer suffer from the loss, but from survivor's guilt. Knowing that I have been left behind when I know in my heart and soul I deserve death more than the ones that have left before me. Numerous times I have tried but failed to end my appeals and volunteer for execution. Every time I think that I'm ready to have it all over, I become a sucker and allow my lawyers to talk me out of it for some reason or another, even though not one of my lawyers have ever been on this side of the wall and have no f...ing clue what they're talking about. They don't understand that the reason I'm hated by the prison officials isn't only for my being caught with a cellphone on Texas Death Row, but because of that dirtball Senator John Whitmire. This man claims to be religious and yet continues to hold his foot to my neck every time I write a letter to the Directors' Review Committee seeking to get my visitation reinstated with my mother and sister every six months. My Grandma passed away years ago, and again I was refused a telephone call home. I have been denied every time I seek to get my visitation back, and yet they never give a reason why. I could be a saint and never get into trouble, and they would refuse me, because of Board Member and State Senator John Whitmire. How can this man claim to be something and yet refuse to forgive me for my actions. It's not like I'm asking to be removed from Texas Death Row or even Death Watch. I am simply asking to be allowed to visit with my remaining family before they too die or something happens to them. And yet they have left me no other option other than to retain a law firm to file a federal lawsuit against them and Texas Death Row, which I have done.

Chapter Twelve

You should never judge someone in prison by appearances. Throughout my time in prison I've known many men who looked and acted strong, but had cores of weakness, and I've known men who seemed timid (like myself) who had shown themselves capable of great strength and of accomplishing terrible things.

Not every day in prison is a bad day, as we each make do with what we have. I try for the most part to treat everyone the same way. It doesn't matter to me if you're a prisoner or an officer. Unlike those around me who see the gray uniform that the officers wear as the enemy, I refuse to see them in that same light. How can I be mad at the officers for doing their job? They didn't put me in this place, my actions put me here. Each officer for his or her part is only doing this job to pay their bills, put a roof over their head or their family's head, and put food on the table. It's not my place to knock them for doing that, as it's more than I have done. My whole life I have been nothing but a failure in the eyes of family and friends, even in the eyes of some of my lawyers, though they refuse to say so. Kindness and compassion should start with us inside these walls, not the other way around. My fellow prisoners get pissed at me for talking with the officers so much, and in a form of retaliation they talk crap trying to get me pissed off. For the most part, I tune it out, though not every time. The old saying is you get more bees with honey than you do crap. Besides, we each have a heart that beats within our chest, it shouldn't matter if the person is black, white, Mexican, yellow, or purple. In stating this, I'm reminded of back in 2019 when Tracy Beaty, also known as "Tray", was housed over here on Death Watch in #5 Cage, and my amigo (friend) Fabian Hernandez, also known as "Spook", was housed over here in #7 Cage. Both of them had execution dates. For the record, my nickname is "Blue", and that is what most everyone calls me here. I was housed in #6 Cage like I am right now.

One day I was in the dayroom, and someone from over in B-Section sent some books over for Tray. I told Tray to shoot his line (fishing line made from braided thread or string) to the dayroom to get these books someone sent him from the other section. He said, "Well hell, Blue, I ain't got no freaking line."

"Man, Tray, you a lazy ass muthaf..." I said, if I tossed them in front of his cell, could he get them in? Yes, he said. So I toss four books in front of his cell and go back to talking to Spook. As I'm talking to Spook, I notice that Tray was able to get the books up into the side of his cell door with a torn piece of sheet. The books are half in his cell but he cannot get them all the way in. Just as I point this out to Spook, the officer walks by and kicks Tray's door, and the books hit the ground. Tray starts going off on the officer and cussing her out. Spook and I are laughing our asses off, cause it's f...ing comical all around. Tray looks like an older Albert Einstein with skin problems due to some tskin conditions. Tray hears us laughing and goes off on both of us, which causes us both to laugh all the more harder.

About three weeks later, we go on a lockdown and are now only getting showers once every other day during the week. Just so happens that the hot water is broke, so the showers are ice cold. Spook goes to the shower first, and you can hear him bitching about how cold the water is. He's telling me, "It's freaking cold as crap, Blue!" I'm not looking forward to taking a cold-ass shower, but I refuse to stink, and it sucks having to use your sink in the cell to take showers if you don't have a shower hose to plug into your sink. (Note: shower hoses made by us are coax cable, removed so you only have the rubber hosing. With this you place a pen top into one end and then jam the pen top into the sink, thus you now have a hose to wash off with.) The thing was, Tray would hardly ever go to the shower.

When the officers come and escort me to the shower, I get in, and that water is beyond freaking freezing! I'm now cursing Spook who's now laughing his ass off. I shut the water off and tell Spook to go along with me in a second. Starting the ice cold water back on and diving under the spray washing really fast, I start talking out loud about how hot the water is and how good it feels. I yell out, "Tray! Tray! Man, Tray, get your ass up, fool!"

"What the hell, Blue?"

"Dude, you've got to come to the shower today, this crap is smokin' hot and feels really good."

When the officers come and escort me back to my cell, they get Tray next. I tell Tray as he passes my cell, just push the button on and dive under the water cause it's hot as hell. We hear the water come on, and next thing you hear is Tray, "Blue, you dick-sucking muthaf..., this water is f...ing cold, muthaf...!! Fuck you, Blue, and F you, Spook!"

I'm laughing so hard I have tears coming out of my eyes. Tray comes out of the shower looking like Grumpy Cat, cursing up a crapstorm. Stops in front of my cell and looks at me, "F YOU, BLUE!" Twenty minutes later he's laughing his ass off too cause someone else was now in the shower that was woken up by the officers for a shower and had no idea the water was freezing. We do our best to entertain ourselves within these walls. At least, I do.

Chapter Thirteen

I have decided to go about telling you everything in no set order. I find this easier than trying to deal with the past because some of the executions are too painful to remember, such as my best friend, Big Tai. What I do wish to explain is what happened to me on this past Friday, May 28th, 2021, at a little after 1:00pm. That racist crap LT. James Sliger was doing escorts along with an OJT (Officer Junior Training.) I had double-checked with him when he came on the pod around noontime that I had a legal telephone call for 1:00 to 2:00pm with my litigation lawyer, David Lane, in Denver, CO. Thinking that by having this fresh in his mind he would come and get me in plenty of time. That ended up not being the case. LT. Sliger was still pissed at me for filing a sexual harassment complaint against him in 2020. I'll get to that in a few. Instead of coming to get me thirty minutes ahead of my scheduled legal call, this asshole waits until 5 minutes to 1:00, knowing that he still has to strip me out and then walk me out of 12-Building all the way to visitation. As he and the OJT are escorting me out of my cell, I simply say, can we speed it up a little. This fool waits until we're off the pod and out of sight of the officers working the pod and the prisoners to stop me and start screaming at me in my face. Screaming with his spittle flying over the side of my face, that if I don't shut the f... up he'll not only slam me but cancel my legal call with my lawyer! What could I say other than stay mute. We get out to my telephone call with my lawyer late. Once out there, I explain to my lawyer what this craphead said and did. What I don't understand though is this: how come all officers act tough against a prisoner only when we're behind a steel cell door or in restraints? The only time this fool ever talks crap is when I'm in cuffs!

Thirty minutes after he escorts me out to visitation to speak to my lawyer on the phone, he's back trying to talk to me as if everything is cool. Crap ain't cool, dicksucker. I told my lawyer that for a hot minute I thought about slipping off my handcuffs to stomp on this piece of crap. What stopped me from doing so is I would have lost a lot, even though I would have felt better after the fact. I have no doubt though that before I'm executed by the State of Texas, sometime I will end up hurting that piece of crap. I mean really, how much crap am I supposed to take from this dude before I say enough is enough? His rank is not going to do anything about everything he does. Truth is, the administration only responds to violence within these walls. Once, and only once, you assault staff do they come around trying to ask why you did this or that to their officers? What a crock of crap.

Then, Saturday morning I awake broken out in some kind of allergic reaction to the Pfizer vaccination shot I took on the 26th. Only when I awake this day, May 29th, 2021. From my head down to my toes I have broken out in a dark red rash-like symptom that not only itches but burns like holy hell, and my throat has swelled to the point I'm unable to eat and swallow foods and can hardly get down water or coffee. A SGT and Officer Karen Woodley come to escort me down over to 10-Building medical. When we get over there, there's this one lady who's always on the pods doing insulin. She asks what I'm there for, and when the SGT tells her, she says that's not an emergency. I stay silent for a second before another lady who is the charge nurse, named Martinez, asks me what the problem is. When I try to explain to her what all is going on and that it's hard for me to swallow, she checks my temperature and slaps a blood pressure cuff on my left arm. Both she and the first lady who spoke with me saying this wasn't an emergency remove my face mask to check my face, and then instead of placing it back on my face properly, just let it slap back half over my eyes and mouth. This is the first time I have ever dealt with either one of them face to face, even though I have been into the ER many times before for both cutting and for allergic reactions. What the charge nurse was supposed to do was call the on-call provider. Instead, she just said I can go back to my cell, that nothing was wrong with me, and that I would be referred to see the provider some time. Even though you can clearly see that I'm messed up and my throat is swollen. As I'm walking out, I heard one of them say I wasted their time. I snapped and stopped walking to turn around and tell them they were a couple of bitches who didn't do crap for anyone unless someone has tried to kill themselves, at which time they send them on Mediflight. "You fucking cunts are worse than the hoes in the mailroom who don't do crap, fuck you bitches!"

At this point, Officer Karen Woodley decides to get up in my face screaming at me, "What the fuck you want them to do?" I want them to call the on-call provider like they should so I can fucking eat without choking, bitch! This chick is crazy! I was going to leave her out of this book, but her actions got her right in it. This chick is from the Islands and is always working the SSI's (Support Service Inmates) who come on the pods cleaning the showers, mopping up and sweeping, cleaning the bars, everything. The way this lady works these prisoners that come back here on Death Row from the general population is like they are fucking slaves. She's always in their faces, talking to them like they ain't going to do nothing but what she tells them to do. How do you expect to talk to grown-ass men who are in prison for anywhere between 10 years and life as if they aren't crap? Just like the men, she only talks her crap when someone is in restraints or behind a steel door. Though I would never put my hands on a female, I would be lying if I said that it's never crossed my mind with some of the females that work inside these prison walls. These women think that they can talk to prisoners any old way.

The thing that makes me laugh a little though is, all the officers only talk crap to prisoners that are locked behind a steel door like Texas Death Row and Ad-Seg on 12-Building. They don't talk the same tough-guy crap out there in the general population because they all know that they'd get their asses handed to them!

This morning I woke up worse than I was the day before, and still medical refused to do anything about the situation even though my throat is swollen and that more than half of my body is covered in a dark red rash that burns like crazy and has my body swollen. Unless I give in to temptation and cut on myself, thus forcing medical to have to see me and then attend to me, I will continue to suffer through the swelling and burning sensation of this allergic reaction from the Pfizer vaccination shot.

Part 2

TEXAS DEATH WATCH

Chapter Fourteen

The day that I was moved over to Death Watch on A-Pod of A-Section was the day that I'll always remember. I was having a spiritual advisor visit with this woman who over the years would become a very dear and great friend to me, named Mary. Once every month, she would drive from Austin, Texas, along with some other men and women that were a part of Friends Meeting of Austin, also known as Quakers. This was/is about a four hour drive one way. During our visit this day, she let me know that my mom wanted me to know that my auntie (Donna Bird) had lost her battle with breast cancer in the hospital in Florida. It was a great loss to everyone that knew her, moreso to her sister, my mom, who was at her bedside when she left to join Jesus in Heaven. After my visit and officers had escorted me back to A-Pod, I thought that I would be going back to B-Section where I had been housed alone for 2 ½ years, but instead I was escorted to Death Watch #14. This was their way of giving me something different to look forward to instead of being isolated now. I wasn't given a telephone call home to check in with my loved ones, nope. I was now being housed on a section that housed only the men with a set execution date. Everyone housed on this section was waiting to be killed by the State of Texas. It was January 2nd, 2011.

Besides myself, there was also at the time two other inmates housed on the section with me. They were ½ Deck and Tito. ½ Deck was housed on One Row in #4 Cell, and Tito was housed also on One Row in #7 Cell while I was upstairs alone. Out of a fourteen man section of single cells and one dayroom that is a bigger cage than our own cells that sits in the front of all the cells. There is also a video camera that watches everyone's moves twenty-four seven in each of our cells. These video cameras are able to be viewed by the officer in the control picket on the pod, officers sitting in the 12-Building control booth at the front of the building that houses Death Row and Ad-Seg, and also from the Major's office, Warden's office, and the Directors' offices in Huntsville, Texas. You never know who is watching you at any time of the day or night. If you're using the restroom, know that you are being watched. It does not matter if you're walking around in your cell butt-naked cause it's so hot in your cell; you are no doubt being watched. At first it took some time getting used to, but after a while, I don't even notice that it's really there, or maybe it's because I no longer care what they see. But back in January of 2011, ½ Deck, Tito, and I had fun with the cameras. Just like in the cells, on the runs (tiers) there are video cameras as well, and there's one in every dayroom that watches us. One day ½ Deck was in the dayroom and Tito and I were in our cells talking to him. We got the idea to cover up the security light out in the dayroom because during the night time when they turned off the lights on the run, that security light shined so bright we each thought it was directed into our cells. The only thing is, neither one of us had any glue at the time to glue something over it. I told Tito that I had some newspapers. If he could find something for ½ Deck to use to hold it up over the light, then shoot it to ½ Deck in the dayroom, I'll shoot him some newspaper.

"1/2 Deck, you feel like climbing up there to do it?"

"Yeah, why not?"

I shot him some newspapers from my cell by sliding it under the cell door to the dayroom bars, where ½ Deck climbed up on the bars to grab them. Tito said he had something in a clear bag that would work and shot it also out to the dayroom for ½ Deck to use. As ½ Deck is opening the bag of goo that Tito sent him to use, you could hear ½ Deck ask Tito, "What the hell is this?"

Tito said it was Colgate toothpaste! "Don't you brush your teeth!?"

"Yeah, but I use something else besides Colgate."

So ½ Deck grabs a page from the sports section of the USA Today that I sent him and the bag of Colgate and starts climbing the bars to the top of the security light. Once he's up there, he smeared a bunch of Colgate all over the light before spreading the newspaper over the Colgate. Seeing that the Colgate was in fact holding the paper to the light, ½ Deck spread more toothpaste over the newspaper and told me to send another page. After I sent another page of the paper to him, he climbed back up and pasted the second page of the paper over the first. Climbing back down, he went to the sink in the dayroom and washed his hands of the Colgate, then came to stand in front of our cells so we could all talk and laugh. ½ Deck was a young white guy, and Tito was on the chubby side for a Mexican, but he could cook! Lol!

Later on that day after ½ Deck was racked up and I was brought to the dayroom after him, I asked Tito if he wanted to cook some tacos for ½ Deck and I? Meaning he would cook for the three of us. He said yeah, but what did I have in mind? "Don't know, let me see what ½ Deck has to chip in with what I got and what you have." (Note: when any of us cook inside these walls, we do so with foods/pouches bought from the prison commissary.) ½ Deck had some cream cheese, jalapeno peppers, and two boxes of roast beef. I told Tito this and that I had some pouches of chili with beans, pickles, couple packs of tortillas, and some Mexican beef pouches. Tito said for us to send it all to him, and he'd hook something up for the three of us for dinner.

When I racked up after my rec time was over, Tito VR'd (Verbally Refused) his rec so that he could cook everything. Cooking food takes time for us. It's not like we have a stove or oven in our cells. Everything we do we do with the aid of our Hotpot bought from commissary. Unless you turn your Hotpot into a lava pot, meaning you bypass the thermostat so that water boils instead of just simply getting hot, to cook the food you place it inside of cook bags (empty chip bags or rice bags.) Also you won't find any knives being sold to us, so we make do with what they do sell us and what the officers give us (razors, broken down for the blades to use as something to cut with.) Using a broken down razor blade, we're able to cut our peppers and pickles and cut bags as well as other things. Everything that a prisoner needs to survive in prison is for the most part sold to us in the commissary. But to get such things to live, you have to have outside support to send you money to your inmate account. Otherwise you'll not only lose tons of weight, but probably get sick eating the food they serve prisoners in Texas.

When Tito was finished cooking that evening for ½ Deck and I, he had each of us shoot our line. This is the term used for us to fish with one another. Fishing consists of each of us using a line that was either spun or braided, that we added either a pole to the end of, or a slider to slide under our cell doors. Once out there, Tito or whoever you're running line with, would send his line to catch yours and pull it in. In my case, with Tito and ½ Deck being on One Row, I would use my fishing pole to shoot over the railing on Two Row. This meant it shoots out my cell door and over the railing to hit on One Row. Tito would then use his line/pole with hooks placed on the end to catch my line and pull me into his cell. The bottom of our cell doors used to have an opening that you could fit your fist out of, but now it's been welded over, so it's harder, but everyone still fishes with their friends or brothers. Like I was saying, when Tito was done cooking, he told ½ Deck to shoot his line. After doing this and being pulled into Tito's cell, Tito would loop on the line two chip bags with two tacos each inside the bags, and then send them out of his cell on ½ Deck's line, who would in turn pull his line into his own cell.

After Tito and ½ Deck finished, I was told by Tito to shoot my line. Practice makes perfect! Being in Cell #14 and him in #7 Cell directly beneath me with the dayroom bars right in front of both our cells, I had to send my pole/line at an angle out over the railing. Once I was sure my line had gone out enough and landed at the base of the stairs, I pulled the slack out of my line, just enough to give it one final hard tug so that it would pop back, and the weight of my pole would cause it to slide right up into the front of Tito's cell so he could grab it with his hand. Being that at the time my fishing line was braided, I was able to pull up a little weight. Tito was able to place both bags of tacos on my line, which I in turn pulled up and over the railing and into my cell. I thanked Tito, as did ½ Deck, and said I'd holler at him later. After putting away my fishing line and cleaning up, washing my hands, I sat at my desk, using my bunk as a seat and enjoyed the tacos my amigo (my friend) Tito made for us, while washing it all down with a can of Coke (wish they sold Pepsi!).

Texas Death Row prisoners do not have TVs, nor are we allowed access to telephones back then. To this day we still have no TVs and though we are allowed to make a five-minute telephone call once a week, this is only due to the Covid-19 pandemic. Before the pandemic, we could only get a telephone call once every 90 days (three months) and the call is collect. Inside of our cells, if you have outside support, you can purchase items such as a radio with headphones, coax cable to hook up to the radio to listen to, or a Hotpot with insert to heat water to drink coffee, make a soup to cook with or heat pouches of certain foods. Basically a Hotpot is our cooking stove/oven in one. You are able to purchase two fans to keep cool in the summer days or whenever you feel hot inside your cell to use. You can buy a nightlight to use to read by inside your cell instead of having to turn on the cell light which is always too bright or knocks out the radio reception when on. All your hygiene items, from soap, shampoo, conditioner, baby powder, lotion, etc., and art supplies for those that like to draw or paint, as well as all correspondence supplies and postage stamps to keep in touch with those on the outside. All kinds of foods and pastries, chips, bottled water, coffee, soups, meats, cookies, etc. Also you can purchase a typewriter and typing ribbons, though it's very costly for the typewriter, $360.00 and $6.50 for ribbons. You can purchase a lot, like I said. Your loved ones and friends can send you reading material from a bookstore or order it online through Amazon.com.

No doubt you're thinking this sounds good for prisoners or it's too easy. Think again. Did I mention that we live in a bathroom? Yeah, each of us sleeps and eats in our own personal restrooms. The same place you go at your home to use the restroom to poop or pee or, when drunk, throw up into the toilet. We have to sleep in one. Thus we're constantly cleaning our cells and the floors, walls, and wiping down everything. Who in their right mind wants to sleep with a toilet less than three feet from where he lays his head, or two feet from where he eats his food? If I were to sit on my cell floor here on Death Watch between my toilet and bunk, I can reach out and touch both as well as my desk. That is how close everything is together. If you don't keep your cell clean, as well as your own personal body, you will get sick, and those you come into contact with will also get sick, or vice versa. The laundry you purchase from commissary, such as t-shirts, gym shorts, boxers, and socks, you wash in your cell sink; they don't do anything for you within these walls other than give you hell or screw you over in whatever way they can get away with.

Besides cooking tacos and just spreading with one another, we can also play either chess or dominoes with one another, though not in the way you think. Each of us must purchase his own board, or 'Bones'. Dominoes must be played while one is in the dayroom and the other in his cell where he can see the 'Bones', thus we play that way. Chess, you each have a board, and it's numbered, and you call your moves by those numbers or some play by numbers and letters. We can pass reading material such as books back and forth, and newspapers and magazines. We share jokes with one another just to enjoy a sense of humor and laugh, because we all know that sometimes laughter is the best medicine for everyone. Sometimes though, even laughter cannot remove the pain and heartache one feels at the loss of friends and brothers. I would come to learn this over many executions in the months to come that would turn into years on end.

Though I had many great laughs with both Tito and ½ Deck, the execution of ½ Deck on February 15th, 2011, a little over one month after getting the news of my auntie's death, would be staggering. Nothing in my life ever prepared me for the pain felt within myself on February 16th, 2011 when I came to the dayroom and yelled out for ½ Deck, forgetting that he had just been executed the night before. Though we all knew of the executions taking place at the Walls Unit in Huntsville, Texas, where the condemned are sent from the Polunsky Unit, it's much more in your face on being housed with that same person who just the day before you were laughing with and eating with.

One week after the execution of ½ Deck, the administration took it upon themselves to start messing with me by moving me out of #14 Cell and over into #13 Cell right next door. No reason was given, and later the same night, another inmate was moved into #14 Cell, named "Youngblood", who had just gotten his own set execution date. Youngblood and I did not talk much, because he was under the impression that I had snitched when I was busted with that cellphone in 2008. He would tell me though that he thought it was messed up that I had called the state senator asking for help with both my appeals and my visitation. This though, I was able to clear up with him, was wrong information, and I showed him paperwork to back it all up. That was always one thing that upset me with everyone. Everyone thought I had went to this fool for help with both my appeals and to see my loved ones. It never made any sense though, because the month of September comes before the month of October. If you all remember from the many previous pages in this book, I had gone back to court in the 264th District Court of the Honorable Martha J. Trudo on September 30th, 2008 to end my appeals and volunteer for execution. And though it greatly saddens me to say and still causes me great heartache and pain, my mom was coming to visit with me the day she was arrested at the Austin airport in October of 2008, for purchasing me minutes for a cellphone so we could talk on the phone. So, why would I be asking for help on either of these issues when I was finished with one and already had visits scheduled? People, even prisoners, will believe what they want to, regardless of the truth. If it was said in the newspaper or on the news, people automatically assume it's the gospel. Malcom X said it best: "The media's the most powerful entity on earth. They have the power to make the innocent guilty and to make the guilty innocent."

Though I kept my distance from Youngblood, we both still passed for one another when a kite (slang for note) came from another section while one was in the dayroom, as well as passing books or anything else that came from another section for each other. For about two weeks, I heard Youngblood asking the prison chaplain for a rosary, and yet he would always get the runaround from the then-chaplain. He even went to his friends that were housed on other sections to see if someone had an extra rosary he could please get. Nobody ever had one for him.

One day while I was in the dayroom, I had been talking to Tito when some volunteer chaplains came onto the pod/section to speak with the fellas on Death Watch, as well as myself. Some of the chaplains that would come around were always cocky, like they could be anywhere else and that they didn't really want to be there talking with us. This would always upset myself and some of the others there with dates. This day though, one of them came to talk with Tito and I by simply talking aloud without first saying "excuse me" or anything. Tito gave me a look that said volumes. He didn't want to speak with the guy and told him so numerous times. The volunteer chaplain just went on talking to Tito like it didn't matter what Tito wanted, he was going to say what he wanted to say. Having enough, and wanting to finish my talk with Tito, I asked the volunteer chaplain, loud enough so he could hear me from right there less than three feet away, what he called that book he was carrying? I was speaking about the Holy Bible he had in his hand but never once opened or tried to share anything from it with Tito. He told me that it was God's Word, the Bible. Being a smartass, and wanting him to leave us alone, I told him that he was wrong. I said something along the lines of it being a Book of Letters, 66 to be exact. How come he didn't open it and try to share anything from God's Word as he said with my friend?

Instead of answering, he turned around and left Death Watch. Tito and I got back to our talk about ½ Deck's execution and how it sucked that he was gone now. Then the officer in the control picket yelled at me to let #14 Cell know that he had a visit. I did this, then thought to ask Tito if I could get his extra rosary he had, along with a piece of paper? He said sure and sent them both to me. I told him I'd be right back and sat at the dayroom table to write out a kite real fast to Youngblood. In the kite, I told Youngblood that I didn't expect him to be my friend, but I had been hearing him asking for a rosary and had gotten my hands on one. Here it was, and I hoped that it helped him relax and to have a good visit. I folded it up with the rosary inside and then climbed the bars and slid it under his cell door. Climbing down, I called his name and told him there was a kite in his cell. After picking up the kite, he asked who it was from, and I said me. He started to say he didn't want anything. I said, "Just read the damn thing, man," and turned away from him.

At that time, the officers that were escorting came onto the section to get him for his visit. As he's walking off the section, I took notice that he had the rosary around his neck and this huge smile on his black face! When he came back a little after two hours later, I was still stuck in the dayroom. He called me over to the front of his cell from up there on Two Row, and told me to climb up and grab the pictures he slid out there. I did as he asked, and he explained that he just had a great visit with his mom and that he wanted to show me the pictures of him and his mom. There in the two pictures is the rosary necklace around his neck, and Youngblood smiling huge with his mom! He told me thanks for the rosary and that it meant a lot to him. As he's speaking to me, he has tears falling down his face. I said that it was no big deal and that I hoped it helped him. He said that his mom and he are Catholic, and he'd been trying to get a rosary for some time but kept getting the runaround. After that, we became friends for the short time he was housed there with me and everyone else on Death Watch. We even cooked for one another and laughed together. On June 21st, 2011, Youngblood was executed by the State of Texas. Less than thirty days later I would lose another amigo, my friend and brother Tito, who was executed on July 7th, 2011. The loss and pain felt after getting to know these three men is something that goes beyond feeling, nor is it really explainable. All I can tell you is that it hurts knowing that someone you know and once laughed with is going to be dead and there is nothing that you can do to stop it or prevent it.

Not long after the execution of Tito, the administration moved one of the infamous Texas 7 into his cell. This would be George Rivas, who everyone just called Rivas. One of the things we all feared about Rivas while he was on Death Watch was him eating some beans with his food or tacos. One day during the month of February, after everyone was done for the day and starting to relax, out of nowhere you heard someone pass gas loud as hell! Nobody said anything like "excuse me" or whatever, then thirty seconds later the same person passes gas again even louder. The officer in the picket looks over to the section, and I guess George felt like something should be said. Right after he farts again, he says, "Exxxxxcuuuuuseeeeee mmmmmeeeeee!!"

When I tell you that everyone busted up laughing, I mean just that. Everyone on Death Watch started laughing so hard, and all of us were asking Rivas, "Dude, what the hell did you eat?"

Rivas: "Beans and more beans!!"

When Rivas wasn't farting around on the section, he could be sharing his skills with all. He was always good for some good jokes, and for hooking up TV on someone's radio. Since Death Row inmates were not allowed TVs, the next best thing for most of us was to hook up or have someone hook TV into our radios so that we could listen to TV throughout the days and nights. Some nights when all was quiet you could hear the sounds of COPS playing over someone's speaker (a speaker is something guys can make back here, and though it's considered contraband, we still make them.) I mean, come on, guys, COPS? Most times though it was some TV series or Judge Judy, or the Simpsons and Family Guy for laughter. One thing he taught me though, and I would use all the time, was how to knock out my video camera inside my cell so that I could have some privacy from the watching eyes of all.

The cameras in the cells back then were different from the ones that they have in our cells now. Back then though, you could take a piece of foil or something that would reflect the light back into the sensors on the camera. By doing this, I was able to knock out my camera whenever I would shut my lights off; it would no longer be able to see me in the dark because it shut off its own night vision.

Rivas wasn't over here for long before he too would be executed on February 29th, 2012. On March 1st, 2012, I was moved back into Cell #14 as a means to start harassing me with moving me into someone's cell that I was friends with or had just been executed. The thing is, that didn't bother me like they thought it would. Right after I moved and Rivas was killed, they moved into his cell a guy everyone called Sarge. Sarge was in the Army at one time for a while. He always had the same haircut when they offered cuts on Death Row by an inmate barber. High and tight was his cut. Sarge used to make so many of us laugh aloud with his sense of humor. Close your eyes and imagine this white guy that's got a high and tight haircut like a soldier, walking around in a dayroom with shorts on and a t-shirt with brown Rhino boots on. He's got this booming laugh. That was what Sarge looked like. He was funny, and yet he was one of the few who I got to know that was also very religious while he was here with us. He had numerous execution dates that never went through because he got stays of executions. I remember him telling us the story of the time he was driven over to the death house in Huntsville Texas. He was being told the way it's going to go down, yada, yada, yada, when he interrupts the Warden of the Walls Unit and says, "Look, I understand all of what you're saying, but let me say this. I'm a grown-ass man who served in the military. One thing I'm telling you that's NOT GOING TO HAPPEN is you putting a butt-plug in me. I'll wear the adult diaper but not a freakin' BUTT-PLUG." Sarge told us that when he said this to them, they all looked at him crazy before asking what the hell he was talking about? Sarge told them that one of the fellas who'd been over here before with a date said that you allow us to choose between the two before executing us. They told him that was not true. Sarge said to himself when he got back he was going to curse Balentine out for this bullcrap. Telling us this story, we all started busting our asses up laughing so hard. I had tears falling cause I was laughing so hard. Balentine is another inmate named John Balentine, who no longer has an execution date but is still housed on A-Pod as I write this out to you. Fact is, he and I laugh a bit when we talk.

Another time while he was housed on Death Watch with me and the other fellas with dates, he was again in the dayroom walking around and just shootin' the breeze with us when we got word that a tour was going to be coming around onto the pod with the wardens and Rank. So we had to get our cells in order if they weren't already. Sarge is telling us we all need to act like fools so they don't come back. I told him to walk around like a dork in the dayroom, like Steve Urkle in that TV show where the young black kid with the big eye glasses is so smart and yet he has his pants pulled way up high and laughs funny. Before we know it, the tour is on the pod, and the wardens are talking about this section and how we all have execution dates and video cameras inside our cells. There are both men and women in the group. They turn around and are facing the control picket as the warden tells them how it's ran. When they turn back around, Sarge is sitting with his pants down around his ankles on the toilet, looks directly at the warden, and says, "Hey, Warden, can I get some crap paper!?" Then makes this loud-ass farting sound. We are all laughing so hard, the warden is turning red in the face, screaming for the officers to rack up Sarge and lock A-Section down for this bullcrap! He can't get the tour off the pod fast enough. We were locked down on this section alone for two weeks for that. But when you think about it, to us it was worth it, and though they don't ask us, we don't like it when they bring tours around to this section to showboat everyone on this section. This is not a zoo where you bring people to see the animals, though that is exactly how they treat us… like animals in a zoo.

On September 25th, 2012, Sarge walked off this section for the last time, never to return to his friends and brothers on Death Row, let alone the rest who knew him on Texas Death Row. Not long after his execution, I was scheduled for a legal telephone call with a new appointed lawyer who was taking on my case. Seems she was appointed by the courts back in May, but I was too busy with the executions of my friends to take good notice. Her name is Marcia Widder, Esq. One thing that I was never good at was getting along with lawyers. I mean, who does, right? Over time though, she, along with some others who would also be appointed at her request to the courts, would get under my skin and become something more than just simple lawyers to me. At the time of her being appointed to work with me, she would be living in New Orleans, LA, and doing private practice for those dumb enough to land in prison or on Death Row in some states. More times than I care to remember, I would get into it with her about my current situation and remaining alive and fighting this losing battle with the State of Texas. However, trying to make her, or any other lawyer for that matter, understand that some people should just be allowed to waive their rights to appeals and volunteer for execution goes beyond her head and those that are with her. Deep down, she's a great person and means well and would do just about anything for someone she believes in or has befriended… such as I. Marcy, as she likes to go by, has been my lead lawyer now for 9 years, and I can tell you it's not been an easy nine years. Numerous times, when I felt that I had reached rock bottom and nobody would listen, I would go back to cutting on myself. Not to end my life, but to release my anger and frustration over the loss of friends/brothers, and over the situation I'm currently in. Being housed on Death Watch without a set execution date. Not being allowed to visit with my mom, sister, and grandma as a further means of punishment by the Texas Department of Criminal Justice and State Senator John Whitmire. When my grandma passed away from cancer years ago, I again was refused a telephone call home to my mom and sister. I took this hard, and feeling with no other choice, I cut myself because I felt something that I hadn't felt since California. I felt a homicidal rage within me to hurt someone in gray (Officer) or the Warden if I could get my hands on them. But deep down, I knew this to be the wrong way to go about something. Hurting the officers or even a warden that in my book deserved to be hurt wouldn't get me anywhere. It wasn't the officers' fault, so why should I take my anger out on them? This is a way for them to put food on the table and a roof over the heads of their loved ones while also paying the bills. However, by harming myself, as they call it here, I was able to not only escape everything within myself when I saw my own blood bleeding out of my body, but it also allowed me to relax and be shipped off the Unit to another prison over in Sugar Land, Texas, called Jester-4.

This was and is a kind of prison hospital for prisoners that need to be there. I didn't go there to get fixed, I would either ask mental health to send me there and they would, or I would do something that would leave them no choice but to send me there. It allowed me to escape the death that I would continue to re-live day after day. People such as other prisoners that were doing time in other prisons throughout Texas had no idea who I was for a while. We were all butt-naked and in single cells. There were both men and women in the cells. The place sucked, and during the wintertime it was freezing, but the officers there treated all the prisoners like they mattered. It didn't matter what you were locked up for or how much time you had, you were treated like a human being and not an animal. Almost all of the officers over there are from Nigeria, and all of them are religious. I would stand at my cell door the first few times I was over there and just listen to the other prisoners talk to one another through their cell doors about how much time they had or what was going on in their lives. Some had lengthy sentences, while others were getting out in months, if not days. Some had serious issues where they snapped and lost their minds. They were smearing feces and urine on themselves or throwing it at other prisoners when they would pass their cells at their Units (Prisons.) To totally lose your mind in prison, I feel, would be the very worst place to do so. Prison is no hospice or hospital; the officers do not want to clean up after you when you crap all over the place, or when you lose the way to think and write because your mind went one way while your spirit went the other way and your body left you. To go insane within prison walls is death in so many ways; and what about the few that lose their minds other ways? Such as the ones who become violent because they're left no other choice but to fight for their own survival within the prison they're spending the rest of their lives? Don't think this happens? Well, then you've never been in prison for any length of time, have you? So you have no honest to gods idea of what you're thinking, just like lawyers. Right now, as I type out my story to you, I can feel the edge of the cliff at my feet. I can taste the edge of sanity going out of me and crazy wanting a place to live. Both of these I refuse to give into, before I lose it all one way or the other. I rather fight to have my appeals dropped, and if that doesn't work…

The real reason for this book though isn't just to share my story and what all I have gone through and continue to go through at the hands of those who keep me here, but hopefully also educate someone out there in society. If you know someone that is looking at going down the wrong path in their lives, be it your child or friend or a neighbor, brother, sister, nephew, niece, anybody, know this. Prison is not the place you want to do it from. This is no life, and when you hear your friends talk about this or that, just know that the minute your butt lands inside these walls, those same friends will no longer know you. Young guys think it's cool walking around with a loaded gun, talking a big game. Just know that when the pressure is on and you've talked yourself into a corner, you'll be tested and forced to do something you don't want to do. By that time it'll be too late to back down or get out of the situation you placed yourself into in the first place. You really want to go through with acting like a badass and carry a weapon of any kind? Then walk your tough little ass down to the local morgue and look at the dead bodies down there. Get up close and personal, knowing that this could very well be you one day, or your friend, or the person you place there. While you're there, listen to their loved ones that come in to identify their next of kin. Talk to the beat cops around your neighborhood about the things they've seen. Or if you really want to know, write to me, and I'll share with you much more than you'll ever read in this book or any other book. My information can be found at the end of this book. Whatever you do, don't throw your life away, cause it's not going to be worth it if you do.

The little control of things you do have out there in society, you'll no longer have within prison walls. Simple things like going to the shower and turning on the hot and cold water, that's gone. The water temp is set at one temp here, that's at 120 degrees, and when it's not set, it's freezing cold like ice water. When your toilet plugs up there in your home with your loved ones, you can contact a plumber to fix it or use a plunger to unplug it yourself. No such thing in prison. Your toilet will remain plugged until they find a plumber, or worse case, it's not only your toilet plugged, but a few of the guys on the run. The piping is screwed up and some idiot keeps flushing his working toilet, which is making the toilets that are plugged back up with feces and urine flooding all over your cell floor, so that you are now standing in it. Think someone is just going to come around and clean that up, you're wrong! You'll either clean up the sewage that came flooding out of your toilet, or you'll bask in it until you do. What about when there is a local water problem where you're at. They tell you to boil the water and you'll be okay, or go to the store and buy some bottled water. Not here in prison. The water goes off, we don't even know about it until it's too late. You wake up in the morning thinking you'll put on some water in your Hotpot to heat and brush your teeth, only you notice the freaking water has been shut off while you're sleeping. Or worse case than that is not only has the water been shut off while you were all sleeping, but before it got shut off something broke, and your cell is now flooded with water. You don't notice this though until you wake up and set your feet on the floor, only to set it right into freaking two inches of water that's running all through your cell and out the door!

Still want to spend your life in prison? Wait until they lock it all down, and you're given only a paper Johnny sack for breakfast, lunch, and dinner, food that wouldn't feed an animal, and this is what you'll get three times a day for weeks if not months, depending on how long they leave you locked down. Oh, and you only get to shower on Monday, Wednesday, and Friday, and that's only when they have enough officers to work and escort you to the shower. Not enough officers, and you're ass out. A homeless person lives better than some of us in prison. Want to spend your life in prison or on Death Row somewhere because you wanted to be accepted by your peers? Take your young ass and go sleep under an overpass like a homeless person. Learn to survive that way, and when you see that you don't like it nor ever want to live this way, take your ass back home and apologize to your loved ones for being an asshole. Take yourself back to school and get an education. Listen to those that love and care about you. I failed to do this. The highest education I got was up to the 11th grade and the streets and homelessness. It not only cost me relationships with family, but also good friends. I lost my best friend due to my stupidity. When he and his parents tried to get me on the right track, I paid no attention. In the end, he went on with his life, and I lost mine in so many ways. Wherever you are, Adam Enos of Turlock, California, I wish you and your loved ones the very best.

 Lost many of my family members when they said they had enough and also turned their backs on me. My older brothers have nothing to do with me, even though I have tried to reach out to them to apologize. The only time both my brothers thought to come into my life was when I had my execution date. They asked me to place them on the visitation list so that they could attend my execution. That's all I am to my brothers now, something for their entertainment, to watch me be executed because I stole and hurt them so much. This is how I took it, my prison mentality is wired this way, yet I was told they only wanted to be there so I wouldn't be alone. I'm alone now, and they want nothing to do with me. The only ones to stick by me after everything, even when I don't deserve them or their love, is my mom, sister, and little niece. Though even my sister and niece have fallen away from me more and more lately, leaving only my mother. Being in prison is a hard and lonely life to live for anyone. Regardless of how tough you are, if you're not mentally tough, it will kill you from the inside of yourself out. People from all walks of life have at one point in time or another reached out to me, wanting to correspond, both men and women. They all talk a good game about how they each care about where you are and what is going on with you, only to break away because they truly do not understand, or they got what they wanted from you. They were fake and insincere in the end.

 For the most part I have stayed away from pen-pal sites since I have been locked up in this sorry state of Texas. Only recently did I contact through one of my lawyers a pen-pal site to place my ad on their site. Not only have these two women been very professional to me, but they have treated me with kindness and compassion. Both of those things in my opinion I'm underserving of, because I'm unable to get over the hatred for myself, for the pain I caused so many and my own loved ones. The trouble I caused for my mom and sister when I was busted with that cellphone, that caused them to get arrested, will never part from my mind/heart. That crap eats at me every day and night of my life. Though my mom and sister have both told me that they forgive me and have moved on, I'm unable to forgive myself nor move on. It's one of the things that's slowly killing me from the inside out. Aside from my loved ones and the ladies who run the pen-pal site at Wire of Hope, Sigrid and Elodie, who can be found at www.wireofhope.com or contact@wireofhope.com, there are very few people in my life right now, because though I used to trust anyone, I am no longer like that, and prison will make you this way. I have become my very own worst enemy.

Chapter Fifteen

When Donnie was moved over to the Death Watch section after getting his own execution date, we said very little if anything to one another because he was also under the impression that I said more, because he was told by other pen pals that I had been talking. Finally one day, when I had had enough, I called him out to the yard so we could talk. The day we were finally able to get out and talk turned out great because he had been baptized recently and wanted to apologize to me about some things. Turns out Donnie was just going with the flow and assuming like everyone else that I was guilty. He told me that he knew just some of the other fellas, that the morning that they kicked in my cell door and found the cellphone, Billy Mason was seen sipping from a cup with no restraints on in the Major's office ten minutes before they busted me, thus letting me know that people knew that Billy Mason had snitched on me. It wasn't only my own stupidity that caused me to get caught by contacting that craphead Whitmire, but Mason too.

After the air was cleared between the two of us, we started playing dominoes on the outside rec yard a few times each week. Throughout the first month while Donnie was housed on Death Watch, I had heard him asking numerous people for a photo album, t-shirt, and an illustration board. Unable to obtain these things before his date that was getting to be three weeks closer, I went about helping him without his knowing it. He was out at a visit one day in early October when I had sent kites around the pod for the things he was asking after. I was able to obtain the t-shirt and illustration board, and the photo-album I took from myself because I had an extra one. Being housed in #14 Cell when Donnie got back from his visit, I yelled at him to shoot his line through the side of the door. Donnie was housed down the run on Two Row with me, but at the far end or near about. He was in Cell #9. Once he shot his line down to me and I pulled it into my cell through the side of my door, I tied on the things that I was able to get for him as well as the photo-album from myself. Once he got everything inside his cell, I told him that he didn't owe me anything and that I had heard him looking and trying to get these items weeks ago. He told me thanks because he needed them for something he wanted to leave his wife and daughter. The next week, after returning from another visit with his loved ones, he asked me to make a list for things to make tacos with for everyone on this section. He said that he would be doing his last spend in the morning, and that while he was at visit the last three days, he wanted to know if I would cook tacos for him, Lizard, Skinny, and myself. I told him that would be okay and went to writing out a list of everything needed. (Note: when someone is doing his last spend, that mean it'll be the last time TDCJ-ID will allow him to make commissary. That's 14 days from his date with death. He can purchase anything from the commissary, so long as he doesn't go over about $150.00. It's also during this time he's pulled out to talk to the Unit Warden and fill out all the proper paperwork, ie. who will be claiming his remains after his execution, picking up his property from the Walls Unit, who will he have witnessing his execution, etc…) When commissary came to deliver Donnie's stuff the next day after he spoke with the Warden and did his paperwork, he shot me everything early so that he wouldn't have to deal with it all later. It's hard work fishing everything through the side of one's cell door! Some things like bags of chips are a pain in the butt.

Before long, Donnie's three days were here. During the last 72 hours while he's housed on Death Watch, the officers have to check on him every thirty minutes and log it down on the paperwork in the control picket. Most of the times though, they do this by looking at the video cameras inside our cells. His last 24 hours, as it is with everyone who has a date, he's checked on both by the video camera inside the cell and by officers walking to his door to double check and to write down what he's doing. For the most part, the officers leave everyone on this section alone. While he was out at visitation, things went like they normally do back here. Loud and crazy. Officers slamming the gates that come onto each section, as well as the cross-over doors that lead from one section to another. Guys being escorted to the shower. Just because someone has an execution date doesn't mean time comes to a stand-still; if anything it seems like it speeds up! I also held up to my end and was cooking food throughout the last three days. On his final morning with all of us on the section, as he was passing by my cell going into the shower, he stopped and dropped some things in front of my cell. Once he was in the shower and the officers had left, I reached out and got the items. Before he started showering he asked me to pass those for him and to let everyone know he'd speak with them when he got out of the shower. I said cool. About that time, Lizard was just being placed in the dayroom, and I told him that I had a kite for him and one for Saint over in C-Section. "See if someone is over there yet, and I will pass it to him."

    I shot both kites for him and Saint to him in the dayroom. The last kite was addressed to me. I left it sitting on my desk, thinking that I would open it after Donnie left for the Walls Unit in Huntsville, Texas. Lizard read his, and when Donnie got out of the shower, he thanked him for the flags (stamps). Guess Lizard had loaned Donnie some flags, and Donnie not only repaid him, but twice as much. Don't know what he sent or said to Saint, but we heard that he got it and yelled back and thanked Donnie as well. Donnie asked me when he got back in the cell what I thought. I told him that I had not opened it yet. He said to open it and let him know. So when I opened the kite from Donnie, he not only wrote me a really kind letter telling me he was sorry for everything that I was going through and hoped that one day these people would let me see my mom and sister at a visit, but he also left me $120.00 in flags. I was beyond touched because I didn't expect anything from him, certainly not something like this. It just goes to show that not everyone on Texas Death Row is an asshole. A lot of us change over time, and for the most part, it's a better change from within ourselves. Donnie was executed later on that night of October 31st, 2012, Halloween night.

    When I set out to tell my story in the form of this book, I didn't think it would be so hard to do. However, I'm finding it greatly painful to re-live the memories of the guys that I got to know as human beings and not the animals the district attorney's office would have you believe we are. Therefore, I will share with you one more in depth who was my best friend back here on Texas Death Row/Death Watch. Before moving onto other topics about this prison and the people who get away with screwing us all over with things such as our legal and non-legal mail. But first allow me to introduce to you the men that have been escorted from this section I have been housed on as a means of further punishment and cruel and unusual punishment for my involvement of being caught with a cellphone back in 2008.

1) Michael Wayne Hall – Executed February 15th, 2011 (1/2 Deck)
2) Timothy Wayne Adams – Executed February 22nd, 2011
3) Cary D. Kerr – Executed May 3rd, 2011
4) Gayland Charles Bradford – Executed June 1st, 2011
5) Lee Andrew Taylor – Executed June 16th, 2011
6) Milton Wuzael Mathis – Executed June 21st, 2011 (Youngblood)
7) Humberto Leal Garcia, Jr. – Executed July 7th, 2011 (Tito)
8) Mark Anthony Stroman – Executed July 20th, 2011
9) Martin Robles – Executed August 10th, 2011
10) Steven Michael Woods, Jr. – Executed September 13th, 2011
11) Lawrence Russell Brewer – Executed September 21st, 2011
12) Frank Martinez Garcia, Jr. – Executed October 27th, 2011
13) Guadalupe Esparza – Executed November 16th, 2011
14) Rodrigo Hernandez – Executed January 26th, 2012
15) George Angel Rivas, Jr. – Executed February 29th, 2012 (Rivas)
16) Keith Steven Thurmond – Executed March 7th, 2012
17) Jesse Jo Hernandez – Executed March 28th, 2012
18) Beunka Adams – Executed April 26th, 2012
19) Yokamon Laneal Hearn – Executed July 18th, 2012
20) Marvin Lee Wilson – Executed August 7th, 2012
21) Robert Wayne Harris – Executed September 20th, 2012
22) Cleve W. Foster III – Executed September 25th, 2012 (Sarge)
23) Jonathan Marcus Green – Executed October 10th, 2012
24) Bobby Lee Hines – Executed October 24th, 2012
25) Donnie Lee Roberts, Jr. – Executed October 31, 2012 (Donnie)
26) Mario Rashad Swain – Executed November 8th, 2012
27) Ramon Torres Hernandez – Executed November 14th, 2012

28) Preston Craig Hughes III – Executed November 15th, 2012
29) Carl Henry Blue – Executed February 21st, 2013
30) Rickey Lynn Lewis – Executed April 9th, 2013
31) Ronnie Paul Threadgill – Executed April 16th, 2013
32) Richard Aaron Cobb – Executed April 25th, 2013
33) Carroll Joe Parr – Executed May 7th, 2013
34) Jeffrey Demond Williams – Executed May 15th, 2013
35) Elroy Chester III – Executed June 12th, 2013
36) John Manuel Quintanilla, Jr. – Executed July 16th, 2013
37) Vaughn Ross – Executed July 18th, 2013
38) Douglas Adam Feldman – Executed July 31st, 2013
39) Robert Gene Garza – Executed September 19th, 2013
40) Arturo Eleazar Diaz – Executed September 26th, 2013
41) Michael John Yowell – Executed October 9th, 2013
42) Jamie Bruce McCoskey – Executed November 12th, 2013
43) Jerry Duane Martin – Executed December 3rd, 2013
44) Edgar Tamayo Arias – Executed January 22nd, 2014
45) Ray L. Jasper III – Executed March 19th, 2014
46) Anthony Dewayne Doyle – Executed March 27th, 2014
47) Tommy Lynn Sells – Executed April 3rd, 2014
48) Ramiro Hernandez Llanas – Executed April 9th, 2014
49) Jose Luis Villegas, Jr. – Executed April 16th, 2014
50) Willie Tyrone Trottie – Executed September 10th, 2014
51) Miguel Angel Paredes – Executed October 28th, 2014
52) Arnold Prieto, Jr. – Executed January 21st, 2015
53) Robert Charles Ladd – Executed January 29th, 2015
54) Donald Keith Newbury – Executed February 4th, 2015 (Lizard)
55) Manuel Vasquez – Executed March 11th, 2015
56) Kent William Sprouse – Executed April 9th, 2015
57) Manuel Fernando Garza, Jr. – Executed April 15th, 2015
58) Derrick Dewayne Charles – Executed May 12th, 2015
59) Lester Leroy Bower, Jr. – Executed June 3rd, 2015
60) Gregory Lynn Russeau – Executed June 18th, 2015
61) Daniel Lee Lopez – Executed August 12th, 2015
62) Juan Martin Garcia – Executed October 6th, 2015
63) Licho Escamilla – Executed October 14th, 2015
64) Raphael Deon Holiday – Executed November 18th, 2015
65) Richard Allen Masterson – Executed January 20th, 2016

66) James Garrett Freeman – Executed January 27th, 2016
67) Gustavo Julian Garcia, Jr. – Executed February 16th, 2016
68) Coy Wayne – Executed March 9th, 2016
69) Adam Kelly Ward – Executed March 22nd, 2016
70) Pablo Lucio Vasquez – Executed April 6th, 2016
71) Barney Ronald Fuller, Jr. – Executed October 5th, 2016
72) Christopher Chubasco Wilkins – Executed January 11th, 2017
73) Terry Darnell Edwards – Executed January 26th, 2017
74) Rolando Ruiz, Jr. – Executed March 7th, 2017
75) James Eugene Bigby – Executed March 14th, 2017

Chapter Sixteen

"That's it, Slim! You are not beating me up anymore! You hear me, Slim!?"

"Dude, Big Tai, you called me out tonight and don't get mad cause I sunk your battleship once again! It's only right I'm kicking your ass right now after the beating you gave me in Hangman!"

"That crap still has me laughing, Slim!"

"Yeah, whatever, foo!"

(Note: Big Tai was the only one to call me by my nickname from California and Florida, Slim. Others call me Blue.)

We had been at it all month, playing games such as Battleship and Hangman while standing at our cell doors here on Death Watch. The two of us had known one another since I rolled up to the prison back in 2007. Big Tai, as we who knew him called him, was a giant black guy about 6 foot 6 and around 240 pounds of muscle, with a shaved head that was so bald you could see your reflection, if you were tall enough, that is. He was also a Five Percenter. Though he was busted here in Texas, he was from Brooklyn, NY, and some family are still out there while some are here in Texas. While he was housed here on Death Watch with me, we had a rule between one another. He would always make the tacos or spreads or gumbo for the two of us, and I'd always make the cheesecakes and drink (hooch) for the two of us throughout his stay over here, in the hopes he would be getting a stay of execution. Also, when either he was in the dayroom or I was, we'd study together. Meaning he would bring his Qu'ran and Bible and dictionary to dayroom, and I'd have mine in the cell. For one hour each day we would study together as not just friends, but as Brothers. People are most afraid of what they don't understand, and too many people are quick to misunderstand another's faith, either cause they're cowards, or because they're ignorant to facts. Both the Holy Bible and the Holy Qu'ran tie into one another. If only people would take the time to study and read instead of passing judgement, life would be so much easier out there in society. But hey, I'm just another Dead Man Walking, so what do I know.

When Big Tai and I weren't studying, we could be found on the outside rec yard playing Run and Shoot with sweat pouring down our faces from busting our asses trying to beat one another for hours on end. Let me explain so you can understand better what the game is. The outside rec yards here on Texas Death Row's 12-Building are two big cages outside that sit side by side to one another. Probably about 30 feet by 15 feet. Each one had a basketball and hoop mounted up on the wall on one side, and a pull-up bar and a urinal/sink to drink water from. Other than that, there is open sky straight up that you can see through the bars. Standing at one end of each rec yard, at the start of the game, you would shoot the ball towards the basket. If you made it, that counted as one shot. You would run to the other end and do it again. The object of the game was to run and shoot points. First one to get ten points won the game. In the two hours we were outside sometimes, you would catch us playing between 60 and 100 games, with little if any breaks in between each set. The other thing that we would do would be when either one of us had a visit, either legal or spiritual in my case, and the same with visits from family with him, we'd bring back each other's favorite goodie/snack from a vending machine that we couldn't buy in the prison commissary. My thing was those freaking Rice Krispy Treats, and his were the Starburst Tropical flavors!

One thing that we couldn't buy in the commissary were game boards like for Battleship or Hangman. So we would make our own boards, and every Friday night he and I would have the music playing on one of our speakers while kicking each other's ass on one game or the other to pass the time when we weren't writing letters to home or lawyers.

One night that we had been planning for for two months came around. Usually it wouldn't be something either one of us would do, but with his upcoming execution date, we decided to get lit and have a good time with some weed and drink, along with some tacos he would be making. We were able to get our hands on three joints and a lighter, and I had made us three bottles of drink each, something that I hardly do because it's too risky. But this night was the only time we felt we could do it and get away with it, and just have fun blocking everything out and his upcoming execution that we both knew was going to go through this time. This night though, it was April 20th, 2017, and we had just finished eating the tacos he made and were sippin' on the second bottle of our drinks as we down the first one to get that good feeling going. Standing at our cell doors, talking with one another and laughing, it was like we were both thinking the same thing at the same time and called each other out for a game of Battleship. Let me tell you young and old people something, don't ever try to play this damn game while drunk and high. For a good many hours we both just talked crap before deciding to play Hangman instead. Standing at the door with a noose around my neck (on the board), it was the first time Big Tai said that a white-looking guy was being hung by a black dude! We both started laughing our asses off, and about that time, one of the officers working the pod decided to walk her rounds. When she made it to our cells there on Two Row on Death Watch, she stopped right in front of our Cells #14 and #13, with this look on her face that said she could smell the weed but wasn't saying anything. Big Tai and I just stood at our cell doors looking at her looking at us, before you hear me tell Big Tai, bet you can't do it again, and if you do I'm not telling nobody! The officer asked us what the hell we were doing up at 3:45am when usually we would both be sleeping by this time. Big Tai and I looked at her said that we were playing… HANGMAN!

That alone had us laughing like little kids caught red-handed, because when you honestly think about it, here you have two grown-ass men on Texas Death Row/Death Watch, and we're playing Hangman like everything is just one big joke or like we could care less about anything right at that moment. We were just enjoying life and the friendship we had.

On July 23rd, 2017, we were both out in the visitation with legal visits and were sitting right next to one another, when our lawyers did the old switch and started talking with us. I started talking with Big Tai's lawyer/paralegal, and he started talking with my lawyer/Investigator; both of us lucked out with two very beautiful women working for us and on our cases. Then, on the day of his execution, I had both of my Investigators come to visit with me so that I could, one, show Big Tai my support by being out in visitation with him when they came to escort him out, and two, because I wanted my legal team to feel what I was feeling and to see how we are truly treated like animals our last day by the administration of Texas Department of Criminal Justice. The day this sorry State executed my Big Homie was the day I felt something else break inside me. Just like when I decided to leave a party late one night with my co-defendant in November of 2004, and I shot and killed two grown men. Then I felt something leave me too. A part of me that I'll never be able to retain, and now this state not only executed someone's son, brother, uncle, dad, but they also took away the only hope and faith I had left in a system I had long been knowing was broken. When they executed my best friend Big Tai on July 27th, 2017 at a little after 6:30pm, making him #76 since I've been housed on this section as a means of further punishment, they might as well have strapped me down on the gurney too. Not a day goes by that I don't think of my friend and look forward to the day that he and I will meet again in Heaven with our other loved ones and friends that have left before each of us. Only now, I know what it is that I suffer from… Survivor's guilt.

77) Robert Lynn Pruett – Executed October 12th, 2017
78) Ruben Cardenas Ramirez – Executed November 8th, 2017
79) Anthony Allen Shore – Executed January 18th, 2018
80) William Earl Rayford – Executed January 30th, 2018
81) John David Battaglia – Executed February 1st, 2018
82) Rosendo Rodriguez III – Executed March 27th, 2018
83) Erick Daniel Davila – Executed April 25th, 2018
84) Juan Edward Castillo – Executed May 16th, 2018
85) Danny Paul Bible – Executed June 27th, 2018
86) Christopher Anthony Young – Executed July 17th, 2018
87) Troy James Clark – Executed September 26th, 2018
88) Daniel Clate Acker – Executed September 27th, 2018
89) Robert Moreno Ramos – Executed November 14th, 2018
90) Joseph Christopher Garcia – Executed December 4th, 2018

91) Alvin Avon Braziel, Jr. – Executed December 11th, 2018
92) Robert Mitchell Jennings – Executed January 30th, 2019
93) Billie Wayne Coble – Executed February 28th, 2019
94) John William King – Executed April 24th, 2019
95) Larry Ray Swearingen – Executed August 21st, 2019
96) Billy Jack Crutsinger – Executed September 4th, 2019
97) Mark Anthony Soliz – Executed September 10th, 2019
98) Robert Sparks – Executed September 25th, 2019
99) Justen Grant Hall – Executed November 6th, 2019
100) Travis Trevino Runnels – Executed December 11th, 2019
101) John Steven Gardner – Executed January 15th, 2020
102) Abel Revill Ochoa – Executed February 6th, 2020
103) Billy Joe Wardlow – Executed July 8th, 2020
104) Quintin Phillippe Jones – Executed May 19th, 2021

Chapter Seventeen

Not every officer that works for the Texas Department of Criminal Justice is a bad officer, nor are some of the ones that work on 12-Building's Death Row/Death Watch section. When this pandemic hit the world and caused widespread panic among society and the administration, you had some officers that would go out of their way to assist myself and many others here on Death Watch. After spending so many years locked up in isolation as a means of punishment, when everyone over here on Death Watch tested negative for Covid-19 during the 2020 and 2021 year, the administration moved prisoners that had tested positive over here with us. That made no sense to any of us, other than the fact that they were hoping some of us would also become sick with Covid-19. As long as the positive were being housed with us even though they shouldn't have been on this section, Death Watch was now being placed on a quarantine lockdown, which further caused much frustration amongst ourselves and those that worked here. It also allowed the Unit mailroom staff, namely Misty N. Sumner, to get out of doing her job and delivering all legal mail and packages to those of us housed over here, as well as for the whole pod. At some point in the past, the United States Supreme Court ruled that correctional officers were not allowed to handle legal mail from lawyers or their law firms that were being addressed to a prisoner. However, the Texas Department of Criminal Justice cares little about what some Justice of the Courts might say or order. By running to the assistant wardens of the Polunsky Unit and the Texas Department of Criminal Justice Mailroom Coordinator in Huntsville, Texas, crying about how A-Pod, and thus A-Section where Death Watch are housed and under quarantine lockdown are, she shouldn't have to go into the section nor anywhere on the Pod to deliver legal mail to us. They agreed with her and thus, she was now allowed to come to the front door of the pod and drop off all legal mail from lawyers and their firms, as well as all packages such as books and other periodicals that were ordered for us from either friends and family, or lawyers through Amazon.com or any bookstore. In doing so, many federal stimulus checks and other legal mail became missing or never made it to the proper inmates. One such piece of mail that had a $40.00 Western Union Money Order enclosed was addressed to my brother and friend Julius Murphy, who we all called Juju. It was stuck together with my legal mail, that wasn't delivered to me until Sunday night around midnight. This was four days after Misty N. Sumner of the mailroom dropped all the legal mail off at the front door to A-Pod. Juju wasn't even housed on this pod. He had been moved two weeks before and was now living on B-Pod in B-Section of that pod. When I tried to give the mail back to the officer that gave it to me, she refused to take it, stating that this crap wasn't even her job and she's not going to be held accountable for it. In the end, I ended up giving it to an LT. that had come walking the pod the next morning. He in turn took it to Juju on B-Pod, who in turn mailed it to one of his lawyers explaining what had happened. This was just one of the times that mail had been sent to the wrong person because the prison mailroom refused to do their job and instead passed off the duties to the officers.

 Texas Death Row used to get tons of mail sent to each of us, but over the years the mailroom has either had much of that mail returned to sender or simply thrown it into the trash without the prisoners knowing this was being done with their mail. She's not the only one doing us this way in the mailroom. Her coworker, who was finally fired by the senior warden, Warden Daniel Dickerson, was also throwing mail out or not delivering it. Her name was Glenda McNiel. Her replacement is another bad apple that worked here before named Mrs. Allen. For the last five years, the mail has trickled down to almost nothing for each pod. Most times we're lucky if we get any mail out of the prison mailroom. Texas Department of Criminal Justice has a contract with www.jpay.com, where our loved ones can go online and send us an email that the mailroom is supposed to print out and deliver to us within 48 hours. This never gets done though. Whenever our loved ones send such an email, something they sat down to type out to their loved ones that they might never see again due to the Covid-19 pandemic or because he's given an execution date, and those same people pay a fee for the email, it matters not to the Unit mailroom staff nor the people in Huntsville, Texas. Unless we're willing to fight for these missing jpay's and risk going to level and losing all personal property, even though we'd be in the right, we'll never see the email our loved ones, or friends, or even lawyers might send us. Their excuse is that they're busy or that they don't do reprints. Hold up, you mean that because you're busy sitting on your ass not doing anything or sending our mail to the wrong person, we're not going to get what's rightfully ours? Thus it's okay for you to break the contract that www.jpay.com has with TDCJ-ID, or that it's okay to screw us and those that send them to us over because in fact you are now stealing. Or what you're really saying is that even though we have been sentenced to Death by the Courts, that we shouldn't even be allowed to get mail that we're automatically being cast aside with no rights; that your life is more important than those of our own, or the officers that come on the sections and pods to feed us, do count each day and night, shower us. That your life, Misty N. Sumner, is more important than even Tracy B. Moye who is the Unit Grievance Officer and who is a young black woman. Your life is more important than hers. She not only does her job without complaint, but during the pandemic, she went along with everyone else by wearing PPE (Personal Protection Equipment) to pick up grievances from all prisoners. This woman goes out of her way to do not only her job, just as her one-time coworker Christina M. Norris had once done before being forced by the prison administration to quit her job, because people actually care about us on Texas Death Row and see us all as human beings. It's okay for the people like Misty N. Sumner and her mailroom coworkers to lie and screw people over in any way they can, regardless of fact or truth. People like the staff in the prison mailroom are no better than the lady that called 911 and lied about the black man who was bird-watching over on the East Coast. When he asked her to place her dog on a leash, this white woman wanted to lie, regardless of the fact that she was caught on video.

If you think that you can get away with screwing myself and everyone else over in regards to their legal mail, jpays, and packages, you'll continue to do so, and the administration and the mailroom coordinator will continue to allow you to do this injustice against those of us condemned.

Yet, not all the officers and staff that work here at the Polunsky are bad apples. You have officers on both the day-shift and night-shift who do their jobs without making us feel like animals or worse. Officers that don't disrespect or name-call in an attempt to draw us out, allowing them to write us a false disciplinary case. I had thought about naming them in this book, but for the simple fact that most still work within these walls, that would not be a good idea on my part. I have no doubt that this book and what I say will be read by prison officials and will be banned from being allowed inside for others to read it. For that reason alone I shall leave their names out of it. They know who they are, and that is all that matters. In the end, they will each be rewarded for their kindness and actions towards myself and others from our Father in Heaven.

Though I'm no saint, I do try my best to have a relationship with God and His Son Jesus Christ. Back in 2019, I had been baptized by a Rabbi from an outside source that was allowed to enter into the prison for this special day. I had become a Messianic Jew. I honestly thought that this is what I was called to be because it felt right deep within my core; and yet not two years later I would be withdrawing from being one such religion because I was seeing how those around me and outside in society were acting and claiming to be the same religion. I would even be knocked down for becoming such, from people of the same religion, as well as Catholics, Christians, etc… Seeing how people were acting when they were any religion was screwing me up even more than I already am. It's not like I can get up and exit my cell to go to church or pick up a telephone and call a Rabbi/Pastor or anyone else for a study or questions. The people who I used to rely on and be able to talk about anything have been removed from my life through execution. The face of many people that they don't want you to see started coming to the surface and showing. The fact that many people both within these walls and out there in society are only hiding behind the Word of God and the Holy Bible is beyond sickening. It hasn't caused me to want to further my faith in any one religion, but has pushed me further away from claiming a religion as my own. How can people claim to be this or that, and then turn around and judge me for where I'm at. Truth is, even though I no longer claim a religion, I do in fact have a strong relationship with our Father in Heaven and His Son Jesus Christ. Daily as well as every night, I speak with Him and ask for His love and strength to get me through each day. I remember the "Footprints in the Sand" picture and poem/saying. When we see two sets of footprints in the sand, that is when we were walking side by side with God. When we saw only one set of footprints, that was when God was carrying us. Throughout my whole life, looking at that picture, I'm only able to see the one set of footprints, because God has been carrying me every step of the way. One day, I hope that I'll be able to make Him proud to the point I climb down off His shoulders, and He says, "Thank you, Jesus, Richard, for getting off. You're damn heavy, son!" One day, God, one day.

Chapter Eighteen

Though I know that my strength comes from our Father in Heaven, it also comes through the people who have remained by my side throughout my life and while I've been housed on Texas Death Row/Death Watch. Mary Hampton came into my life around ten years ago. She's with a group called Friends Meeting of Austin, also known as the Quakers. Once a month, she and others will drive down from Austin, Texas to visit with those of us on Texas Death Row. Slowly over the years, she and I would become great friends. Though I'm not allowed to visit with my mother or sister, Mary always brings me messages from them when she comes to visit so that I know what is going on and how they're doing. I can correspond with them, but I don't always get their mail or the Warden's office withholds my incoming as well as my outgoing mail to them for weeks at a time. When Mary and I visit, we talk about all kinds of things, even the bad times and the times we are frustrated with life in general. She's always been there to send me books from the local bookstore or take some pictures of us during our visit so that I can mail them home to my mom and sister and my little niece, as well as any artwork or property I am wanting to send home or to anyone else. Just as she is an anchor in life to her family, she has also become one for me. I'm thankful for having her in my corner, as she's not only been there for myself but for my mom too. No doubt that our friendship is not easy on her, because, trust me, I can be and am a handful! One thing she always talks about during our visits is her love for her family and their new dog, Daisy, being bossy. If it wasn't for her friendship, as well as the others I have made, though they are few, I have no idea where exactly I would be or if I would even still be here.

Because like her, there is also my long-time friend from Glasgow, Scotland, named John Dougan. For just as long as I have been friends with Mary, John and I have also been friends, and corresponding from overseas to here is no easy task. The mail system sucks, but when I'm feeling at my lowest and I reach out to John, he's always been there with his ear lowered and kind words to send back over the waters to me. He is also very understanding of what all is going on with me and how I have been and continue to be mistreated by the prison administration.

Patrick Pease, who is from here in Texas as well, but further up north. I first met Pat, as he likes to be called, when he reached out to Donald Newbury (Lizard), wanting to write him and see if he could attend his execution. Pat wanted to know what it would be like witnessing such a thing. Instead of responding to him, Lizard shot me Pat's letter, and I responded to him. Thinking I wouldn't hear anything back from him, I said a lot to him in the letter. I was in for a shock when a couple of weeks later I got a return letter. From that point on we've been corresponding back and forth and become friends. Pat even drove down from up north a couple of times for visits and to attend my federal court hearing back in 2018 in Austin, Texas. Pat is also a good person who has a huge family, tons of kids and grandchildren that he's always telling about keeping him busy.

Someone else that is special to me and reached out to me after my friend Big Tai was executed, only because I hadn't known he was doing so, but Big Tai reached out to this very special woman and told her about his little homie (Slim) and that if they went through with his execution, would she please be there for his friend. Her name is Sister Cordia Klein, of Germany. She is always writing to me and telling me that she has a candle burning in the Chapel for me and that Jesus loves me, as she does too. Though her English is not great, she does her best to translate the words from German to English whenever she writes. Whenever I get her letters, I can feel the love she has for our Father and that same love she sends my way. Though we've never met, I know that one day she and I will meet up with Big Tai once again when this life is over.

The lawyer who was appointed to my case back in May of 2012, Marcia Widder, she too has become more than just my lawyer. Let me tell you something about how far a lawyer will go to get what she wants. We all know tons of lawyer jokes, and we all know that most lawyers are crooks, some even worse than their clients. But, with Marcy, she brings a whole new caliber to the table. I had been fighting to end my appeals and wanting a hearing in federal court. I got my wish and was at a hearing in federal court in Austin, Texas before the Honorable Robert Pitman back in 2018. As I'm waiting for the U.S. Marshals to come and get me to escort me into the courtroom, being one of my lawyers, Marcy was allowed into the back with me to talk about things. She, along with a couple of my other lawyers and this other little doll named Cassandra, were doing everything that they could to get me not to go through with it. Marcy, seeing that I wasn't going to fold, pulled out a last minute stunt against me. Her daughter, Sasha, had hand-written me a card and drawn a picture on it, telling me that she didn't want me to be killed and that I should let her mommy continue to work on my case! Who in the hell uses their kid as a weapon like that to get what they want! That was a low blow, man. So now, as I'm sitting in front of Judge Pitman and others attending my hearing, I'm thinking about this little girl and the card she did for me, that her mother is using to get her way.

If that's not enough, also in the courtroom is another dear friend and lawyer/investigator named Cassandra Belter. If Sasha and her mother weren't enough, then Cassandra was the next best thing to get me to fold. When I first met Cassandra, I did everything within my power to push her away and not allow her to get close to me as a person. I went so far as to write a short story fiction urban book that I never published, but had her playing in a sex scene with me! I did everything I could to piss this chick off and keep her away, only to have her in the end and over the years become so close to me that she is now invading my dreams and most of my thoughts. Though I know she is way off limits, we've become very close friends, and she, like Marcy and Mary, is someone that I'm able to go to for anything at any time when I need them/her. Her only fault is that she is a Georgia Bulldog fan, and she is a slave to her cat, Master Hopkins!

Let me not fail to mention my friend Luis Batiz, who is also a part of my legal team and who at one time was my paralegal and has since become one of my investigators. He too has become more than just a legal team member. He was also friends with my Big Homie Big Tai, as was Cassandra through me. When I first met Luis, or I should say, when I heard he was my paralegal and that if I needed anything I should write to him at the Capital Habeas Unit Office in Philadelphia letting him know, I wrote to him asking that he please send me an S.A.S.E. (Self-Addressed Stamped Envelope) so that I could mail some legal documents back. He does this, but he also sealed the envelope he was sending me! How was I now supposed to send the legal documents back now with the envelope sealed shut. I in turn drew him a picture of a Rook upon a chess board and nicknamed him Rookie! From that point on, he and I would also become fast friends, and this would turn into more than him just being a part of my legal team. He, along with his wife and their daughter and the daughter's boyfriend, would become like an extended part of my own family. The story we share with one another when we're not talking about legal work or my appeals is truly one of a kind. Like myself, Luis also loves to ride motorcycles. During one of our visits one day, he shared with me about how his daughter accidentally hit a motorcyclist there in Philadelphia. I laughed so hard and told him it was a good thing he no longer rides while she's on the road! The stories that come from his family are one of a kind and truly special. I'm thankful that they are a part of my life. Though we honestly know who wear the pants in their house is his wife Joycet!

The true ones that have also stuck by my side through the thick and the thin of it all, though sometimes they too have a hard time of doing so, and I wish they would be more in contact with me, is that of my mom, sister, and little niece. I know that my situation isn't easy on them and that they too have their own lives to live. I just wish that they would try to write a little more often than they do. However, I'm grateful for the time and effort that they have put into being there for me all these years, when God knows I don't deserve their love nor their continuing support. I cannot begin to imagine what it's like for them as they sit out there living their lives to their best ability, while knowing that one of their loved ones is guilty of Capital Murder and is sitting on Texas Death Row. Knowing that I have failed them in life though keeps me from doing better because it just eats away at my core and spirit, as it does when I think about how I've let so many others down in this life.

The last person to come into my life is my lawsuit lawyer, David A. Lane. I did an art piece for him after retaining him in my lawsuit against Texas Death Row/Texas Department of Criminal Justice. As my other lawyers that were appointed by the courts fight not only to keep me alive while also fighting against me fighting against them and the courts, David has become a friend who is more understanding about the crap I go through within these prison walls. He does his best to keep the peace between my appeal lawyers and I while also getting something done about the way I'm being treated on Death Row by all prison officials and not be allowed to visit with my mom and sister for over 13 years now. It's with his okay that at the back of this book I have added a copy of my current lawsuit as well as that of one with written permission of an Ad-Seg inmate also housed within the walls of the Polunsky Unit. This way you not only are able to read the hell I have gone through and continue to go through, but to read about how others are treated as well. I have never met Mr. Hope, nor do I know anything about him and his life. Word of mouth and his situation got back to me, and I took it upon myself to reach out to his lawyers.

It is my sincere hope that something in this book will help someone out there that is going through a bad time in life or is headed down the wrong path to stop, and know that it can always become worse than what you're currently going through in life. I have no idea what will become of my life, if I'll allow my lawyers to keep fighting to get me off Texas Death Row/Death Watch, or if I'll throw in the towel. At this point in my life, I want everyone to know about my side of the story about my life and what it was and is like for me to live it. Before I close this out, allow me to share one last thing with you from the book Just Mercy, written by Bryan Stevenson, that was sung to him by one of his first Death Row clients in Georgia and used here with permission:

> "I'm pressing on, the upward way
> New heights I'm gaining, every day
> Still praying as, I'm onward bound
> Lord, plant my feet on Higher Ground.
> Lord lift me up, and let me stand

By faith on Heaven's tableland
A Higher plane, that I have found
Lord, plant my feet on Higher Ground."

Richard L. Tabler

This is a picture of Big Tai on his last day of life visiting with one of his brothers
(R.I.P.Big Tai)

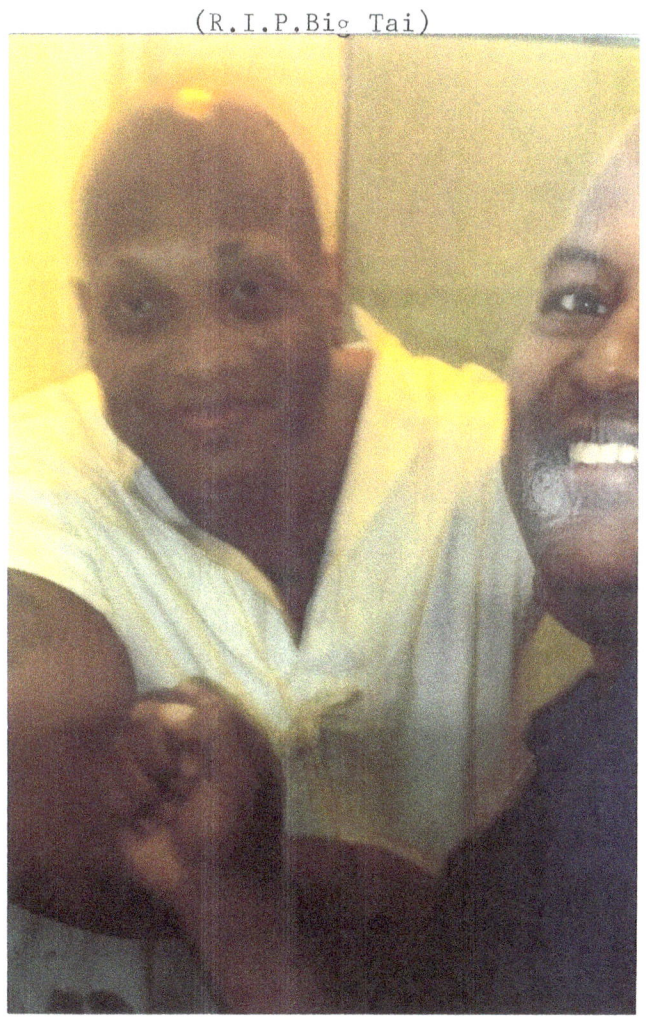

Mary Hampton & I during a visit. That's me holding my Jewish Bible

This is a picture of me taken in 2020 while visiting with Mary

This is a picture of my mom, sister and little niece having a day at the beach.

This is Marcy and her daughter Sasha who are my friends/support

Richard L. Tabler

My friend/lawyer/Investigator
Cassandra L.Belter & Master Hopkins

This is a picture
of my friend/Sister Cordia Klein

Lawsuits

IN THE UNITED STATES DISTRICT COURT
FOR THE EASTERN DISTRICT OF TEXAS
LUFKIN DIVISION

RICHARD TABLER, Plaintiff,	)))
v.	) Civil Action No. _____
	)
LORIE DAVIS, Director, Correctional Institutions Division, Texas Department of Criminal Justice, in her official capacity. Defendant.	)))))

COMPLAINT AND JURY DEMAND

Plaintiff, by and through his attorneys, David A. Lane and Reid Allison of KILLMER, LANE & NEWMAN, LLP, and Richard Burr, BURR AND WELCH, PC, hereby brings this Complaint and alleges as follows:

INTRODUCTION

1. For nearly a decade, Richard Tabler has been housed in the Death Watch section of the Texas Department of Criminal Justice's ("TDCJ") death row, at the Polunsky Unit. He has spent 22 hours per day alone in a small cell. His family is prohibited from visiting him. Besides guards, the people he has interacted with in the Death Watch section have been executed within weeks of their being housed near Mr. Tabler.

2. This is an extreme and torturous existence for any person, which is why those for whom Texas has scheduled an execution spend only a limited, determinate amount of time in the Death Watch section—typically no more than 60-180 days. Studies on prolonged solitary confinement have indisputably shown that such housing significantly damages a person's

physical, mental, and emotional health, while risking heightened levels of anxiety, depression, and exacerbation of pre-existing mental health problems. In recent years, Supreme Court Justices have recognized that prolonged solitary confinement "exact[s] a terrible price," "literally drives men mad," and "raises serious constitutional questions." *Davis v. Ayala*, 135 S. Ct. 2187, 2210 (2015) (Kennedy, J., concurring); *Ruiz v. Texas*, 137 S. Ct. 1246, 1247 (2017) (Breyer, J., dissenting). Justice Sotomayor has recently quoted Charles Dickens' observations that "very few" are "capable of estimating the immense amount of torture and agony which this dreadful punishment [solitary confinement], prolonged for years, inflicts upon the sufferers." *Apodaca v. Raemisch*, 139 S. Ct. 5, 9-10 (2018) (Sotomayor, J., statement on denial of certiorari).

3. For Mr. Tabler, this is a personalized torture, profoundly exacerbating his longstanding severe mental health issues. This cruel, protracted housing has not only significantly worsened his mental health, it has also led him to attempt to take his own life multiple times.

4. Mr. Tabler's continued, indeterminate housing in the Death Watch section: (1) is Cruel and Unusual Punishment, in violation of the Eighth and Fourteenth Amendments; (2) unconstitutionally denies him Due Process, guaranteed by the Fourteenth Amendment, to prevent the atypical and significant hardships he suffers in the Death Watch section; and (3) violates his rights under the Americans with Disabilities Act ("ADA"). He must be immediately transferred out of the Death Watch section.

JURISDICTION AND VENUE

5. This action arises under the Constitution and laws of the United States and is brought pursuant to 42 U.S.C. § 1983 and the Americans with Disabilities Act ("ADA"), 42 U.S.C. §§ 12101 *et seq*.

6. This Court has jurisdiction pursuant to 28 U.S.C. § 1331. Jurisdiction supporting

RICHARD L. TABLER

Plaintiffs' claim for attorneys' fees and costs is conferred by 42 U.S.C. § 1988.

7. Venue is proper in the Eastern District of Texas pursuant to 28 U.S.C. § 1391(b). At all relevant times, Mr. Tabler has been incarcerated within the State of Texas, in the Eastern District, all housing decisions made by Defendant affected him there, and all of the parties were residents of the State of Texas at the time of the events giving rise to this litigation.

PARTIES

8. Plaintiff Richard Tabler has been, at all relevant times, a state prisoner in custody of the TDCJ and housed in the Death Watch section of death row in the Polunsky Unit, Livingston, Texas.

9. Defendant Lorie Davis is the Director of the Correctional Institutions Division ("CID") of TDCJ. As Director of the CID, Defendant Davis is responsible for housing decisions, planning, direction, and coordination of all programs and operations of Texas state prisons, including death row and the Death Watch section at the Allan B. Polunsky Unit ("the Polunsky Unit"), located at 3872 FM 350 South, Livingston, Texas, 77351. Defendant Davis interpreted laws, policies, and operational procedures relevant to all employees at the Polunsky Unit and death row. As part of her directorship of the CID, Defendant Davis authorized and/or condoned the unconstitutional housing of Mr. Tabler. As such, she directly and proximately caused the constitutional and statutory violations set forth below. At all relevant times, Defendant Davis was acting under color of state law, as an official representative of the TDCJ.

FACTUAL ALLEGATIONS

I. Mr. Tabler's Cruel and Unusual housing

10. Mr. Tabler has been housed in the Death Watch section of TDCJ's death row at the Polunsky Unit since January 2, 2011.

11. The Death Watch section houses those TDCJ inmates who have an imminent

execution date, scheduled within 60-180 days. Therefore, inmates spend only a limited, pre-determined amount of time in the Death Watch section.

12. Mr. Tabler does not have an execution date and has not had one scheduled at any point during his nearly ten years housed in the Death Watch section.

13. Mr. Tabler is in the Death Watch unit as punishment for his having been caught with a cell phone approximately ten years ago.

14. The restrictions within the Death Watch section are extreme.

15. Mr. Tabler is held in solitary confinement conditions for 22 hours every day, in a miniscule, 60-square-foot cell.

16. He is provided meals through a slot in the door of his cell.

17. He spends his limited recreation time in a pen separate from other inmates.

18. Mr. Tabler is allowed virtually no face-to-face contact with other inmates.

19. The harshness of these death row conditions, designed intentionally to limit human contact, is substantially exacerbated by Mr. Tabler's unusual status among death row inmates—though he is not scheduled for execution, he is housed exclusively among inmates who are within months of their own scheduled executions.

20. Death row inmates can communicate to a limited extent with other inmates. Given their years- and decades-long waits for execution, these limited communications allow inmates to form relationships and friendships, providing at least some human contact.

21. Perversely, aside from impersonal communications with prison guards, the only people with whom Mr. Tabler is permitted to communicate are sent to be executed within weeks of meeting him. Rather than the comfort that other inmates are permitted to draw from their limited society with one another, Mr. Tabler is confronted with an endless procession of men who are put to death as soon as he is able to form an attachment to them.

22. Indeed, while Mr. Tabler has been housed in the Death Watch section, TDCJ has executed over 90 inmates. Mr. Tabler had formed friendships with at least a dozen of those who were then executed. On average, once a month an inmate has been executed, after spending his final weeks housed in the Death Watch section with Mr. Tabler.

23. Though this bizarre and torturous circumstance would no doubt take a severe toll on the mental well-being of any inmate, Mr. Tabler's specific mental health problems are such that he suffers an unusually elevated level of stress and mental anguish from the loss of people to whom he has become attached.

24. The conditions for Mr. Tabler in the Death Watch section are so severe and have such a profound impact on his mental health that in 2011, a federal judge denied his request to drop his habeas appeals and be executed, after finding that his conditions of confinement coerced him to that decision.

25. Despite the judge's explicit finding that Mr. Tabler's conditions of confinement were so onerous as to coerce him into an effective suicide by dropping his habeas appeals, Mr. Tabler remains housed in the Death Watch section.

26. Mr. Tabler has never been afforded a meaningful process in which to challenge his housing in the Death Watch section and argue for a transfer to Texas' less restrictive standard death row, where he might at least find relief from his constant loss of friends to the death chamber under his current conditions.

II. Mr. Tabler's severe mental health issues

27. Throughout Mr. Tabler's incarceration, TDCJ has known of his substantial mental health issues.

28. Mr. Tabler has long been diagnosed with Fetal Alcohol Spectrum Disorder (specifically, Alcohol-Related Neurodevelopmental Disorder) and Klinefelter Syndrome. These diagnoses reveal that Mr. Tabler suffers multiple central nervous system dysfunctions, resulting in decreased impulse control, heightened anxiety, mood lability, low frustration tolerance, depression, and executive function impairment. TCDJ has been aware of these diagnoses for nearly five years.

29. With respect to his Fetal Alcohol-Related Neurodevelopmental Disorder, Mr. Tabler suffers difficulty with social skills, including lack of stranger fear, naivete and gullibility; inappropriate choice of friends; immaturity; difficulty understanding the perspective of others; and poor social cognition.

30. Mr. Tabler also meets the criteria for Bipolar Disorder and Attention Deficit Hyperactivity Disorder.

31. In addition to these significant mental health issues, he has suffered repeated traumatic brain injuries.

32. This particular combination of mental health disorders, resulting in emotional instability for Mr. Tabler at the best of times, leaves him without the emotional and cognitive ability to effectively process the loss of people close to him. In the Death Watch section, such losses are frequent and unavoidable and subject Mr. Tabler to undue suffering well beyond what a neurotypical inmate might experience.

33. Mr. Tabler has repeatedly expressed mental distress, including suicidal ideation, and has displayed physically self-harming and suicidal behaviors since his placement in the Death Watch section, often in connection with the frequent loss of friends as a result of their execution. What follows are a few examples of his significant mental health deterioration between 2011 and 2015 due to his housing in the Death Watch section.

34. On February 22, 2011, security and medical personnel contacted Mr. Tabler after he intentionally cut his right arm open.

35. In addition to his overt attempt to kill himself, Mr. Tabler made multiple suicidal statements during that contact with jail personnel.

36. A nurse who spoke with Mr. Tabler noted that she believed Mr. Tabler's suicidal statements might be genuine, and that he should be evaluated by a mental health professional.

37. Mr. Tabler asked the nurse for help with his suicidal impulses and was placed in a psych observation cell.

38. While housed in the observation cell, Mr. Tabler spoke with mental health staff. Mr. Tabler stated that a friend of his from death row had been executed a week earlier, and that another friend was being transported to Huntsville to be executed. Mr. Tabler discussed how difficult he found it to deal with the losses.

39. Asked whether he felt that other inmates' lives were more important than his own life, Mr. Tabler responded affirmatively. The mental health staff who interviewed Mr. Tabler noted that he was surprised by the question and that his eyes filled with tears as he answered.

40. Mr. Tabler recounted a conversation with another death row inmate during which Mr. Tabler voiced a desire to trade places with that inmate so that he could be executed.

41. On November 29, 2012, mental health staff noted that Mr. Tabler vented concerns about recent executions.

42. On February 20, 2013, mental health staff assessed Mr. Tabler after he made suicidal statements in a letter directed to his family and attorney, including a statement that he intended to complete suicide on March 11.

43. During the February 20, 2013 mental health assessment, Mr. Tabler indicated that one of the reasons he wanted to kill himself was that a friend of his was going to be executed the

following day.

44. On October 4, 2013, Mr. Tabler was assessed for urgent mental health needs after he threatened to cut himself with razor blades. Mr. Tabler informed mental health staff that he no longer felt that he was in control and asked to be transferred to the Jester IV inpatient psychiatric facility. The transfer was ordered the same day for the purposes of crisis management.

45. On October 8, 2013, during Mr. Tabler's stay at the Jester IV facility, Mr. Tabler informed staff that he remained very upset and needed to get some things off his chest. He stated that five out of six recently executed inmates had been friends of his, and that their loss had affected him deeply.

46. On October 9, 2013, still at the Jester IV facility, Mr. Tabler reported increased depressive symptoms, including irritability, disturbance of his sleep pattern, decreased appetite, and thoughts of hopelessness. During the same interaction, Mr. Tabler noted his concerns about his housing in the Death Watch section, the pod where death row inmates with imminent execution dates are housed. Mr. Tabler stated that he becomes close with the offenders housed near him, only to lose them to execution, and again referenced his friendship with five of the past six inmates executed. Mr. Tabler explicitly connected the loss of these five inmates with an increased sense of hopelessness and feelings of depression during this conversation.

47. On October 10, 2013, still at the Jester IV facility, Mr. Tabler again indicated his plans for self-harm to mental health staff, and he again explicitly connected his feelings of depression to the fact that several of his friends had been executed over the previous six months.

48. On October 14, 2013, still at the Jester IV facility, Mr. Tabler once more indicated that his poor mental health was connected to the loss of his fellow death row inmates, noting that he had seen 27 men executed.

49. On October 15, 2013, still at the Jester IV facility, mental health staff asked Mr.

Tabler to verbalize his principal problem that would be the focus of his clinical attention. Mr. Tabler asked staff to let him stay at Jester IV for a while rather than returning to the Death Watch area of death row, stating that he needed a break from Death Watch. He again expressed distress related to five of the past six men executed having been his friends. He told mental health staff that he would attempt to harm himself if and when he was returned to Death Watch.

50. Mr. Tabler also told mental health staff that he had been experiencing auditory hallucinations, hearing his friends who had been executed. He stated that he had most recently heard the auditory hallucinations the day after another offender had been executed.

51. On October 17, 2013, Mr. Tabler reported that his problems originated from his housing in the Death Watch section, and that he had seen 40 inmates executed over the course of his incarceration. He further reported that he had experienced auditory hallucinations in conjunction with his friends being taken to be executed, and stated that he felt upset that he would continue to live while his friends were executed. The mental health staff noted that Mr. Tabler's concerns appeared reflective of survivor's guilt.

52. On April 1, 2014, having returned to the Death Watch section, Mr. Tabler was seen by mental health staff after the facility's mail room again reported that Mr. Tabler had made suicidal statements in outgoing mail. Mr. Tabler once again told mental health staff that he was upset by being forced to witness other offenders being taken to die, an inevitable result of his housing in the Death Watch section. He indicated that he had been giving away his property as a precursor to an approaching suicide attempt.

53. On April 2014, Mr. Tabler expressed a desire to stop consuming food and liquids, noting that he was tired from watching executions. Mental health staff noted that Mr. Tabler appeared to desire to go into renal failure and seemed depressed.

54. On February 12, 2015, Mr. Tabler reported that he was feeling down about a

recent execution.

55. On numerous other occasions, and until the present day, Mr. Tabler's mental health has been substantially worsened by his housing in the Death Watch section, and he has continued to exhibit suicidal behaviors throughout his time in the Death Watch section.

56. Indeed, he attempted suicide and very nearly succeeded in June 2019. Mr. Tabler sliced his arm open from wrist to shoulder and nearly died. This was just the most recent in Mr. Tabler's established history of suicide attempts to escape his present torturous day-to-day experience in the Death Watch section.

57. As referenced above, the conditions remain so severe that a federal district judge has previously refused to allow Mr. Tabler to drop his habeas appeals, finding that his conditions of confinement were coercing him to seek execution rather than continue living in the Death Watch section.

58. Plaintiff has fully, properly, and timely exhausted all available administrative remedies in connection with the events described herein.

STATEMENT OF CLAIMS FOR RELIEF

FIRST CLAIM FOR RELIEF
42 U.S.C. § 1983 – Violations of the Eighth and Fourteenth Amendments
Cruel and Unusual Punishment

59. At all times relevant to this action, the Defendant was responsible for promulgating and implementing policies, practices, and procedures relating to inmate classifications and housing decisions.

60. The Defendant's decision to house Mr. Tabler in prolonged solitary confinement, among men due to be executed in mere weeks, in the Death Watch section has deprived and continues to deprive him of basic human needs. Mr. Tabler's continued, indeterminate housing in the Death Watch section is cruel and unusual punishment because this housing deprives him of

basic human needs, imposes serious and irreparable psychological and physical injury on his person, and violates present-day standards of human dignity.

61. The indefinite duration of Mr. Tabler's housing in the Death Watch section poses significant risks of incapacitating him and causing him permanent mental and psychological injury.

62. The Defendant's housing Mr. Tabler in the Death Watch section inflicts disproportionate punishment on him.

63. Housing him in these cruel conditions serves no valid, legal purpose and lacks penological justification.

64. The Defendant's infliction of mental and physical harm on Mr. Tabler strips him of his dignity and worth, transgresses civilized society's notions of decency, and is a practice that is disavowed in contemporary society.

65. The mental and psychological anguish inflicted on Mr. Tabler as a result of his housing in the Death Watch section are obvious to Defendant and any other reasonable person. Defendant knows that Mr. Tabler is suffering substantial and ongoing injury.

66. As a direct and proximate result of Defendant's constitutional violations, Mr. Tabler will continue to be irreparably injured. He will suffer irreparable harm unless Defendant is enjoined from continuing this unconstitutional housing decision.

SECOND CLAIM FOR RELIEF
42 U.S.C. § 1983 – Fourteenth Amendment Due Process Violation

67. Plaintiff Tabler incorporates all other paragraphs of this Complaint for purposes of this Claim.

68. Defendant has substantially increased the punishment suffered by Mr. Tabler by placing him permanently in the Death Watch unit.

69. Defendant has sporadically conducted hearings for inmates facing unusual increased levels of security within the prison system. The Defendant has created a liberty interest through the implementation of hearings, which give inmates the chance for less restrictive confinement and by maintaining a standard death row at the Polunsky Unit, as well as the Death Watch section in which Plaintiff Tabler has been housed for nearly a decade.

70. Plaintiff Tabler has this liberty interest in a due process hearing which may result in a less restrictive and torturous confinement and therefore must be afforded sufficient due process before the interest can be refused.

71. Plaintiff Tabler has not been provided sufficient process to argue for transfer to the less restrictive standard death row and exercise this liberty interest, in violation of his Fourteenth Amendment right to Due Process.

72. By denying him meaningful review of his protracted, indefinite housing in solitary confinement in the Death Watch section and never affording him the opportunity to be considered for transfer to the less restrictive death row, Defendant is denying Mr. Tabler liberty without due process of law.

73. Indefinite confinement in the isolated Death Watch section, with no prospect of meaningful review for transfer to the less restrictive death row unit, imposes atypical and significant hardship on him in relation to the ordinary incidents of prison life.

74. Every other prisoner in Mr. Tabler's Death Watch section has been promptly executed, and no other prisoner has ever been subjected to housing in this unit indefinitely.

75. Defendant's acts and omissions are the proximate cause of the violation of Plaintiff Tabler's rights under the Fifth and Fourteenth Amendments.

76. The acts or omissions of Defendant were conducted within the scope of his official duties and employment.

77. As a direct and proximate result of Defendant's acts or omissions, Plaintiff Tabler has suffered harm and is at risk of suffering harm going forward, until he is provided sufficient process to consider him for transfer to the less restrictive and torturous standard death row unit.

THIRD CLAIM FOR RELIEF
42 U.S.C. § 12132, *et seq.* – Violation of Title II of the Americans with Disabilities Act of 1990, as Amended
Unlawful Discrimination and Failure to Reasonably Accommodate

78. Plaintiff hereby incorporates all other paragraphs of this Complaint as if fully set forth herein.

79. The Americans with Disabilities Act (hereinafter referred to as the "ADA"), 42 U.S.C. §§ 12101 *et seq.*, and specifically 42 U.S.C. §§ 12131-12134, prohibits discrimination in public services on the basis of disability. 42 U.S.C. § 12132 provides:

> Subject the provisions of this subchapter, no qualified individual with a disability shall, by reason of such disability, be excluded from participation in or be denied the benefits of the services, programs, or activities of a public entity, or be subjected to discrimination by any such entity.

80. The ADA defines a "public entity" to include any state or local government or any department, agency, special purpose district, or other instrumentality of a State or local government, 42 U.S.C. § 12131(1). The Texas Department of Criminal Justice is a "public entity" within the meaning of the ADA.

81. Mr. Tabler is a person that Defendant knew had a disability, including severe mental health issues and suicidal ideation, that substantially limits his major life activities.

82. Plaintiff, with or without reasonable modifications to rules, policies or practices, met the essential eligibility requirements for the receipt of services or the participation in programs or activities provided by the Defendant. Thus, Plaintiff was a "qualified individual with disabilities" within the meaning of the ADA, 42 U.S.C. § 12131(2).

83. Plaintiff was qualified to participate in the services, programs, activities, and benefits provided to inmates in the TDCJ's custody within the meaning of Title II of the ADA.

84. Defendant was on notice regarding Mr. Tabler's serious mental health issues, suicidal state of mind, and repeated suicide attempts.

85. Defendant failed to reasonably accommodate Mr. Tabler's disabilities despite knowing of his suicidal ideation, and related impairments and conditions.

86. An obviously reasonable accommodation exists, that TDCJ has failed to provide Mr. Tabler: moving him out of the Death Watch section and back to death row.

87. Defendant's actions and inactions violated clearly established law under Title II of the ADA and its implementing regulations.

88. Defendant had no legitimate basis for violating Mr. Tabler's ADA rights.

89. Defendant's actions and inactions are objectively unreasonable in light of the circumstances.

90. Defendant's actions and inactions are the proximate and legal cause of Plaintiff's injuries.

91. Plaintiff has been and continues to be damaged by Defendant's unlawful conduct under the ADA.

PRAYER FOR RELIEF

WHEREFORE, Plaintiff respectfully requests that this Court enter judgment in his favor and against Defendant, and grant:

(a) Appropriate relief at law and equity;

(b) Declaratory and injunctive relief, as well as other appropriate equitable relief;

(c) Attorneys' fees and the costs associated with this action, including expert witness fees, on all claims allowed by law;

(d) Any further relief that this Court deems just and proper, and any other relief as allowed by law.

PLAINTIFF HEREBY DEMANDS A JURY TRIAL ON ALL ISSUES SO TRIABLE.

Dated this 16th day of March 2020.

KILLMER, LANE & NEWMAN, LLP

s/ David A. Lane
David A. Lane
Reid Allison
KILLMER, LANE & NEWMAN, LLP
1543 Champa Street, Suite 400
Denver, Colorado 80202
(303) 571-1000
(303) 571-1001
dlane@kln-law.com
rallison@kln-law.com

BURR AND WELCH, PC

s/ Richard Burr
Richard Burr
Texas Bar No. 24001005
Burr and Welch, PC
PO Box 525
Leggett, Texas 77350
(713) 628-3391
(713) 893-2500 fax
dick.burrandwelch@gmail.com

ATTORNEYS FOR PLAINTIFF

CERTIFICATE OF SERVICE

The undersigned certifies that a true and correct copy of the foregoing pleading was served electronically upon Kristen Worman (kristen.worman@tdcj.texas.gov), General Counsel for the Texas Department of Criminal Justice and counsel for Respondent, this 16th day of March, 2020.

/s/Richard H. Burr
Counsel for Plaintiff

IN THE UNITED STATES DISTRICT COURT
FOR THE EASTERN DISTRICT OF TEXAS
LUFKIN DIVISION

RICHARD TABLER,
    Plaintiff,
 	
v.
 	
LORIE DAVIS,
Director, Correctional Institutions
Division , Texas Department of
Criminal Justice, in her official capacity,
    Defendant.
	)
	)
	)
	) Civil Action No. 1:20-cv-111
	)
	)
	)
	)
	)
	)

MOTION TO TRANSFER CASE TO PROPER DIVISION

Plaintiff RICHARD TABLER respectfully requests that the Court transfer this case to the Lufkin Division. The causes of action have arisen in the Lufkin Division. Undersigned inadvertently filed in the Beaumont Division.

                            Respectfully submitted,

s/ David A. Lane
David A. Lane
Reid Allison
Killmer, Lane & Newman, LLP
1543 Champa Street, Suite 400
Denver, Colorado 80202
303-571-1000
303-571-1001 (fax)
dlane@kln-law.com
rallison@kln-law.com

s/ Richard Burr
Richard H. Burr
Texas Bar No. 24001005
Burr & Welch PC
P.O. Box 525
Leggett, Texas 77350
713-516-5229
713-893-2500 (fax)
dick.burrandwelch@gmail.com

<u>Counsel for Petitioner</u>

CERTIFICATE OF SERVICE

The undersigned certifies that a true and correct copy of the foregoing pleading was served electronically upon Kristen Worman (kristen.worman@tdcj.texas.gov), General Counsel of the Texas Department of Criminal Justice, and counsel for Defendant, this 17th day of March, 2020.

/s/Richard H. Burr
Counsel for Plaintiff

IN THE UNITED STATES DISTRICT COURT
FOR THE EASTERN DISTRICT OF TEXAS
BEAUMONT DIVISION

RICHARD TABLER	§	
VS.	§	CIVIL ACTION NO. 1:20cv111
LORIE DAVIS	§	

TRANSFER ORDER

This action came on before the Court, and the issues having been duly considered and a decision having been duly rendered, it is

ORDERED and **ADJUDGED** that this action is **TRANSFERRED** to the Lufkin Division of this court.

SIGNED this 20th day of March, 2020.

Zack Hawthorn
United States Magistrate Judge

IN THE UNITED STATES DISTRICT COURT
FOR THE EASTERN DISTRICT OF TEXAS
LUFKIN DIVISION

RICHARD TABLER, *Plaintiff,*	§ § §	
v.	§ §	CIVIL ACTION NO. 9:20-cv-00049
LORIE DAVIS, *Defendants.*	§ § §	

DEFENDANT LORIE DAVIS'S MOTION TO DISMISS PURSUANT TO FEDERAL RULES OF CIVIL PROCEDURE 12(b)(1) AND 12(b)(6)

Defendant Lorie Davis, Director of the Texas Department of Criminal Justice—Correctional Institutions Division (TDCJ-CID), as sued in her official capacity, files this motion to dismiss pursuant to 12(b)(1) and 12(b)(6) of the Federal Rules of Civil Procedure in response to Plaintiff's Original Complaint. ECF No. 1.

I. Statement of the Case

In his Original Complaint, Plaintiff Richard Tabler sues Lorie Davis, Director of TDCJ-CID, in her official capacity for cruel and unusual punishment in violation of the Eighth Amendment, denial of due process, under 42 U.S.C. § 1983, and for violation of his rights under the Americans with Disabilities Act ("ADA"). ECF No. 1. Tabler seeks "appropriate relief at law and equity," "declaratory and injunctive[1] relief, as well as other appropriate equitable relief," and attorney's fees and costs. *Id.* at 14. Tabler does not seek compensatory damages.

---

[1] It is unclear what form of injunctive relief Plaintiff is seeking. It seems that he is seeking to be moved out of the "Death Watch" section. See ECF No. 1 at 14 ("An obviously reasonable accommodation exists, that TDCJ has failed to provide Mr. Tabler: moving him out of the Death Watch section and back to death row.").

II. Statement of Facts

Plaintiff Richard Tabler is an offender in custody of TDCJ housed at the Polunsky Unit in Livingston, Texas. ECF No. 1 at 3. Tabler was sentenced to death on April 2, 2007 for capital murder. While he was at the Polunsky unit, Tabler was convicted of smuggling in a cell phone and using it to call and threaten Senator Whitmire. He was also convicted of retaliation. According to the Complaint, Tabler has been housed at the Polunksy Unit in the "Death Watch" section of death row since January 2, 2011. ECF No. 1 at 3. Usually, offenders housed in the Death Watch cells are scheduled to have an execution date; however, Tabler's execution date is still not scheduled. *Id.* at 4. Tabler asserts he has been housed on Death Watch as "punishment" for being caught with the cell phone ten years ago. *Id.*

In October of 2013, Tabler was transferred to TDCJ's Jester IV unit, an inpatient psychiatric facility, for making multiple suicide attempts. *Id.* at 7–8. Tabler remained at the Jester IV unit, where he told mental health staff that he would attempt to harm himself if he was returned to Death Watch. *Id.* at 9. Tabler asserts that his mental health issues originated from seeing 40 inmates executed over the course of his incarceration,[2] and mental health noted Tabler's concerns appeared reflective of "survivor's guilt." *Id.* After being housed at Jester IV for about 1.5 years, Tabler returned to the Death Watch section at the Polunsky Unit in April of 2014. *Id.* at 9. Tabler again was expressing suicidal ideations in went on hunger strike in April of 2014. *Id.* Tabler notes that on numerous other occasions, and until the present day, his mental health has been substantially worsened by his housing in the Death Watch section, and he has continued to exhibit suicidal behaviors throughout his time in the Death Watch section. *Id.*

Plaintiff Tabler sues Lorie Davis, the Director of TDCJ-CID, in her official capacity, alleging that she is responsible for housing decisions, planning, direction, and coordination of all programs

---

[2] Throughout his Complaint, Tabler makes many statements similar to being "tired from watching executions." ECF No. 1 at 9. The death chamber is not at the Polunsky unit, but rather at the Huntsville Unit, where Tabler would not witness any executions.

and operations of Texas state prisons. *Id.* at 3. Tabler further alleges that Ms. Davis interpreted the laws, polices, and operational procedures relevant to all employees at the Polunsky Unit and death row, and authorized and/or condoned the unconstitutional housing of Mr. Tabler. *Id.*

III. Standards of Review

Motions to dismiss under FED. R. CIV. P. 12(b)(1) are reviewed under the same standard as a motion to dismiss failure to state a claim upon which relief can be granted under Rule 12(b)(6). *Rivas-Hernandez v. U.S.*, EP-98-CR-345-DB, 2000 WL 33348738, at *1 (W.D. Tex. Oct. 30, 2000) (citing *Benton v. United States*, 960 F.2d 19, 21 (5th Cir. 1992)). Rule 12(b)(1) allows a party to move for dismissal of an action for lack of subject-matter jurisdiction. The party asserting that subject-matter jurisdiction exists bears the burden of proof on a 12(b)(1) motion. *Crowell v. Lahood*, CIV.A. H-09-1788, 2011 WL 147913, at *1 (S.D. Tex. Jan. 18, 2011) (citing *Ramming v. United States*, 281 F.3d 158, 161 (5th Cir. 2001)), *cert. denied sub nom. Cloud v. United States*, 536 U.S. 960 (2002). The court may determine whether subject-matter jurisdiction is lacking by any of three approaches: "(1) the complaint alone; (2) the complaint supplemented by undisputed facts evidenced in the record; or (3) the complaint supplemented by undisputed facts plus the court's resolution of disputed facts." *Ramming*, 281 F.3d at 161.

When evaluating a motion to dismiss under Rule 12(b)(6), the complaint must be liberally construed in favor of the plaintiff and all facts pleaded therein must be taken as true. *Leatherman v. Tarrant Cnty Narcotics Intel. & Coordination Unit*, 507 U.S. 163, 164 (1993); *Baker v. Putnal*, 75 F.3d 190, 196 (5th Cir. 1996). A complaint must nevertheless contain sufficient factual matter, accepted as true, to "state a claim to relief that is plausible on its face." *Bell Atlantic v. Twombly*, 550 U.S. 554, 570 (2007). This plausibility standard is not simply a "probability requirement," but imposes a standard higher than "a sheer possibility that a defendant has acted unlawfully." *Ashcroft v. Iqbal*, 556 U.S. 662, 679 (2009).

The standard is properly guided by "[t]wo working principles." *Id.* First, although "a court must accept as true all of the allegations contained in the complaint," that tenet "is inapplicable to legal conclusions" and "[t]hreadbare recitals of the elements of a cause of action, supported by mere conclusory statements do not suffice." *Id.* at 667–78. Second, "[d]etermining whether a complaint states a plausible claim for relief will . . . be a context-specific task that requires the reviewing court to draw on its judicial experience and common sense." *Id.* at 679. In considering a motion to dismiss, therefore, the court must initially identify pleadings that are no more than legal conclusions not entitled to the assumption of truth, then assume the veracity of well-pleaded factual allegations to determine whether those allegations plausibly give rise to any right to relief. If not, "the complaint has alleged— but it has not shown—that the pleader is entitled to relief." *Id.* (internal quotations omitted).

IV. Arguments and Authority

A. Plaintiff's 42 U.S.C. § 1983 claim against Ms. Davis in her official capacity must be dismissed for failure to state a claim and lack of jurisdiction.

Plaintiff Tabler claims that Ms. Davis's decision to house him in the Death Watch section has deprived him and continues to deprive him of his basic human needs, imposes psychological and physical injury on his person, and violates present-day standards of human decency. ECF No. 1 at 10– 11. In sum, Tabler asserts that his housing inflicts a "disproportionate punishment"[3] on him, with no valid, legal purpose and lacks penological justification. *Id.* Additionally, Ms. Davis, is entitled to

---

[3] Plaintiff alleges he is housed on Death Watch as punishment for having a cell phone. A review of his public profile on the TDCJ "Offender Search" shows that he was convicted of capital murder and sentenced in 2007. https://offender.tdcj.texas.gov/OffenderSearch/offenderDetail.action?sid=07420770. While he was incarcerated, he was convicted of having a prohibited item in a correctional facility and retaliation; he was sentenced for 10 years for each crime in 2009. *Id.* To the extent that receiving the relief requested in this lawsuit, i.e., moving his housing, would invalidate his conviction or sentence, his claims are Heck-barred. *Heck v. Humphrey*, 512 U.S. 477, 487 (1994) ("[w]hen 'a judgment in favor of the plaintiff would necessarily imply the invalidity of his conviction or sentence,' . . . § 1983 is not an available remedy. . . 'But if . . . the plaintiff's action, even if successful, will not demonstrate the invalidity of [his conviction or sentence], the [§ 1983] action should be allowed to proceed . . . '").

Eleventh Amendment immunity for the 42 U.S.C. § 1983 claims, and this Court lacks jurisdiction over the ADA claim altogether due to sovereign immunity. All claims are barred by the statute of limitations.

1. Defendant Davis is entitled to Eleventh Amendment Immunity for claims brought against her in her official capacity.

Title 42, United States Code, Section 1983 authorizes the assertion of a claim for relief against a person who, acting under the color of state law, allegedly violated the claimant's rights under federal law. *See* 42 U.S.C. § 1983. In Section 1983 suits, government officials may be sued in either their individual or official capacities. A claim against a state or municipal official in his official capacity "generally represent[s] only another way of pleading an action against an entity of which an officer is an agent." *Kentucky v. Graham*, 473 U.S. 159, 165 (1985) (citation omitted). Individual or personal capacity suits "seek to impose personal liability upon a government official for actions he takes under color of state law." *Id.* (citation omitted).

Plaintiff only brings suit against Defendant Lorie Davis in her official capacity. *See* ECF No. 1. Defendant Davis moves to dismiss the § 1983 claims brought against her in her official capacity because she is entitled to sovereign immunity pursuant to the Eleventh Amendment of the United States Constitution. *See Warnock v. Pecos Cnty.*, Tex., 88 F.3d 341, 343 (5th Cir. 1996) ("Eleventh Amendment sovereign immunity deprives a federal court of jurisdiction to hear a suit against a state."). The Texas Department of Criminal Justice, as a state agency, enjoys sovereign immunity under the Eleventh amendment. As previously mentioned, official capacity suits "generally represent only another way of pleading an action against an entity of which an officer is an agent." *Graham*, 473 U.S. at 165 (citation omitted). Thus, "an official capacity suit is, in all respects other than name, to be treated as a suit against the entity." *Id.* at 166. Consequently, the Eleventh Amendment bars suits against state officials and employees of state entities, acting in their official capacities. *See K.P. v. LeBlanc*, 627 F.3d 115, 124 (5th Cir. 2010) (citations omitted); *Green v. State Bar of Tex.*, 27 F.3d 1083,

1087 (5th Cir. 1994) (plaintiff cannot evade Eleventh Amendment by suing state employees in their official capacity).

a. Plaintiff Tabler does not meet the elements of the *Ex Parte Young* exception

The Supreme Court has carved out a narrow exception for suits for injunctive or declaratory relief against individual state officials. *Ex parte Young*, 209 U.S. 123, 155–56 (1908)); *see also Nelson v. Univ. of Tex. at Dallas*, 535 F.3d 318, 321-22 (5th Cir. 2008) ("Pursuant to the Ex Parte Young exception, the Eleventh Amendment is not a bar to suits for prospective relief against a state employee acting in his official capacity."). Under the *Ex Parte Young* exception, "claims against state officials for prospective injunctive relief under § 1983 . . . are not barred by sovereign immunity." *Kobaisy v. Univ. of Miss.*, 624 F. App'x 195, 198 (5th Cir. 2015) (citing *Nelson*, 535 F.3d at 324); *see May v. N. Tex. State Hosp.*, 351 F. App'x 879, 880 (5th Cir. 2009) (citing *Aguilar v. Tex. Dep't of Crim. Justice*, 160 F.3d 1052, 1054 (5th Cir. 1998) (stating that the *Ex Parte Young* exception "applies to suits that allege a violation of federal law that are 'brought against individual persons in their official capacities as agents of the state, and the relief sought must be declaratory or injunctive in nature and prospective in effect.'").

The *Ex Parte Young* exception only applies "when (1) the suit is against a state official and (2) the plaintiff seeks only prospective injunctive relief (3) in order to end a 'continuing violation of federal law.'" *Thomas v. Texas*, 294 F. Supp. 3d 576, 592–93 (N.D. Tex. 2018). Here, Tabler asserts in his Complaint that he "has suffered harm and is at risk of suffering harm going forward" and that he will "continue to be irreparably injured" until he is "provided sufficient process to consider him for transfer to the less restrictive and torturous standard death row unit." ECF No. 1 at 11, 13. However, as explained below, Tabler's relief does not fit the *Ex Parte Young* exception because he does not allege a continuing violation of federal law.

b. Plaintiff fails to state a persistent widespread policy or practice implemented or enforced by Defendant Davis

"[I]n an official-capacity suit the entity's 'policy or custom' must have played a part in the violation of federal law." *Graham*, 473 U.S. at 166. A § 1983 claim asserting a violation of the plaintiff's federal constitutional rights may proceed in federal court as long as the relief sought against a state official in official capacities is "declaratory or injunctive in nature and prospective in effect." *NiGen Biotech, L.L.C. v. Paxton*, 804 F.3d 389, 394 (5th Cir. 2015). "The failure of plaintiff to allege specific facts showing precisely how each of the named defendants was personally involved in the alleged [violations of a plaintiff's constitutional rights] does not furnish a basis for the dismissal of this action." *Barnes v. Givens*, Civil Action No. SA-17-CA-1071-XR, 2019 U.S. Dist. LEXIS 187059, at *13 (W.D. Tex. Oct. 29, 2019) (citing *Bagwell v. Livingston*, No. SA-15-CV-584-DAE, 2016 U.S. Dist. LEXIS 11173, 2016 WL 393553, at *2 (W.D. Tex. Feb. 1, 2016)).

To establish liability against a state employee in their official capacity pursuant to § 1983, a plaintiff must demonstrate that an official policy is the "moving force" behind the employee's allegedly unconstitutional act. *See Monell v. Dep't of Soc. Servs.*, 436 U.S. 658, 694 (1978); *Piotrowski v. City of Houston*, 237 F.3d 567, 578 (5th Cir. 2001). "To establish liability for a policy or practice, a plaintiff must prove that (1) the local government or official promulgated a policy; (2) the decision [or policy] displayed 'deliberate indifference' and proved the government's culpability; and (3) the policy decision lead to a particular injury." *In re Foust*, 310 F.3d 849, 861 (5th Cir. 2002) (citation omitted). An official policy is either a formal statement officially adopted by a municipality or a persistent widespread practice of municipal employees which is common and well established. *Id.*; *see Powers v. Clay*, No. V-11-051, 2012 U.S. Dist. LEXIS 184738, at *27-28 (S.D. Tex. Nov. 21, 2012) (dismissing claims against TDCJ defendants in their official capacities on the grounds that that plaintiffs failed to show that the policy in place for prison shakedowns do not reflect "deliberate indifference" and is "facially innocuous").[4]

Here, Tabler has not shown or alleged any specific TDCJ policy that deprived him of either a cognizable property or liberty interest. First, he has pointed to no state statute that creates property interest in his housing or classification. In fact, there is much law to the contrary as explained below. Second, Tabler has not stated a claim that Ms. Davis, or TDCJ, have deprived him of a cognizable liberty interest, because his classification on death row does not impose "atypical and significant hardship…in relation to the ordinary incidents of prison life." *Sandin v. Conner*, 515 U.S. 472, 483-484 (1995). Even if he did provide a policy, Tabler failed to allege that policy constituted deliberate indifference. Further, Plaintiff Tabler has failed to state an Eighth Amendment claim, as discussed below.

2. Plaintiff's allegations of conditions of confinement must be dismissed

Here, Tabler is essentially asserting a condition of confinement claim under 42 U.S.C. § 1983 by alleging that he has been deprived and continues to be deprived of basic human needs. The required substantial showing of the denial of a constitutional right must have some footing in the law. *Ruiz v. Davis*, 850 F.3d 225, 228 (5th Cir. 2017). The Fifth Circuit in *Ruiz* was not aware of any court that has found an Eighth Amendment violation occasioned by years on death row while a prisoner pursues his

---

[4] To the extent that Plaintiff seeks to sue Ms. Davis because of her supervisory capacity, he fails to state a claim. "Personal involvement is an essential element of a civil rights cause of action." *Thompson v. Steele*, 709 F.2d 381, 382 (5th Cir. 1983). There is no vicarious or *respondeat superior* liability of supervisors under section 1983. *Thompkins v. Belt*, 828 F.2d 298, 303-04 (5th Cir. 1987). *See also Carnaby v. City of Houston*, 636 F.3d 183, 189 (5th Cir. 2011) (the acts of subordinates do not trigger individual § 1983 liability for supervisory officials). "Supervisory officials may be held liable only if: (1) they affirmatively participate in acts that cause constitutional deprivation; or (2) implement unconstitutional policies that causally result in plaintiff's injuries." *Mouille v. City of Live Oak, Tex.*, 977 F.2d 924, 929 (5th Cir. 1992). Thus, a supervisor who is not personally involved is liable only if he has implemented "a policy so deficient that the policy itself is a repudiation of the constitutional rights and is the moving force of the constitutional violation." *Thompkins*, 828 F.2d at 304. "Mere knowledge and acquiescence on a supervisor's part is insufficient to create supervisory liability under § 1983." Doe v. Bailey, No. H-14-2985, 2015 U.S. Dist. LEXIS 136508, 2015 WL 5737666, at *9 (S.D. Tex. Sep. 30, 2015) (citing *Iqbal*, 556 U.S. at 677).

direct and collateral appeals. *Id.* The Fifth Circuit's jurisprudence on the subject is well-known: "[t]here are compelling justifications for the delay between conviction and the execution of a death sentence… [Prisoners who have] benefited from this careful and meticulous process . . . cannot [later] complain that the expensive and laborious process of habeas corpus appeals which exists to protect [them] violate[s] other of [their] rights." Here, it seems that Plaintiff Tabler's habeas appeals are still pending. ECF No. 1 at 5. Much like the case here, Ruiz alleged that he had been in solitary confinement for the majority of time he was on death row. *Ruiz*, 850 F.3d at 229. The Ruiz court dismissed his claims, citing several cases. *See Knight v. Florida*, 528 U.S. 990 (1999) (Thomas, J., concurring) (concurring in denial of certiorari in extended death-row confinement claims and, in response to Justice Stevens's "invitation to state and lower courts to serve as 'laboratories' in which the viability of this claim could receive further study," arguing that courts "have resoundingly rejected the claim as meritless"); *see also Stafford v. Ward*, 59 F.3d 1025, 1028 (10th Cir. 1995) ("We conclude that Appellant has failed to show that executing him after fifteen years on death row, during which time he faced at least seven execution dates, would constitute cruel and unusual punishment."); *Johns v. Bowersox*, 203 F.3d 538, 547 (8th Cir. 2000) (holding that, even if petitioner's *Lackey* claim were not barred, "[a]bsent evidence that the delay was caused intentionally to prolong the defendants time on death row, we [have] held that it [does] not even begin to approach a constitutional violation"); *Smith v. Mahoney*, 611 F.3d 978, 998 (9th Cir. 2010) (holding, in the context of AEDPA review, that "the Supreme Court has never held that execution after a long tenure on death row is cruel and unusual punishment"). *Ruiz*, 850 F.3d at 228, n.10.

Plaintiff Tabler has failed to state a claim that rises to the level of a constitutional violation because he has not identified any "basic human need" which he was denied for an unreasonable period of time. In *Crawford v. Epps*, No. 4:12CV38-M-A, 2014 U.S. Dist. LEXIS 68436 (N.D. Miss. Feb. 28, 2014), Crawford, a death row inmate, alleged a multitude of claims falling under the category of general conditions of confinement. *Id.* Specifically, he alleged: (1) intermittently available hot water, (2) unsatisfactory laundry service, (3) lack of incentive programs for death row inmates, (4) unreasonably high prices at the prison canteen, (5) improperly conducted fire drills in the building housing death row inmates. *Id.* at *12. [T]he Eighth Amendment may afford protection against conditions of confinement which constitute health threats but not against those which cause mere discomfort or inconvenience." *Wilson v. Lynaugh*, 878 F.2d 846, 849 (5th Cir. 1989), *cert. denied*, 493 U.S. 969 (1989) (citation omitted). "Inmates cannot expect the amenities, conveniences, and services of a good hotel." *Id.* at 849 n.5 (citation omitted). It is clear that prison officials have certain duties under the Eighth Amendment, but these duties are only to provide prisoners with "humane conditions of confinement," including "adequate food, clothing, shelter, and medical care..." *Woods v. Edwards*, 51 F.3d 577, 581 n.10 (5th Cir. 1995) (quoting *Farmer v. Brennan*, 511 U.S. 825, 832 (1994)). The court in *Crawford* found that none of these claims amounted to a constitutional violation.

Specifically, as to the "fire drill" claim for death row inmates, the court wrote:

> A prison policy or practice will not be found unconstitutional as long as it is reasonably related to a legitimate penological objective of the facility. *Hay v. Waldron*, 834 F.2d 481, 487-87 (5th Cir. 1987). Though a different, more thorough, method of conducting a fire drill in Crawford's unit would be a more accurate measure of the ability of prison officials to evacuate the unit, the State's interest in the safety and security of both prisoners and prison staff is readily apparent. Transporting death row inmates is fraught with risk for both guards and prisoners. Therefore, the court will not second-guess the decision by prison administrators to use the procedure they have chosen to carry out fire drills.

Id. at *15–16. The court in Crawford found there was a legitimate penological interest in the State's interest in the safety and security of the prisoners and prison staff.

In another case, brought under the ADA but with similar complaints regarding the conditions of confinement on death row is *Scheanette v. Riggins*, No. 9:05cv34, 2005 U.S. Dist. LEXIS 41777 (E.D.

Tex. Dec. 14, 2005). In *Scheanette*, the plaintiff alleges there was a policy of discrimination against inmates on Death Row, including: the denial of access to television, the taking of blood samples in the dayroom, no spoons or cups are given to Death Row inmates, other inmates have been gassed while hanging themselves, inmates are not provided with any kind of educational programs, inmates are strip searched regardless of the weather, inmates are housed in segregation for 22 1/2 hours per day, strip searches are conducted every time inmates leave their cells, the medicine of an inmate Dione Summerlin was confiscated even though Summerlin had previously attempted suicide, Death Row inmates are locked down twice a year for shakedowns, Death Row inmates are moved from cell to cell yearly while inmates in general population stay in the same cell throughout their incarceration, Death Row inmates are not permitted to go to the law library, information about Death Row inmates is placed on the Internet, the Death Row inmates get clothes that say "D.R." on them, they are not allowed to practice their religion with other inmates of the same faith but must do it by themselves or with a minister at the cell, they are not allowed any inmate to inmate contact, and they receive different I.D. numbers beginning with 999. *Id.* at *6. In a *Martinez* Report provided by the prison officials, the prison officials stated legitimate, non-discriminatory reasons having to do with legitimate penological reasons to explain the conditions in which the plaintiff complained. *Id.* at *10.

The *Scheanette* court reasoned that the Fifth Circuit has held that indicia of confinement constituting cruel and unusual punishment include wanton and unnecessary infliction of pain, conditions grossly disproportionate to the severity of the crime warranting imprisonment, and the deprivation of the minimal civilized measures of life's necessities. *Wilson v. Lynaugh*, 878 F.2d 846, 848 (5th Cir.), cert. denied 493 U.S. 969 (1989). The Supreme Court has held, however, that to the extent that prison conditions are restrictive and even harsh, they are part of the penalty that criminal offenders pay for their offenses against society. *Rhodes v. Chapman*, 452 U.S. 337, 346–47, (1981). In compliance with the Supreme Court's opinion, the Fifth Circuit has stated that the Eighth Amendment does not afford protection against mere discomfort or inconvenience. *Wilson*, 878 F.2d at 849.

As to Scheanette's complaint regarding being housed in segregation for 22.5 hours a day, the court responded that inmates convicted of capital murder represent a significant risk to the security of the institution, and the segregation of such individuals, for the protection of staff, other inmates, and themselves, is reasonably related to a legitimate penological purpose. *Id.* at *24–25. The court dismissed Scheanette's claims as he failed to state a claim under the ADA.

This Court should apply the same standard. Tabler is not housed on death row in a restrictive cell to make friends but is a penalty that criminal offender pay for their offenses against society. Although his mental health has suffered in this environment, the Eighth Amendment does not afford protection against discomfort and inconvenience, and the removal of Tabler from the restrictive housing will do more harm than good to anyone.

3. Plaintiff's allegations of due process violation must be dismissed because he lacks a liberty interest in his housing.

"To state a Fourteenth Amendment due process claim under § 1983, a plaintiff must first identify a protected life, liberty or property interest and then prove that governmental action resulted in a deprivation of that interest." *Morris v. Livingston*, 739 F.3d 740, 750 (5th Cir. 2014). Prisoners have no constitutionally protected liberty interest in a particular housing assignment. *See Nathan v. Hancock*, 477 F. App'x 197, 199 (5th Cir. 2012) (no liberty interest is implicated by a prisoner's change in custody status, placement in segregation or lockdown and consequent restrictions on privileges). Liberty interests protected by the Due Process Clause are "generally limited to freedom from restraint which ... imposes atypical and significant hardship on the inmate in relation to the ordinary incidents of prison life." *Sandin v. Conner*, 515 U.S. 472, 483-484 (1995); *see also Meachum v. Fano*, 427 U.S. 215, 225 (1976) (no protected liberty interest in housing at a particular prison facility); *Nash v. Wilkinson*, 124 F. App'x 254, 255 (5th Cir. 2005) (no liberty interest in housing assignment); *Adeleke v. Heaton*, 352 F.

App'x 904 (5th Cir. 2009) ("Adeleke's allegations fail to state a claim for deprivation of due process of law arising out of his change in housing or arising out of the lockdown after the transfer of housing units. Adeleke's due process challenge to his transfer from one unit to another are without merit; prison officials exercise sole discretion over inmate unit placement, and inmates do not have a constitutionally protected property or liberty interest in housing in certain facilities.").

In *Bisby*, the punishments imposed on the inmate plaintiff, Bisby, included a reduction in classification status, a change in housing assignment, and the loss of 180 days good time credits. *Bisby v. Dir., TDCJ-CID*, No. 6:10cv358, 2010 U.S. Dist. LEXIS 139281, at *8 (E.D. Tex. Nov. 15, 2010). The punishments of reduction in classification status and a change in housing assignment do not impose atypical and significant hardships on an inmate in relation to the ordinary incidents of prison life. *Id.* (citing *Wilson v. Budney*, 976 F.2d 957, 958 (5th Cir. 1992) (no protected liberty interest in custodial classification); *Bradley v. Mississippi Department of Corrections*, 283 F. App'x 250, 2008 WL 2489905 (5th Cir., 2008) (no liberty interest in housing assignment); *Wilkerson v. Stalder*, 329 F.3d 431, 435–36 (5th Cir. 2003); *Moody v. Baker*, 857 F.2d 256, 257–58 (5th Cir. 1988)). In a similar case, in which a death row inmate complained about his custodial status, this Court found that the did not have a protected liberty or property interest in his classification status. *Robertson v. Thaler*, No. 9:12cv58, 2013 U.S. Dist. LEXIS 66135, at *11 (E.D. Tex. May 9, 2013). The inmate argued that the Death Row plan gave him a "state created liberty interest" in being present for his classification hearings, but this Court found that there was no constitutional violation in the fact that he was not allowed to be personally present at the classification hearing because he had no liberty interest in his custodial classification. *Id.*

Here, Tabler was placed in restrictive housing on death row due to smuggling in a cell phone and then using that cell phone to threaten a state senator. *See Tabler v. Stephens*, 588 F. App'x 297, 300 (5th Cir. 2014). An inquiry into the call ultimately led to an investigation into cell phone smuggling in the prison, which purportedly resulted in threats and harassment from prison staff and fellow inmates. *Id.* Due to his illegal actions of smuggling a cell phone, threatening a senator, and retaliation while he incarcerated in TDCJ,[5] prison officials exercised their discretion over Tabler's housing placement when he was placed in the restrictive housing area of death row.

B. Defendant Davis is entitled to sovereign immunity under the ADA.

Defendant Davis is entitled to sovereign immunity under the ADA because it's Eleventh Amendment immunity has no been abrogated. The doctrine of sovereign immunity "bars an individual from suing a state in federal court unless the state consents to suit or Congress has clearly and validly abrogated the state's sovereign immunity." *See, e.g., Perez v. Region 20 Educ. Serv. Ctr.*, 307 F.3d 318, 326 (5th Cir. 2002); *Kimel v. Florida Bd. of Regents*, 528 U.S. 62, 72–73 (2000) (stating that "for over a century now, we have made clear that the Constitution does not provide for federal jurisdiction over suits against nonconsenting States"); *Bd. of Trustees of Univ. of Alabama v. Garrett*, 531 U.S. 356, 363 (2001) (stating that "[t]he ultimate guarantee of the Eleventh Amendment is that nonconsenting States may not be sued by private individuals in federal court"). Congress, however, has the power to "single-handedly strip the states of their Eleventh Amendment immunity and thereby authorize federal court suits by individuals against the states." *Pace v. Bogalusa City School Bd.*, 403 F.3d 272, 277 (5th Cir. 2005). "When Congress does this, it is exercising its power to abrogate Eleventh Amendment immunity." *Id.* In addition to Congress' power to abrogate immunity, a state can also be sued if it has "waive[d] its Eleventh Amendment protection and allow[ed] a federal court to hear and decide a case" by consent. *See Idaho v. Coeur d'Alene Tribe of Idaho*, 521 U.S. 261, 267 (1997). In this case, it is undisputed that TDCJ is an arm of the State of Texas and can assert sovereign immunity as a defense from suit. *Sherwinski v.*

---

[5] See TDCJ Offender Search, https://offender.tdcj.texas.gov/OffenderSearch/offenderDetail.action?sid=07420770 (Last visited May 22, 2020).

Peterson, 98 F.3d 849, 851 (5th Cir. 1996). Here, Plaintiff has failed to allege any claims under § 504 of the Rehabilitation Act and thus has not stated a waiver of immunity for TDCJ-CID under the ADA.

    1. Plaintiff fails to state a claim under the ADA/RA.

    The Supreme Court has set out a three-part test to determine whether or not Title II of the ADA abrogates a state's sovereign immunity. *United States v. Georgia*, 546 U.S. 151, 159 (2006). First, the district court must consider which aspects of the State's alleged conduct violated Title II. *Id.* After making this determination, the court must ask to what extent such misconduct also violated the Fourteenth Amendment. *Id.* If the State's conduct violated both Title II and the Fourteenth Amendment, then Title II validly abrogates state sovereign immunity. *Id.*, *see also Hale v. King*, 642 F.3d 492, 498 (5th Cir. 2011). If the conduct only violates Title II and not the Fourteenth Amendment, the court must then consider whether Congress' purported abrogation of sovereign immunity as to that class of conduct is nevertheless valid. *Id.*

    Abrogation of sovereign immunity is not "absolute" in in a Title II ADA claim. *Brigham v. Tex. Dep't of Criminal Justice*, No. 1:15-CV-440, 2016 U.S. Dist. LEXIS 135674, at *16 (E.D. Tex. Aug. 29, 2016). The first step for the Court is to consider whether the plaintiff has state a claim for relief under Title II. Here, Plaintiff has failed to allege any violation of the Eighth Amendment or state a claim under Title II for the reasons set forth below. Thus, Ms. Davis retains sovereign immunity and this Court lacks jurisdiction over the ADA/RA claim.

    To state a claim under the ADA or RA, the Plaintiff must allege that the decedent was (1) is a qualified individual; (2) who was excluded from participation in or denied the benefits of services, programs, or activities of a public entity; and (3) that the exclusion, denial, or discrimination was because of his disability. *See Blanks v. Southwestern Bell Communications*, 310 F.3d 398, 400 (5th Cir. 2002). Here, Tabler's Complaint fails to state a claim against Ms. Davis in her official capacity under the

ADA/RA because he fails to assert nothing but conclusory allegations and includes nothing but threadbare recitals of the elements needed to plead a claim under the ADA/RA.

a. Plaintiff fails to state a disability as required by the ADA.

With respect to the first element, the ADA defines the term disability as: (1) a physical or mental impairment that substantially limits one or more major life activities of such individual; (2) a record of such an impairment; or (3) being regarded as having such an impairment. 42 U.S.C. § 12102(1). Although the 2008 Amendment to the ADA statute provides broad coverage to the meaning of "disability," the Fifth Circuit has recognized that "it does not absolve a party from proving [a disability]." *Neely v. PSEG Tex., Ltd. P'ship*, 735 F.3d 242, 245 (5th Cir. 2013). Courts look to 29 C.F.R. § 1630 for detailed guidance on what constitutes a disability. *See* 29 C.F.R. § 1630.1–16. Section 1630.2 defines disability as "[a] physical or mental impairment that substantially limits one or more of the major life activities of such individual." A substantial impairment under the ADA is one that limits an individual's ability to perform a major life activity as compared to most people in the general population. *Garza v. City of Donna*, 2017 U.S. Dist. LEXIS 103118, (S.D. Tex. July 5, 2017) at *14 (citing 29 C.F.R. § 1630.2(j)(1)(ii)); *See also Weed v. Sidewinder Drilling, Inc.*, 245 F. Supp. 3d 826, (S.D. Tex. 2017) ("[T]o be substantially limited means to be unable to perform a major life activity that the average person in the general population can perform or to be significantly restricted in the ability to perform it."). "Neither the Supreme Court nor [the Fifth Circuit] has recognized the concept of a *per se* disability under the ADA, no matter how serious the impairment; the plaintiff still must adduce evidence of an impairment that has actually and substantially limited the major life activity on which he relies." *Salcido v. Harris Cty.*, No. H-15-2155, 2018 U.S. Dist. LEXIS 169034, at *141 (S.D. Tex. Sep. 28, 2018); *Griffin v. United Parcel Service, Inc.*, 661 F.3d 216, 223 (5th Cir. 2011).

Here, Tabler has alleged that TDCJ "failed to reasonably accommodate his mental health issues despite knowing his suicidal ideation and related impairments and conditions." ECF No. 1 at 14. Tabler asserts that an "obviously reasonable accommodation exists, that TDCJ has failed to provide Mr. Tabler: moving him out of the Death Watch section and back to death row." *Id.* Tabler alleges that he has been diagnosed with Fetal Alcohol Spectrum Disorder and Klinefeleter Syndrome, which effect his central nervous system, resulting in decreased impulse control, heightened anxiety, mood lability, low frustration tolerance, depression, and executive function impairments.[6] Tabler states that his combination of health disorders result in "emotional instability at the best of times" and "leaves him without the emotion and cognitive ability to effectively process the loss of people close to him. In Death Watch section, such losses are frequent and unavoidable…". ECF No. 1 at 6. Tabler has "repeatedly expressed mental distress, including suicidal ideation, and displayed physically self-harming and suicidal behaviors since his placement in the Death Watch section." *Id.* In his Complaint, Tabler then gave several examples of mental health deterioration between 2011 and 2015. *Id.*

Construing these allegations in the light most favorable to the Plaintiff, he has alleged that he suffers from mental health impairments that causes her to be potentially dangerous to himself and others. But allegations of suicidal risk are not sufficient, without more, to show than an impairment is disabling. *Wade v. Montgomery Cty.*, No. 4:17-CV-1040, 2017 U.S. Dist. LEXIS 216522, at *20-21 (S.D. Tex. Dec. 6, 2017); *see Garza v. City of Donna*, Cause No. 7:16-CV-00558, 2017 U.S. Dist. LEXIS 103118, 2017 WL 2861456 (S.D. Tex. July 5, 2017) (stating that "a person's 'risk of suicide' is not a life activity" sufficient to maintain an ADA claim); *Martin v. The Brown Schools Edu. Corp.*, Cause No. 3:02-CV-0144G, 2003 U.S. Dist. LEXIS 3942, 2003 WL 21077454 (N.D. Tex.

---

[6] Many of these symptoms, including his decreased impulse control and low frustration tolerance perhaps lend to more of a reason as to why Tabler should be watched and not let in to less restrictive housing.

August 6, 2003) (Fish, C.J.)(noting that the plaintiff "fail[ed] to even show how being 'suicidal' translates into a perceived impairment and to designate any major life activity in which she is substantially limited by the unidentified impairment"); *Steele v. Rowles*, 2009 U.S. Dist. LEXIS 80711, 2009 WL 2905903, at *10 (E.D. Tex. Sept. 3, 2009) (Crone J., adopting magistrate's recommendation) (holding that a plaintiff who expressed suicidal intent did not show that he was disabled), aff'd, 389 Fed. Appx. 347 (5th Cir. 2010). Similarly, allegations of depression, without any evidence that it substantially limits a life activity, are also insufficient. *Lottinger v. Shell Oil Company*, 143 F. Supp. 2d 743 (S.D. Tex. 2001) (noting that "depression . . . is not considered a disability per se" when it only occasionally affected the plaintiff's ability to sleep and eat) (citing *Schneiker v. Fortis Ins. Co.*, 200 F.3d 1055, 1061 (7th Cir. 2000)).

Tabler's allegations here detail several impairments, but they do not describe how those impairments substantially limit any major life activity. For that reason, Tabler has not alleged facts from which it can be reasonably inferred that he is disabled, as defined by subsection A of the ADA definition. *Hale*, 642 F.3d at 501–502 ("Absent allegations that [plaintiff's] ailments substantially limited him in the performance of a major life activity, [he] has failed to state a claim for relief under subsection A of the ADA's definition of disability."); 42 U.S.C. § 12102(1)(A) ("'disability' means . . . a physical or mental impairment that substantially limits one or more major life activities"); *see also Wade*, 2017 U.S. Dist. LEXIS 216522, at *21-22.

Tabler has also failed to allege sufficiently that she is disabled under subsection B of the ADA's definition of disability. A plaintiff proceeding under subsection B must allege that she "has a record of an injury or impairment" and that the "impairment limited a major life activity." *Dupre v. Charter Behavioral Health Sys. Of Lafayette, Inc.*, 242 F.3d 610, 615 (5th Cir. 2001). Plaintiff claims that he was diagnosed with mental illnesses before these events, so he has alleged that she has a record of impairment. However, as noted, Tabler has not alleged facts from which it can be reasonably inferred that those impairments substantially limited a major life activity. Again, for that reason, she has not alleged a necessary element to show that she is disabled under subsection B of the ADA's definition of disability.

b. Plaintiff fails to allege he was excluded from participation in or denied the benefits of services, programs, or activities provided by TDCJ-CID.

Plaintiff Tabler has failed to adequately plead that he was denied access to any programs or services necessary to support an ADA claim. The Rehabilitation Act defines a "program or activity" as "all of the operations of…a local government." *Frame v. City of Arlington*, 657 F.3d 215, 225 (5th Cir. 2011) (citing 29 U.S.C. § 794(b)(1)(A) (2014)). As it relates to prisons, "[t]he Supreme Court considered the text of Title II as it is 'ordinarily understood,' and reasoned that 'prisons provide inmates with recreational 'activities,' medical 'services,' and education and vocations 'programs,' all of which at least theoretically 'benefit' the prisoners." *Frame*, 657 F.3d at 225.

Significantly, while a public entity may not deny a qualified individual the opportunity to participate in, or benefit from, an aid, benefit, or service, it also cannot afford a qualified individual with an opportunity to participate in, or benefit from, an aid, benefit, or service that is not equally afforded to others. 28 C.F.R. §35.130(b)(1)(i)-(ii) (2011); *see also Borum v. Swisher Cty*, No. 2:14-CV-127, 2015 WL 327508, at *9 (N.D. Tex. Jan. 26, 2015) (finding prisons not required to provide *new* services or programs for a disabled prisoner, but only that a disabled prisoner have meaningful access to *existing* services and programs) (emphasis in original). Furthermore, public entities responsible for the operation or management of correctional facilities shall ensure offenders are housed in the most integrated setting appropriate to their needs, and not be designated to a medical area unless actually receiving in-patient medical care or treatment while at the TDCJ Unit. 28 C.F.R. § 35.152(b)(2)(ii) (2011); 28 C.F.R § 35.130(d) (2011); *see also* TEX. GOV'T CODE § 499.055, Population Management Based on Inmate Health.

The only accommodation that Tabler alleges TDCJ failed to accommodate is placing him in a housing assignment that is less restrictive. This relief does not correspond to his disabilities, except to say that he "might" find relief from the loss of his friends. ECF No. 5 at 5. Moving him to less restrictive housing does not accommodate his alleged disability, but rather accommodates his lack of friends and loss he experiences therefrom.[7]

c. Plaintiff fails to plead a cognizable injury in fact.

A mere violation of the ADA alone does not establish injury. *DeLeon v. City of Alvin Police Dep't*, No. H-09-1022, 2011 U.S. Dist. LEXIS 1354, at *11 (S.D. Tex. Jan. 6, 2011). Rather, a plaintiff is obligated to show, by competent evidence, that a defendant's violation of the ADA proximately caused her actual injury before she can recover. *Id.*; *see Armstrong v. Turner Indus., Inc.*, 141 F.3d 554, 562 (5th Cir. 1998) (holding "that damages liability [under the ADA] must be based on something more than a mere violation of that provision. There must be some cognizable injury in fact of which the violation is a legal and proximate cause for damages to arise from a single violation."). Here, even if the Court finds that the Plaintiff properly plead he was disabled within the meaning of the ADA and he was denied services for which TDCJ was responsible, the Plaintiff has failed to establish the third element of his *prima facie* case because he has not plead sufficient facts that Defendants discriminated against him "by reason of his disability" or caused him any cognizable injury.

---

[7] "Discrimination" includes "not making reasonable accommodations to the known physical or mental limitations of an otherwise qualified individual with a disability who is an applicant or employee, unless such covered entity can demonstrate that the accommodation would impose an undue hardship on the operation of the business of such covered entity." *Id.* § 12112(b)(5)(A); *Daugherty v. City of El Paso*, 56 F.3d 695, 696 (5th Cir. 1995). Here, if TDCJ were to move the Plaintiff into a less restrictive housing area, it would put the rest of the prison and prison officials, and possibly the public at risk. Plus, it would be opening the door for any inmate who wants to get off death row or out of restrictive housing to bring a lawsuit to have their housing assignment changed for the possibility they may feel less anxious or depressed or be able to make friends.

Case 9:20-cv-00049-RC-KFG Document 9 Filed 05/27/20 Page 21 of 29 PageID #: 64

C. Plaintiff is not entitled to injunctive relief because he cannot meet the standard required for injunctive relief.

To obtain a preliminary injunction, the applicant must show (1) a substantial likelihood that he will prevail on the merits, (2) a substantial threat that he will suffer irreparable injury if the injunction is not granted, (3) that his threatened injury outweighs the threatened harm to the party whom he seeks to enjoin, and (4) that granting the preliminary injunction will not disserve the public interest. *See Planned Parenthood of Houston & Southeast Texas v. Sanchez*, 403 F.3d 324, 329 (5th Cir. 2005). For a permanent injunction to issue the plaintiff must prevail on the merits of his claim and establish that equitable relief is appropriate in all other respects. *See Dresser-Rand Co. v. Virtual Automation Inc.*, 361 F.3d 831, 847 (5th Cir. 2004) (citing *Amoco Prod. Co. v. Village of Gambell*, 480 U.S. 531, 546 n. 12 (1987) (recognizing that the standard for a permanent injunction is essentially the same as for a preliminary injunction with the exception that the plaintiff must show actual success on the merits rather than a mere likelihood of success)). Injunctive relief in the form of "superintending federal injunctive decrees directing state officials" is an extraordinary remedy. *Morrow v. Harwell*, 768 F.2d 619, 627 (5th Cir. 1985). Here, Tabler seeks injunctive relief either in the form of due process by "sufficient process to consider him for transfer to the less restrictive and tortuous standard death row unit" or simply by "moving him out of the 'Death Watch' section and back to death row." ECF No. 1 at 13 (¶ 77), 14 (¶86).

In a similar case, the plaintiff, Watson, was an offender in custody of TDCJ who was placed in protective housing after he provided information to prison officials about illegal drug operation by a prison gang. *Watson v. Quarterman*, No. H-06-3260, 2008 U.S. Dist. LEXIS 15169, at *2 (S.D. Tex. Feb. 27, 2008). As a result, Watson was put on the gang's "hit list." *Id.* Because of the threats made against his life, Watson has been in protective custody since that time. *Id.* Watson filed suit under 42 U.S.C. §1983 against Nathaniel Quarterman in his official capacity as Director of TDCJ, along with the unit warden. *Id.* at *3. Watson complained that the conditions of confinement in protective custody are more restrictive than the conditions placed on inmates housed in general population. As a result of these restrictions, Watson complained that his constitution rights were violation in the follow manners: 1) he was denied "legal visits" with other inmates and therefore denied his right to access the courts; 2) he was denied access to adequate medical care for a hearing impairment because the transportation policy is unsafe; 3) he was denied routine mental health screening that is exempt from the co-payment prisoners are required to pay. *Id.* at *4. He also complained generally that in comparison to inmates housed in the general population, inmates assigned to protective custordy do not have sufficient access to a variety of privileges featured at the prison. *Id.* Watson sought injunctive relief in the form of changes to TDCJ policy concerning the privileges extended to inmates in protective custody. *Id.* The court denied his request for injunctive relief for failure to meet his burden on proving the elements needed for injunctive relief. *Id.*

In coming to its conclusion, the court in *Watson* noted several paragraphs of pertinent case law, which applies to the facts in the present case as well:

An inmate's placement in protective custody implicates the duty imposed on prison officials under the Eighth Amendment to the United States Constitution to maintain institutional security and to keep prisoners safe from conditions that pose a substantial risk of serious harm. *See Farmer v. Brennan,* 511 U.S. 825, 834 (1994); *see also Helling v. McKinney,* 509 U.S. 25, 33 (1993) (observing that a prison official's duty under the Eighth Amendment is to ensure "'reasonable safety'"). The Eighth Amendment standard associated with this duty incorporates due regard for prison officials' "unenviable task of keeping dangerous men in safe custody under humane conditions." *Farmer,* 511 U.S. at 846 (citations omitted).

The Supreme Court has explained that "[t]he very object of imprisonment is confinement" and, as such, "many of the liberties and privileges enjoyed by other citizens must be surrendered by the prisoner." *Overton v. Bazzetta,* 539 U.S. 126, 131 (2003). While an inmate is not "stripped of all constitutional protection as he passes through the prison's gates," *Jones v. North Carolina Prisoners' Labor Union, Inc.*, 433 U.S. 119, 137 (1977) (C.J. Burger, concurring); *see also Turner v. Safley*, 482 U.S. 78, 84 (1987) ("Prison walls do not form a barrier separating prison inmates from the protections of the Constitution."), it is well established that an inmate does not retain rights inconsistent with proper incarceration. *Overton*, 539 U.S. at 131. As the Supreme Court has repeatedly held, the United States Constitution permits greater restrictions on inmates' rights than it allows elsewhere and affords substantial deference to the professional judgment of prison administrators. *See Beard v. Banks*, 548 U.S. 521 (2006) (citing *Overton*, 539 U.S. at 132; *Turner v. Safley*, 482 U.S. 78, 84–85 (1987)).

Deference to prison regulations is required based on the recognition that "courts are ill equipped to deal with the increasingly urgent problems of prison administration and reform." *Turner*, 482 U.S. at 84 (citing *Procunier v. Martinez*, 416 U.S. 396, 405 (1974)). As the Supreme Court has acknowledged, "the problems of prisons in America are complex and intractable, and, more to the point, they are not readily susceptible of resolution by decree." *Id.* (quoting *Martinez*, 416 U.S. at 404–05). "Running a prison is an inordinately difficult undertaking that requires expertise, planning, and the commitment of resources, all of which are peculiarly within the province of the legislative and executive branches of government. Prison administration is, moreover, a task that has been committed to the responsibility of those branches, and separation of powers concerns counsel a policy of judicial restraint." *Turner*, 482 U.S. at 85. Further, where a state penal system is involved federal courts have "additional reason to accord deference to the appropriate prison authorities." *Id.* (citing *Martinez*, 416 U.S. at 405).

It is settled that safety and institutional security are legitimate penological interests. *See Washington v. Harper*, 494 U.S. 210, 225 (1990) ("There can be little doubt as to both the legitimacy and the importance of the governmental interest presented here. There are few cases in which the State's interest in combating the danger posed by a person to himself and others is greater than in a prison environment, which, 'by definition,' is made up of persons with 'a demonstrated proclivity for antisocial criminal, and often violent, conduct.'") (quoting *Hudson v. Palmer*, 468 U.S. 517, 526 (1984) (citations omitted)). Accordingly, courts are required to show great deference to prison administrators' adoption and implementation of policies needed to ensure order and security. *See Pell v. Procunier*, 417 U.S. 817, 827 (1974); *see also Oliver v. Scott*, 276 F.3d 736, 745 (5th Cir .2002) (noting that prison administrators' judgments regarding institutional security are accorded "great deference").

In the present case, Tabler was placed in a section of death row for at least smuggling in a cell phone and threatening a senator. As stated above, safety and institutional security are legitimate penological interests. Washington, 494 U.S. at 225. The Complaint itself shows the danger Tabler presents to himself and others within the prison. Thus, courts are required to show great deference to prison administrator's adoption and implementation of policies needed to ensure order and security. *See Pell*, 417 U.S. at 827.

In assessing the elements needed for Tabler to obtain injunctive relief, he fails to meet the standard for a permanent injunction. The standard for a permanent injunction is essentially the same as for a preliminary injunction with the exception that the plaintiff must show actual success on the merits rather than a mere likelihood of success. *Amoco Prod. Co. v. Village of Gambell*, 480 U.S. 531, 546 n. 12 (1987). The first element being that he must show actual success on the merits, which he fails to do as illustrated by the argument made below.

As to the second element, Tabler does not show from his Complaint that he will suffer an irreparable injury if he is not taken off of "death watch." Tabler contends that being on death watch "imposes serious and irreparable psychological and physical injury on his person." ECF No. 1 at 11. This is because he has been suicidal in the past and due to the friendships he has formed and then lost on death row, his "specific mental health problems are such that he suffers and unusually elevated level of stress and mental anguish from the loss of people to whom he has become attached." *Id.* at 3.

Case 9:20-cv-00049-RC-KFG   Document 9   Filed 05/27/20   Page 25 of 29 PageID #: 68

In fact, he has been taken off death watch before, when he was at the Jester IV unit for 1.5 years, but allegedly still suffered suicidal ideations while at Jester IV and when he went back to Polunsky Unit. See ECF No. 1. Further, even if Tabler is given "due process" (to which he is not entitled because he has no liberty interest in his housing), it is still not guaranteed that he will be moved from death watch. Still, even if he was removed from death watch and housed in a general cell on death row, the offenders housed on death row are still sentenced to death but may receive an execution date and be moved to death watch at any time. Tabler includes no facts or assertions in his Complaint, other than pure speculation, the moving him into the "less restrictive" death row would help his mental health. In fact, Tabler states in his complaint that he seeks "transfer to Texas' less restrictive standard death row, where he *might* at least find relief from his constant loss of friends to the death chamber under his current conditions." ECF No. 5 at 5 (emphasis added). *See Kirby v. Johnson*, 243 Fed. Appx. 877, 2007 WL 2228616 (5th Cir. 2007) ("Injunctive relief is inappropriate when sought to prevent injury that is speculative at best.") (citing *Carter v. Orleans Parish Public Schools*, 725 F.2d 261, 263 (5th Cir. 1984)); *Taylor v. Milton*, 124 F. App'x 248, 2005 WL 352637 (5th Cir. 2005) (noting that, where a prisoner failed to allege any facts that would render the likelihood of a future injury any more than a remote and speculative possibility, he failed to state a valid Eighth Amendment claim for injunctive relief) (citing *Society of Separationists, Inc. v. Herman*, 959 F.2d 1283, 1285 (5th Cir. 1992)).

The third element that Tabler must overcome is that his threatened injury outweighs the threatened harm to the party whom he seeks to enjoin, which in this case would be TDCJ as whole (through his suit against Lorie Davis in her official capacity). As Tabler has been deemed a security threat through at least two crimes he has committed while in prison, and his free-world crimes put him on death row, his threat to the rest of the prison population and the threat he would pose to prison officers and officials would substantially outweigh the threatened harm to himself while in the custody of a more restrictive housing on death row. The Complaint does not state that he is not receiving medical and/or mental health treatment, nor that he is not allowed recreation time or showers, or access to the law library, or medical if he needs it. Instead, the Complaint actually states that he is allowed out of his cell 2 hours per day, he is provided meals, and that he is allowed recreation time.[8] ECF No. 1 at 4.

The fourth element Tabler needs to meet to qualify for injunctive relief is to show that the relief will not disserve the public interest. Again, as stated above, Tabler is capital murderer capable of many manipulation and violent acts and threats to other offenders and prison officials, even senators. Common sense dictates that it is not in the interest of the public that placed in less restrictive housing. There can be no dispute that inmates on Death Row are among the most significant security risks within the prison. *Scheanette v. Riggins*, No. 9:05cv34, 2005 U.S. Dist. LEXIS 41777, at *20 (E.D. Tex. Dec. 14, 2005); *See, e.g., Jeffries v. Reed*, 631 F. Supp. 1212, 1217 (E.D. Wash. 1986). Tabler's request for injunctive relief in the form of less restrictive housing should be denied.

D. Plaintiff's claims are barred by the statute of limitations

The Fifth Circuit determines the accrual date of a § 1983 action by reference to federal law. *Walker v. Epps*, 550 F.3d 407, 414 (5th Cir. 2008) (citing *Wallace v. Kato*, 549 U.S. 384 (2007)). Federal law holds generally that an action accrues when a plaintiff has "'a complete and present cause of action,'" or, expressed differently, "when 'the plaintiff can file suit and obtain relief.'" *Id.* (quoting *Bay Area Laundry and Dry Cleaning Pension Trust Fund v. Ferbar Corp. of Cal.*, 522 U.S. 192, 201 (1997) (citations omitted)). As the Fifth Circuit has stated, the limitations period begins to run "the moment the plaintiff becomes aware that he has suffered an injury or has sufficient information to know that he has been injured." *Piotrowski v. City of Houston*, 237 F.3d 567, 576 (5th Cir. 2001) (quoting *Russell v. Bd. of Trustees*,

---

[8] Ironically, Tabler complains that he has to spend his recreation time separate from other inmates and is allowed virtually no face-to-dace contact with other inmates, while at the same time he becomes too "attached" to these inmates, such that they become "friends" and he hears them in his dreams. ECF No. 1.

968 F.2d 489, 493 (5th Cir. 1992), cert. denied, 507 U.S. 914, (1993)). The Fifth Circuit in *Walker* held that there is no exception for § 1983 actions seeking only equitable relief. *Id.* at 414.

Because Congress has not adopted a statute of limitations for § 1983 actions, the limitations period is determined by reference to the appropriate state statute of limitations and coordinate tolling rules. *Board of Regents, Univ. of N.Y. v. Tomanio*, 446 U.S. 478, 483-84 (1980). In § 1983 actions, district courts apply the forum state's personal injury limitations period. *Moore v. McDonald*, 30 F.3d 616, 620 (5th Cir. 1994). The Texas general personal injury limitations period is two years. *Id.*; Tex. Civ. Prac. & Rem. Code Ann. § 16.003(a) (Vernon Supp. 2008); *see also Lee v. Valdez*, Civil Action No. 3:07-CV-1298-D, 2009 U.S. Dist. LEXIS 43381, at *8–9 (N.D. Tex. May 20, 2009). The two-year statute of limitations also applies to claims brought under Title II of the ADA. *Frame v. City of Arlington*, 575 F.3d 432, 441 (5th Cir. 2009).

In this case, Tabler alleges he has been housed in the Death Watch section of death row at the Polunsky Unit since January 2, 2011. ECF No. 1 at 3. According to the Complaint, the conditions in the Death Watch section are so severe that in 2011, a federal judge denied Tabler's request to drop his habeas appeals an be executed, after finding that his conditions of confinement coerced him to that decision. *Id.* at 5. Tabler alleges that TDCJ has known of his mental health conditions and detioration for five years. *Id.* at 6. Between 2011 and 2015, Tabler made several suicide attempts ad suicidal statements. *Id.* at 7. He was even seen multiple times by mental health where he apparently explained his issues with living on Death Watch. *Id.* Tabler stayed at a psychiatric facility, where he expressed his concerns regarding his mental health and the toll Death Watch was taking on him for over a year before he was transferred back to Death Watch in 2014. *Id.* at 9. The last specific event that the Complaint states happened on February 12, 2015, when Tabler reported he was feeling down about a recent execution. *Id.* at 9–10. Then, Tabler makes a vague and conclusory statement that "on numerous other occasions, and until the present day" his mental health has been substantially worsened by his housing in the Death Watch section. *Id.* at 10. Finally, Tabler reports that he attempted suicide in June of 2019. *Id.*

Tabler had notice of his §1983 the moment he became aware that he suffered an injury, which would be in 2011 when he entered Death Watch and the habeas judge found that his conditions of confinement made him want to commit suicide. Indeed, if it wasn't in 2011, Tabler had notice anytime between 2011 and 2015 during any of the events in which he alleged he expressed his mental health concerns, including in October of 2013 when he was transferred to the Jester IV unit for crisis management. Tabler filed this lawsuit on March 16, 2020. ECF No. 1. At the most, this lawsuit is seven years passed the statute of limitations. At the least, this lawsuit is four years passed the statute of limitations. Nevertheless, all of Tabler's claims should be dismissed because his claims were subject to a two-year statute of limitations and he far exceeded that date.

V. Conclusion

Plaintiff Tabler fails to state a claim under the ADA/RA, leaving this Court with no jurisdiction over those claims because TDCJ is entitled to sovereign immunity. Tabler also failed to state a claim under § 1983 for due process and conditions of confinement because he does not have a liberty interest in his housing. Tabler fails to meet the standard needed for the injunctive relief he seeks. Additionally, all claims are barred by the statute of limitations and should be dismissed with prejudice.

Respectfully submitted.

KEN PAXTON
Attorney General of Texas

JEFFREY C. MATEER
First Assistant Attorney General

RYAN L. BANGERT
Deputy First Assistant Attorney General

DARREN L. MCCARTY
Deputy Attorney General for Civil Litigation

SHANNA E. MOLINARE
Chief, Law Enforcement Defense Division

/s/ Briana M. Webb
BRIANA M. WEBB
Assistant Attorney General
Texas State Bar No. 24077883
Briana.webb@oag.texas.gov

Law Enforcement Defense Division
Office of the Attorney General
P. O. Box 12548, Capitol Station
Austin, Texas 78711
(512) 463-2080 / Fax No. (512) 370-9814

Attorneys for Defendant Davis

Certificate of Service

I, Briana M. Webb, Assistant Attorney General of Texas, do hereby certify that a true and correct copy of the above and foregoing has been served via ECF/PACER to all counsel of record on May 26, 2020.

/s/ Briana M. Webb
BRIANA M. WEBB
Assistant Attorney General

IN THE UNITED STATES DISTRICT COURT
FOR THE EASTERN DISTRICT OF TEXAS
LUFKIN DIVISION

RICHARD TABLER,
    Plaintiff,

v.   Civil Action No. 9:20-cv-00049

LORIE DAVIS, DIRECTOR OF
CORRECTIONAL INSTITUTIONS DIVISION,
TEXAS DEPARTMENT OF CRIMINAL
JUSTICE,
in her official capacity;
    Defendant.

PLAINTIFF'S RESPONSE TO DEFENDANT LORIE DAVIS'S MOTION TO DISMISS
[ECF No. 9]

Plaintiff, by and through his attorneys, David A. Lane and Reid Allison of KILLMER, LANE & NEWMAN, LLP, and Richard Burr, BURR AND WELCH, PC, hereby submits the following Response to Defendant's Motion to Dismiss [ECF No. 9] ("*Def's Mot.*").

I. INTRODUCTION

Plaintiff Richard Tabler filed this lawsuit to achieve a very simple goal: to be moved from the nearly uniquely torturous housing he has been subjected to for almost a decade. He is not asking to be moved out of death row, altogether; he is not asking to be released. Reading Defendant's pending motion to dismiss could easily give the wrong impression of the very limited injunctive relief Mr. Tabler seeks. Viewed properly, Mr. Tabler has plausibly alleged violations of his federal constitutional and statutory rights that must be allowed to proceed to discovery.

II. FACTS ALLEGED

Mr. Tabler has been housed in the Death Watch section of the Texas Department of Criminal Justice's ("TDCJ") death row since January 2, 2011. *See Complaint* [ECF No. 1], at ¶ 10. The restrictions within this unit are extreme and include 22-hour per day solitary confinement in a tiny 60-square foot cell. *Id.* at ¶¶ 14-15. Mr. Tabler's meals are provided through a slot in the door, and he is allowed virtually no face-to-face contact with other prisoners. *Id.* at ¶¶ 16-18. The Death Watch section is reserved for prisoners who have an imminent execution date, scheduled within 60-180 days. *Id.* at ¶ 11. Therefore, every other prisoner that Mr. Tabler has had contact with in the last ten years has been killed by the state within mere months. *Id.* Mr. Tabler does not have an execution date and has not had one scheduled at any point during his decade in Death Watch. *Id.* at ¶ 12.

These conditions are designed to limit human interaction and do so to a severe degree. *Id.* at ¶ 19. However, there is a special cruelty in Defendant's treatment of Mr. Tabler, as the limited interaction he has is with prisoners who are at their last extremity and are only months away from being killed. *Id.* at ¶ 21. "Rather than the comfort that other inmates are permitted to draw from their limited society with one another, Mr. Tabler is confronted with an endless procession of men who are put to death as soon as he is able to form an attachment to them." *Id.* at ¶ 21. While Mr. Tabler has been housed in Death Watch, TDCJ has killed over 90 prisoners. *Id.* at ¶ 22. Mr. Tabler was able to form brief friendships with at least a dozen of these doomed men. *Id.*

These conditions are severe and would take a toll on the mental health of any prisoner. *Id.* at ¶ 23. But the conditions are particularly cruel to Mr. Tabler, because of his underlying mental disabilities, which are both obvious and well known to TDCJ and Defendant. *Id.* at ¶¶ 23, 27. Mr. Tabler suffers "an unusually elevated level of stress and mental anguish from the loss of people to whom he has become attached." *Id.* He has been diagnosed with both Fetal Alcohol

Spectrum Disorder and Klinefelter syndrome. *Id.* at ¶ 28. These mental disabilities cause Mr. Tabler "decreased impulse control, heightened anxiety, mood lability, low frustration tolerance, depression, and executive function impairment." *Id.* Mr. Tabler's mental disabilities also cause him "difficulty with social skills, including lack of stranger fear; naivete and gullibility; inappropriate choice of friends; immaturity; difficulty understanding the perspective of others; and poor social cognition." *Id.* at ¶ 29. Mr. Tabler also meets the criteria for Bipolar Disorder and Attention Deficit Hyperactivity Disorder, and he has suffered repeated traumatic brain injuries. *Id.* at ¶¶ 30-31.

Mr. Tabler's idiosyncratic combination of mental health disabilities leaves him completely unable to process the loss of people close to him. *Id.* at ¶ 32. The toll this housing has taken on him is so severe that he has experienced auditory hallucinations, hearing those who have been executed during his time in Death Watch. *Id.* at ¶ 50. His housing in Death Watch, therefore, subjects him to undue suffering well beyond what a neurotypical prisoner would experience. *Id.* at ¶ 32.

The combination of the conditions in Death Watch and Mr. Tabler's serious mental disabilities has compelled him to attempt to kill himself multiple times. *Id.* at ¶¶ 33-55. Mr. Tabler has repeatedly made clear to TDCJ that his mental health is being savaged by his housing in Death Watch and being forced to see over 90 people, including over a dozen friends, taken to be executed, soon after he meets them. *Id.* at ¶¶ 33, 38-41, 43, 45-54. These attempts have continued and include a June 2019 incident in which he sliced his arm open from wrist to shoulder and nearly died. *Id.* at ¶ 56.

In 2011, a federal judge found that Mr. Tabler's conditions in the Death Watch section were so severe that they were coercive as a matter of law—i.e. the conditions had effectively forced him into dropping his habeas appeals in order to be executed sooner. *Id.* at ¶ 24. These conditions have not changed, and Mr. Tabler remains housed in the Death Watch section in the same torturous conditions that the judge concluded coerced him into seeking a speedy death. *Id.* at ¶¶ 25, 57. Mr. Tabler has never been afforded meaningful process to challenge his housing in the Death Watch section and argue for transfer to TDCJ's less restrictive death row. *Id.* at ¶ 26.

Defendant has no valid penological justification to continue to house Mr. Tabler in Death Watch indefinitely, and his housing there inflicts disproportionate punishment on him. *Id.* at ¶¶ 62-63. Mr. Tabler's housing inflicts serious and irreparable psychological injury and violates present standards of human dignity. *Id.* at ¶¶ 60-61. Defendant's housing of Mr. Tabler indefinitely in Death Watch imposes atypical and significant hardship on him in relation to the ordinary incidents of prison life, and no other prisoner has been held indefinitely in Death Watch as Mr. Tabler has been. *Id.* at ¶¶ 73-74. Therefore, he is entitled to meaningful process to attempt to argue to be moved back to death row, and he has never received this process. *Id.* at ¶¶ 70-72.

III. LEGAL STANDARD

Federal Rule of Civil Procedure 12(b)(6) allows for dismissal of a complaint for "failure to state a claim upon which relief can be granted." "To defeat a Rule 12(b)(6) motion to dismiss, a plaintiff must 'nudge[ ] their claims across the line from conceivable to plausible' by pleading 'enough facts to state a claim to relief that is plausible on its face.'" *Wilson v. Bradshaw*, No. 9:16-CV-112, 2017 U.S. Dist. LEXIS 156993, at *3 (E.D. Tex. Aug. 10, 2017) (quoting *Bell Atlantic Corp. v. Twombly*, 550 U.S. 544, 570 (2007)). In reviewing a Rule 12(b)(6) motion, the Court "accepts all well-pleaded facts as true, viewing them in the light most favorable to the plaintiff." *Sonnier v. State Farm Mutual Auto. Ins. Co.*, 509 F.3d 673, 675 (5th Cir. 2007).

"It is axiomatic that a motion to dismiss an action for failure to state a claim upon which relief can be granted admits the facts alleged in the complaint, but challenges plaintiff's rights to relief based upon those facts." *Madison v. Purdy*, 410 F.2d 99, 100 (5th Cir. 1969). Under the appropriate standard, "[a] motion to dismiss on the basis of the pleadings alone should rarely be granted." *Id.* The same standard applies to Defendant's motion to dismiss Plaintiff's complaint under Federal Rule of Civil Procedure 12(b)(1). *See, e.g., Benton v. United States*, 960 F.2d 19, 21 (5th Cir. 1992).

IV. Argument

Plaintiff has plausibly alleged violations of his federal constitutional and statutory rights. Defendant's arguments in the present motion are founded on (1) minimizing the psychological torture that Mr. Tabler continues to undergo while housed in Death Watch and (2) implying that Mr. Tabler is asking for something more than transfer to death row and that a ruling in his favor would open the floodgates on litigation from other death row prisoners. This Court must reject Defendant's attempts to rewrite and contradict Mr. Tabler's allegations and must allow his claims to proceed to discovery.

A. Plaintiff has plausibly alleged violations of his Eighth and Fourteenth Amendment rights.

Mr. Tabler has plausibly pled violations of his right to be protected from cruel and unusual punishment in the conditions of his confinement. Defendant's continued housing of him in the Death Watch Unit is catastrophic for his mental health, Defendant has continued to house him there years beyond any penological reason for doing so, and Defendant's conduct for the last decade (as well as Defendant's argument in the present motion) make clear that Defendant has every intention of keeping Mr. Tabler housed there indefinitely.

"The Constitution does not mandate comfortable prisons, but neither does it permit inhumane ones." *Gates v. Cook*, 376 F.3d 323, 332-33 (5th Cir. 2004). Courts must analyze prison conditions according to "'the evolving standards of decency that mark the progress of a maturing society' and not the standards in effect during the time of the drafting of the Eighth

Case 9:20-cv-00049-RC-KFG Document 11 Filed 06/24/20 Page 6 of 27 PageID #: 84

Amendment." *Id.* (quoting *Estelle v. Gamble*, 429 U.S. 97, 102 (1976)). As part of the analysis of humane conditions, a prisoner's "mental health needs are no less serious than physical needs." *Gates*, 376 F.3d at 332-33.

A prison official violates the Eighth Amendment when she "1) shows a subjective deliberate indifference to 2) conditions posing a substantial risk of serious harm to the inmate." *Gates*, 376 F.3d at 332-33. "Whether a prison official had the requisite knowledge of a substantial risk is a question of fact subject to demonstration in the usual ways, including inference from circumstantial evidence, and a factfinder may conclude that a prison official knew of a substantial risk from the very fact that the risk was obvious." *Id.*

"Conditions of confinement may establish an Eighth Amendment violation 'in combination' when each would not do so alone, but only when they have a mutually enforcing effect that produces the deprivation of a single, identifiable human need." Moreover, the Supreme Court has stressed that "the length of confinement cannot be ignored.... A filthy, overcrowded cell ... might be tolerable for a few days and intolerably cruel for weeks or months." *Hutto v. Finney*, 437 U.S. 678, 686-87 (1978). A plaintiff "need not show that death or serious illness has occurred." *Helling v. McKinney*, 509 U.S. 25, 32 (1993) ("It would be odd to deny an injunction to inmates who plainly proved an unsafe, life-threatening condition in their prison on the ground that nothing yet had happened to them.").

    1.   *Mr. Tabler's conditions of confinement in Death Watch pose a substantial risk of harm to him.*

Mr. Tabler has plausibly alleged that Defendant housing him indefinitely in Death Watch is cruel and unusual punishment that violates his constitutional rights. Plaintiff's conditions of confinement are severely restrictive and cause obvious and well-known destruction to his mental health. *See generally Complaint*, ¶¶ 10-57. What limited human interaction he has had in the last decade has been almost entirely with men who are on the verge of being killed by the state. After certain of his fellow prisoners have been killed, Mr. Tabler has suffered auditory hallucinations, during which he hears their voices. These conditions have compelled him to attempt to kill himself multiple times during his housing in Death Watch. The conditions also led him to attempt to drop his habeas appeals so as to hasten his death at the hands of the state. Fortunately, a federal judge recognized the severe conditions of Mr. Tabler's confinement and found that the conditions had coerced him to such action. *Id.* at ¶¶ 24, 57.

Mr. Tabler's conditions of confinement are at least comparable to those found to violate the Eighth Amendment in by a court of this circuit in 1999. *See Ruiz v. Johnson*, 37 F.Supp.2d 855, 914 (S.D.Tex.1999), *rev'd on other grounds*, 243 F.3d 941 (5th Cir. 2001), *adhered to on remand*, 154 F.Supp.2d 975 (S.D.Tex.2001). In *Ruiz*, the court found violations of the constitutional rights of prisoners in TDCJ administrative segregation because the conditions cause them to "suffer actual psychological harm from their almost total depravation of human contact, mental stimulus, personal property and human dignity." *Id.* The court reasoned that it was clear in 1999 "that under American jurisprudence, deprivation of activity, exercise, mental stimulation and activity, at some level, is the denial of a basic human necessity." *Id.* The court quoted liberally and correctly from another federal judge, establishing:

> We thus can not ignore, in judging challenged conditions of confinement, that all humans are composed of more than flesh and bone--even those who, because of unlawful and deviant behavior, must be locked away not only from their fellow citizens, but from other inmates as well. Mental health, just as much as physical health, is a mainstay of life. Indeed, it is beyond any serious dispute that mental health is a need as essential to a meaningful human existence as other basic physical demands our bodies may make for shelter, warmth or sanitation.

Id. (quoting *Madrid v. Gomez*, 889 F. Supp. 1146, 1261 (N.D. Cal. 1995).

"As the pain and suffering caused by a cat-o'-nine-tails lashing an inmate's back are cruel and unusual punishment by today's standards of humanity and decency, the pain and suffering caused by extreme levels of psychological deprivation are equally, if not more, cruel and unusual. The wounds and resulting scars, while less tangible, are no less painful and permanent when they are inflicted on the human psyche." *Ruiz*, 37 F.Supp.2d at 914. Finally, the court noted that segregation and severe solitary confinement may be necessary in some circumstances for legitimate penological interests, but when conditions are so extreme as to violate the United States constitution and "the remedial powers of a federal court are invoked to protect the constitutional rights of inmates, the court may not take a 'hands-off' approach." *Id.* at 914-15.

Other courts in the years since *Ruiz* that have examined similar solitary conditions have made clear that "[t]he same standards that protect against physical torture prohibit mental torture as well - including the mental torture of excessive deprivation." *Wilkerson v. Stalder*, 639 F. Supp. 2d 654, 677-79 (M.D. La. 2007) (quoting *Ruiz*, 37 F.Supp.2d at 914. Regardless of what earlier cases said on similar subjects, "[t]he standard for determining whether prison conditions satisfy the Eighth's Amendment objective component, whether the condition is 'sufficiently serious,' is not static" and instead "focuses on whether the conditions are contrary to 'the evolving standards of decency that mark the progress of a maturing society.'" *Wilkerson*, 639 F. Supp. 2d at 677-79 (quoting *Farmer*, 511 U.S. at 833-34).

Specifically, the court in *Wilkerson* reasoned that:

> Such things as food, sleep, clothing, shelter, medical attention, reasonable safety, sleep, and exercise have been recognized by courts as basic physical human needs subject to deprivation by conditions of confinement. While the defendants urge the court not to recognize social interaction and environmental stimulation as basic human needs, the failure to identify them would be inconsistent with jurisprudence recognizing mental health as worthy of Eighth Amendment protection, and the requirement that Eighth Amendment protections change to reflect "evolving standards of decency that mark the progress of a maturing society." *Ruiz v. Johnson*, 37 F.Supp.2d 855 (S.D.Tex.1999), citing *Rhodes*, 452 U.S. at 346, 101 S.Ct. 2392. Additionally, recognizing social interaction and environmental stimulation as basic human needs is hardly going out on a radical limb, as defendants would suggest. In *Ruiz*, the district court found that the defendants were "deliberately indifferent to a systemic pattern of

extreme social isolation and reduced environmental stimulation," and social interaction and environmental stimulation have been identified as basic psychological human needs, either directly or indirectly, by other courts.

Id.

Since at least 1999, courts in this circuit have correctly determined that "in light of the maturation of our society's understanding of the very real psychological needs of human beings, courts have recognized the inhumanity of institutionally-imposed psychological pain and suffering" and that such recognition is not defeated by previous cases' focus on "the basic components of physical sustenance - food, shelter, and medical care." *Ruiz*, 37 F. Supp. 2d at 914. Moreover, courts around the country have rightly reasoned that it is not "rocket science" that "prolonged isolation from social and environmental stimulation increases the risk of development of mental illness." *Shoatz v. Wetzel*, 2014 U.S. Dist. LEXIS 9386, 2014 WL 294988, at *4, n.3 (W.D. Pa. Jan. 27, 2014) (quoting *McClary v. Kelly*, 4 F. Supp.2d 195, 209 (W.D.N.Y. 1998)); *see also Grissom v. Roberts*, 902 F.3d 1162, 1176 (10th Cir. 2018) (Lucero, J., concurring) ("[s]ocial interaction, environmental stimulation, and activity are basic human needs" and "[p]sychologically, solitary confinement is devastating."); *H'Shaka v. O'Gorman*, 2020 U.S. Dist. LEXIS 42908, *50-55 (N.D.N.Y. March 12, 2020) (collecting cases as establishing social contact and environmental stimulation as basic human needs for the purposes of the Eighth Amendment analysis).

Moreover, "[b]oth the Supreme Court and the Fifth Circuit have recognized that certain conditions that would pass constitutional scrutiny if imposed for a short period of time may be rendered unconstitutional if imposed for an extended period of time." *Wilkerson*, 639 F. Supp. 2d at 679; *see also Meriwether v. Faulkner*, 821 F.2d 408, 416 (7th Cir. 1986) ("[T]he duration of a prisoner's confinement in administrative segregation or under lockdown restrictions is certainly an important factor in evaluating whether the totality of the conditions of confinement constitute cruel and unusual punishment."). Mr. Tabler has suffered these conditions for nearly a decade, and there is no end in sight. Defendant obviously intends to keep him housed in Death Watch until he is either executed or succeeds on his still-pending habeas appeals. Whether or not being housed in solitary confinement and restricted to very limited human contact with only other prisoners who are soon to be executed would violate Mr. Tabler's constitutional rights, such housing for ten years and counting, with the expectation that such housing will continue for as long as Mr. Tabler is alive, is cruel and unusual punishment.

> 2. *Defendant is deliberately indifferent to the substantial risk of harm, and Defendant's Eighth Amendment arguments are erroneous.*

It is also clear (and does not appear to be disputed) that Defendant knows of the substantial harm to Mr. Tabler and yet persists in housing him in Death Watch. Indeed, "the extensive scholarly literature describing and quantifying the adverse mental health effects of prolonged solitary confinement that has emerged in recent years" strongly indicates that such risks are obvious. *Porter v. Clarke*, 923 F.3d 348, 361 (4th Cir. 2019) ("[g]iven [State D]efendants' status as corrections professionals, it would defy logic to suggest that they were unaware of the potential harm that the lack of human interaction on death row could cause."). Defendant is aware both (1) of Mr. Tabler's mental disabilities and recurring serious mental health crises and (2) that his housing in what amounts to solitary-plus (a place in which all of your peers are killed within months) is calamitous to his mental health.

In response to Plaintiff's allegations of torturous indefinite solitary confinement among those who are soon killed, Defendant Davis now indicates that Mr. Tabler has been housed in the Death Watch Unit for a decade in order to protect him from harming himself. *Def's Mot.* at 17 n.6. However, later in the same motion, Defendant Davis insists that "if TCDJ were to move the Plaintiff into a less restrictive housing area, it would put the rest of the prison and prison officials, and possibly the public at risk." *Id.* at 20 n.7. All of which is to say, Defendant Davis has no reason why Mr. Tabler must continue to be confined in the Death Watch Section, and Mr. Tabler has plausibly pled that others could be protected from his vague, ominous malice perfectly effectively in the normal Death Row (which is in no way un-restrictive). *See Complaint*, at ¶ 63. Defendant's lack of justification for continuing to house Mr. Tabler in Death Watch indefinitely also makes clear that this is exactly the type of "unnecessary and wanton infliction of pain" that is prohibited by the Eighth Amendment. *See, e.g., Hernandez v. Velasquez*, 522 F.3d 556, 560-61 (5th Cir. 2008); *see also H'Shaka*, 2020 U.S. Dist. LEXIS 42908, *50-55 (collecting cases for the proposition that indefinite confinement in solitary conditions "that is based on past [] conduct, and that fails to take into account a lack of more-recent serious disciplinary infractions over a lengthy period of time, suggests a violation of the Eighth Amendment."). Moreover, the question of whether Defendant has a legitimate justification for Mr. Tabler's indefinite housing in Death Watch is not one for this Court to decide on a motion to dismiss. *See, e.g., Wilkerson*, 639 F. Supp. 2d at 668-69 (accepting plaintiff's argument that defendants had no legitimate penological interest in continuing to keep them in solitary confinement for the purposes of the Eighth Amendment and rejecting defendants' generic assertion that the need for facility safety provided a legitimate penological interest under the circumstances).

Defendant also makes light of both Mr. Tabler's serious mental disabilities and the nightmarish conditions he has lived in for a decade, asserting without basis that allowing this suit to proceed into discovery "would be opening the door for any inmate who wants to get off death row or out of restrictive housing" to sue based on "the possibility they may feel less anxious or depressed or be able to make friends." *Id.* at 20 n.7; *see also id.* at 26 n.8 (finding irony in Mr. Tabler's nightmares). Plaintiff is not asking to be moved out of Death Row, altogether. He is not asking to be freed. And despite Defendant's baseless hints to the contrary, Mr. Tabler is not a threat to anyone else and certainly not to such a degree that he could not be comfortably managed in standard Death Row. Read correctly, Mr. Tabler's lawsuit does not threaten the parade of horribles that Defendant conjures.

Defendant relies heavily on *Ruiz v. Davis*, 850 F.3d 225, 228 (5th Cir. 2017) as dispensing with Mr. Tabler's § 1983 conditions of confinement claim. *See Def's Mot.* at 8-9. However, *Ruiz* has nothing to do with Mr. Tabler's case. There, a Death Row inmate sued on the eve of his execution, alleging that the significant delay between his conviction and execution the multiple previous stays of execution that he had been granted made the "ultimate punishment [of execution] cruel and unusual." *Ruiz*, 850 F.3d at 228. The Fifth Circuit denied him a certificate of appealability, noting that Ruiz had been granted two previous stays to consider his claims, and that his current argument amounted to an attack on capital punishment itself. *Id.* at 229-30. Importantly, the Fifth Circuit made clear that it did not "address the conditions death row inmates, in Texas or elsewhere, face generally. The solitary confinement of prisoners has long been at issue in suits challenging prison conditions." *Id.* at 229. The Court also noted that, "[d]espite being a named plaintiff in a § 1983 method-of-execution suit challenging Texas's lethal injection protocol filed last year, Ruiz voiced no concern regarding Texas's death row conditions of confinement, this at a time that would have allowed him to develop his claims in the district court. Had he done so, we might be properly situated to determine the merit of such claims." *Id.*

Read properly, *Ruiz* has no relevance to Mr. Tabler's claims; Mr. Ruiz sought relief declaring his imminent execution unconstitutional. He did not challenge the actual conditions of confinement of Texas' death row, let alone the even more restrictive and harsh conditions in Death Watch. Mr. Tabler is clearly not seeking any comparable relief in this case. For similar reasons, Defendant's string cite of purportedly similar cases has no relevance to Mr. Tabler's suit and cannot be grounds to dismiss his § 1983 claim. Mr. Tabler is not suing to be released from Death Row.

In general, the tone of Defendant's arguments regarding conditions of confinement make them seem as though they were written at least twenty years ago. *See Def's Mot.* at 11-12. For example, Defendant states that "to the extent that prison conditions are restrictive and harsh, they are part of the penalty that criminal offenders pay for their offenses to society." *Id.* at 11. Of course, this statement—citing a 1981 Supreme Court opinion as support—begs the question presented by Mr. Tabler's lawsuit. It is not, in fact, true as Defendant's definitive statement would make it seem that there are no conditions so restrictive and/or harsh as to violate the United States Constitution. Indeed, Mr. Tabler has alleged such conditions, and he has done so according to the evolving standards of decency that have progressed well beyond the state of the law in 1981. In recent years, courts around the country have recognized "that solitary confinement poses an objective risk of serious psychological and emotional harm to inmates, and therefore can violate the Eighth Amendment." *Porter*, 923 F.3d at 355-64 (collecting cases); *Reynolds v. Arnone*, 402 F. Supp. 3, 16-20 (D. Conn. August 27, 2019).

Finally, Defendant completely diminishes, misconstrues, and contradicts Mr. Tabler's allegations by stating that "the Eighth Amendment does not afford protection against discomfort and inconvenience" and that "removal of Tabler from the restrictive housing will do more harm than good to anyone." *Def's Mot.* at 12. Mr. Tabler has not alleged "discomfort and inconvenience;" he *has* alleged that he has been housed in a uniquely torturous environment for ten years and that there is every indication that Defendant intends to house him there for the rest of his life. For the reasons stated above, this Court should deny Defendant's motion to dismiss Plaintiff's claim of unconstitutional cruel and unusual punishment.

B. Plaintiff has plausibly alleged violations of his constitutional right to Due Process.

Mr. Tabler's conditions of confinement are some of the most restrictive and atypical that exist in any prison in this country. Indeed, his conditions of confinement are nearly unique among the living. By definition, his conditions are shared only by those who will soon be killed by the state. This existence continues to wreak havoc on his mental health and subject him to hardships that not even those in death row suffer. He has not been provided process to state his case to be moved from this terrible existence back to TDCJ's standard death row.

Defendant Davis now argues that Mr. Tabler has no liberty interest in avoiding these conditions by being housed in death row rather than Death Watch. *Def's Mot.* at 12-14. The Supreme Court has made clear that an inmate *does* have a protected Due Process liberty-interest in the conditions of his housing, if that housing "imposes atypical and significant hardship on the inmate in relation to the ordinary incidents of prison life." *Wilkinson v. Austin*, 545 U.S. 209, 222-23 (2005). "[T]he touchstone of the inquiry into the existence of a protected, state-created liberty interest in avoiding restrictive conditions of confinement is not the language of regulations regarding those conditions but the nature of those conditions themselves 'in relation to the ordinary incidents of prison life.'" *Id.*

In *Wilkinson*, the Supreme Court examined Ohio Supermax conditions, including the facts that "almost all human contact is prohibited, even to the point that conversation is not permitted from cell to cell; the light, though it may be dimmed, is on for 24 hours; exercise is for 1 hour per day, but only in a small indoor room." *Id.* at 223-24. In addition to these conditions, the Court noted that such housing was of indefinite duration and was only reviewed annually, and transfer to the facility eliminated an inmate for parole eligibility. *Id.* The Court was "satisfied that assignment to OSP imposes an atypical and significant hardship under any plausible baseline." *Id.* Finally, the Court noted that even if the harsh conditions could be viewed as necessary, "[t]hat necessity . . . does not diminish our conclusion that the conditions give rise to a liberty interest in their avoidance." *Id.*

Mr. Tabler's conditions of confinement are similar to *Wilkinson*, as well as the other cases discussed in the previous section. He is subject to severe solitary confinement, with minimal human contact. Importantly, Mr. Tabler has been housed in Death Watch for nearly a decade, and it is clear that Defendant intends his housing there to be indefinite. This factor was fundamental to the Supreme Court's decision in *Wilkinson* and has been central to court's analyses of similar housing ever since. *See, e.g., Wilkerson v. Goodwin*, 774 F.3d 845, 855-56 (5th Cir. 2014); *see also Sandin v. Conner*, 515 U.S. 472, 486 (1995) (holding that there was no liberty interest in part because a 30-day period of disciplinary segregation was not of atypical, excessive duration). And like *Wilkinson*, even if a factfinder were eventually to deem this housing necessary, Mr. Tabler is still entitled to due process to avoid the severely restrictive conditions.

Mr. Tabler's conditions of confinement on Death Watch are also similar to those examined in *Wilkerson v. Goodwin*. 774 F.3d 845, 855-56 (5th Cir. 2014). In that case, the Fifth Circuit confronted prison conditions, including solitary confinement conditions for 23 hours per day, "significant limitations on human contact, and placement is indefinite." *Id.* The Court concluded that the conditions were sufficiently severe, despite the prisoner being allowed "some contact visits, telephone privileges, peer counseling, and correspondence courses." *Id.* Viewing the extended solitary isolation, limited human contact, and many years that the plaintiff had been subject to these conditions "collectively" the Court held that "there can be no doubt that these conditions are sufficiently severe to give rise to a liberty interest under *Sandin*." *Id.* The Fifth Circuit held that this conclusion was particularly true because the plaintiff's housing was "effectively indefinite," reasoning that this was a "significant factor" in the Supreme Court's decision in *Wilkinson*. *Id*. For the same reasons, Mr. Tabler's indefinite confinement in conditions with severely limited human interaction and 22-hour solitary confinement in a tiny cell pose "atypical and significant hardships" such that he has a liberty interest and a concomitant Due Process right to be afforded an opportunity to avoid such confinement and be moved to death row.

Defendant argues that Mr. Tabler has not pointed to a state policy that creates such a liberty interest. *See Def's Mot*. at 8. However, that line of reasoning has been outmoded for at least 15 years. In *Wilkinson*, the Supreme Court noted its previous, sometime, focus on what policies a state did or did not have regarding housing and transfer. *Wilkinson*, 545 U.S. at 222-23. The Court reasoned that such a focus "creat[ed] a disincentive for States to promulgate procedures for prison management." *Id*. Therefore, the Court adopted the "atypical and significant hardship" standard and explicitly rejected myopic examination of prison policies. *See id*. ("the touchstone of the inquiry into the existence of a protected, state-created liberty interest in avoiding restrictive conditions of confinement is not the language of regulations regarding those conditions.").

Defendant also cites to an unpublished Fifth Circuit case, dismissing a *pro se* prisoner's appeal as frivolous to contend that "[p]risoners have no constitutionally protected liberty interest in a particular housing assignment." *Def's Mot*. at 12 (citing *Nathan v. Hancock*, 477 F. App'x 197, 199 (5th Cir. 2012)). However, as in the previous section, this statement begs the question and is simply not true as a matter of law. As explained above, a prisoner does have a "constitutionally protected liberty interest in a particular housing assignment," when he can establish that his housing "imposes atypical and significant hardship on the inmate in relation to the ordinary incidents of prison life." *Wilkinson*, 545 U.S. at 222-23.

What each of the cases Defendant cites lacks is an indefinite duration of the severe conditions present here. Mr. Tabler has been housed in these torturous conditions for nearly a decade. And it is clear that Defendant intends to keep him in these conditions indefinitely. In examining similar conditions of solitary confinement and/or segregation, the Fifth Circuit has indicated that "two and a half years of segregation is a threshold of sorts for atypicality." *Bailey v. Fisher*, 647 F. App'x 472, 476-77 (5th Cir. 2016). The Fifth Circuit has also noted that eight years or more of such solitary confinement has been found sufficient to establish a liberty interest, especially where there is no prospect of transfer to less restrictive housing. *See Wilkerson*, 774 F.3d at 855-56.

Finally, Defendant's argument that Mr. Tabler's current and continued housing in Death Watch in 2020 is justified by the misdeeds that got him placed there in the first place (over a decade ago) makes clear that Defendant will never move Mr. Tabler. *See Def's Mot.* at 12-14. This exact argument has previously been viewed as establishing an indefinite housing decision, with substantial importance to the Due Process analysis. *See, e.g., Wilkerson*, 774 F.3d at 855-56 (holding that a review board's repeated insistence on continued confinement based on the original infraction made clear that the reason for such housing could never change and was in fact indefinite). For the same reasons, Mr. Tabler's indefinite housing in Death Watch poses atypical and significant hardships; he is, therefore owed due process to challenge his continued housing in Death Watch, rather than in death row with all other prisoners who, like him, have been sentenced to death but do not yet have an execution date.

C. **Defendant is not entitled to sovereign immunity.**

Defendant Davis is not entitled to sovereign immunity on Plaintiff's claims seeking injunctive relief for continuing violations of his federal constitutional and statutory rights. "Sovereign immunity is not limitless, and this case involves an important caveat—the *Ex parte*

Young exception." *Williams v. Reeves*, 954 F.3d 729, 735-36 (5th Cir. 2020). *Ex Parte Young* allows a plaintiff to sue a state official in her official capacity, as long as the plaintiff "seeks prospective relief to redress an ongoing violation of federal law." *Id.* "Though an *Ex parte Young* suit has an 'obvious impact on the State itself,' it is an essential mechanism for affirming the supremacy of federal law." *Id.* (quoting *Pennhurst State Sch. & Hosp. v. Halderman*, 465 U.S. 89, 104-05 (1984)).

The Fifth Circuit has noted three requirements for an *Ex Parte Young* suit—it "must: (1) be brought against state officers who are acting in their official capacities; (2) seek prospective relief to redress ongoing conduct; and (3) allege a violation of federal, not state, law." *Williams*, 954 F.3d at 735-36. As a fundamental matter, the state official who is named as defendant must have a "sufficient connection [to] the enforcement" of the unconstitutional acts. *City of Austin v. Paxton*, 943 F.3d 993, 998 (5th Cir. 2019).

Defendant does not appear to dispute that she has a "sufficient connection" to the federal constitutional and statutory violations Mr. Tabler has alleged; she clearly has the power to order Mr. Tabler moved. *See generally Def's Mot.* at 4-6. Instead, Defendant's argument that *Ex Parte Young* does not allow Mr. Tabler's suit is based on the conclusory assertion that he "does not allege a continuing violation of federal law." *Def's Mot.* at 6. The above facts and legal discussion should make abundantly clear that Mr. Tabler is absolutely alleging a continuing violation of federal law. And fundamentally, "the inquiry into whether suit lies under *Ex Parte Young* does not include an analysis of the merits of the claim." *Williams*, 954 F.3d at 735-36. If a complaint alleges an ongoing violation of federal law (as Mr. Tabler's does) and seeks relief properly characterized as prospective (as Mr. Tabler's also does), the suit complies with the requirements of *Ex Parte Young*. *See id.*

18

D. Plaintiff has plausibly alleged violations of his rights under the ADA.

Mr. Tabler has plausibly alleged violations of his rights under the Americans with Disabilities Act ("ADA"). Defendant again asserts that she is entitled to sovereign immunity. However, with respect to an ADA claim, the issue of sovereign immunity is bound up with the merits. *See, e.g., Hale v. King*, 642 F.3d 492, 497-98 (5th Cir. 2011). In such a case, a court considers "which aspects of the State's alleged conduct violated Title II [of the ADA]" and then determines whether the State's conduct "also violated the Fourteenth Amendment." *Id.* at 498. "If the State's conduct violated both Title II and the Fourteenth Amendment, Title II validly abrogates state sovereign immunity." *Id.*

"A plaintiff states a claim for relief under Title II if he alleges: (1) that he has a qualifying disability; (2) that he is being denied the benefits of services, programs, or activities for which the public entity is responsible, or is otherwise discriminated against by the public entity; and (3) that such discrimination is by reason of his disability." *Id.* at 499.

Mr. Tabler has plausibly alleged that he is an individual with a qualifying disability. Courts throughout this circuit have recognized that serious mental illness can constitute a qualifying disability for purposes of an ADA discrimination claim. For example, in *Williamson v. Larpenter*, the court determined that plaintiff had plausibly alleged a qualifying disability based on his mental illness, "including depression, suicidal tendencies, [and] mood and behavior alterations." No. 19-254, 2019 U.S. Dist. LEXIS 133628, at *35-36 (E.D. La. July 15, 2019). In reaching this conclusion, the court noted that "[d]epression and other mental illnesses can qualify as disabilities for purposes of the ADA." *Id.* (quoting *Stradley v. Lafourche Commc'ns, Inc.*, 869 F. Supp. 442, 443 (E.D. La. 1994)). The court also found that plaintiff's "history of depression and multiple suicide attempts indicate that his mental impairments limited his ability to engage in the most basic life activity there is — keeping himself alive." *Williamson*, 2019 U.S. Dist.

Case 9:20-cv-00049-RC-KFG Document 11 Filed 06/24/20 Page 20 of 27 PageID #: 98

LEXIS 133628, at *35-36. Based on these allegations, the court determined that plaintiff's "impairments of depression and mental illness constitute a qualifying disability under the ADA." *Id.*

Similarly, in *Carter v. Cain*, the court considered claims that the prisoner-plaintiff was disabled due to his "mental illness, psychosis, paranoia, acute anxiety, [and] hallucinations," and that he "was at high risk of suicide." No. 17-201-SDD-RLB, 2019 U.S. Dist. LEXIS 27293, at *33-35 (M.D. La. Feb. 21, 2019). The court reasoned that such disabilities could substantially limit plaintiff's ability to engage in "major life activities," like "caring for oneself, performing manual tasks, walking, seeing, hearing, speaking, breathing, learning, and working." *Id.* The court specifically determined that "Plaintiff's allegations describe how Terrance Carter's mental illness caused him debilitating anxiety and even interfered with his ability to perceive reality," and that based on these allegations "a reasonable factfinder could conclude that Carter had a 'qualified disability' under the ADA." *Id.*

Lastly, a court of this circuit has determined that a plaintiff-prisoner plausibly alleged an ADA claim based on her housing in solitary confinement, despite her known mental illness. *See Wade v. Montgomery Cty.*, No. 4:17-CV-1040, 2017 U.S. Dist. LEXIS 216522, at *15-17 (S.D. Tex. Dec. 6, 2017). In that case, plaintiff alleged that her placement in solitary confinement constituted disability discrimination because it exacerbated her mental illness. *Id.* The court concluded that

> This allegation also plausibly states a claim upon which Plaintiff could recover. *See Wright v. Texas Dept. of Criminal Justice*, Cause No. 7:13-CV-0116-O, 2013 U.S. Dist. LEXIS 176222, 2013 WL 6578994 (N.D. Tex. Dec. 16, 2013) (holding that jail failed to reasonably accommodate inmate's mental disability when it placed him in a solitary cell where he was able to attempt suicide, and that was sufficient to show a prima facie violation of the ADA and Rehabilitation Act); *Lee v. Valdez*, Cause No. No. 3:07-CV-1298-D, 2009 U.S. Dist. LEXIS 43381, 2009 WL 1406244 (N.D. Tex. May 20, 2009) (noting that a jail's refusal to accommodate an inmate's mental health needs constitutes an impermissible

denial of benefits or services); *McCoy v. Tex. Dep't Crim. Justice*, Cause No. C-05-370, 2006 U.S. Dist. LEXIS 55403, 2006 WL 2331055, at *7, n.6 (S.D. Tex. Aug. 9, 2006) ("In the prison context, failure to make reasonable accommodations to the needs of a disabled prisoner may have the effect of discriminating against that prisoner because the lack of an accommodation may cause the disabled prisoner to suffer more pain and punishment than non-disabled prisoners.").

Id. The court then reasoned that "[b]ecause these allegations 'are to be taken as true,' they suffice to establish both the second and third elements of a Title II claim," and determined that "[a] fact finder could plausibly conclude from these allegations that Defendant discriminated against Wade by denying her benefits and services due to her alleged disability, and by not accommodating that alleged disability." *Id.* The court reached this conclusion, despite plaintiff not ruling out "benign explanations for her treatment," while stressing that "at this stage of the proceeding, [plaintiff] need not prove her claims, nor must she negate all potential defenses that the County may have. Wade need only allege facts that make her claim plausible." *Id.* (citing *McCoy v. Texas Dep't Crim. Justice*, 2006 U.S. Dist. LEXIS 55403 (S.D. Tex. Aug. 9, 2006) for the proposition that the reasonableness of the requested accommodations was a question for the jury to decide).

As a fundamental matter, pursuant to its statutory authority to issue regulations to carry out the ADA, 42 U.S.C. § 12116 (1994), the Equal Employment Opportunity Commission has refined the definition of "disability" to include "any mental or psychological disorder, such as . . . emotional or mental illness." 29 C.F.R. § 1630.2(h)(2) (1996). The EEOC has expressly characterized major depression, anxiety disorders, bipolar disorder, and personality disorders as disabilities under the ADA. *See* EEOC Enforcement Guidance: Psychiatric Disabilities and the

Americans With Disabilities Act, 2 EEOC Compl. Man. (BNA), filed after Section 902, at 15 P 1 (Mar. 25, 1997).[1]

With respect to exclusion from "services, programs, or activities," courts have been careful to stress that the "only reasonable interpretation of Title II is that law enforcement officers who are acting in an investigative or *custodial* capacity are performing 'services, programs, or activities' within the scope of Title II." *Williams v. City of N.Y.*, 121 F. Supp. 3d 354, 368 (S.D.N.Y. 2015) (emphasis added). As such, "the phrase services, programs, or activities has been interpreted to be 'a catch-all phrase that prohibits all discrimination by a public entity.'" *Noel v. N.Y.C. Taxi & Limousine Comm'n*, 687 F.3d 63, 68 (2d Cir. 2012) (quoting *Innovative Health Sys. v. City of White Plains*, 117 F.3d 37, 45 (2d Cir. 1997)); *see also Seremeth v. Bd. of Cty. Comm'rs Frederick Cty.*, 673 F.3d 333, 338 (4th Cir. 2012) (reaching the same conclusion while noting that the Department of Justice's regulations confirm that Title II is meant to apply to anything a public entity does). Safe housing in conditions of confinement that are not ruinous to the mental health of mentally disabled prisoners would seem to be among the most fundamental "services" that a prison provides to prisoners.

This view also comports with a broad reading of the ADA consistent with its status as a comprehensive remedial statute, which courts around the country have insisted upon when interpreting the scope and application of the ADA. *See, e.g., Hason v. Medical Bd.*, 279 F.3d 1167, 1172 (9th Cir. 2002) (holding that a narrow construction of the phrase "services, programs,

---

[1] Moreover, courts have accepted that fetal alcohol syndrome (one of the many mental disabilities that Mr. Tabler suffers) can be a qualifying disability under the ADA. *See, e.g., Sims v. Najera*, No. 1:12-cv-00466- AWI- JLT, 2012 U.S. Dist. LEXIS 123098, at *5-7 (E.D. Cal. Aug. 28, 2012) ("[h]ere, Plaintiff's allegation that he suffered from Fetal Alcohol Syndrome is sufficient to demonstrate that he is an individual with a disability."); *see also Lester v. M&M Knopf Auto Parts*, No. 04-CV-850S, 2006 U.S. Dist. LEXIS 70371, at *32-34 (W.D.N.Y. Sep. 28, 2006).

or activities" ran contrary to "the remedial goals underlying the ADA."); *see also Mary Jo C. v. N.Y. State & Local Ret. Sys.*, 707 F.3d 144, 160 (2d Cir. 2013); *Steger v. Franco, Inc.*, 228 F.3d 889, 894 (8th Cir. 2000); *Arnold v. UPS*, 136 F.3d 854, 861 (1st Cir. 1998).

Lastly, the question of whether Defendants refused to provide Mr. Tabler a reasonable accommodation is a question of fact that is to be decided by the factfinder. *See, e.g., EEOC v. Universal Mfg. Corp.*, 914 F.2d 71 (5th Cir. 1990). Mr. Tabler has plausibly alleged a reasonable accommodation that Defendant has refused—transfer out of Death Watch and back to death row. *See Complaint*, ¶ 86. "[T]he Fifth Circuit has held that a defendant's failure to make the reasonable modifications necessary to adjust for the unique needs of disabled persons can constitute intentional discrimination under the ADA and the RA." *Hacker v. Cain*, No. 3:14-00063-JWD-EWD, 2016 U.S. Dist. LEXIS 73014, at *40 (M.D. La. June 6, 2016) (citing *Melton v. Dall. Area Rapid Transit*, 391 F.3d 669, 672 (5th Cir. 2004) and *Garrett v. Thaler*, 560 F. App'x 375, 382 (5th Cir. 2014)). That said, as in all such disability discrimination cases, this question is "highly fact-specific and varies depending on the circumstances of each case, including the exigent circumstances presented by criminal activity and safety concerns." *Bahl v. Cty. Of Ramsey*, 695 F.3d 778, 784-85 (8th Cir. 2012) (citing *Bircoll v. Miami-Dade County*, 480 F.3d 1072, 1086 (11th Cir. 2007)).

Because Mr. Tabler has plausibly alleged Defendant's violation of his rights under Title II of the ADA, this Court must consider whether Defendant's conduct violates the Fourteenth Amendment. *See United States v. Georgia*, 546 U.S. 151, 159 (2006). If Defendant's misconduct also violates the Fourteenth Amendment, then Defendant is not entitled to sovereign immunity because Title II has validly abrogated such immunity under the facts of this case. *Id.* As explained above, Defendant's conduct has violated and continues to violate multiple protections afforded to Mr. Tabler by the Fourteenth Amendment. Moreover, "Congress' power 'to enforce' the [Fourteenth] Amendment includes the authority both to remedy and to deter violation of rights guaranteed thereunder by prohibiting a somewhat broader swath of conduct, including that which is not itself forbidden by the Amendment's text." *Arce v. Louisiana*, 306 F. Supp. 3d 897, 909 n.36 (E.D. La. 2017) (quoting *Bd. of Trustees of the Univ. of Ala. v. Garrett*, 531 U.S. 356, 365, 121 S. Ct. 955, 148 L. Ed. 2d 866 (2001)). "In other words, Congress may enact so-called prophylactic legislation that proscribes facially constitutional conduct, in order to prevent and deter unconstitutional conduct." *Nevada Dep't of Human Res. v. Hibbs*, 538 U.S. 721, 727-28, 123 S. Ct. 1972, 155 L. Ed. 2d 953 (2003). Plaintiff has plausibly alleged that Defendant's conduct violates both the ADA and the Fourteenth Amendment; therefore, Defendant is not entitled to sovereign immunity, and Plaintiff's ADA claim should not be dismissed.

In the alternative, if this Court were to conclude that Plaintiff has not plausibly alleged a violation of his rights under the ADA, he should be allowed a chance to amend his complaint to remedy any deficiencies. In a similar disability discrimination case, a district court in this circuit explained the necessity of amendment and allowed plaintiff to amend to cure deficiencies in her pleading. *See Wade*, 2017 U.S. Dist. LEXIS 216522, at *24-26. In *Wade*, the court explained:

> The court should freely give leave [to amend the pleadings] when justice so requires. FED. R. CIV. P. 15(a)(2). A decision on whether to permit amendment "is entrusted to the sound discretion of the district court." *Wimm v. Jack Eckerd Corp.*, 3 F.3d 137, 139 (5th Cir. 1993). Nevertheless, the Fifth Circuit has commented that the term "discretion" "may be misleading because FED. R. CIV. P. 15(a) evinces a bias in favor of granting leave to amend." *Mayeaux v. Louisiana Health Serv. & Indemn. Co.*, 376 F.3d 420, 425 (5th Cir. 2004)(citation omitted). "[A]bsent a 'substantial reason' such as undue delay, bad faith, dilatory motive, repeated failures to cure deficiencies, or undue prejudice to the opposing party, 'the discretion of the district court is not broad enough to permit denial.'" *Id.* (citation omitted).
>
> If a plaintiff's complaint fails to state a claim, the court should generally give her at least one chance to amend it under Rule 15(a), before dismissing the action with prejudice. *Great Plains Trust Co v. Morgan Stanley Dean Witter & Co.*, 313 F.3d 305, 329 (5th Cir. 2002)("District courts often afford plaintiffs at least one opportunity to cure pleading deficiencies before dismissing a case, unless it is

clear that the defects are incurable or the plaintiffs advise the court that they are unwilling or unable to amend in a manner that will avoid dismissal."); *United States ex rel. Adrian v. Regents of the Univ. of Cal.*, 363 F.3d 398, 403 (5th Cir. 2004)("Leave to amend should be freely given, and outright refusal to grant leave to amend without a justification . . . is considered an abuse of discretion.").

Wade, 2017 U.S. Dist. LEXIS 216522, at *24-26; *see also Hale*, 642 F.3d at 503 (remanding to allow plaintiff "opportunity to amend his Title II claim after being alerted to its deficiencies.").

For the reasons stated above, Plaintiff's ADA disability discrimination claim should be allowed to proceed, or he should be allowed to amend after being alerted to any deficiencies.

E. **Plaintiff's claims are not barred by any statute of limitations.**

Finally, Mr. Tabler's claims are not barred by any statute of limitations. Defendant asserts that Mr. Tabler's claims are barred by that statute of limitations for § 1983 claims. *See Def's Mot.* at 26-28. "This argument mischaracterizes the nature of harm that Plaintiff allegedly suffered. Plaintiff has pled a continuing injury. In a continuing injury case, the wrongful conduct continues to create an additional injury to the Plaintiff until the conduct stops." *Foddrill v. McManus*, Civil Action No. SA-13-CV-00051-XR, 2013 U.S. Dist. LEXIS 125837, at *7-9 (W.D. Tex. Sep. 4, 2013). As the Fifth Circuit has made clear, "[w]hen a tort involves continuing injury, the cause of action accrues, and the limitation period begins to run, at the time the tortious conduct ceases." *Donaldson v. O'Connor*, 493 F.2d 507, 529 (5th Cir. 1974). "In Texas, a continuing tort occurs where 'the wrongful conduct continues to effect additional injury to the plaintiff until that conduct stops.'" *Whitaker v. Collier*, 862 F.3d 490, 496 (5th Cir. 2017).

Mr. Tabler is not challenging his initial placement in the Death Watch section. He is also not challenging any other discrete-in-time decision by Defendant, especially considering he has not been provided process due to him to challenge his indefinite housing. Instead, he is challenging his continued housing in the Death Watch section, without due process and without reasonable accommodation to his known and obvious mental disabilities. As the various above discussions should make clear, he has plausibly alleged that every day he is kept in the Death Watch section is a new, compounding injury. His suit is similar to other challenges to indefinite solitary confinement that have involved long periods of time between the beginning of such restrictive confinement and the filing of suit. *See, e.g., Wilkerson*, 774 F.3d at 855-56 (addressing decades-long solitary confinement and collecting cases of similar years-long, indefinite confinements). The injuries that Mr. Tabler has suffered and continues to suffer can only be remedied by Defendant Davis ordering that he be moved out of Death Watch and back to death row. Therefore, Mr. Tabler's claims seeking only that prospective relief are not barred by the statute of limitations.

V. Conclusion

For the reasons stated above, Plaintiff respectfully requests that the court deny Defendant's motion to dismiss and allow his claims to proceed to discovery.

Respectfully submitted this 24th day of June 2020.

KILLMER, LANE & NEWMAN, LLP

/s/ *David A. Lane*
David A. Lane
Reid Allison
KILLMER, LANE & NEWMAN, LLP
1543 Champa Street, Suite 400
Denver, Colorado 80202
(303) 571-1000, Fax: (303) 571-1001
dlane@kln-law.com
rallison@kln-law.com

Richard Burr
Burr and Welch, PC
PO Box 525
Leggett, Texas 77350
(713) 628-3391
(713) 893-2500 fax
dick.burrandwelch@gmail.com

ATTORNEYS FOR PLAINTIFF

CERTIFICATE OF SERVICE

I certify that on this 24th day of June 2020, I filed the foregoing via CM/ECF which will generate a notice and service to all counsel of record.

/s/ David A. Lane
David A. Lane
KILLMER LANE & NEWMAN, LLP

IN THE UNITED STATES DISTRICT COURT
FOR THE EASTERN DISTRICT OF TEXAS
LUFKIN DIVISION

RICHARD TABLER	§	
VS.	§	CIVIL ACTION NO. 9:20cv49
LORIE DAVIS	§	

ORDER

The defendant previously filed a motion to dismiss (doc. no. 9). The defendant has now filed a motion (doc. no. 12) seeking an extension of time to file a reply to the response.

After due consideration, it is

ORDERED that the motion is **GRANTED**. The defendant is granted an extension of time, December 30, 2020, to file a reply. Pending the filing of a reply, the motion to dismiss is **DENIED** for statistical purposes only.

Plaintiff previously filed a motion (doc. no. 10) seeking an extension of time to file a response. As a response was subsequently filed, this motion is **DENIED** as moot.

SIGNED this the 12th day of January, 2021.

KEITH F. GIBLIN
UNITED STATES MAGISTRATE JUDGE

IN THE UNITED STATES DISTRICT COURT
FOR THE EASTERN DISTRICT OF TEXAS
LUFKIN DIVISION

RICHARD TABLER, *Plaintiff,*	§ § §	
v.	§ §	CIVIL ACTION NO. 9:20-cv-00049
LORIE DAVIS, *Defendants.*	§ § §	

DEFENDANT LORIE DAVIS'S RESPONSE
TO THE COURT'S ORDER OF JAN. 12, 2021

Defendant Lorie Davis, Director of the Texas Department of Criminal Justice—Correctional Institutions Division (TDCJ-CID), as sued in her official capacity, files this response to the Court's Order of January 12, 2021. ECF No. 13.

In his Original Complaint, Plaintiff Richard Tabler sues Lorie Davis, Director of TDCJ-CID, in her official capacity for cruel and unusual punishment in violation of the Eighth Amendment, denial of due process, under 42 U.S.C. § 1983, and for violation of his rights under the Americans with Disabilities Act ("ADA").[1] ECF No. 1. Tabler seeks injunctive relief in the form of a housing reassignment from "Death Watch" to death row. *Id.* at 14.

On May 27, 2020, Defendant Davis filed a motion to dismiss pursuant to Fed. R. Civ. P. 12(b)(1) and 12(b)(6). ECF No. 9. After a short extension, Plaintiff Tabler filed a response on June 24, 2020. ECF No. 11. Defendant Davis then filed a motion for extension of time to reply to Plaintiff Tabler's response, making the reply due July 15, 2020. ECF No. 12. On January 12, 2021, the Court

---

[1] Lorie Davis has retired from TDCJ. Bobby Lumpkin is the new Director of TDCJ's Institutional Division. A motion to substitute will be filed shortly.

granted Defendant's extension, ordering the reply due by December 30, 2020. ECF No. 13. Upon further consideration, Defendant informs this Court she will not be filing a reply brief.

Respectfully submitted,

KEN PAXTON
Attorney General of Texas

BRENT WEBSTER
First Assistant Attorney General

GRANT DORFMAN
Deputy First Assistant Attorney General

SHAWN E. COWLES
Deputy Attorney General for Civil Litigation

SHANNA E. MOLINARE
Division Chief, Law Enforcement Defense Division

/s/ Briana M. Webb
BRIANA M. WEBB
Assistant Attorney General
Texas State Bar No. 24077883
Briana.Webb@oag.texas.gov

Law Enforcement Defense Division
Office of the Attorney General
P. O. Box 12548, Capitol Station
Austin, Texas 78711
Office (512) 463-2080 / Fax (512) 370-9814

Attorneys for Defendant Davis

Certificate of Service

I, Briana M. Webb, Assistant Attorney General of Texas, do hereby certify that a true and correct copy of the above and foregoing has been served via ECF/PACER to all counsel of record on January 14, 2021.

/s/ Briana M. Webb
BRIANA M. WEBB
Assistant Attorney General

IN THE UNITED STATES DISTRICT COURT
FOR THE EASTERN DISTRICT OF TEXAS
LUFKIN DIVISION

RICHARD TABLER, *Plaintiff*,	§ § §	
v.	§ §	CIVIL ACTION NO. 9:20-cv-00049
LORIE DAVIS, *Defendants*.	§ § §	

DEFENDANT LORIE DAVIS'S MOTION TO SUBSTITUTE

Defendant Lorie Davis, in her official capacity as the Director of the Correctional Institutions Division of the Texas Department of Criminal Justice, submits this motion to substitute the parties pursuant to FED. R. CIV. P 25(d)(1).

Lorie Davis was named as a Defendant in above-styled and numbered cause in her official capacity only. Lorie Davis has now retired from State service. Effective, August 10, 2020, Bobby Lumpkin became the new Director of the Correctional Institutions Division of the Texas Department of Criminal Justice.

Bobby Lumpkin, accordingly, must be substituted for Lorie Davis, in his official capacity only.

Defendant Lorie Davis respectfully requests that this Court recognize the substitution of party adding Bobby Lumpkin as Defendant and removing Lorie Davis.

Respectfully submitted,

KEN PAXTON
Attorney General of Texas

BRENT WEBSTER
First Assistant Attorney General

GRANT DORFMAN
Deputy First Assistant Attorney General

SHAWN E. COWLES
Deputy Attorney General for Civil Litigation

SHANNA E. MOLINARE
Division Chief, Law Enforcement Defense Division

/s/ Briana M. Webb
BRIANA M. WEBB
Assistant Attorney General
Texas State Bar No. 24077883
Briana.Webb@oag.texas.gov

Law Enforcement Defense Division
Office of the Attorney General
P. O. Box 12548, Capitol Station
Austin, Texas 78711
Office (512) 463-2080 / Fax (512) 370-9814

Attorneys for Defendant Lumpkin

Certificate of Service

I, Briana M. Webb, Assistant Attorney General of Texas, do hereby certify that a true and correct copy of the above and foregoing has been served via ECF/PACER to all counsel of record on January 21, 2021.

/s/ Briana M. Webb
BRIANA M. WEBB
Assistant Attorney General

Special Thanks

I want to give all the thanks and glory to God, His Son Jesus Christ and the Holy Spirit. Also my love and thanks to: Lorraine, Kristina, Justine, Greg, Austin, Sean, Laura, Jacob, David Lane, Mari Newman, Darold Killmer, Maddie Lips, Colleen Kulas, Debbie Sebastian, Reid Allison, and the rest of the staff of Killmer, Lane and Newman, LLP, Marcy and Sasha Widder, Luis Batiz, Claudia Van Wyk, Cassy Stubbs, Travis Mulhauser, Shawn Nolan and those at the CHU, Ally, Josina S. Wiesner, Mary Hampton, Sister Cordia Klein, John Dougan, Sigrid, Soren and Alan Wade, Elodie, Wire of Hope, Veronique Scauflaire, Stacey and Jimmy Smith, Troup Foster, Damon Lewis, Fabian Hernandez, Billy Tracy, Moran Kabaso-Beatty, Inside Out Prison Ministry, Li'l Blue, John Montana, Tom Mooney, Bikers For Christ, Braynn Trejo and Kingdom Muzic Family, Eric Genuis, Jay Dan Gumm and Family, Forgiven Felons, Tony F. Jones, Rochelle and Family, Kevin Salwen and Family, Frank Reuter and Cadmus Publishing, Director Dickerson, Warden A. Enrriques, Director Hazelwood, Chaplain Gay, Captain N. Neyland, Captain H. Watson, Major G. Hunter, Ruth Davis, Julius Murphy, Tai'Chin Preyor (R.I.P.)

Questions and comments you can reach me at:

Texas Department of Criminal Justice
Richard L. Tabler #999523
Polunsky Unit
P.O. Box 660400
Dallas, TX. 75266-0400

ABOUT THE AUTHOR

Richard L. Tabler is an individual that made serious mistakes in and throughout his life before finding the strength to write his own first book, "Within the Shadows of Life", in 2021. Those mistakes have cost him his freedom, and pain and suffering for others. It wasn't until Mr. Tabler turned 43-years-old that he was able to forgive himself and love himself to fully accept Jesus Christ into his life and heart. It's through the Grace of God that he is able to write the book you now hold in your hand and that those in society live and care about Mr. Tabler's voice as he suffers from survivors' guilt here on Texas' Death Row.

RICHARD L. TABLER

www.ingramcontent.com/pod-product-compliance
Lightning Source LLC
Chambersburg PA
CBHW071947070526
44583CB00015B/1101